Flying the Frontiers

Volume III
Aviation Adventures Around the World

Shirlee Smith Matheson

Detselig Enterprises Ltd.

Calgary, Alberta, Canada

Flying the Frontiers, Volume III

© 1999 Shirlee Smith Matheson

Canadian Cataloguing in Publication Data

Matheson, Shirlee Smith

Flying the frontiers: aviation adventures around the world

ISBN 1-55059-176-2

1. Air pilots -- Canada -- Anecdotes. 2. Aeronautics -- Flights. I Title.
TL539.M37   1999   629.13'092'271   C99-910182-X

Detselig Enterprises Ltd.
210-1220 Kensington Rd. N.W.
Calgary, AB T2N 3P5
Telephone: (403) 283-0900
Fax: (403) 283-6947
e-mail: temeron@telusplanet.net
www.temerondetselig.com

Detselig Enterprises Ltd. appreciates the financial support for our 1999 publishing program, provided by Canadian Heritage and other sources.

Printed in Canada
ISBN 1-55059-176-2
SAN 115-0324
Cover painting & cartoon illustrations by Wally Wolfe
Cover design by Dean Macdonald

Dedication and Acknowledgement

This book is dedicated to those whose stories appear herein, who trusted my discretion as well as my talent to portray the drama and poignancy of their aviation experiences.

A heartfelt thank you to Clark Seaborn, P.Eng., who checked out the collection.

Shirlee Matheson and Clark Seaborn, Aviation Day,
Calgary, Alberta, May 30, 1999, with Clark's pride
and joy – 1929 Fokker Super Universal (CF-AAM).

Other books by Shirlee Smith Matheson

Nonfiction

Youngblood of the Peace

This Was Our Valley

Flying the Frontiers, Volume I

Flying the Frontiers, Volume II

A Western Welcome to the World (a history of the Calgary International Airport)

Juvenile/Young Adult Fiction

Prairie Pictures

City Pictures

Flying Ghosts

The Gambler's Daughter

Table of Contents

Preface

"The last time I flew with a woman pilot, it was snowing," the grizzled prospector notes to the female pilot as they take off in the Super Cub from Whitehorse. "We crashed." He indicates a patch over the eye lost in that accident. "So I'm sure glad the weather's good today."

As they cross over to the far side of the mountains it starts to snow . . . .

Aviation adventures have excited readers since human beings first took to the air strapped to crude kites. The wild times have continued, even with the advent of sophisticated machines to transport us from the ocean's depths to the airless void of space, allowing us to explore the farthest frontiers.

Good stories contain conflict and challenge, and these abound in the aviation field. As one pilot noted dryly, "Nothing is more useless than the airspace above you and the runway behind you."

In the three volumes of *Flying the Frontiers* I have sought stories that portray adventures on all sides of the flying field – old stories and new, heroic and imprudent, during times of peace and war. These aviators and engineers have taken to the air in fixed- and rotary-wing aircraft, and even in a space shuttle with a goal of attaching a docking module onto the Russian space station Mir – the ultimate in "field work."

In Volume III, "Aviation Adventures Around the World," readers meet 12 Canadians and one American who fly and fix all types of flying machines.

A Saskatchewan family follows two of Canada's most historic occupations, the fur trade and the exploration of remote northern rivers by canoe. In keeping with modern times, however, they expedite their goods by air, and one son is an aircraft pilot and engineer.

A helicopter pilot decides to catch 40 winks in the passenger seat of a helicopter parked on the beach of a remote Arctic Island – and awakens to discover that a polar bear has assumed the pilot's position.

Readers will join a BC coastal pilot in a Beaver aircraft on floats when he is forced to seek harbor on the black, choppy waters of an unknown channel. Life or death for him and his passengers depends on courage, training and clear-thinking, and the ultimate Will of God.

We'll take a flight in a vintage tanker over the searing flames of a forest fire, and watch the fire die under the assault of 6000 gallons of water per drop. This story features the Martin Mars aircraft, and the Herculean human efforts made to rescue these beautiful, and highly effective, flying tankers from the junk-pile.

We'll also meet two masters who have combined lifetime skills of working in the aviation industry to restore old beauties for the topnotch Alberta Aviation Museum.

What makes flying physicians different from ordinary pilots? That question and others are examined by a worldwide, not-for-profit society with a mandate to promote safety, education and science-oriented research and human interest projects related to aviation. The story features the experiences of an 86-year old charter member who, after losing a leg, is busy relearning his flying skills.

We'll also follow the development of a "flying family," on whom aviation has bestowed their greatest joys, and also their deepest sorrows.

A northern airline is deeply affected by Transport Canada's mandate to sell off its airports. With whom lies the ultimate responsibility of maintaining necessary, but unprofitable, airports? Who holds the winning position, and is there one?

How does one turn knowledge of aviation, and the northland, into everlasting works of art? transform the fun of flying into cartoons and learning-activity books for children? One pilot has followed this route, and now his artwork appears in both public and private galleries . . . as well as on the covers of all three volumes of *Flying the Frontiers*.

The adventures chronicled in Volume III go beyond our dominion boundaries, however, to take in world-wide air rallies, and explorations of land, sea, air and space.

Some, inevitably, involve wartime memoirs.

"Before you start writing my story, watch the movie, 'The Great Escape,'" instructs the World War II ex-Prisoner of War. "James Garner played me." The story recalls an Alberta airman's five long, but oddly active years spent in the wire-bound world of Stalag Luft III.

Also during World War II, when a call goes out for pilots with skill, training and experience to fly DC-3s over the Burma Road, only those who love travel, romance, danger, daring and adventure respond. In this story we trace the heroic missions of two Canadian-born brothers of Chinese ancestry who flew the Burma Hump, called the "world's worst graveyard of the air," as members of the famous Flying Tigers.

This book also relates first-hand accounts of two Canadians who "embrace space." Like sailors of old, the astronaut works in incredible isolation, and many risks are involved when breaking the bonds of gravity and confronting the final frontier.

I feel honored to have met the people who lived these stories, and to dramatize their adventures. A thorough manuscript review was provided by Clark Seaborn, a Calgary engineer, pilot and restorer of vintage aircraft (such as the fabulous Fokker Super Universal, CF-AAM), and I am thankful for his close attention to detail.

Since the release of *Flying the Frontiers: Volume I, A Half-Million Hours of Aviation Adventure* in 1994, and *Volume II, More Hours of Aviation Adventure* in 1996, inevitable changes have occurred in the lives of some of the people I've written about. Five have "slipped the surly bonds of earth": Phil Lucas and his lifelong friend Joe Irwin, Weldy Phipps, Roy Staniland and Mike Thomas. With their friends and families I mourned their passing, while being grateful for the privilege of chronicling their adventures of flying the frontiers.

"What do you want to do? Live forever?"

"I figure I was about three years old when I heard the strange noise outside," recalls Cedric Mah. "In those days they had plank sidewalks in Prince Rupert, and I went running down them to see where that noise was coming from. I saw something zoom up and waggle its wings. Then a hand wearing a glove waved from the window. I remember saying to myself, 'One day I want to be up there in a thing like that!'"

This incident occurred in 1925. The pilot who waved as he flew over Kaien Island on Canada's northwest Pacific coast, where the town of Prince Rupert had been incorporated just 15 years earlier, unknowingly sparked a lifelong interest in the small boy.

From that time on, Cedric became a self-described "aviation nut."

Eager to fly, Cedric's brother Albert attended California Flyers Aviation College in Los Angeles as a paying student. In 1941, at age 19, Cedric followed and became one of the college's first student pilots to receive his training from a female instructor. "From what she mentioned, at that time aviation was pretty much male-dominated."

Cedric had helped to pay for Albert's flying instruction by working in the family business, Sunrise Grocery, and now Albert helped his brother. Following his training at California Flyers, Albert also paid for Cedric to take an advanced instrument course in Fort Worth, Texas. By 1942, Cedric held private and commercial licenses, and, combined with instrument training and 300 flying hours, his qualifications were top-notch.

At this time, the British Commonwealth Air Training Plan (BCATP) was in full swing, training air crews for the allied war effort from bases across Canada. Albert had become an instructor, through Canadian Pacific Air Lines, at No. 2 Air Observer School (AOS) in Edmonton, and later at No. 8 AOS at Ancienne Lorette, Quebec City.

When Cedric finished his course in Texas in 1942 he returned to Prince Rupert, "grabbed $150, and headed to Edmonton to see if I could get a job. There I was," Cedric says, "fat, dumb and happy! What I didn't know was that practically all the commercial outfits were shut down for the war. My intention was to be a bush pilot; I liked the open country, but all the bush outfits were shut down. The heavy equipment had been taken out of the mines, so there was no mining activity. Not only that, but once fall came, darkness set in up North. There were no lighted airstrips. You had to wait until it froze up. But I didn't know, I just headed for Edmonton, the Gateway to the North, where there might be that type of work."

He finally scored a job through the BCATP training bomb-aimers, photographers and navigators at No. 5 AOS in Winnipeg, operated by the former Starratt and Wings airways (which in 1941 had become part of the Canadian Pacific Air Lines group). The

BCATP provided an excellent opportunity for young pilots, and especially Chinese-Canadians who'd not been readily accepted in the military, to build hours. "In Canada, to December 7, 1941, there were less than 1200 licensed Canadian pilots. Very few people knew how to fly in Canada in those days," Cedric recalls.

Meanwhile, in December 1941, Japan had invaded Burma and Thailand.

The Flying Tigers

"The term 'Fei Hou,' or 'Flying Tigers,' comes from ancient Chinese history," Cedric notes. "A fighting man, a person who resists, is called a 'Tiger'."

In 1931 when Japan attacked Manchuria, local people volunteered to fight. But in 1937 when Japan attacked the second time, volunteers came from all over the world and were given the name 'Tigers'.[1]

Cedric, after instructing in Winnipeg for a year, paid a visit in the fall of 1943 to his chosen base of Edmonton, where Captain Wilfred (Wop) May, OBE, DFC, was in charge of No. 2 AOS. "Wop May and I were good friends," Cedric relates, "so when Wop said, 'How do you like it in Winnipeg?' I said, 'I'm a coastal boy, a mountain boy, and I prefer to have a few mountains to climb.' He laughed and said, 'Well, if you can talk to somebody here maybe you can get a transfer,' so of course he fixed it so I could come back."

The following spring, Wop May approached Cedric. "Come and see me after you get back from your flight."

When Cedric arrived in his office, Wop opened the conversation with a surprise revelation. "Did you know I once had a chance to fly in China? Right after the war – that is, World War One?" Cedric knew that during the Great War, Wop had been just a fledgling airman when the 'Red Baron,' Manfred, Freiherr von Richthofen, got Wop in his sights. Luckily, Canadian airman Roy Brown intercepted and brought down the Red Baron (apparently with assistance from Australian ground fire) before he pulled the trigger.

"How come you didn't go to China?" Cedric asked Wop.

"I tried but they wouldn't let me."

"Who were *they*?" Cedric said, his interest piqued.

"The government. When I applied for a passport and told them I had a job in China they refused to export me, wouldn't give me a visa." He leaned forward. "So, if you get a chance you should go there. That country is just ripe for aviation."

The USAAF China National Aviation Corporation (CNAC) Transport Group had been formed to airlift personnel and supplies such as aviation fuel, equipment, explosives, ammunition and money to the Nationalist Chinese government, and bring out tin,

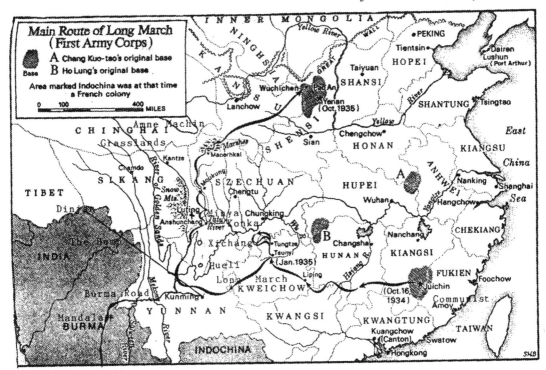

tung oil, tungsten, tea, mercury, silk and hog bristles. The flight plan crossed over the Burma "Hump," from Dinjan, Assam Province, direct to Kunming. This route, in good weather with no enemy interception, took about three hours and 20 minutes to cover the 550 miles, flying through the mountain passes at 16 000 feet.

The CNAC flights over the Himalayas had begun in 1942 with Douglas C-53s – DC-3s with superchargers (and early in 1945 with Curtiss Commando C-46 Transports, on a contract basis, packing freight for the American Military Commission in China). Pan American Airways jointly owned the CNAC (the China division of Pan Am) and were busy recruiting and training pilots to fly the Burma Hump run, supplying Chiang Kai-shek's Nationalist armies.

"This work was a special call," Cedric says. "After the Burma Road fell, Chiang Kai-shek asked for 50 DC-3s. No other type would do. In February 1942, a few months after Pearl Harbor, President Roosevelt requisitioned 25 DC-3s. These DC-3s had been leased to the airlines that flew the Rocky Mountains, such as American Airlines which flew into Flagstaff, Arizona, and Trans World Airlines that landed at Denver, Colorado. High blowers, or super-chargers, would allow these aircraft to top Mount Everest (29 000 feet). The Burma Road passes crested at 10 000 feet."

But for many reasons the air route over the Hump became known as the "graveyard of the air," and the logistics of making a successful run required serious strategy, and aircrew with nerves of steel.

The 681-mile Burma Road had been completed in 1938 by the sweat of 200 000 laborers using primitive hand tools. Winding through the high mountains between Burma and Kunming, China, the road became China's only surface supply link to the outside world when the Japanese held the Chinese coastal areas.

The CNAC desperately needed pilots who could navigate in bad instrument weather and fly at night in order to avoid detection from the Japanese fighters. Being multilingual would also help, and copilot and radio operators were expected to speak from five to seven different languages or dialects. But there were very few trained pilots and the attrition rate was high.

On Wop May's advice, Cedric communicated with Pan American Airways in New York and was apprised of the intense situation overseas. His brother, Albert, was already flying in Burma.

"I've got to have some relief!" Albert wrote to Cedric. "I've been out here more than a year, I've got to have a break, this is war activity!"

Thus, it was Albert who again led Cedric to the next stage of his career. Cedric was ready. When he inquired if Pan American Airways could use his services, their reply was an eager invitation: "Need you right away." Cedric showed the letter to Wop May, who offered to present it on his behalf to the government office. "If they'll give you a Labour Exit Permit, you can go."

With Wop pushing the application – "Here's a guy who wants to go fly in the Pacific theatre, it's part of the war effort. We have to keep China in the fight and we have very few people with the necessary experience to operate in high altitudes," – Cedric was accepted. Although he did not have much high altitude experience, his instrument training enabled him to do night-flying, and he had taken every opportunity to build up this experience while instructing at No. 2 AOS.

Cedric left Edmonton for New York by rail in April of 1944. After training, he flew on the new DC-4 Atlantic Service from New York to Newfoundland, the Azores, Casablanca, Tripoli, Cairo, Iraq, to Abadan in Iran, Karachi, Delhi and Agra, to finally report for duty in October at the Air Transport Command of the CNAC's maintenance, overhaul and supply facilities base at Dum Dum airport in Calcutta. At 22 years of age, Cedric was one of the youngest pilots there. Air transportation duties were given only to those with top priority.

"In wartime you don't have too much time to train," Cedric acknowledges, "and we'd gone through all the things they were doing there anyhow, with the BCATP."

Cedric received notice that Albert was up at the operating base in Dinjan, Assam Province, India, in the Northeast Frontier Agency. During the short time the brothers were both associated with Transport Wing, they did trips together in DC-3s to familiarize the new pilot with the awesome territory.

Cedric recalls his introduction to flying the Himalayas.

"'You fly!' Albert said. Jeez, I'd maybe had two landings on a DC-3 and here I've got this heavily loaded transport filled with ammunition, gasoline and other war supplies, in pelting rain and cloying heat!"

The absolute darkness of the jungle was another shock. "In Canada we have a degree of actinic light, star-shine, glacial-glow and reflective light from the sun, moon and stars that gives us a horizon. But, in the jungle, the forest canopy absorbs all. I'd never seen it so pitch black in all my life."

Cedric turned the aircraft to the east, and Albert said, "Now, we'll go up this 90-degree valley."

"How high are these mountains?" Cedric asked.

"Oh, left side about 18 000 feet and right side about the same."

Cedric checked his altitude. "We're only 6000 feet in the air!" he yelped. "How do you tell you're going straight through the mountains? Is there any radio bearing or any beam?"

"Oh, no, we just go down there," Albert replied casually, "but if you don't get up to 16 000 feet by so many minutes out you'll have to circle and spiral up. Don't continue on if you haven't enough altitude because the mountains are all around us."

The prospects looked bleak as Cedric circled up to gain altitude. He couldn't see a thing in the black, starless sky. He had to rely totally on instruments with nobody guiding him, no radio, just his brother's experienced voice in the dark cockpit beside him.

"Let me see a map," Cedric said.

"We don't have a map."

Cedric now understood the reason for the high attrition rate.

After about two hours out they were cruising at 16 000 feet. "How high are the mountains here?" Cedric asked again.

"Oh, there's an 18 000 foot range we've got to cross."

"How can you tell when we've crossed it?"

"In a few minutes you'll see," was Albert's reply.

Moments later, Cedric's stomach dropped as the airplane began to rock and shake. "What the hell is that?" he gasped, when he caught his breath.

"We just crossed that 18 000 foot range of mountains," Albert informed him.

"At 16 000 feet??"

"Yeah. That shows we got through the pass okay. What made us jump around was the jet stream hitting this mountain, and cascading down the other side. In about 50 minutes we should be able to see Kunming."

Cedric was well aware of the desperate situation of those who had flown the Burma Hump before his arrival. He'd read the statistics and heard the stories. These strong winds could rip off wings or flip airplanes over onto their backs, and he'd heard of down-drafts so violent that an airplane could drop 3000 feet in a single plunge. If you crashed it was game over. There were headhunters and enemy troops on the ground to kill you if the crash hadn't done the job.

Cedric also discovered that the pilot on the Transport Wing's DC-3s was also the navigator. It was a simple matter of logistics: the space and weight of a second man could be better be used to transport another few gallons of fuel and more belts of ammunition. "Here, in Canada, we were training navigators, but when we got over there you couldn't afford the luxury of one," Cedric says. "You did the all the work yourself."

When Cedric arrived at the Chinese base in Kunming, Yunnan, the old Burma Road terminal, he was exhausted. He'd been up since six o'clock that morning and now it was five o'clock the next morning. From spending 10 days in India where the heat had been so oppressive it was impossible to sleep, now, on the Yunnan Plateau at 6120 feet, the air was lovely and cool. "I just want to sleep," he told his brother.

Albert laughed. "Yeah, we all do the same. We try to overnight on the China side and then only spend a few nights in the jungle. That way we can last longer."

"I also want to have a look at these damned mountains by daylight!" Cedric said.

The Trans-Himalayas run east and west, but on the China end, between Burma and China, a spur, the 'Hump,' runs north and south, Cedric explains. In order to get from India or Burma into China, you had to cross over this range. Because it backs up all the monsoon winds that come in from the southwest you get tremendous rains, cumulonimbus buildups (thunderheads), severe icing, turbulence, powerful winds and generally horrible weather. And beneath all this are jungle, mountains, rivers, crags and rocks.

"We had to fly over the corrugations cut through the Trans-Himalayas by three giant rivers that exit Burma, Annam [Vietnam] and China. The Jade Dragon range is 20 000 feet; the Great Snowy Mountains 25 000 feet, so this gives you the feel for the routes."

Ced Mah in Dinjan, Assam Province, Northeast Frontier Agency, India, 1945. The aircraft is a Curtiss Commando C-46. Note the parking area paved with perforated steel mats, interlocked. This was to keep the aircraft from sinking out of sight in the monsoon downpours. (Photo: Ced Mah collection)

Cedric viewed the azure-blue Dali Lake on the east side that gave rise to the violent katabatic winds. The downward flow of cold air spilled over the mountain into this lake to give their aircraft a sudden drop. He couldn't see the wind, but he knew the downdraft was there. But, in the afternoon the mountains seemed beautiful and serene. "So, once I saw the enemy, I kind of settled down," Cedric recalls.

Cedric and Albert had one month together, from October to November 1944. When Albert was released from duty, after flying 420 return trips over the Hump in 18 months, he returned home to Canada and became a North Atlantic Treaty Organization (NATO) instructor based at a school near Montreal. But the training he gave his younger brother in Burma was essential. "He kept his eye on the course that I was steering, on the instruments," Cedric says. "He'd know what direction I was going. If I started to stray off course he'd come back, 'Thataway mountains.'"

Cedric's orders were to fly DC-3s loaded with supplies for the allied troops, the Americans, British and Chinese. "Our theatre of operations was the Northeast Frontier Agency, Assam Province, at the base of the Himalayas where Bramputra River debouches out of Tibet. Our base was Dinjan, a tea plantation, and it featured the first paved airstrip in Northeast India."

Adventures in the High Country

And so the 22-year-old pilot went to work, flying the notorious Burma Hump. On one trip, while transporting $866 million in Chinese paper money over the mountains, ice built up on his aircraft. Then a hydraulic line sprung a leak, causing an undercarriage wheel to let down and create drag. Shortly thereafter the right engine quit, to triple the problem.

Cedric's first thought was to order the crew to jump, but then he remembered they were over Lolo Nosu country, populated by a national minority of ethnic hill people. They were known to be notoriously hostile and treated all captives as slaves. Even if the crew escaped capture, the chances of walking safely out of the mountains and disease-infested territory were almost nil. Cedric had one other choice: to dump his load over the mountains.

With only a single engine, the C-46 plummeted from 22 000 feet to 12 000 feet. At 10 000 feet, in cloud, they rounded a peak into a valley with a lake, leading to a dead-end. Cedric circled above the lake, contemplating his choices: a belly landing on water with a dragging wheel, or a crash landing on the side of a mountain. In the lower altitude, however, the ice began to melt off the wings. He tried the dead engine. It coughed and miraculously fired. He had full power again but not enough fuel to make it to Chungking. He turned south-east and just made it to Kunming, still dragging the wheel.

The money has never been recovered. "Kind of spendthrift, don't you think?" Captain Mah wrote to his brother. His aircraft, a Curtiss Commando, was at that time the largest twin-engine transport in the world. "We traded $866 000 000 Chinese for a $300 000 aircraft and our lives – a fair price."

On another flight, when he encountered turbulence while flying a load of lead ingots, his cargo began bouncing "like corks in an ocean." The result was holes in the roof as well as some ingots becoming embedded in the floor (*Star Weekly*, Sept. 11/54).

One stormy night, January 6-7, 1945, he was part of a 300-airplane contingent that flew into a "monsoonal nightmare," a storm with billowing clouds and strong updrafts, "a granddaddy, a big one," with heavy icing. A reported 35 aircraft were lost over the Hump that night.

Cedric quickly learned the tricks of survival in this wild country.

Teng Chun, Japan's most northerly fighter base on the Burma Road, allowed their Zeros to reach into Tibet and intercept the Transports. Only in overcast and bad weather could CNAC fly direct. At all other times, they were forced to fly further north over higher mountains, turn right to the south-east, and complete the "dogleg" to land at Chonqing or Kunming, Cedric says.

"This was at a time when they figured stratospheric flight was still 10 to 20 years away. Initially, there were no oxygen masks. The Yanks got them from the British, as they had developed them for the Battle of Britain aircraft that had to engage in dog-fighting at rarefied altitudes.

"Everybody thought the Douglas DC-4s flew the high, or true, Hump. However, the C-54s, a cargo DC-4 with long range, were first pressed into overseas service in the spring of 1944. Later the C-54s were put to use over the lower Hump, flying from Calcutta on the Gangetic Plains, which were sea level, to bases on the Yunnan Plateau in the southwest region of China which were 6-7000 feet high," Cedric adds. "We were flying C-47s, or cargo DC-3s, and also Curtiss Commando C-46s equipped with high blowers, super-chargers, that would carry us up to 35 000 feet on westbound headings, using updraft thermals inside thunderheads."

"We used to say that when flying the Burma Hump there may be only one day a month when you earn your salary," Cedric says, "and that's the day when the you-know-what hits the fan. You have navigation, weather – thunderclouds and everything – and enemy action. You try to dodge all these impediments but you can't dodge them all. Sometimes we'd get to the China side and they'd say, 'Ai! Those guys are running into a big roadblock down the Burma Road. You've got to fly ammunition, guns and fuel in there.' Then you begin food drops, and get mortared and shelled and shot at and everything else.

"Then, on another trip, it might start out to be a beautiful day but the wind would jump up to 150 mph and you can't believe you should be going that fast. One guy flying in overcast skies from Dinjan to Kunming ended up in the Gulf of Tonkin. He looked down and there was Haiphong, the seaport for Hanoi. These guys were recruited from the United States and elsewhere, a lot of them had been mainly teaching students before.

Now suddenly they are in the airplane and it's night, completely black, and dawn breaks and you look down and Jeez! that's a big lake! And you look and see there's no end to that lake. It's the Pacific Ocean! You've picked up a tail wind. You've over-flown China!"

But with "bombers' moon" nights, one's cover would be blown. No need for flare pots or landing lights, for moonlight exposed everything. "You are clear to land when suddenly the tower crackles, 'Three balls overhead! Lights out. Take cover.'" As you set down there's a plop! plop! sound behind and flashes all around. It's the Japanese Sally Bombers from Hanoi! They are in the airfield circuit every moonlit night. You quickly shut off your navigation lights so they can't see where you are, pull off the runway and jump out."

Remembering the warning, 'anything moving on the airfield is shot at,' Cedric quickly stopped his aircraft, clambered out and hid down behind the tires. His hiding place offered little protection. The aircraft above him was filled with fuel, in both its wings and on board, along with the ammunition he was ferrying.

"I lay out there on the runway while they dropped bombs all over, knowing that being beneath the aircraft wasn't all that much help – in fact, I'd burn faster," Cedric says. "But I thought, first of all, they're shooting at Fifth Columnists setting fires outside the airfield. Secondly, it's harder to shoot a gopher lying under something on the ground than an eagle sitting in the tree, so I got close to the ground and lay flat and made myself harder to hit."

One time, he landed at an airstrip just as enemy shells moved within range. Cedric left one engine running and, while ground crews unloaded, he dived for a dugout to escape the shrapnel. When the airplane was off-loaded he raced from the dugout, jumped in, and started for takeoff down the runway while bringing in the second engine.

Nearly every day, airplanes were being hit and fellow crewmen killed. "My brother Albert was landing in Dinjan when the tower said, 'There's a Zero on your tail!' He dove down to the top of the jungle canopy and the copilot shouted, 'He's veered off!' They turned 90 degrees right to observe a P-40 fighter taking off and the Zero diving. Before the P-40 rotated, the Zero fired. The P-40 crashed in a ball of flame alongside the runway. So the P-40 got it instead of my brother. Another couple of seconds it could have been rapping on his plane.

"When Albert came back to Canada in November of 1944, just a month after I got out there, he got the name of this pilot and found he was from Buffalo, New York. He went there to console his fellow pilot's mother. She was overwhelmed. 'That's the most wonderful thing ever.' she said. 'We know our son is gone but at least we know he didn't die in vain.'"

Fate had intervened, with one man alive and the other dead, the vagaries of war.

One morning in February of 1945, as they took off in a C-47, the pilots received a strange order: they were to buy 10 000 horses. Only three places in the Far East would have such a number: Lijiang in the Jade Dragon Mountains north of the Burma Road – but they wouldn't be sending airplanes there because it was accessible by truck; the great Gobi Desert north of the Himalayan Mountains – but that was 4000 or 5000 miles away; and the mountainous area of Tibet – 500 miles as the crow flies.

"Next thing we knew, our orders were Destination Ying Guan La – Eagle Pass Mountain," Cedric says. "We were to take off from Xichang at 3:00 a.m. from a grassy pasture in the dark of night by the headlights of a single Jeep. The track north was up the Wolong River and the only navigation aid would be Gongga Shan [Minya Konka]. At 24 900 feet it would be easily recognized as the tallest peak in continental China. We were to land at daybreak on a landing strip 12 000 feet high, where boulders had been rolled off the riverbank."

Portrait of Captain Ced Mah in May 1946, on return from flying the Himalayan Hump from India over Burma to China in World War II. The picture was taken in New York in the dress uniform of China National Aviation Corp. (CNAC). (Photo: Ced Mah collection)

Because Western China is 90 percent mountains and hills, the animals were needed for the planned October 1945 landing and invasion of Haiphong, in French Indo-China. Tibetan horses are small and wiry, being of Mongolian stock, and it was the plan of the American veterinarian officers to drive the horses to Xichang over the 16 000 foot passes.

Lack of oxygen en route to Gongga Shan forced the passengers to lie on the floor of the aircraft and not move. When an oxygen leak developed in the line, Cedric and his copilot had to share the little that was left. It ran out, and they flew for the last 20 minutes breathing only the thin air in the cockpit until an opening appeared in the clouds and they could lower the aircraft.

The aircraft banked beneath the snow and hanging glaciers, and set down in the pink dawn of the Tibetan morning. Cedric was awestruck by the beauty of mountain peaks wreathed in mist above lengthy purple shadows, and the sight of the sparkling white monastery clinging to the side of the steep hill. The golden-robed abbot and lamas came running out, their faces etched in the string of lights from their lamps fueled with yak butter.

So Long Busong, the pilots' Tibetan Chieftain and guide, moved to greet them as curious children came near to tentatively touch the "giant Gorak" (eagle) aircraft.

The Jeep they had brought in the aircraft was unloaded and the veterinary officers departed to buy horses as the pilots blasted off again into the cool morning air.

"What a delight to get away from the Assam jungle!" Cedric wrote in a memoir. "To experience the spring-like Yunnan Plateau, and to get to view the Himalayas from Kham, Tibet's easternmost province. A once-in-a-lifetime experience, one I intend to someday retrace by land." (He did make the return trip in June 1945, and has written eloquently about the experience).

On August 8, 1945, Cedric received an order that later proved significant. "You've got a trip to Chonqing with 20 passengers. You're to stay with them and take them anywhere they want to go."

Something was strange. He'd seen the uniforms of these passengers before, but where? Suddenly he knew: on the corpses of Japanese who had been killed when Teng Chun was taken in the fall of 1944! When B-25s were bombing overhead, P-51 fighter-bombers were knocking down the walls, and CNAC Transports had been flying dynamite and ammunition! These people were Japanese!

When the passengers had boarded, Cedric was given specific orders. "You're going to Shui Long Po, not San Hu Pa, the sandbar at the bottom of the Yangtze gorges." Odd. At the sandbar was a good runway of about 2000 feet, paved with tombstones taken from graves to make a hard landing surface.

"Shui Long Po! That's a military field! Chiang Kai-Shek's private airstrip," Cedric said.

"That's right," came the reply. "They know you're coming."

Cedric surmised that his passengers, the enemy, had been captured. He duly flew them in to the Yangtze gorge south of the town. At 4:00 the next afternoon, August 9th, he was cleared back to Kunming, but informed that his passengers would be staying. When he finally asked their identity he was simply told that they were "a military mission."

Many years later, Cedric discovered that on the night of August 6th, after a United States Army B-29 had dropped the atomic bomb on Hiroshima, the younger brother of Emperor Hirohito, Prince Haulik, Kai Hirohito, flew from Tokyo to Nanjing, China.

From Nanjing they'd set course for Chihkiang, a town and an airstrip located between the Japanese-occupied lands and free China. (The aircraft flown by the Japanese was a DC-2 "Tabby," built by licence agreement under Nakajima Aircraft). From the Japanese headquarters at Chihkiang , a US DC-3 had picked them up and flown them to Kunming, and there Cedric had been employed to take them further to Chongqing. He had flown the delegation that had come to talk surrender terms with China!

In total, Cedric completed 337 return flights over the mountains of Burma with the Flying Tigers in 1944 and 1945, and again in the spring of '46. For each of these missions he had to psyche himself up with the oft-repeated phrase ringing in his ears: "You're expendable, don't you know?" When asked if he was ever afraid that the next might be the final flight, he shrugged. "This is what we said during the war: 'So? What do you want to do? Live forever?' In other words, you become a fatalist. 'What do you want to do, live forever? You're expendable, don't you know?'

"And you *did* know it was the most hazardous, dangerous air route, because of weather, winds, altitude, war . . . and against a very disciplined, very sophisticated enemy. Over there, as the Tiger says, 'Don't forget to respect your enemy.' They're nothing like the cartoons, where they have myopic vision. They're fierce, fierce fighting men. You're out there doing your job, you know what you have to do and nothing matters except survival. If you don't survive, no story."

Many of Cedric's comrades, and the airplanes, didn't survive. "Towards the end of the war we had a fleet of 22 aircraft; but our attrition rate was so high that we'd lost 66 aircraft during the war. In other words, that fleet was replaced three times over. It was also hard on the human beings. They were killed, or they quit, wore out or just broke down."

Release from one's tour of duty in Burma was almost impossible, unless you were shot down, wounded or could get someone to relieve you. For round-the-clock flying, five complete crews were needed per day to man each aircraft.

In late September 1945, Cedric was hurriedly dispatched from Burma with arms and troops through China and Beijing, to the Siberian border. The United States was afraid that Russia would march right through Manchuria and enslave China. Therefore 60 000 US Marines had landed in Tianjin to race to The Great Wall and cordon off North China. The Chinese Communists were moving their capital from Yan'an into China's three northeast provinces. The Russians were disarming the Japanese, and, although they controlled the cities and railroads, the Chinese "Reds" had seized the ammunition dumps in the outlying areas. The Civil War moved into the open, and by October 1945, Cedric was over Kaifeng, air-dropping supplies along the Yellow River. The Nationalists were holding the cities and attempting to maintain communications.

It became difficult, indeed, to recognize the face of the enemy. Cedric acknowledges that "the internal war became quite a tangled sky."

When the war officially ended, the story did not conclude for CNAC, nor for Cedric Mah. He kept on flying the Hump until the end of November. Then the US Air Transport Command shut down and began the demolition of all war installations, hangars and runways.

When Cedric came out of Burma, he had built up 6000 hours flying time. "We flew every day that we possibly could and gained a lot of experience. Well, that's what we went over there for. We figured if we survived it, we'd have experience and memories."

Post-War Adventures

Cedric's post-war work included flying out government ministries from inland war-torn Chongqing to Nanjing, the pre-war Nationalist capital. He took a brief holiday in April 1946 following the signing of peace treaties, but soon found himself returning to the fray.

"I went back towards the end of 1946, when they were pioneering overseas routes for airlines into French Indo-China, Siam, Burma and Calcutta," Cedric says. "I'd moved over from CNAC – Pan American Airways – to Central Air Transport Company [CATC] – Eurasia, a subsidiary of Lufthansa Airlines. We engaged in all campaigns, air-dropping supplies into Manchuria when the Communists cut off their rail and road routes."

"After Manchuria fell, the Communists moved their offensive to Central China," Cedric continues. "Days without end, I was overhead, from November 6, 1948, when the Communists launched their final attack, to the last day, January 10, 1949, when the slaughter on the Yellow River plains ended."

That last day of fighting involved 400 Transports flying in the dark at 6:00 a.m.

"Our call for grid coordinates netted silence," Cedric recalls. "Slowly, the fleet of wingtip lights orbited, wondering where to drop the fuel, food, guns, shells and ammunition. There was no answer. Then, in the half-light, a ring of fire erupted and the voice of the Ground Controller came on: 'Woy Nanjing! Woy Nanjing! Return Nanjing! Return Nanjing!' Chen Yi and Vice-Commander Deng Xiaoping had prevailed.

"With dawn, defeat and surrender flickered in the split windshields of the Dodge trucks forming a 10-mile diameter, or larger, circle. The Nationalists had put to the torch all the supplies we had dropped."

Cedric flew the last airplane out of Nanjing before the Communists captured the airport, and also was the last pilot to fly out of Shanghai before it fell.

"We had flown all the refugees out of Shanghai to Hong Kong and I came back in and said to the station agent, 'Any more passengers?' 'No more,' he said, 'but don't try to go back to your house. The Communists are there, on the western outskirts.' I jumped in the car and headed down the Bubbling Well Road and came to a 10-foot board fence. I asked the soldier standing there, 'What is this?' 'That's a bandit wall to keep the Communist bandits out.' He didn't want to call them 'the opposite side' or the 'enemy.' I said, 'You mean I can't go through there?' 'No,' he said. 'We don't let the Communists through, why should we let you sneak through?' So everything I had was lost. I was wearing a set of underwear that I'd put on three weeks before, I'd slept in the C-46 airplane day and night while flying back and forth. Everything I had in the house, the Communists got."

This included the loss of a major portion of his earnings, two cars, and the house.

"I got out with only the shirt on my back. But I was smart enough to throw my photograph album and my movie film into a steamer trunk and put it in the bottom cargo compartment of the aircraft, so that's why I still have the pictures I took up in Tibet, when I flew American veterinary officers up there to buy horses," Cedric says.[2]

"After the conquest of China by the Communists, I – a capitalist and entrepreneur with money in the bank, not a Communist with holes in my pockets – departed Hong Kong to arrive back home in April 1950, to start a business in Canada," Cedric concludes.

Reality of Return

Wars are expensive: planes and personnel must be paid for and the United States had carried a large part of the expense. Cedric's salary had been deposited at the Bank of America in New York. Carrying out these high-risk jobs had resulted in good money, including bonuses for particularly dangerous trips. Cedric reported in the *Star Weekly* (ibid.) that in one three-month period he had received $10 000.

Some history books have called them mercenaries or soldiers of fortune, because neither Canada nor the US was at war with Japan at the time these fighting forces were established.[3]

Although Albert was awarded the Distinguished Flying Cross and the Air Medal for path-finding the uncharted 'Hump' and Himalayas, those who "volunteered" to fly and fight in Burma have only recently been acknowledged, and honorably discharged from service, some 50 years later in 1995.[4]

"When Albert reached 75 years of age, they finally decided to fire him," Cedric says with a smile. "Then, when I got to be 75 a couple of years later, they fired me, too."

Cedric's letter, dated July 2, 1997, from the Department of the Air Force Headquarters personnel center at Randolph Air Force Base, Texas, reads:

Congratulations on your discharge from the Air Force as a former member of the China National Aviation Corporation (CNAC). This discharge entitles you to the Asiatic-Pacific Campaign Medal, American Campaign Medal, and World War II Victory Medal. We are extremely pleased to provide you with these awards, as well as the World War II Honorable Service Lapel Button.

The letter, signed by Georgia A. Wise, DAFC, Recognition Programs Branch, closes with a note of "sincere appreciation for your faithful service to a grateful nation."

Cedric now had vast experience flying DC-3s, C-46s and the early Convair 240s which came out in 1949, in the worst conditions imaginable. It came time to consider his future. His favorite aircraft was the DC-3 and they were being used with good success in Canada's North.

"We all loved the DC-3. The C-46 was a little bit more difficult to handle, you couldn't kick it around like the DC-3. In gusty and windy conditions they go the way the big gale leads it. With the DC-3 we had more maneuverability, we could pilot those airplanes just like the bush pilots were piloting Beavers."

He said farewell to his surviving fellow Tigers, and returned to Canada to relax and do some long-awaited hunting and fishing. Some of his colleagues went to Indonesia, some to Burma, but Cedric notes that many of these fellows are not around today, men who had become famous for their bravery and flying ability, such as Earthquake McGoon. This giant of a man, who stood six-foot-six and weighed around 300 pounds, during World War II flew an F-4U bent-wing fighter. Cedric later heard that McGoon had also served in the Vietnam war. One day he was over Dien Bien Phu when his Fairchild Packet took a round of ack-ack. The machine hit the side of a hill and exploded. It was just an example of the odds catching up

Cedric, himself, had grown tired of "always being shot at."

"That's why I say, nothing else matters except survival," he says, about his decision to leave the drama of wartime flying. "Other than that you're just a statistic. After a while, you become cynical. It affects you for a long time.

"It took about five years before I could adapt to living in Canada. Five years, I'd wake up with my pyjamas all skewed and buttons pulled, still fighting the war – 'Watch that right engine, eh? Stay away from the flak, there!'"

It was a strange time of readjustment. Unlike other returned servicemen, his service time wasn't immediately recognized because he was, basically, nobody's employee. While overseas, it was always understood that "If you were shot down, nobody knew you. We were just doing a job out there."

Civilians back home couldn't imagine the scenario. "Nobody could acknowledge it because they didn't know what life I'd gone through. Their life was the same every day. There were no decorations or rewards for us. And, by that time, everything had gone to pot. Because you're not on the winning side, nobody wants to know you. We were flying for China, and China had fallen."

He decided to reestablish his life in Vancouver, a bustling coastal city that offered opportunity for the entrepreneur. He bought property on Hastings Street and Clark Drive, and built the Playdium Bowling Alley which he ran for 15 years. When competition went wild, with people building 100-lane – and even talking about 200-lane – bowling alleys, Cedric had to decide between raising a few million dollars to equal or better the competition, or get out. He sold and moved to Edmonton in 1964, to fly the bush.

In the meantime, he'd kept up his flying credentials by signing on with various airlines each year from spring until fall during the slack bowling season. From 1951-54 he'd

Cedric Mah, 1951, on Norseman in Kildala, BC, with pet crow Blackie. (Photo: Ced Mah collection)

flown with Central BC Airways (which later became Pacific Western Airlines) to and from the Kemano project near Kitimat. Noted as the largest civilian project in the world at the time, the Kemano hydroelectric project provided power for the Alcan aluminium smelter at the head of the Douglas Channel via a dam on the Nechako River, which diverted the flow westward through a tunnel to the Kemano generation station. The Duke of Edinburgh opened the massive project.

Cedric was flying Beavers and Norsemen for Central BC Airways on the Kemano project when Carl Agar brought in the first helicopter, and began to experiment with mountain flying. Cedric put a few hours on helicopters himself, but that type of work was not for him. "I'm a 'place and people' person," he says. "I like to go from one place to another. I liked the helicopter itself but I didn't like sitting in the muskeg all summer, and going from there to someplace up on the mountain to bring in a few drill rods or whatever. I remember on one job, for three weeks I never saw a bathtub. So, I never did take it up."

His work entailed flying personnel around the project and making trips from Vancouver to Kitimat and Kemano. He agrees that the coast is a tough route to fly, perhaps easier than the Himalayas, but "each has its own problems."

Again, climatic conditions were extreme: fog, sleet, snow, wind and rain – and other coastal problems

Ced Mah, 1952, Kemano, BC, in Beaver aircraft. (Photo: Ced Mah collection)

such as high waves or other sea-situations. "It might be 3:00 in the morning and you're skidding down the channel," Cedric says. "The inlets get real calm and smooth and you're down low trying to stay underneath the fog, but the whale is sleeping, just under the surface. It looks like a slick of water or maybe a rock or something. Then the whale feels your vibrations. All of a sudden you see something black off the horizon and this is the tail fluke [horizontal tail fin] as it's diving, trying to get away from the buzz. You could easily hit the tail if you didn't pull up."

Cedric spent 20 years flying the Pacific West Coast area, and was featured in a Toronto publication, *The Star Weekly*, on September 11, 1954, as reputedly being Canada's only Chinese-Canadian bush pilot. His adventures included flying RCMP personnel around the remote coastline searching out "log rustlers." Cedric would zigzag up and down inlets seeking out the thieves, then circle above a fishing boat he spotted towing the booty. One time, when the robbers saw the aircraft they desperately tried to saw the identifying brands off their stolen logs. But Cedric quickly zoomed in, and the offenders were arrested and loaded onto the airplane for a trip to the Kitimat jail.

A mountain in BC's coastal range has been named "Ced Mah Mountain" in honor of his outstanding service in transporting and supplying a government survey party to this area under difficult flying conditions. "People all over the world know me as 'Ced.' In the Orient, the people don't use, or can't pronounce, the letter 'r'. It also saves paper," Cedric adds with a grin.

The best thing he remembers about coastal flying is "I got in lots of fishing."

"When we'd get a few hours off on a charter flight, we'd fly over the mountains into pristine lakes and catch steelhead and salmon and stuff like that." Cedric is a rockhound and has an interest in geology, gemstone cutting and minerals. Other pilots report seeing him haul "about 600 pounds" of rocks and cutting equipment in the tail of his aircraft.

In 1957, Cedric had married Maimie Lee, the daughter of a high ranking official for the Hong Kong-Shanghai Bank Corporation. The romance had blossomed since 1944, when they were introduced by mutual friends in Calcutta, between the wealthy, educated city girl and the dashing, but poor, Canadian pilot. "She had millionaire suitors stacked up 10 deep," Cedric recalls. "I told her she should marry one of those because when I got back to Canada I wanted to be a bush pilot."

Maimie, who had always lived in large cities such as Shanghai with its 14 million people, considered Vancouver to be little more than a hick town. Instead of being the daughter of a high-ranking bank official, entertaining international business people, she was now the wife of a bowling-alley owner whose customers represented the working class and a bush pilot who was away from home for long stretches of time. "It was not easy," Cedric concedes. The marriage with Maimie Lee lasted from 1957 to 1964, and no children were born. When they separated, Maimie went to New York to work for the

United Nations, and Cedric sold the bowling alley. The following year he headed to Edmonton to pursue his bush flying career in earnest.

Bush Pilot

Cedric Mah took jobs with a number of airlines to achieve his dream of being a Northern pilot. On one job, flying north out of Edmonton for Gateway Aviation in 1967, he made national headlines when he and a geologist went missing for 10 days in the Arctic. "We ran into severe snow squalls, heavy snow showers, icing conditions, no visibility and winds up to 40 and 50 miles per hour," Cedric recalls. "It was like the curtain being drawn across Shakespeare's last stage." A search and rescue operation involved RCAF airplanes as well as civilian searchers. "We knew where we were – it was the other planes that were lost," Cedric said at the time. His hard-won survival skills kept them alive, although he lost 20 pounds.

During the summer months Cedric flew for smaller airlines in BC and the Yukon, even flying one summer for legendary pilot Herman Peterson of Atlin.

Cedric laughs. "From a big city like Vancouver I wound up in Atlin, where on a busy summer night, when all the prospectors and natives and everyone would come in, there'd be 75 people in town! But I enjoyed the fishing in the summer, and the scenery."

In June 1960, Cedric was flying for the Geological Survey of Canada in BC's Tatshenshini region (Mount Logan 19 850 feet), now Kluane National Park. He received orders to fly to Telegraph Creek and pick up the Forestry Warden and take him to McClure Lake near Telkwa, BC. The Smithers district had been on high fire alert since April and water bombers and float planes were assembled. Most surprising was to learn that his home town of Prince Rupert, usually considered the wettest spot on the Pacific coast, was also tinder-dry. A hectic summer was spent at McClure Lake and the Smithers headquarters, fighting fires until fall.

"I flew a Beaver," Cedric recalls. "I had to have a machine that could get in and out of those small lakes and rivers. We had 65-gallon tanks on either float. We'd skim across the lake and the probes, like straws bent forward, would scoop up the water. We'd go up and down, up and down. Our water dumps kept the fire cooled down a bit, so they could get the helicopters in with the firefighters."

Cedric also flew C-46s for Russ Baker's company, Pacific Western Airlines, on the DEW Line, flying out of Yellowknife and Hay River.

On another job, Cedric took to the Arctic with the federal government's Polar Gas project to do a game survey, counting musk ox and polar bears and other wildlife in the Arctic Islands. "They were trying to run a pipeline from the Arctic Islands down past James Bay to Sarnia, Ontario."

Next season, he flew for the Polar Continental Shelf Expedition. Departing Resolute, they would fly west and cover the Arctic Coast to Point Barrow, Alaska. Then, they'd turn northeast and follow the permanent ice pack to a point 300 miles south of the North Pole. "We flew scientists from Ward Hunt Island east to Greenland, threaded past Ellesmere Island to Baffin Island and Lancaster Sound, and chased the Northwest Passage through Prince of Wales Straits to the base at Tuktoyaktuk," Cedric recalls. "On other trips, they photographed the hogback and glaciers of Ellesmere Island from a high level, and mapped Devon Island's Polar Ice Cap for global warming."

For this work, the government used a Super Beechcraft 18, Model "H," especially crafted for the T. Eaton Company. In addition to regular tanks it also sported nose tanks, giving it a range of 10 or 11 hours. Cedric liked flying this "luxury liner," and was amused by the respectful way the aircraft was treated compared to the other commercial airplanes he'd flown in the North, "where we beat them all to pieces hauling fish and bloody caribou and everything else."

This type of flying involved being in the air for eight to 10 hours at a time, at speeds of 200 mph, covering the entire Arctic region. "We had a female glaciologist with us, and her job was to sit for maybe two months on an ice floe on an Arctic Island, all by herself, fighting off amorous polar bears!"

Nothing is mentioned about fighting off amorous pilots, but Cedric laughingly explains that the type of work they did, and in those particular conditions, "didn't allow you to put your arm around them for too long."

One of the "particular conditions" was "burgy bits," pieces of ice 10 or 12 feet in diameter, smaller than "growlers" which were around 15 feet or more. Normally, pressure ridges didn't reach much higher than 75 feet, but that was the altitude they maintained when they were trying to sneak around the large icebergs doing ice patrol.

Cedric explains that the icefields and glaciers on Ellesmere Island and Greenland could be the size of Vancouver Island, with ice 10 000 to 12 000 feet deep. "Their weight keeps oozing them down. By the time they come out of the valley and into the sea, the summer warmth causes them to candle, break and slough off into the sea as icebergs."

So again he was flying in challenging conditions, but this time there was no human enemy gunning for him, just nature with its quick temper and hidden surprises.

But, like everything else, flying in the North changed, with more airlines setting up operations, and with better radio communication and faster aircraft that no longer required crews to spend much time in northern posts, getting to know each other.

"Before that, northern aviation was like a big club," Cedric recalls. "In the old days you told each other about fuel caches. You had your names on the barrels. If you used one you told the owner immediately that you'd used so many gallons of their fuel, and would replace it on a certain date, and that the other pilots who might depend on that cache should be informed. But, airlines were ambitious, everyone wanted to break in to the business everywhere. It got so that nobody trusted anybody. And soon, fuel started going missing."

Although Cedric had been for a time employed by a company often accused of such shenanigans, he does not want to be tarred with that same brush. "Us old-timers would never just use up other people's fuel, but there were a lot of hungry people there at that time. It takes a lot of money to cache fuel up there and it was just like the world is right now: everything was money. You never got an increase in pay until you said, 'I think I'm going to quit,' and then you'd hear, 'Oh, then we'll give you more money.'"

But Cedric loved the life of a northern bush pilot. When he was airborne he was free; it was the people on the ground who were scrapping for money. Although Cedric had the intelligence and acumen to rise in business, he chose to stay in the bush and fly. "That's my life," Cedric says simply. "They'd ask me to run different places and I'd always say no. I'd say to them, 'If I ran this business, I'd have to talk to you guys and all you talk about is money. This way, I can go talk to guys like 'Midnight' Anderson and Herman Peterson and other northern bush pilots. I speak their language.' I prefer to be able to walk anywhere and not have a dollar sign in my eye."

Cedric married again, in 1970, to Ruth Gronlund. Two children were born, a daughter Cheryll in 1970, and a son, Jonathan Christopher, in 1974. The marriage lasted 13 years to 1983, but with Cedric up North most of the time and the family living in Edmonton, strains were placed on this marriage as well.

"That's the life of a pilot," Cedric says. "They're gone all the time. She wasn't too happy with that."

Following his contracts with the federal government, Cedric flew on contract in 1975 for Bradley Air Service. But he was now 53 years old, and he began to think about retirement plans. He decided to visit his old home town of Prince Rupert. Perhaps, by going back to his birth-city, he might discover something to interest him in the years to come.

En route, he stopped at Smithers, and found himself employed by Smithers Air as their chief pilot. "Geez, I'd rather just fly," Cedric said, but as the company lacked anyone who held licenses for flying and fixing, Cedric had the job whether he wanted it or not. "I had to do everything there. I was the mechanic to the gas boy to the pilot. They had a Beaver, a seven-passenger Piper and a Beech 18."

When asked if he had any adventures with this company, he laughs. "It was all a total adventure. I didn't stay very long."

The company's lack of funds for top-quality maintenance made Cedric uneasy. "When I quit they brought a young fellow in there. He made a few mistakes that resulted in burnt out engines and a few accidents. After all these accidents the owner finally had to sell."

When Cedric reached Prince Rupert, he was again offered jobs. He flew there for North Coast Air while researching his past to lay groundwork for the future.

But, before he attacked his stacks of books and volumes of notes, Cedric decided to make some "farewell trips" into the Arctic before calling it quits to his flying career. He flew for a tourist lodge at Great Bear Lake near the Arctic Circle, an area he'd flown 25 years previous. Then he flew single Otters and Cessna 185s for Rae-Com Air out of Yellowknife. It was great fun, just flying. No more rolling barrels of fuel up bobbing ramps into Beavers on floats, no more loading and unloading blood-soaked caribou or heavy steel rods. "I'd done my share of rolling and loading. Now I could just fly – walk on and walk off."

Cedric's brother, Albert, had also continued with his aviation career. He flew a Canso (San Francisco-Hawaii-Japan), then switched to C-46s to service the Nationalist troops that had retreated to the Golden Triangle (Burma-Laos-Thailand) opium land. He also flew on the DEW (Distant Early Warning) Line and in the bush. He now owns and operates an apartment building in Montreal.

New Routes on Old Paths

At 65 years of age, Cedric let his medical go, retired from flying and sat down to write a family history that goes back almost to the dawn of time.

When asked if he feels he made good career choices, Cedric says, "Well, I flew until I was 65 and I can still smile. I was going to fly another five years after that, I figured I was healthy enough to do it, but there were no more helpers! Before, you could get an eager young fellow interested in aviation to work for minimum wage or a few dollars to come help you load and fuel and work on the airplane, or swamp with you, or you could maybe grab a few minutes' nap while he kept the airplane in the sky. But pretty soon, these kids discovered they could make $20 or $25 an hour working in a mine, so

Cedric Mah with his vintage Pontiac Parisienne in front of the Alberta Aviation Museum, Edmonton, 1998. (Photo: Shirlee Matheson)

why would they hang around the dock? And airplanes didn't interest them anymore. Life changed, and the kids weren't air-minded anymore."

Cedric Mah's flying career is now on hold, but there's always a possibility that it could be reactivated. "I could get a physical, maybe go up with some young shaver to check me out to see if I can fly or not, and spend a couple of dollars flying around the airport." Then Cedric laughs. "Who knows? Maybe he, with his 500 hours, will think I don't know how to fly! But, the secret is longevity. I didn't want to be the best pilot in the world, but I did want to be the oldest."

Cedric isn't exactly sure of the number of flying hours he has accumulated. "I quit adding them up after about 30 000. Records have been lost in the wars and numerous evacuations. I made many little short trips from here to there. I suppose it would be somewhere around 30 000 plus fishing trips."

That's a lot of hours, especially the kind of flying he has done – 337 missions over the Burma Hump and a civilian flying career that was not without drama. When asked if he's ever crashed an airplane, his response is instantaneous: "All the time! But every one was a controlled crash. I'd get it there – where it went after that was beside the point. So many close shaves!"

He expands by describing tricky landings on the Mackenzie River. "You go down and bounce two or three times to make sure the ice can hold you, come back and land, and all of a sudden the wing dips in, hits that goldarn aileron horn. You pop back up, 'What the hell was that?' and you spin around on the ice. You look behind and discover that, as you'd landed, a big chunk of ice 10 feet thick had broken. You see, when it gets cool, the ice freezes and the water gets lower, so the ice is hanging there. By the time you go in, March or April, it's hanging with no water underneath to support it."

He hasn't "written off" aircraft, just "knocked off a wheel, maybe, here or there," and he's justifiably proud of his record. "I don't have a scratch on me and I never injured anybody."

Now back in Edmonton to work on his research, Cedric maintains his connection with the aviation world through membership in the local flying club and the aviation museum.

"I was minding my own business, rewriting some of these stories, when one day I bumped into Chuck MacLaren and Gordy Cannam. 'Hey, put out $25! They're going to roast me!' Gordy said. I said, 'I'll be there.' So I went to the 'roast' and all of a sudden some people came up and said, 'Are you a Flying Tiger?' and before I could open my mouth they said, 'I heard you were here. We've got to come and talk to you.'"

Cedric hasn't yet found the time to do any volunteer work with the air museum, aside from "helping them drink their coffee," because he's been working six days a week on his writing project. But the "yakking" that goes on in Marie's Place, the coffee shop at the back of the museum, allows him to renew old friendships and meet new people in a field that Cedric has embraced for most of his life.

His views on aviation in Canada yesterday and today centre on the radical changes he has seen from the cockpit. "In the late 1920s and early '30s they started bush flying, so I was there at the start, even though I was just a three-year-old kid seeing this gloved hand waving out a window from the thing in the sky. I knew I wanted to be up there, like a bird, and I've done that.

"During World War II, bush flying in Alaska just disappeared out the window. Mainline flying took over. When every village and hamlet had carved out an airstrip, ski-planes and float-planes began to service the outlying settlements, with sportsman guides and pilots by the thousands. With all these landing strips, pilots lost the feel for flying where you were just as comfortable landing on a sandbar as on an airfield.

"Now, a lot of the Forestry work we did is being done by helicopters and fire detection units. We used to fly around and eyeball where a fire was starting by seeing a red glow. Now a satellite picks it up; lightning strikes are recorded by a central agency, so all of that has changed."

Cedric reflects on the short history of the "by guess and by God, seat-of-the-pants" style of bush flying: "We thought it was going to last forever, but it's gone. We should be content that we were able to put in 50 or more years doing what we'd dreamed about. Very few people are able to match that."

Cedric Mah has flown nearly every kind of airplane, in civil, commercial and military ventures. "I flew commercial aircraft in the Far East, pioneering the routes into Thailand, Laos and French Indo-China. But every time I got back to Shanghai, I knew I preferred the warfront, so I'd be up near the Siberian border in Manchuria."

He could easily have gone with an airline and become a captain. "I have a wire here from Trans Pacific Airline in Hawaii saying they could employ me as pilot, starting as copilot. But can you imagine, after flying thousands of miles of barren lands, over Arctic landscape, me going to Hawaii where the longest route in the Hawaiian Islands is 300 miles? I wanted to see the rest of the world, and the rest of the world isn't in the middle of the Pacific Ocean."

Would he change anything if he could look back and turn himself left or right at a certain point?

"I don't think so," Cedric replies. "As a three-year old kid I knew what I wanted to do. No, I don't think I'd change anything, even with all the hardships.

"I was born a Gemini, and was destined to roam," Cedric says philosophically. "An unknown author wrote this epitaph, which I guess would be quite fitting for mine:

'Adventure was his coronal, and all his wealth was wandering.'"

Footnotes:

[1]A concise history of the formation of the Flying Tigers is contained in: Seagrave, Sterling, *Soldiers of Fortune*, Time-Life Books Inc., The Epic of Flight Series, Alexandria, Virginia,

USA, 1981. "Tigers in the Asian Sky," pp. 73-108. The author spent much of his child-hood in Burma where his father, Dr. Gordon Seagrave, won fame as a medical missionary and as the author of *Burma Surgeon*.

[2]The horses of Tibet, bought in February/March of 1945 and driven over the high passes to Xichang for a planned autumn invasion of Haiphong on the French Indo China coast, never saw action. At war's end they were declared surplus.

[3]A favorite poem of Claire Lee Chennault, the American who initially led the Flying Tigers, was said to be "Epitaph on an Army of Mercenaries" by British poet A.E. Houseman:

These, in the day when heaven was falling
The hour when earth's foundations fled,
Followed their mercenary calling
And took their wages and are dead.
Their shoulders held the sky suspended;
They stood, and earth's foundations stay;
What God abandoned, these defended,
And saved the sum of things for pay.

[4]A letter and certificate, sent to Albert Mah from the Department of the Airforce, Washington, DC, 20330-5020I dated February 24, 1995, refers to "Special Order GD132."

By direction of the President, and with approval of the Secretary of the Airforce, each of the following China National Aviation Corporation personnel is awarded the Air Medal for meritorious achievement while participating in aerial flight during the period indicated [4th of July, 1943 to 29th of November, 1944].

The letter is signed by Kevin A. Collins, Colonel, USAF, Director of Information Management, for the Secretary of the Airforce. Albert, arriving in Burma 18 months before Cedric, was the first to receive this award.

The letter goes on to finally ascertain his Honorable Discharge from the Armed Forces of the United States of America.

This is to certify that Albert Mah, 221-03-3590, USAF China National Aviation Corporation ATC Group, was honorably discharged from the United States Airforce on the 29th day of November, 1944. This certificate is awarded as a testimonial of honest and faithful service.

For further details of the contribution to the war effort of captains Albert and Cedric Mah, and other Chinese Canadians, see, Wong, Marjorie: *The Dragon and the Maple Leaf, Chinese Canadians in World War II*. Pirie Publishing, Box 39073, London, ON, N5Y 5L1.

A Grassroots Love of Aviation

Gertrude "Trudy" Alvina Jenkyn always felt that aviation would play an important part in her life. She loved the idea of flying, and in 1944 when she finished her courses at Sarnia Collegiate Institute & Technical School in Sarnia, Ontario, she considered becoming a stewardess, one of few opportunities for women to get into the air at that time. A friend, Lois Soper, who lived in the United States and was a stewardess with United Airlines, thrilled Trudy with descriptions of the cities she was visiting and the fun she was having. But Trudy began making good money working in offices, first at Dow Chemical, then at Polymer Corporation.

Neil J. Armstrong was a field engineer who worked for Trudy's boss, and it was part of her job to advise him of meetings and provide other professional information. When the young couple began dating, their common interest in aviation immediately became apparent. When she told Neil about her friend Lois and how she, too, might like to work for an airline, Neil was very encouraging and supplied her with addresses of airlines and advice on who she should contact.

"At the time I remember thinking, 'Well, does he want me out of here, or what?'" Trudy says, laughing.

She never did get to be a stewardess. Trudy and Neil were married on June 20, 1953, when Trudy was 25 and Neil 33.

Trudy Jenkyn was born in the small town ("about 600 people on a busy day") of Courtright, Ontario, located 12 miles south of Sarnia on the St. Clair River. Trudy's and Neil's personal backgrounds were not dissimilar, although his eight-year seniority had given him the opportunity to clock a number of adventures by the time he and Trudy met. Neil J. Armstrong was born April 15, 1920, in the nearby small town of Alvinston, Ontario. He joined the Royal Canadian Mounted Police and served in Ontario, Manitoba and Saskatchewan before entering the military in 1943. He graduated as an RCAF commissioned officer and pilot, and instructed pilot trainees until his discharge in 1945.

Neil took a mining engineering degree from the University of Toronto, graduating in 1949 with majors in geology and geophysics. His career sent him to the Northwest Territories to work for Eldorado Mining and Refining, to Manitoba with the International Nickel Company, and back to Sarnia to work for Polymer Corporation. By the time Neil and Trudy were married, he had begun working as a geologist for Hudson's Bay Oil and Gas in Calgary.

For their honeymoon the couple flew from Ontario to Calgary in Neil's Cornell aircraft (CF-FLY), a low-wing trainer commonly used during the war. Upon landing at Calgary International Airport they were met by Neil's friends, Bill and Florence (Ginger) White. They landed the Cornell on the east side of the airport and made arrangements to store it at the Calgary Flying Club while on their honeymoon. "But almost immediately, Neil got a call to go on a well in Edson, Alberta! So, I stayed with the Whites in Calgary while he went up there – and that was the beginning of many, many years of such separations," Trudy says.

Later in 1953 Neil changed jobs again, leaving his work as a geologist to become a pilot for Spartan Air Services Limited. He had his pilot's licence for fixed wing, but he wanted to learn to fly helicopters and Spartan offered him that opportunity.

Flying On Her Own

The Armstrong family settled in Ottawa where their first child, J. Bradford, was born in 1954. At the time, Neil was in the Barren Lands where Spartan had sent him, under contract to the Geological Survey of Canada, to fly on Operations Baker (Lake) and Thelon (River), where they were mapping 100 000 square miles of uncharted territory. Left to her own devices, Trudy decided to sign up for flying lessons herself.

"When he was up North, I went flying on my own," Trudy says simply. "I took lessons at Carp, near Ottawa, through Bradley Air Services. There were not as many women doing it then.

"It's hard to believe, but there was not any ground school. I had Neil's reports and papers on meteorology and navigation, and I studied from Sandy Macdougall's book, *From the Ground Up*."

With famed Northern pilot Dick deBlicquy as her instructor, Trudy trained on an old two-place Aeronca, a tail-dragger, and soloed in five hours. "I had a great instructor. Dick deBlicquy and I had good rapport with each other," Trudy recalls.

"Like all fledgling pilots, I was so happy on the day that I soloed! On my way home I came to a stop sign and did a sort of 'California stop,' slow down and glide through, no traffic, but a short piece up the highway I was stopped by an Ontario Provincial policeman. I said, 'Oh, you can't do this to me! I just soloed!' 'Yeah, yeah, lady.' He didn't even say, 'Congrats.'

"But it was exciting, it truly was, because Neil was so proud of me."

Trudy wrote the usual exams, administered by the Department of Transport, and received her private pilot's licence in 1955.

Neil encouraged Trudy's achievement, which complemented his keen interest in aviation. Now they could fly together, as they still had the Cornell, although it was stored in Calgary. When they received news that the Calgary Flying Club had burned to the ground, they figured they'd lost their airplane. As luck would have it, the Cornell had been pushed out of the hangar because they owed two months rent, so was saved.

The next few years were extremely busy for Trudy, with moves back and forth from Ottawa to Calgary to accommodate her husband's work with Spartan. Three more boys were added to the family in rapid succession: J. Neil, simply called "JN," was born in Calgary in 1957, J. Trekker in Calgary in 1959, and J. Corcoran, usually called "JC" or "Corky," in Ottawa in 1964.

J. Corcoran was named for Trudy's beloved mother, "Mayme" Corcoran Jenkyn. Trudy and her mother were always very close and, following the death of Trudy's father, Mayme spent part of the year with the Armstrongs in Calgary and the rest with one of Trudy's sisters in Detroit.

"Mom died on my birthday, April 2, in 1963," Trudy says "Neil and I went down for the funeral in a Comanche. On takeoff from Detroit City Airport a few days later, we flew directly over the beautiful cemetery where mother had just been buried. I looked down and said to myself, 'I'm going to have another baby, and when I do I'm going to call that baby Corcoran after you, whether it's a girl or a boy.' And that's how Number 4 son got his name."

Finding The Next Fluffy Cloud

Trudy's next ambition was to get her gliding licence, which she accomplished in 1965.

"Gliding is very exciting," Trudy says. "Glider pilots always give power pilots a hard time, and vice-versa, saying, 'My type of flying is *more pure* than power flying," and power fliers replying, 'Yes, but you've got to get *towed* to be in the air.' It's very exhilarating. You see, there's no engine and you climb on thermals."

Trudy Armstrong at the glider base at Pendleton, east of Ottawa, 1965. (Photo: Trudy Armstrong collection)

She began taking lessons outside Ottawa at Pendelton when Number 4 son, Corky, was five months old. She would take him out to the airport, place him safely in a playpen, then go into the air while friends kept an eye on the baby and her other toddlers.

It wasn't easy for a mother of four young children to arrange some time for herself. Mega-preparations must be made. "Before I'd go out in the morning I would make sandwiches, with all kinds of goodies, plus drinks – you can imagine how much would be needed for all of us. When you glide, you're involved with everyone, you don't just go flying and then stand around. It's a community.

"It's not like flying where you pay for your hours, have your instructor tell you what your flying is going to be for that day, how much time you have, then when it's over you are free to just walk away. Gliding, on the other hand, means that you're committed to the day, and to everyone's activities. If you're going gliding on the weekend, you're there early Saturday morning when everyone is hauling out the gliders. When the gliders land you grab the wings and walk with them, babysit them. There's a lot of work involved."

With the kids on the ground and mom in the air, Trudy still managed to keep a maternal eye on her brood. "Rather than striving for long flight duration, I didn't stay up too long or leave the airport with all those kids down there. I kept it in sight, and made sure I had access to it, because there was no way I could turn on the power to get down in a hurry."

So, Trudy started her gliding lessons, and the fun began. "One has to have so many hours. Your instructor has to know that you are capable of being towed aloft alone, releasing, and doing circuits or whatever is expected of that particular flight. You have to be able to land the glider with the spoilers, to judge speed and distance, and to land without damaging anything. In short, your instructor has to know that you are a safe glider pilot!"

While she was learning, the instructor would demonstrate how to pull down the Plexiglas canopy and strap herself in. "You're not wearing a helmet, but you do wear a shoulder harness," Trudy says. "You climb in, stretch out your legs, the rudders are way down so you're sitting back, stretched out. It's not like an aircraft where you see the whole cockpit as you get in. It's more like a kayak, really!" In other words, it's a tight fit.

Training gliders have basic instruments (airspeed, altimeter and compass) on the panel. The release knob has a simple hook and catch release, and the glider is connected to a tow plane trailing a 150-foot rope. The skill is to keep straight and level behind the tow plane as it tows you into the air. "You don't spin or anything, but you can oscillate way over to one side or the other, or be above or below the tow plane. Formation flying, but directly behind the tow aircraft," Trudy says.

"Once you feel you're at the height you want to be – usually a designated height of 1500 to 2000 feet or maybe less – you release your tow rope and turn to the right while the tow airplane turns to the left, goes around and lands."

Under normal circumstances there is no signal to indicate to the pilot that you have released, Trudy says, because he's ahead of you – you see only the back of the pilot's head if you can see him at all. He knows by the weight, by the lack of pull, that you're gone.

"Then you try to find some thermals to keep you aloft! By that I mean updraft winds. You try to find a nice little puffy cumulus cloud, because usually there are thermals under there. Quite frankly, if I couldn't find a thermal right away to play around in, I'd just do my circuit while I still had my altitude and come back in.

"The whole idea with the pure glider pilots, which I am not," Trudy clarifies, "is to remain aloft at an astonishing height and travel for miles on the thermals."

Trudy never had any scary moments while gliding. "My scary moment was coming back down to see if the kids' diapers were clean!" she says with a laugh.

Her philosophy is that "gliding is a sport, like surfing, whereas flying is usually to get from A to B. My only destination in gliding was just to find the next puffy cloud. I wasn't out looking for new records, I was looking to get my glider pilot's licence, and I did."

Now having both fixed-wing and glider licenses, Trudy found gliders to be more thrilling. "When you solo in a glider you are relying on yourself. I suppose you are in a single aircraft, too, but in a glider one is impressed by that odd 'sound of silence'. Actually, there's the whistle of the wind going by, but it's a monotone, not hard or blustery."

Trudy acknowledges that she sometimes became philosophic while gliding. "You sit there and look down, you're on your own and you think, 'Oh God, it's just me and the world.' It's a neat experience."

Neil decided to join in the fun, too, and the whole family would go out to the old Pendelton airport east of Ottawa on a weekend, with the kids watching mom and dad fly away in the rented gliders.

"I'm trying to think of how Neil felt about gliding versus fixed wing, because his life was fixed wing – no, I can't assume. But I'm sure he found the power of fixed wing much more to his liking – there, I am assuming. He always felt gliding was okay but it was a weekend thing."

Daughter Nonnie Le'e was born in Ottawa in 1965, nicely completing the Armstrong family. "And then," says Trudy," my life just got complicated with children. When we moved to Calgary on a permanent basis in 1967, although there was a lot of gliding being done at Pincher Creek south of Calgary where the mountains give you great lift, I didn't do any more gliding."

Liftair International Ltd.

When Neil was first transferred to Calgary as the western manager for Spartan Air Services in 1957, he had met the Chairman of the Board, Fred McConnell, who owned Velocity Surveys, a geophysical company. When Spartan Air Services acquired that company, Fred and Neil began working together. It was the beginning of a lifelong friendship. As a result, when Spartan dissolved in 1969 and the Armstrongs were permanently located in the West, Neil and Fred decided to start Liftair International Ltd., a helicopter leasing company.

The work with Spartan Air Services, and the formative years of Liftair, took both Neil and Fred away a lot, as Neil was considered to be the first combination helicopter pilot-geologist in the North.

Trudy went on as many trips as possible but usually as copilot, in the right seat. "I wouldn't take those hours. Neil wanted them and as far as I was concerned that was fine. And besides, my flying had diminished – mainly because I couldn't get behind the dumb yoke, usually being pregnant! I mean, gee whiz, there were five children in 11 years, so my flying took second priority – but it was never a second priority with Neil and later with the children. They all began flying cross-country from Alberta to Ontario when they were little, like seven or eight."

The Armstrongs had a busy, busy life. In the early 1970s Trudy joined The Ninety-nines: an International Organization of Women Pilots, and in 1971 the group sponsored the first Canadian Powder Puff Derby to depart from a Canadian venue, flying from Calgary to Baton Rouge, Louisiana. She became an active member of that committee, which gave her the chance to meet other accomplished women. "Eleanor Bailey was chairman, and Neil's former secretary at Spartan, Rita Sinclair, was co-chairman. It was very exciting, intense work, and short-lived."

There was also a women's organization in Calgary called Cross-Winds. "It was to bring familiarity among the women whose husbands were well-known to each other," Trudy says. "This group gave the women, the distaff side, a chance to know each other and included anyone who was associated with the airport. You have to remember that it was a male-dominated airport, outside of the women who did secretarial work.

"Then, the Women's Airport Association of Calgary (WAAC) was formed, and was open to anyone associated with the airport, not necessarily pilots. I joined that. It allowed us to network with other women through meetings, and to hear speakers, socialize, etc."

While Trudy enjoyed the camaraderie of these women, she was simply too busy to take any executive position. "Like any organization, one finds that they become time-consuming, and once you volunteer you usually can't get out of your job."

The Armstrong family was extremely active. "Neil was a member of many organizations," Trudy says. "He was with the Canadian Owners and Pilots Association

(COPA) for years – I was too, as a member, but he was on the board for over 25 years. And we mixed a lot, and did a lot of travelling – to Europe, Africa, India, Australia, Singapore, etc. – so I wasn't feeling that I was left at home, 'barefoot and pregnant,' no!"

While Trudy was supportive of her husband's work, she did not take an active role in the businesses. "I knew all the staff and saw them socially, but I was not involved with the day-to-day running of the business. Neil and his partner, Fred McConnell, were very busy."

After Liftair was sold they started Fanair International, which leased helicopters to various corporations. "Most of the companies would fly them under their own names, but they were actually purchased by Fanair and then leased." Fanair was comprised of three partners: Fred McConnell; Andy Gray, a local orthodontist; and Neil Armstrong ("fan" was an acronym based on the first letter of each owner's Christian name). The company offices occupied No. 5 hangar, sharing the building with the budding Aero Space Museum where Trudy worked for 10 years after the children were grown.

Growing Up, Flying

As the years passed and the Armstrong children grew, aviation became a natural part of their lives. "They were in it all the time. Rather than our children saying, as you do in a car when you're on a holiday, 'Are we there yet?' they were in an airplane saying, 'Are we there yet?'" Trudy recalls with a smile. "We used to fly from Calgary to Ontario a lot. I felt that the children would get a real feeling for geography flying across

L. to R.: JN, J Corcoran, J Bradford, Trudy, Nonni, J Trekker, in front of Cessna 172 at Claresholm around 1972. (Photo: Armstrong collection)

the country, but you know children! They'd fight with each other, or sleep, or read, or listen to whatever!"

The children "just naturally gravitated" toward learning to fly. "There was no question, it was just going to happen. Flying would be part of whatever they did. And every one of them loved it, and are in it still."

All five began taking flying lessons before they were 16, and soloed on their 16th birthdays. At age 17, when they became eligible to apply for private pilot's licenses, each got one. "Number 1 son, Brad, when he was in university, also got his helicopter rating, and flew helicopters as a university student," Trudy says. "First he worked for Floyd Glass, owner of Athabaska Airways in Prince Albert, Saskatchewan, just to be around airplanes, and then flew helicopters for his father, for Liftair, on contracts, as did No. 2 son, JN."

The development of each Armstrong child's interests and accomplishments shows the deep commitment of the family to aviation.

"Number 1, Brad, always had an airplane. He went into family medicine, first practicing in Ontario then in Yellowknife, NWT, now in Hinton, Alberta. His wife, Peggy (Margaret) Allan, also in medicine, was taking flying lessons when they met in Yellowknife. Brad's flying is just for pleasure. He had a Cessna 210, which he sold and recently bought a partnership in a Cessna 172, stored at a small airport at Entrance near Hinton.

"Number 2 son, JN, has a Cessna T210, same as Brad's but a turbo. JN pursued advanced flying, including getting his ATR [airline transport rating] after he got his medical degree. He's doing anesthesiology now in Calgary at the Peter Lougheed Hospital. He also flies his T210 to and from Yellowknife, where he's on contract to do anesthesiology at the hospital there."

JN also flies a helicopter for Alberta Shock Trauma Air Rescue Society (STARS). His duties are strictly as pilot, but his combined knowledge of medicine and flying make him an integral member of this noteworthy organization that has saved many lives.

After university, Number 3 son, J. Trekker, joined Trans-Canada Pipelines Limited (TCPL) in Calgary and is currently their Manager of Information Technology. He flies Corky's little yellow Taylorcraft, which is hangared at Airdrie airport. "It's a classic, built in 1946. It's a neat little aircraft, a keeper," Trudy says.

Number 4 son, J. Corcoran, soloed at 16 and then began his university education, gaining a Bachelor of Science degree. "We always had an airplane, a 172 or whatever, in the family," says Trudy, "so he flew our aircraft until he built up his hours and got the tickets he needed for commercial flying.

"He flew out of Yellowknife for a while with LaRonge Aviation, starting as a 'hangar-rat', or a 'dock-rat' I guess you'd call it, working around the float planes," Trudy explains. "Then he flew Twin Otters for Kenn Borek Air Ltd. He spent time over in Baghdad, Iraq, flying on contract with United Nations through Kenn Borek Air, leaving Baghdad the day before the Gulf War. Then, also with Kenn Borek Air, he flew for several years in Antarctica. He also had his airline transport rating [ATR]. He did a number of trips flying Twin Otters across the Atlantic Ocean.

"After university he went directly for an aviation career," Trudy concludes. "He did love flying."

Corky retained his single status and thus freed himself to explore the world, through aviation. He was hired by the Italian National Antarctic Program through Kenn Borek Air Ltd. to aid in their study of weather patterns. Norway had been chosen as typical of some of the weather experienced in Antarctica, and Corky made several trips there flying the Twin Otter, on different contracts.

Number 5 child, Nonnie, also got her private pilot's licence, but her time became taken up by gaining three university degrees, a Bachelor of Science (B.Sc.), a Bachelor of Fine Arts (French) (BFA) and then a degree in physiotherapy (B.Sc.PT). She and her partner have a physiotherapy clinic in the Westhills area of Calgary. With these heavy time commitments she did not actively continue to fly.

Tale Heavy

The COPA *Canadian Flight* newspaper for 20 years carried a regular column, "Tale Heavy," authored by Neil Armstrong. Filled with news, stories of flights taken, anecdotes, historic insights and general chat from their 25-year board member, the newsy column was popular reading for subscribers.

In the December 1994 issue Neil expresses excitement at being contacted by Ramon Sagaceta (nicknamed "Moncho"), a Chilean friend of Corky's. Moncho worked as an air traffic controller and ham operator in Punta Arenas, Chile, and during the transmission Neil could hear sounds of PT6 turbines. Then his son's voice came on the HF radio patched through by Moncho, as Corky, accompanied by an engineer, piloted a Twin Otter en route from the South Pole. Corky stated that they'd first be landing at an abandoned German science station, then flying for another three hours to Patriot Hills, Antarctica.

"At that moment, they were cruising at 12 000 feet with their GPS silently counting off direction and miles," Neil writes. "He closed off with 'Merry Christmas! I'll probably see you in February.' What a Christmas present that was for us, one you can't buy at the mall!"

Neil explains that Corky enjoyed flying for this Calgary-based, "aggressive company, Kenn Borek Air Ltd., with contracts in many far-flung areas," and adds that they had one of the largest Twin Otter fleets in the world, the type of aircraft that Corky usually flew. The winter of 1994-95 was Corky's third season in the Antarctic.

Neil goes on to chart the route Corky took from Calgary to Punta Arenas, Chile.

Twin Otter flown by J. Corcoran Armstrong in Antarctica. (Photo: Armstrong collection)

"First, a customs stop in Great Falls, Montana; 1363 NM (nautical miles) to a RON (Rest Overnight) in Houston, Texas; 1032 NM to a RON in Georgetown, Cayman Islands; 1295 NM to a RON in Guayaquil, Ecuador; 1253 NM to a RON in Arico, Chile; 718 NM to Serena, Chile, 711 NM to Puerto Montt, Chile; and 781 NM to Punta Arenas – his home away from home – and a city of over 100 000 people with weather similar to that of the Alaska panhandle."

By this point, they had flown 7000 miles on a combination of wheels, wheel/skis, and straight skis.

At Punta Arenas, they'd changed to wheel/skis to fly over an area considered to be the roughest stretch of water in the world, the Drake Passage. Here, Corky reported seeing icebergs and ice pans but none large enough to land on in case of emergency. The end of the trip was Marsh, on the tip of the Antarctic peninsula.

"The ice cap can be 9000 feet thick and at that altitude, with a blizzard blowing, they could be tenting in -30°F with a severe wind chill," Neil writes. "If fuel and weather permit, they can go on to the British Base, Rothera, on Adelaide Island, replacing their wheel/skis with straight skis, and from there to various destinations. On his initial trip down, No. 4 son and the captain, Henri Perk, were weathered in at Rothera for 22 days."

Neil goes on to describe the methods of transportation that must be relied on in this inhospitable area. Dogs were used for transportation until 1994 when they were disallowed for not being indigenous to the area. Even horses had been used at one time, although it's hard to imagine. Now most often seen are airplanes and snowmobiles, which are eyed with curiosity by indigenous penguins.

Neil concludes by stating, "Antarctica is an area that holds much fascination for me . . . Where else can the airplane play a better role? No. 4 son says he may someday be able to show me some of the sights down there. Should one seat only become available, I would, of course, have to arm-wrestle with three of his brothers for the trip. Will seniority help?

"Fly safely, friends."

When a seat did come available for the trip, Neil got it.

"Neil looked so forward to the trip, and everybody was happy for him," Trudy says. "He was doing all the neat things he wanted to do, plus being with his son Corcoran. He was going to stay at Patriot Hills, Antarctica, which had nothing to do with the project that Corcoran was on, and then join a company out of New Zealand that brings tourists to the Patriot Hills to see penguins. The trips are quite expensive but intriguing, and that's exactly what Neil was going to do."

Following the tour, he planned to fly back to Calgary on a commercial airline.

"They spent some time in Punta Arenas prior to flying over to Antarctica, and Neil met a number of people there, such as Captain Mike Egan and Pilot Jim Conn, who were on a 'Polar Flite' around the world." Trudy recalls. "They later said that JC, as they called Corcoran there, with his knowledge of the area helped them so much because they hadn't been to Antarctica before. Neil had written about them . . . "

What happened next is beyond Trudy's ability to tell the story. Garnered from secondary sources, this is what occurred:

The Twin Otter departed Calgary on November 8, 1994, en route to Antarctica where it was to complete a radio echo survey for the Italian National Antarctic Program.

From Punta Arenas they would go to Rothera, then to Patriot Hills, Byrd, McMurdo and Terra Nova Bay, about 2000 NM. Delays dogged the journey, first in Houston to replace a fuel control unit and because of weather, and also in Punta Arenas due to weather. They finally arrived in Rothera on November 23rd, after a seven hour, four minute flight.

According to the British Aircraft Accident Inquest Board (AAIB) report, published in Transport Canada's Aviation Safety Letter (Issue 3/95), on arrival at Rothera they were notified of a 100-foot-high iceberg floating off the end of Runway 18, on the centre line. The crew of four (Captain J. Corcoran Armstrong, his dad, Neil, and crew members Dale Fredlund of Calgary and Erik Odegaard of Vancouver) flew a low circuit to examine the iceberg and landed at the Rothera airport without incident.

They ate lunch, refueled, then prepared to take off after a two-hour rest to fly another seven hours to their next stop. They discussed their departure with local Rothera pilots, and received advice that it would be safest to turn gently to the right immediately after takeoff, to fly past the right side (from the pilot's perspective) of the massive iceberg.

The AAIB report states that, "The wind was down the runway at 20 knots as power was applied against the brakes. After brake release, the ground-roll measured 1335 feet and the aircraft climbed toward the iceberg.

"At an altitude of about 100 feet, the wings rocked and the climb decreased to become a shallow descent. As the aircraft approached the nearest ridge of the iceberg the wings rocked again, the nose pitched up to a very steep attitude, and the aircraft sank in this attitude to impact at the very top of the far ridge of the iceberg. As it slid back into the ice-ravine a fire started and the aircraft exploded as it reached the floor of the ravine."

Rescue was impossible. All four people aboard perished.

The impact on family, friends, and associates from around the world was one of indescribable shock and sadness. Trudy, having lost both her husband and son, was inconsolable, as were the children.

Also deeply affected was Corcoran's Chilean friend, Ramon (Moncho). In a faxed message sent from Punta Arenas, Chile, to Brad Armstrong in Hinton, Alberta, on November 12, 1996, he thanks the family for their letters and a picture sent of Corcoran. "He has been in my mind so much, especially when working night shifts and I am alone and I feel his presence sitting in the Center/Radar seat talking to me, having some coffee, waiting for weather info., or making jokes of course.

"I remember he told me that Henri Perk suggested he contact me when he came for the first time, 'because if you have a problem in Antarctica, he [Ramon] can save your life.' But, God didn't want it that way and I feel very sorry for that, it hurts me, too. We consider him a brother."

Ramon goes on to recall the last day he spent with Corcoran and the thrill of meeting his father, Neil. "You know they were proud of each other and I was proud to be their friend." They had lunched together at the airport, and at two o'clock JC and crew flew on to Rothera. When Ramon returned home, he contacted JC on the radio. "I made some phone patches to him, we made jokes . . . Your dad was listening because he had a headphone but without a microphone – JC said he was waving his hands to us."

The Twin Otter arrived at Rothera at 22:30 and Corcoran called Ramon from the ground (runway), saying they were planning to stay an-hour-and-a-half, eat and fuel up the aircraft. Ramon told him to call again because he'd have the radio on in his computer. JC did call, again from the ground, after a 20 minute delay and minutes from midnight, November 23, 1994. "Moncho, we are a little bit delayed. I am starting engines and I'll call you when airborne."

"My friend who was with me listening heard a noise on the HF," Ramon reports, "probably a PTT [push to talk], but we can't say what it was and that's the last transmission I had. After that I called Rothera by telephone [inmarsat - satellite phone] and I talked to Paul Rose [Commander, British Antarctic Survey]. He didn't want to tell me anything but when you have been working as ATC [air traffic control] for years you don't have to be smart to realize what happened. I didn't know what to do. I called to Bill Houghton [of Kenn Borek Air] and I wanted to call your mother [Trudy] but he told me not to do it because the company will take care of it. I felt very sorry for that. My kindest regards to your mom and family."

Guilt often follows such tragedies, whether deserved or not. "If only" are words that reverberated in many peoples' minds following this tragedy. An e-mail letter from Anne Kershaw, of Adventure Network International (ANI), reiterates Ramon's, and others', deep regret.

"JC was more than a pilot to us. He was a dear friend and one of the few people who could make me laugh for hours on end. Trust me, he is sorely missed. I am actually the person who agreed to take your father out from Patriot Hills when JC delivered him – a decision I have long since regretted and often wonder if I could have made things different. I remember having tea with them both and thinking that JC got a lot of his looks, kindness, and humor, from your dad."

Kershaw's husband, too, had died in an aircraft accident in Antarctica (in 1990) and this accident brought back that time "with a sharp blow of reality."

Letters, phone calls and messages of condolence poured in from all over the world. James M. Conn, Command Pilot, Polar Flite, in a letter drafted November 26, 1994, recounted the good visit he'd had with JC and Neil at Punta Arenas prior to their departure. "Even though not mentioned by JC, I could tell that the ongoing weather delay in not being at Terra Nova Bay was beginning to bother him from an obligation standpoint," Conn writes. "I hasten to add that he felt no pressure from Kenn Borek [Air] to depart and several times mentioned his pride in his company and what a good company they were to work for. . . . I noted JC throughout the evening in animated conversation with all of us – having a good time – but with his left hand always periodically patting his dad on the back and right shoulder. You could see the pride and respect they held for each other throughout our time with them in PA."

Conn elaborates on the flight planning undertaken by JC, commenting on the conscientious manner in which he gathered information on weather and his caution as he developed his strategy for a safe flight to his Antarctic destination. "His decision to go was sound and based upon improving weather conditions at Rothera and beyond."

True to his promise, JC called Conn inflight, via HF phone-patch through Moncho, to help them with an update on the en route weather. "He reported 1H 52M Rothera ETA with 105 KT ground speed at the time," writes Conn. "We did not hear about the tragedy until Anne Kershaw from ANI called us the next morning at 1015Z." He concludes by offering his deepest condolences. "I have now seen the associated severe consequences when even the best plan and the most professional piloting skills are skewered by the unpredictable nature of flight in these parts."

These first-hand observations contrasted sharply with the British AAIB report (who were in charge of the investigation because the accident occurred in British air space), reproduced in the aforementioned Transport Canada Aviation Safety Letter. Their report said that detailed calculations made by AAIB investigators proved that the aircraft had been extremely overweight at takeoff. "The aircraft had taken on 5100 pounds of fuel at Rothera into the mains and two ferry tanks. Based on runway conditions, wind temperatures, aircraft performance and the measured takeoff run, the AAIB investigators calculated the takeoff weight of the aircraft to be between 18 600 and 18 700 pounds. The approved flight manual MTOW (maximum takeoff weight) is 12 500 pounds. The actual aircraft weight was more than 6000 pounds above the MTOW."

Although there is no airworthiness authority in Antarctica, a Canadian-registered aircraft is required to operate within Canadian regulations. Calculated takeoff performance proved that the aircraft could have attained an altitude of 50-64 feet by the time it reached the 100-foot high iceberg, but they concluded that at the calculated weights the aircraft was not capable of climbing over the iceberg.

"It is impossible to determine why the captain elected to climb directly over the iceberg instead of turning gently to the right as discussed prior to departure," the report states. "However, immediately after takeoff, the extreme overweight conditions would have limited his ability to maneuver without stalling. The aircraft was seen rolling from side to side and pitching nose up – a typical characteristic of entry to a stall, particularly in the turbulence which may have existed in the lee of the iceberg."

The report concludes by noting that the crew had already flown for seven hours that day, and the investigators could only wonder why it was decided to carry on for another seven-hour leg, and if "fatigue had clouded judgment."

The article published in the Transport Canada Aviation Safety Letter, and based on the preliminary accident report by the British Aircraft Accident Investigation Bureau, was a blow to all concerned: family, friends and the companies involved. Although it did not mention names or aircraft registration, because of the

J. Corcoran Armstrong and Neil Armstrong. (Photo: Armstrong collection)

media publicity surrounding the accident it was not difficult for readers to make the connection.

A formal inquest held in London, England, in April 1995 was attended by Neil's and Trudy's three sons – Corcoran's brothers – Brad, J. Neil and Trekker. As well, attendees were Paul Rose, Base Commander of Rothera, various members of his staff who had witnessed the take-off, other pilots of the British Antarctic Survey (BAS) who had been in Rothera and representatives of the British Aircraft Accident Investigation Bureau.

Following the inquest, the final British Aircraft Accident Report was modified to reflect new findings. The aircraft "although heavily laden" was, in fact, within legal operating (ferry) weight and not over gross. The pilot had just had the prior three days off and was well within the Canadian guidelines for Pilot Flight Times.

The most likely cause of the accident was wind-shear or downdraft coming over the iceberg, which was very close to the end of the runway. The aircraft had rotated for take-off at a respectable distance down the runway, as witnessed by BAS Twin Otter pilots. As well, it had climbed at what appeared to these pilots to be a reasonable angle. In fact, by the time it was approximately two-thirds down the length of the runway, it had out-climbed the iceberg, as witnessed by staff from the top of the ridge beside the runway. From that point on, however, the aircraft had lost lift (probably because of the down-draft) and started descending. Although it flew over the first ridge of the iceberg, it impacted a second ridge only some 10 feet from the top.

In the final analysis, the Accident Report indicated that the cause was indeterminate.

When the Armstrong family requested that the Transport Canada Aviation Safety Letter publish these new discoveries, however, they were refused on the grounds that the information available at that particular time had been correctly published. Further, no one had actually been named in the Letter. The themes of "aircraft weight" and "pilot fatigue" were general points of concern that they wished to get across to readers.

It was gratifying for the family to hear the British Antarctic Survey pilots declare the respect they held for the Kenn Borek Air crew. But they added that the Antarctic weather, wind, terrain and vast distances caused it to be one of the most challenging and unpredictable places in the world in which to fly.

Trekker Armstrong later reported to the Calgary *Herald* (July 21, 1995) that, "one of the major amendments to the original report had to do with the weight of the aircraft. The weight limit for Twin Otters is normally 5682 kilograms [12 500 pounds], but when the plane is used for long-range ferrying, the manufacturer's limit is 7955 kilograms [17 500 pounds]. Transcripts from the three-day inquest indicate the plane's weight was below maximum. Even using the worst-case approach of assessing weight, it was still under the maximum ferry weight for that aircraft."

Trekker also read from the transcript, quoting the coroner as saying, "so far as I'm concerned this aircraft, insofar as the weight is concerned, was within parameters normally considered safe. Although by the testimony of all the witnesses who have appeared before me, it was heavily laden."

J. Neil Armstrong agrees, and vowed to the *Herald* reporter that the family would strive to have the report corrected. "The findings indicate the crash was purely accidental, and that the cause was indeterminate. Obviously we'll have to notify Transport Canada of the error."

The memorial service was massive. Neil was a member of Canada's Aviation Hall of Fame, as well as being well-known and respected for his work in geology, in his various aviation businesses and his much-enjoyed columns in the COPA newspaper, *Canadian Flight*. Corcoran was known for his flights "from pole to pole," and for his endearing good nature. Neil was 74, and Corcoran 30, when they died on November 23, 1994.

Trudy was left in despair, and with business decisions that involved a mountain of paperwork. With the help of friends and family, she slowly picked up the pieces.

Fanair International was sold. Neil and pilot Bill Watts had co-owned a Piper Arrow aircraft. Now Trudy became Bill's partner. They rented the aircraft to the Calgary Flying Club, and in the spring of 1998 sold it to the club. Bill Watts then convinced Trudy to resume her volunteer job with the Aero Space Museum. She'd worked there for 10 years prior the accident; they needed her and she needed them. Nearly everyone who came into the museum knew the Armstrong family and were glad to see her back. Trudy is modest about her popularity at the museum. "Well, if you hang around long enough you become one of the artifacts!" she says lightly.

The author and Trudy Armstrong at the Calgary Aero Space Museum. (Photo: Calgary Airport Authority)

Trudy continues to be involved in aviation. "I'm still a member of COPA. It's almost like a family," she says. "I've known the recently-retired manager, Bill Peppler, for years and years."

In 1995, Calgarian Ken McNeill (then COPA director for Alberta and Northwest Territories, and 1998-99 Chairman of the Board of Directors) initiated the annual Neil Armstrong Scholarship Award, and Trudy sits on the nominating committee. "It started out to be a $3000 flight-training scholarship (won in 1998 by Bruce Haycock), but there was a donation made by the outgoing-president and his wife, Jim and Barb Snow, to the first runner-up (Shannon de Coninck Smith) for a $2000 scholarship, and to the second runner-up (Kyle Doerksen) of $1000. We're aiming for a total of $100 000 so it can be self-perpetuating."

Bill Watts, with Trudy and Neil Armstrong. (Photo: Armstrong collection, by Allan F. McQuarrie)

The Aero Space Museum also honors recipients of an annual Neil Armstrong Memorial Achievement Award, and Trudy sits on that nominating committee as well. These awards are given to deserving Calgarians in honor of lifetime achievements in aviation. Bill Watts was the first recipient, in 1996, followed by Ken Lett and Franz McTavish (posthumously) in 1997, and David Dover and Stan Green (posthumously) in 1998.

What has flying meant, to Trudy and her family? She considers the question for a moment.

"We all just feel such a love of aviation," she finally says. "I love it when I hear someone at the museum say, 'Oh, that old, old aircraft! How did they ever fly a DC-3?' or whatever, because the public now is so oriented toward jet and space travel. But the older aircraft are still there. For weekend flying a little aircraft like the Taylorcraft, or the

Cessna 172, are still part of the aviation community and are at people's grassroots love of aviation. I think the Museum itself represents a sort of grassroots love of aviation.

"Neil was a hard worker in aviation. It was his love, and mine, and our children's.

"It's part of who we are."

Mister Cargo

William John Thomas Cove was once the youngest licensed bus driver in Canada.

A further appellation was "Mister Cargo."

And friends who've heard Cove relate adventures of transporting people and freight by surface and air throughout British Columbia's wild west coast area also call him the "Bob Hope of Vancouver Island."

Bill Cove's energetic personality, laced with an abiding sense of humor and backed by topnotch training, skill and luck, has given him, his family and friends some memorable rides.

Growing Up Years

Bill Cove was born on March 29, 1933, in Regina, Saskatchewan, the son of John Bennett Cove, a mechanic for Greyhound Bus Lines, and Rose Edith Cove (née Jackson).

When Bill was 12, the family moved west to Vancouver Island for the duration of the war.

He entered the full-time work world at age 15 as a copy boy at the Victoria *Daily Colonist*, but in August 1950 moved on to C&C (Cameron and Caldwell) Transportation Co. Ltd. The company operated a diversified fleet of taxis, buses, limousines, tow-trucks and ambulances from Government Street, and had a contract with Trans-Canada Airlines (TCA) to haul freight and passengers on the airport run. When they acquired a new 1950 half-ton pickup for Bill to drive, they bestowed on him the title "Mister Cargo."

Bus Driver

Bill Cove waited patiently for his 21st birthday, when he could apply for a licence to drive a bus with passengers. That morning he was standing in front of the motor vehicles branch office before it opened to take his written and road tests. Finally, with licence in hand and an "A" badge on his cap, he emerged to be met by a *Times Colonist* reporter. The evening paper's headline read, "Bill Cove – Youngest Bus Driver in Canada."

The airport run involved four trips per night, and there Cove came to know TCA pilots Al Dodds and Bill Spratt, who flew the company's DC-4s (Northstars). Spratt would joke with the young driver. "I hear you got pinched the other day for speeding! Why don't you become a pilot where you wouldn't have to worry about that kind of thing?"

The youngest bus driver in Canada!
(Photo: Cove collection)

"Hey, interesting," was Cove's response, but surely it was impossible for an ordinary person to get a pilot's licence. "I thought you had to be out of the airforce, and walk hand in hand with God, to touch these things!" Cove says, laughing. "But after they'd coaxed me for a while, I went over to the Victoria Flying Club and talked to Gordie Jeune, one of their four flying instructors."

When Jeune learned that Cove drove a bus, he said they loved having bus or truck drivers as students because they were used to judging distances and operating big equipment. Cove promptly signed up for lessons.

"Gordie Jeune took me under his wing and I trained on a Fleet Canuck, one of those old fabric-covered, tail-wheel, marvelous airplanes," Cove says. "To this day, I've never had any trouble with Grumman Goose-type airplanes with tail wheels, because I learned to fly on one. It was great experience."

Cove gained his private licence in 1956 and immediately began working toward his commercial. Meanwhile, he continued to work at C&C as passenger and cargo agent, dispatcher, personnel administrator and driver. He also became an unofficial agent for Queen Charlotte Airlines and met many of their pilots who were flying scheduled ("sked") flights on the Vancouver-Nanaimo-Victoria run. Because this airline came in just twice a day, they couldn't afford their own station staff.

And so Bill Cove became familiar with both ground and air transportation. When he attained his commercial pilot's licence in 1957, with float plane endorsement, he began to seriously consider getting a job in the aviation industry.

Victoria Flying Services Ltd.

With Trans-Canada Airlines laying off pilots, however, jobs were scarce. When Cove asked his friends at TCA for advice, they said, "Go float flying," convincing him he'd never be out of work if he could fly floats, "whereas the instrument-flying types of jobs would always come and go."

When it seemed obvious there were no jobs to be had with the existing airlines, Cove and flying instructor Ray Schofield came up with a plan. They would start their own company, with Ray running the flying school and Bill the charter business.

"Ray and I became convinced there should be an airline operating out of Victoria, so we decided to call Bill Sylvester, who'd started, owned and then sold BC Airlines. I'd had contact with him before so I phoned him up and said, 'Bill, you know Ray Schofield? He and I want to meet with you.' He said, 'Be at the Sussex Hotel at 9:00 Tuesday morning.'

"When we arrived, he was outside sitting on this wooden bench on the city street in front of the hotel! 'This is my office,' he said, patting the bench. 'We're going to put this airline together at this office.' We looked at one another. 'What do you mean, put together an airline? How did you know what we came here to talk to you about?' He said, '*Everybody* comes to me to talk about starting an airline! And you guys are no different.'"

W.B. Sylvester had sold BC Airlines with a clause in the contract stipulating that he could not be involved in aviation for five years, and this was just the first year of the agreement. Nonetheless, he asked Schofield and Cove to tell him what they had in mind. "What experience do you have?" Sylvester asked Cove. He honestly replied, "None." Sylvester laughed. "What about money?" "None." Then Sylvester said he and his wife were leaving immediately for a trip to Hawaii. "Be here when I get back."

"We were there, at the bench, the morning of his arrival," Cove says, "and he started to rhyme off his plan: the company is this and this, the directors are this guy and this guy – all the old BC Airlines people. He'd set it all up! He had gone to his financial advisor and accountant, Eric Cox, and said, 'Hire Stan Scurrah to be our bookkeeper.'"

Victoria Flying Services Ltd., a concept that Ray Schofield and Bill Cove "had dreamed up in the beer parlor," and put into action by Bill Sylvester, became a going concern. Before Sylvester left on his vacation he had reportedly said to Stan Scurrah, "I'm going to Hawaii and I'll be gone for two weeks. When I get back I want a company formed, I want it called Victoria Flying Services, but I want you to look into this contract that I've signed when I sold BC Airlines and find out if I can do this. I won't have any shares, my wife will have the shares."

The five directors, who'd originally put up money for BC Airlines, were called back in: Do you want to make another fortune? They said yes. Cove recalls that it was set up to cost $10 000 for shares and $10 000 for a shareholder loan, or $20 000 from each member, bringing in $100 000 plus some other money.

"We were spellbound," Cove says. "We didn't know these people, we didn't have any money, but Bill Sylvester said, 'It's your company, you're expected to make this work so you should put some money into it. However, if you don't want to, we can work it so you're just employees.' It became so overwhelming, so quickly. I was just 24 years old, driving a transport truck at the time to pay for my flying bills, so I opted out [of a shareholder's position]. I thought the best thing for me was to just be a pilot and try to get a flying job out of this. As matter of fact, he wanted that, too. Bill was such a believer that this was going to be another BC Airlines."

Victoria Flying Services held an Open House on August 30 and 31, 1959, where old hands and new welcomed the hordes of people who came to check out the facilities. The company had a fleet of seven aircraft for charter work, offered five government-approved flying courses, and also became the Cessna dealership.

In addition, Sylvester owned a Luscombe 8E, "the smallest one you could buy, with a tail wheel," and then acquired a second one. "We discovered they weren't right for the school, to match the Fleet Canucks," Cove says. "They were unstable, you could ground-loop them very easily, so Bill placed orders for a new Cessna 150 and 172, to be delivered in a few weeks from the factory."

Bill Sylvester personally checked Cove out on the Luscombe 8E on its narrow floats. "We went around the Gulf Islands and he picked all the dirty spots." Cove vividly recalls a bay on Saturna Island where there is a continual outflow. Going in was no problem, but coming out one had to take off downwind and get airborne quickly. "Make sure you're in the air when you get to the rough water, because if you're not and you start tumbling it's too late," Sylvester warned. "The big waves can take you over, capsize the airplane, or pound so hard the floats will buckle under you."

Ganges, on Saltspring Island, was another tough one. A pilot generally flew in over the town and landed facing out, against the wind. With the Luscombe, Cove learned to get behind boats or log booms. "Bill spent about 10 hours showing me what not to do, that was the secret," Cove recalls. "After that he said, 'Just get in the airplane and go. You're going to make mistakes.'"

Victoria Flying Services – open for business! Bill Cove with Cessna 180 amphibian, 1958. (Photo: Cove collection)

The first one he made was scratching a wingtip on a boat. "I couldn't quite get it out of the narrow, confined area."

Cove had less than 200 hours, with virtually no experience, when Sylvester gave him his first flying job, but he proved to be a quick study. "After I got 100 hours on that Luscombe I could go anyplace." Soon, he was flying all over the west coast.

One day, he'd made a successful landing in the Luscombe at the dock at Alert Bay (up-island, just south of Port McNeill) after winning a fight with a blustery southeaster, when he noticed a man standing beside a Beech 18, watching him intently. He introduced himself as Jack Moul of Pacific Western Airlines. "I want you to come to see me in the spring. If you can fly that little popcorn plane in this gale, you can fly anything we've got," Moul said. Cove thanked him, but thought no more about it.

He continued flying the Luscombe, as well as the new Cessna 150 and the 172, on wheels. "The 172 was my big airplane. I did numerous charters at night, which weren't legal at that time, and still aren't, on a single-engine aircraft," Cove says. "Charter work at night has to be done in a twin-engine airplane. We didn't have one and we weren't planning on getting one for a long time down the road."

He learned, however, that he could "rent" the airplane, as long as he didn't actually charge a fare, to fly a passenger over to Vancouver. "TCA would continually phone us to help with connections – we called them 'cons' – to fly people over to Vancouver when they'd missed their flights. I could take two at a time in the 172.

"We got $27 for that flight in the 172. It became so bad that Bill Sylvester's wife, Joan, who was running the company, would say, 'Bill, you stop that! You're not going to do any more night flights!' She knew the rules," Cove laughs.

No one ever left the aircraft without paying. " I would be hustling the baggage into the terminal and come out to find money on the seat or in the ashtray, and usually more than $27," Cove says. "We did this for two years! I made more money at night than I did in the daytime, and at the same time I logged valuable night time. It *was* legal! Nobody said I couldn't 'rent' that airplane and fly to Vancouver."

For some trips he used the Cessna 180 amphibian, which had wheels and floats, so Cove got the rental rate for it as well as float experience. "I could juggle the log books a bit to say I'd had all this float experience even though it was under the 'amphib' column," he explains.

The fledgling airline was doing well on three fronts: the flying school, sked flying, and maintenance – everything except the charter business. "It was coming but it was very, very slow."

Cove was busy nearly 24 hours a day. "When we started up the flying school, we'd got away from the old stuffy type of flying club where nobody ever invited you in," Cove says. "We took out an extensive advertising program inviting people from Port

Victoria Flying Services, with Cessna 180 amphib. L to R: Bill Cove, charter pilot, Joe Holroyd, engineer, Gordy Jeune, instructor and chief pilot. (Photo: Cove collection)

Angeles in Washington, and Victoria and other places, to fly in. We'd put on free breakfasts or barbecues.

"I was always doing sales promotions. We'd give people an hour's flight for $5 to pique their interest. I was forever taking somebody up, letting them have the controls, doing some turns. When we came down, they'd sign up for lessons with Gordie Jeune, who'd come to work for us. We signed up 40 or 50 new people who had the intent to take flying lessons."

Morris Punt had always wanted to learn to fly. His son had a private licence, and when he read about Victoria Flying Services' upcoming breakfast fly-in, he came to see what it was all about. Bill Cove promptly signed him up.

Although Cove was extremely busy, it didn't prevent him from noticing Morris Punt's comely, dark-haired daughter, Beverley, who often accompanied her father when he came to take his lessons.

While Morris was in the air, Bev and her mother would come to the office and have coffee – personally brewed and served by Bill Cove. They noted the spotless office, waiting room and counter, meticulously cleaned by the energetic Bill Cove, while Ray Schofield ensured that the washrooms sparkled, and Gordie Jeune attended to the general hangar. "We all had our little duties," Cove explains. "By the time the ladies arrived I'd have the coffee made, and I'd 'wine 'em and dine 'em', as we used to call it!"

Bill and Bev were wed on October 1, 1960. "Her mother was a big influence," Cove laughs. "I fell in love with her mother – she just doted over me. It was a marvelous family."

Jack Moul was an important figure in BC aviation, being the founder in 1946 of Port Alberni Airways, and was now Chief Pilot, VFR, with Pacific Western Airlines. Bill Cove began to consider Moul's invitation to see him at the PWA offices in the spring.

"Bill Sylvester was paying me a pittance. I was getting $250 a month for base salary, and three cents a mile for flying – but there was no flying," Cove recalls. "Most of my hours spent were in the office, dispatching, being the agent and getting what flying work I could beg, borrow or steal from Trans-Canada Airlines. Beverley was making more money as a hairdresser at Eaton's than I was!"

Realizing it was time to look seriously to his future, which now included the responsibilities of a family man, Cove decided to explore Moul's offer. On the day he flew to Vancouver to pay him a formal visit, however, Moul had just left for Prince Rupert. Oddly, fate intervened.

"I came out of Jack Moul's office to see Bill Waddington sitting across the way in his office, in the big new BC Airlines hangar that Bill Sylvester had built just before he sold out. He spotted me and asked what I was doing there. I told him Jack had offered me a job and I'd heard he wanted to send me to Prince Rupert.

"'You know what's going to happen?' Bill Waddington said. 'You're going to get up to Rupert and you won't like it, your family is in Victoria. I'll give you a job, and I'll send you to Port Alberni. You'll be home every night.' Then he asked what Jack was going to pay me. I said, '$450 a month and three cents a mile.' He said, 'Bill, I'm so short of amphib pilots, I'll give you $450 and four cents a mile, but you've got to go to Port Hardy.' I said, 'That's not so bad. I had the Cessna 180 amphib up there last week, and I liked it.'"

Waddington pressed his case: "You would be much better off with BC Airlines than with PWA."

He called dispatch right then and asked someone to take Cove around the block for an evaluation flight. Hardly able to believe what was happening, on April 13, 1961, Bill Cove went out with Al Eden in a Cessna 170 Doyne Conversion and made two landings at Steveston (just south of Richmond). After a 15-minute flight Eden said, "This is a waste of time and money, let's go back." He'd blown it! But, when they walked into Waddington's office, Eden said, "You'd better hire this guy."

"Okay," Waddington said, "Let's make a deal right here. I can guarantee you 10 000 miles a month." Wow! At four cents a mile that was $400, plus $450 a month salary – $850! He was presently making around $300.

"It's a deal," Cove said.

He reported the news to Bev. "I'm going to Port Hardy. Until we see what this outfit's like, you'd better stay here."

BC Airlines

Bill Cove began his employment with BC Airlines in April 1961. Beverley moved back with her folks in Victoria while her husband left, on April 27th, to seek his fortune in Port Hardy.

"I've never flown with anybody better than BC Airlines," Cove says of his experience with this company, although he acknowledges that it had been difficult to leave

Victoria Flying Services. "Even the day I left, Bill Sylvester sat on the ramp and said, 'What's it going to cost to keep you here? Give me a price.' I said, 'Bill, it's too late. We've talked about this for 100 days now, and there was always 'going to be' more money. You should have been talking about this four months ago!'"

Cove then revealed to his ex-boss his hopes and dreams for the future. "This isn't over money, though. If I'm going to get anywhere in this industry I've got to go to somebody who's got some good, bigger airplanes, like a Beaver. I'm going to get a chance to fly a Beaver and other stuff in Port Hardy. I have to go and see what's out there. If I'm not happy, I'll come back."

Bill Sylvester didn't need to be told that his young employee wasn't making enough money with Victoria Flying Services to support a family; he also knew that the hours Cove had worked to get the company on its feet had been brutal. And so, he wished him well and waved good-bye as Cove flew off to new adventures.

The first question asked him by Frank McCarville, the base manager at Port Hardy was, "Are you married?" When Cove replied that he was, McCarville, unknown to Cove, made his plans. "Okay, this is the guy I'll send to Port Alice."

He had been there only one day when McCarville, who hadn't yet given him a check ride on the 180 amphib, ordered, "Go fly that airplane!" based on the check Al Eden had given him. Cove made a couple of trips. Then McCarville took him in the Beaver up the coast to Namu where they dropped off passengers, and told Cove to climb into the left seat. They flew back to Warner Bay, picked up some people, flew to the airport, and landed. "Go out and do a couple of touch-and-goes, on wheels," McCarville said. "Tomorrow we'll do some float work." The next day Cove's order was to take a load to Alert Bay. "But, we were going to do some float work!" Cove replied. "We did it," was the base manager's laconic response. And so, Bill Cove was "checked out" on the Beaver.

"We didn't need an endorsement in those days," Cove notes. "I had never read a manual on a Beaver. The idea was, 'If you can handle the airplane, you can have the airplane. Just don't get lost.'"

Bill Cove's innate sense of humor got him through his next career phase, but barely. There were five deHavilland DHC-2 amphibious Beavers on the base and increasingly Cove was assigned trips from Port Hardy to the communities of Port Alice and Holberg on the northern end of Vancouver Island.

He recalls that it was a good run, except for "this terrible little hump of 800 feet." One could get from the Rupert Arm side through the little pass, not more than an indent in the ground, at 850 feet – you might clip a tree but you'd get to the other side – even in snow or rain storms, or fog, but it was difficult to shuttle the airplanes back and forth Therefore, they came up with the idea of leaving one aircraft at Port Alice. If the weather was bad they could fly into Coal Harbour and a Volkswagen bus would come to take passengers to the airport at Port Hardy. For that reason, a Beaver was based in Port Alice, the home-base assigned to Cove by Frank McCarville.

Before Cove's arrival in Port Alice, there had lived a resident log-broker whose wife had a roving eye. Her gaze lit on the local BC Airlines base pilot, and the mood was reciprocated. The lovers decided to blow town, but the night of their planned escape the fog rolled in and the entire coast was blanketed. Undaunted, they took possession of an amphibian Beaver aircraft sitting at the dock in Port Alice (there were no airport runways at Port Alice, all flying was 'water work').

Unable to fly out because of the fog, they taxied for 21 miles on the water – down the inlet, through the rapids, past the Indian village, through the narrows, across the open water, to Coal Harbour. There, they tied the airplane to the dock and hired a taxi to take them to the airport. They bravely entered the terminal, nodded to people they knew, and bought tickets on PWA's morning flight to Vancouver.

In the meantime, BC Airlines was desperately making calls. Where was their airplane? Later that day, the missing Beaver was spotted, tied to the dock in Coal Harbour where the star-crossed lovers had left it.

Now that their base pilot was obviously gone from Port Alice the company needed a replacement. Along came Bill Cove, and thence the reason for McCarville's immediate question, "Are you married?" and his decision to send him there.

Knowing nothing about the situation, Cove looked forward to his new residence. But he soon discovered that his predecessor's actions had prejudiced the entire town against all BC Airlines pilots, and he had difficulty finding accommodation until Stan Becker, the local airline agent, took pity on him.

"You're going to be okay here," Becker said, "but why don't you get serious about bringing Bev up? You can have my cabin at the lake. It will be rough, but if she doesn't mind, you're welcome to it. No charge."

Bill wrote to his bride, describing the cabin in the enthusiastic terms of a husband who wanted her there. He skimmed over the fact that it was three-and-one-half miles from town up a logging road and over an 800-foot high pass, and perched on stilts above a wilderness lake in an area teeming with wildlife, including cougars. And that she'd be there all by herself while he worked 12-to-14-hour days, seven days a week.

Bill Cove's workday started at daybreak. He would arrive at the office, discuss the day's schedule with Stan Becker, then get airborne. If he was going out to the logging camp at Mahatta River he'd make that run before leaving on the sked flight into Port Hardy.

"You were like a taxi, sitting at the dock for anybody who wanted to go somewhere in the area," Cove recalls. "Port Alice was totally isolated, no road. If you wanted to get in or out of town you either came on the water taxi speedboat or by airplane, and 90 percent went by airplane. In those days our flights were always full. It took 15 minutes to fly to Port Hardy airport. Coming back it took 12 or 13 minutes."

The weather was usually atrocious. "Sometimes I'd just be skimming along the water to get to Coal Harbour. I'd put off the passengers and then go over to Mahatta. It was a three-fingered arm, with Port Alice at the end of one, the open ocean or Winter Harbour out Mahatta way, and then Holberg arm, a long sliver-inlet. At the head of that was a huge logging camp, Rayonier of Canada, and a Distant Early Warning (DEW) radar airforce camp.

"We were busy," he notes, in an understatement. "We had five Beavers and this was before any helicopters were working on the coast. The hospitals at Alert Bay, Port Alice and Holberg were extremely busy. It was not uncommon to have a full day's work lined up moving people into or out of camps, and then be called for emergency cases, or 'hospital-hops' as we called them [now called Medevacs].

"We'd be doing the mail runs and then get a hospital-hop call, drop everything, and go. I recall one day when all five Beavers were on hospital-hops. Two had dead bodies on board and the other three, including mine, had stretcher cases. I was on my way to Vancouver and the other pilots were taking their patients into Campbell River. It virtually meant that the airline came to a standstill, leaving all these people stranded who'd had bookings maybe months in advance. It was a zoo some days."

The accident rate in logging camps at that time was extremely high. "I'd often transport people with arms missing. One fellow had been working on a barge when two logs came together and squashed his head right off. He was dead, of course. The head had to come in a separate container. These accidents were gory."

Bev arrived in Port Alice and moved into the little cabin in the woods. It was not a "honeymoon cottage", as she soon discovered. There was neither electricity nor running water so she washed their clothes in a tub, then hung them in a basket over the porch, on stilts above the water, to rinse in the fresh-water lake.

One night while they were in bed they heard noises beneath the cabin. In the morning they discovered both deer and cougar tracks, and surmised that a cougar had been tracking a deer. The pioneering couple were in the cabin for three months.

When Stan Becker built a new office right by the dock, with a coffee shop, two upstairs suites, and a space he hadn't yet filled, Cove suggested he install a beauty salon. Beverley, a licensed hair stylist, was delighted. They moved into one of the suites at Christmas and Beverley open her salon. It soon became a busy place. Cove flew in Beaver-loads of women from the Mahatta logging camp who were very pleased to have their hair professionally attended. Her work became so popular that Bill would fly her into the camps on Saturdays to do haircuts.

Mister Cargo became the official "go-fer" of northern Vancouver Island. "If I got to a place where someone was selling fresh corn-on-the-cob, I'd buy a bunch and haul it

"A LITTLE LOAD PROBLEM?"

back. Anything I brought in was snapped up, at cost. I had friends all over."

One late, dark afternoon after a busy day, Cove was returning from Zeballos. But, there was no sense in coming home empty. "I went to the liquor store and got 25 boxes of beer and two cases of hard liquor. A cab brought it out to the airplane, then I called Port Alice on the radio to say I was coming in with this 'stretcher case' of booze."

Dorothy, Stan Becker's bookkeeper, was working on radio dispatch. She caught on, but somehow Stan also heard the message, picked up the words "stretcher case," and phoned the hospital. "Stretcher case landing at the dock!" When Cove landed, there to meet the plane were a nurse, doctor and helpers from Port Alice Hospital.

"Usually in such cases, the medical personnel would spot the first aid man looking out the window. The stretcher would be laid down one side of the aircraft, with the patient's head beside the pilot on the folded-down copilot's seat. But this time they couldn't see an attendant! Now they're really worried. Maybe it's a dead one."

Cove pulled into the dock and hopped out. "What's up?" he asked brightly.

"We've come to get the stretcher case," the doctor said.

"What stretcher case?"

When it was discovered that the only thing laid out in the aircraft were party supplies, the medics stomped off the dock, muttering nasty – and totally unwarranted – comments about pilots in general and Cove in particular.

"Bill Cove flies at 100 mph from party to party," the joke ran, with good reason.

But balanced with the fun were risks of flying in remote areas in weather that could turn in a instant, and death be a heartbeat away.

The Angel of Death

One day in 1962, Cove was at Mahatta in the Beaver when he received a call: "Go in to Port Alice, you've got a stretcher case. Stan will talk to you."

An elderly patient, Mrs. Murray, was hemorrhaging seriously and the Port Alice Hospital – as well as other up-island hospitals – had run out of blood supply. Dodi Maher, the head nurse and hospital matron, would accompany them on an emergency flight to Vancouver. As Cove was leaving the dock at Port Alice, Becker took him aside. "You know, this woman hasn't got much of a chance."

Cove was into the air at 2:33 p.m., figuring on a regular, but urgent, flight. At this time of year it would be pitch black by 5:00, but he should be past Comox before then, leaving a half-hour or so to fly on to Vancouver in darkness.

"We never checked weather, we just went and did the trip," Cove says. "It had been a nice day with a bit of breeze, so weather was the last thing on my mind as I flew from Port Alice across the hills, fairly high, direct to Beaver Cove. If the day had been worse, I'd have been much lower and flying out towards Alert Bay."

He was going down Johnstone Strait toward Kelsey Bay when it started to snow. He was forced to fly over by the islands a bit, but no problem. Then, it began to snow hard. He was down on the water, just crawling, yet reasoning, "If I could get back around Rock Bay and Chatham Point, I've got 'er made." He knew, however, that this was a notoriously bad area for heavy rain, snow and fog.

As he flew down Johnstone Strait he was forced down even lower. After flying for a while in snow, the weather seemed to improve until he was flying along at a normal 500 feet. Campbell River radio had even said, 'Keep coming, it's okay here.'

But suddenly, just 25 minutes flying time north of Campbell River, near Jackson Bay by Hardwicke Island, the weather got worse, a hard wind accompanied by heavy, wet, snow. He had no choice but to "plunk 'er down" on the water.

As he landed he called back to Dodi, "How are you doing back there?"

Her response did nothing to cheer him. "Not good. I hope it's not going to be much longer."

"I hope not, too."

What Dodi didn't say was that her patient was hemorrhaging profusely and getting very, very, close to running out of blood. Dodi had applied numerous towels and compresses until she had no more absorbent materials. Now they were trapped in the amphibious Beaver, bobbing about helplessly on the black water.

Cove had landed amongst a hopeless mix of islands and channels and, as they drifted about on the floats, he could no longer be sure of his exact location. He felt nervous that any moment a ship might come along and run them down, or a wave knock them over. "I'd look out and think I could see a rock or an island going by, or a piece of driftwood. Even with the wind blowing hard enough to stop us, I could see how fast the tide was going when I'd spot a piece of wood going by, something that wasn't affected by the wind," he explains.

With the increase in snowfall the wind died down, but at times the airplane would move about when a breeze blew by. Heavy wet snow continued to fall from a black sky. Worried about the affect of the snow's weight on the aircraft, Cove clambered out to stand on the float and clear it off.

"I had no broom or anything, so I tried to get rid of the snow using the paddle as best I could. Wet snow carries a lot of weight and I knew it could sink us. If the airplane got too low and the water started coming over the floats, they could take on water and everything would go down."

The snow continued to fall heavily and the plane drifted about as the tide rushed up and down the channel, carrying them along with other flotsam.

Dodi's voice echoed from the back of the plane. "Bill, have you any idea where we are?"

"I haven't got a clue," he replied honestly. "I saw some stars a few minutes ago but I've lost them."

He looked over at the patient. Blood was streaming from her nose, her ears, from everywhere. "What's the chance?" he whispered to Dodi. The nurse just shook her head.

He clambered out again to clear snow from the airplane, the only positive thing he could do in an increasingly hopeless situation. The snow clumped down in handfuls. He'd radioed Stan Becker after Stan had called various hospitals up-island. None had any blood. "Make it to Vancouver if you can."

"Okay," Cove had promised, "I'll get her to Vancouver."

Campbell River called in. "You'll have to come in and land at Campbell River now, it's dark."

"Jesus! He's telling me it's dark now," Cove thought. "I'm looking outside and I can *see* it's dark! He's worrying about me landing at Vancouver, I'm just worrying about getting off this water." He shut off the radio, partly in fear of running down the battery if the radio and lights were kept on and then the plane not starting, and partly to shut off useless advice.

He couldn't taxi, even if he knew where to go, for fear of running into a boat. He was in one of the main channels where there were tugboats, and even passengers ships. He had never felt more downhearted in his life. What if it kept snowing until 2:00 in the morning? He'd been informed that the weather to the south was okay, other than this band of snow between Port Hardy and Campbell River.

It snowed and it snowed, seemingly forever.

Dodi switched on the cabin light and Cove knelt on his seat to look back. He nearly passed out at the sight. The patient was fighting while Dodi tried to calm her, and both women were covered in blood. If Cove thought the situation was hopeless before, now he had shocking proof. As he watched, the patient slumped back and lay still. "Is she gone?" he asked.

"No, I still get a pulse," she said. Dodi, too, seemed ready to expire. She looked at Cove and in a quiet voice asked, "What do we do now?"

For first time in his life Cove had to say, "I don't know." What was there to do? He didn't know when it might quit snowing, when they could get flying or even if the airplane would start. It was horrible, horrible. He felt sick to his stomach. A hospital smell permeated the airplane, plus a reeking odor of voiding, discharge, and they were cooped up in this mess together until fate dictated the next move.

Dodi's voice was drained of energy and her face, seen in the pale glow reflected from the snow falling outside the window, was a pasty white. She, like everyone else, was over-worked and bone-tired. She'd been running the hospital all morning, and now this. Cove wondered how he'd ever got into this predicament. How could he get them out? He could almost see the image of the Angel of Death hovering over their aircraft, as they tossed about in the black water.

It was now 7:00 in the evening. Cove turned the master switch on the radio to call Campbell River and let them know they hadn't yet sunk. Harry Brown, the base manager, was still standing by, dutifully waiting until this airplane had finished its flight. Vancouver dispatch was also standing by.

"How're you doing, Bill?" Harry Brown asked.

"Not good. I can't get off the water."

"Well, when you do get airborne you've got to come in to Campbell River here."

That was the last thing Cove wanted to hear. He feared landing in Campbell River, amidst the channels and sand bars. The town had no airport at this time, just a waterway. He envisioned hitting a sand bar and flipping over, and all three drowning. He made up his mind, at that moment, with Brown waiting for his response, that if and when he got airborne he would head directly for the military base at Comox. This was an emergency – they'd have to let him in!

He informed Dodi of his plan to try for Comox rather than Campbell River, and of the risks involved. "Just do your best," was her response.

Minutes passed, 10, 20, 30. Stars! He could see stars! Maybe they were getting a break! Cove again climbed out to clear snow from the wings knowing that if he fell, both he and his passengers were gone, but with snow weight the airplane wouldn't fly properly and could stall. He climbed up above the windshield and moved along cautiously, grasping onto the hand-holds. He stepped onto the engine housing, and from there to the wing. With nothing to hang on to now he stayed in the centre, creeping on his knees as he pushed off the heavy snow with his paddle. When he stretched out toward the wingtip, the airplane began to lean from his 182-pound weight. He cautiously pushed at the bulk of the snow, hoping the rest would eventually blow off.

The water was still black, but calm, with minimal wave motion. He could see a few stars. A few minutes ago he hadn't been able to see his hand in front of his face for the thick white snowfall, but now he could almost say, "Hey, it's not a bad night out here!" But, how long would it stay like this?

He went back inside, then climbed through the little pilot's door to clear off one side of the tail while standing on the flat but slippery float, then through the copilot's door to clear the other side, being unable to use the centre doors because of the stretcher. He moved to the back of the float, reaching with the paddle to clear off the tail. When the job was done he got back into the aircraft, cold and soaked to the skin.

All was silent. "Dodi?"

A faint, "Yes?"

"I'm going to give it a try."

The engine started, a major relief, and the radio also worked. He called Campbell River. "We're getting going here."

"You're coming in to Campbell River," Harry Brown confirmed.

"Yeah, whatever," Cove replied.

He got airborne and was flying okay, but he knew a new crisis could develop at any moment. He couldn't tell what amount of snow still remained on the wings; some might have come off, some might still remain. He hoped it would come off both wings evenly, otherwise he could experience a stall. He recalled another time, when a deadly combination of rain and snow, with some ice, had clung to the outside of one wing while the other had cleared. Cove had found himself flying in a crazy circle. When he'd landed he'd had to chip the hardened snow off the wing with a paddle in order to fly straight.

He became airborne and saw a light, but still had no idea where he was. The Beaver had no ADF, nothing but a radio, a compass and a directional gyro set from compass and radio information. Nothing to navigate with other than the seat of his pants.

He recognized the light as a marker for tugboats, and thought, "Ah, civilization!" but which marker was it? Which channel was he in? He had no marine chart to help him decipher the flashes, to identify the rock he'd reached. He flew by, recognizing nothing.

By instinct he chose to fly up the right side of this channel, hoping it would take him to the main channel that ran between Kelsey Bay, Chatham Point and Campbell River, where all the big boats went. He'd be better off there than amongst all the islands.

He worked his way over and instinct proved right. He entered the channel and encountered another light which he figured to be the light by Chatham Point. He worked his way to another light, Hendricks Rock. This lead him to the next, until he thought he could see Chatham Point.

"Dodi, hang on!" he called back.

No response. Mrs. Murray still hadn't regained consciousness, and Dodi was just barely hanging on herself. With her patient now quiet, and the drum of the engines, she'd succumbed to sleep.

Bill Cove knew he'd soon be approaching a gigantic set of wires that ran across the narrows, about 200 feet off the water where they dipped in the centre and were higher at each end. With no alert company, and with a better chance for failure than success in this flight with no end, Cove began to talk to himself. "Bill, it's going to be okay if you can just get by those damned wires." It would be impossible to see the wires in the pitch-black night, but he felt he'd have a better chance by going under them rather than over, so he hugged the right shoreline. He had to be high enough to not hit the water, yet low enough to not hit the wires.

He switched on the radio to hear Harry Brown still clamoring, "Come in to Campbell River! We've got the lights on for you!"

"Harry Brown, Captain Smart, if I hear one more word from you I'm going to tell you over the radio what I think about you!" Cove muttered to himself, but he flipped the transmitter switch and asked, "What do I need to safely get under these wires?"

"One hundred feet," was the response. "If you're no higher, you'll be safe."

That's what Cove wanted to hear, someone else to confirm that it was possible to fly under the wires in the dark. His compass told him he was at 50 feet. A trickle of confidence returned.

Just prior to his reaching the wires, Brown called again. "We've got everything set up for you to land!"

Cove did not respond. He was, at that very moment, flying under the wires.

Vancouver now came on the radio. "What are you doing?"

"I'm going to Comox," Cove replied. "I've talked to Comox tower and they'll allow me to land but I have to stay on the runway." The Canadian Forces Base, Lazo, three miles northeast of the town of Comox, did not normally lay out the welcome mat for general or commercial aviation. Cove had heard that if one even approached the airport without permission the military could, and would, throw everyone in jail. The base practiced high security.

He continued south until he could see the lights of Campbell River. Still, the thought of landing in their harbor amid the sand bars frightened him although he'd done it a couple of times before. But if he should goof and hit a sandbar and flip over, there would be no possibility of saving Dodi and Mrs. Murray as well as himself. It only made sense to go on to Comox where there was a good hospital. The military, while not being exactly welcoming, surely would not let somebody die while parked on their runway asking for help.

"I'm declaring an emergency landing," Cove informed the Comox tower. "I have a very, very sick woman who has probably no blood left. Can you get me on tonight?"

"Yes, keep coming," was the response. "We'll get you on the runway and then somebody will meet you."

The station then went on high-alert mode, with the tower in constant contact. "Radar says you're now 12 miles back." "Radar says you're eight miles back, keep coming. It's a beautiful night down here."

Cove could see Middlenatch light, he could see the light over at the big island of Texada by Powell River, then the marine lights at Comox. He briefly thought of continuing to Vancouver but with his patient dead or nearly so, and Dodi totally fatigued, they had to quickly see a doctor.

He landed on the Comox runway, on wheels in the amphibian Beaver, to be greeted by a sharp military order, "Stop right there! Don't move." Vehicles of every description surrounded the aircraft and armed men leaped upon the airplane. One man looked inside. "My God, what the hell mess is this?" he gasped. He jumped back to give a hand up to the pilot, as paramedics rushed to help Dodi and issue orders for Mrs. Murray's placement on a stretcher. "Get her into the ambulance quick, there's nothing we can do here." Both Mrs. Murray and Dodi were whisked into an ambulance that raced across the tarmac, sirens blaring.

An officer turned to Bill Cove. "Leave the airplane here, you've got to come with me." They climbed into a military police car and sped back to the hangar. Then, just as they got inside, a message came in. No one knew how to tow the airplane off to the hangar – they'd never seen such a craft before, with both wheels and floats! They brought Cove back and allowed him to get in and taxi his airplane to the hangar.

Then, as the officer observed the bedraggled, wet, cold and totally exhausted pilot who stood before him, a look of sympathy flashed in his eyes. "What you need is a good drink," he said, and took him to the officers' mess.

After he'd been fed and watered, Cove was given a comfortable room where he fell into a deep, and well-deserved, sleep. In the morning, when he went out to see his airplane he hardly recognized it. They'd had it completely cleaned, inside and out.

He discovered that after the medical personnel had stabilized both Dodi and Mrs. Murray, they'd loaded them into a DC-3 and flown them to the hospital in Vancouver, saving the patient's life.

Bill Cove's voice still chokes at the memory of that ghastly night, and how close they came to meeting the Angel of Death.

A month later, Mrs. Murray came back to Port Alice, her health restored. But the experience bothered Cove for many, many years . . . the images of Dodi fighting to keep her patient alive and herself conscious, the dank, blood-spattered interior of the aircraft, and Cove's dreadful fear that all would die if he failed.

"That experience touched me for years, it really did," says the usually-jovial pilot. And then he falls silent, remembering.

Pine Island

At times, Bill Cove had doubts about his career when he considered the number of hours he was putting in and the type of flying he was doing.

One day, when he pulled up to the ramp at Port Hardy with the Beaver, Doug Hudson, the agent/dispatcher, handed Cove a routing form. He was to pick up an RCMP constable at Alert Bay and then fly him along the coast.

"Just a standard trip?" Cove asked. Hudson nodded.

At Alert Bay, they were taxiing away from the dock when the policeman said, "They told you, eh?"

"Told me what?"

"That we're going up to Pine Island?"

Cove nodded. He knew the island was located 45 miles west of Alert Bay in the Queen Charlotte Strait.

"The lighthouse keeper has spotted a body in the kelp bed," the constable added.

"Uh, what are we doing with this body?"

"We're loading it into the airplane and bringing it out."

"Oh no!" Cove said. "No dead people get in my airplane unless they're wearing a body bag. We're going back to the dock to negotiate this!"

Following discussion, Cove outlined a plan. "You get a tarp from someone, a fisherman, lots of people have them for covering their boats, and some rope, and a hook or a pick." Cove then called Mrs. Emma Kenmuir, who operated a radio service in Alert Bay. "Would you send a police car down here? With a tarp?"

They circled Pine Island to see the lighthouse keeper standing out on the rock, signaling. The body could be spotted from the air, still hung up in seaweed that floated about the rocks. The rubbery tentacles of the kelp, long and stringy, captured objects that came their way, from logs to bodies, and now had caught this unfortunate soul.

The sea was rough, so Cove landed around the corner and taxied back to the site. If the lighthouse keeper couldn't get his boat in the water it would be extremely difficult for Cove and the policeman to wrestle the body from the kelp and up onto the float.

The kelp held the aircraft fairly steady, even though it rose and fell alarmingly with three and four-foot swells coming in from Japan. The lighthouse keeper managed to get his boat into the water and came over to help. Using a probe and paddle, they brought the body alongside the float, forced the tarpaulin underneath and around, pulled it up onto the float and secured it with ropes.

"It was a horrible sight," Cove says, "all bloated and ballooned with gasses, and black and blue. We had no gloves, in those days they didn't supply us with anything like that, but we did the best we could with what we had.

"But those were the kinds of situations we found ourselves in by being members of a five-Beaver operation, with maybe seven or eight pilots on the base."

Nimpkish Lake

Bill and Bev left Port Alice in April of 1964 when he took over the base at Nimpkish Lake, across from Alert Bay in the Port McNeill-Port Hardy area. Again, he was Mister Cargo, hauling everything from groceries to booze.

"Nimpkish Lake turned out to be the best place for Bev and I to live," Cove says on reflection. "It sat 32 air miles from Port Hardy, 22 miles from Zeballos, 30 miles from Tahsis, and 84 from Campbell River, so we were in the hub of this big wheel with all these bases around. I could almost say goodbye to Port Hardy, although for control I still answered to that base."

He would leave Nimpkish at 7:00 in the morning and go to Woss Lake, Vernon Lake and Campbell River airport to meet the PWA flight arriving from Vancouver. Then he flew the route in reverse, through Nimpkish, Beaver Cove, Alert Bay, Sointula, to Port Hardy. He would work out of Port Hardy all day, then come back. "I'd have big camp moves and everything, so I was able to have these tremendously high revenues, with back-hauls."

Cove has great praise for Mrs. Kenmuir, the radio dispatcher at Alert Bay, who the pilots came to know and respect for her innate knowledge. On her retirement at age 72, aviation news reporter Ramsay Milne described her operation as one of the world's most unusual radio stations: a collection of ordinary trade-name radio receivers to monitor weather reports and a transmitter to relay weather data and other information to pilots.

Cove would call and in a jovial voice ask, "Hello, Mrs. Kenmuir! How's your wind and water?" Back would come an absolutely accurate report. "She had an uncanny knack of predicting the weather. When she said to expect cloud level to be down to 500 feet, believe me it was just that. I'd be flying the Beaver out of Nimpkish Lake wondering if I'd get back at night, and Mrs. Kenmuir would tell me to come right on. She could tell if the weather and the light would hold on just long enough for me to set the Beaver down on the lake. I had great faith in her judgment."

The Coves left Nimpkish on Christmas Eve, 1965. A farewell letter from the townspeople paraphrased Sir Winston Churchill to convey their feelings toward the family: "Never was so much owed by so many to so few."

"You have always been 'inside' the camp activities, pitching in to help us in our private lives or in community affairs," the letter read. "Your assistance, encouragement and happiness has been an integral part of the lasting friendships you cultivated in our Valley."

The Cove family, which now included two sons, Willie born in 1963 and Danny in 1964, moved to Ladner on the mainland until they bought a house in Richmond in January of 1967. Daughter Melenie was added to the family in 1968.

Still, Bill Cove's working hours were extraordinary, including night flying in the Beaver. When his boss, Wally Russell, commented, "You know, Bill, it's illegal to fly at night," his response was, "No, it's only illegal to *take off and land* because there are no lights on lakes or inlets." According to air regulations at that time, 1965-66, the two minutes spent getting off the water was the illegal part; once airborne everything was fine. "You can fly an 'amphib' Beaver at night, on floats, from airport to airport. There's nothing illegal about that," Cove protested.

He described for his urban boss the conditions on the west coast inlets. "These nights are black! There is no civilization so there's no light other than what you might get out of the moon. You start letting down to land on the water, shut the engine off and yell, 'Hey!' You hear this voice way off in the distance, so you start up and taxi until you finally see a light, a match strike.

"I find my passengers sitting in the dark, cold and wet, no campfire because they're tucked in at the bottom of a sheer cliff waiting for me to pick them up. They stand on the floats and I taxi them across the bay, and go back and forth until I've got all their stuff, and it's the middle of the night by now."

Incredibly, Bill Cove did not experience any serious accidents – "No, touch wood, not at that time," – although he had a couple of close calls caused by heavy weather and/or unruly passengers.

"Coming out of Ocean Falls in the Mallard in June 1967, we had a person who tried to jump out of the airplane," Cove says. He explains that the Mallard is similar to the Grumman Goose but larger. "The Goose carries 10 people – nine plus the pilot. The Mallard would carry 14. It's high wing, and has two big round 'reciprocal' [reciprocating or radial] engines, a beautiful airplane to fly."

On this trip, copilot 'Red' Croisdale was in the right seat. They left Ocean Falls with 11 people on board, entered cloud, did the turn tracking to Vancouver and came out of the cloud on the top of the climb. It was 11:30 a.m. – time for lunch!

"I had just set out my sandwich on the glare shield and got my tea poured when the airplane started to wobble," Cove recalls.

He turned, alarmed, to Croisdale. "Red, I think they're fighting back there! The tail's kind of moving."

There were no flight attendants, just the two pilots, and the door was closed, so Cove asked Croisdale to go back and find out what was happening. They were now over Burke Channel next to Dean Channel, near Ocean Falls in the Namu area, pointing directly to Vancouver.

Suddenly a passenger screamed, "Some guy back here is trying to jump out!" Croisdale confirmed the news, adding, "He's so strong, I don't think we can hold him!"

"Take the fire extinguisher and talk to him," Cove said. "If he doesn't listen, hit him between the eyes. We're heading for Port Hardy."

Cove called dispatch and stated their emergency – "We have a passenger trying to get out of the airplane and we're at 11 000 feet in solid cloud!" The airplane began to fishtail. With the cloud, and no distance measuring equipment, he couldn't pinpoint their position. "We started to commence our descent, and when I got a fix on the Pine Island lighthouse with my ADF I started rushing," Cove says. "Then Red came back into the cockpit, locked the door and announced that they had the man stabilized – the passengers were sitting on him."

When dispatch called from Ocean Falls, Cove discovered that this man was known to be unstable but had been sedated before the flight. "You didn't tell us that!" Cove responded angrily.

They got down through the clouds, did an instrument approach and landed at Port Hardy. For over two hours the pilots watched attendants struggle with the unruly man, trying to get him out of the aircraft. "He got his legs wrapped around the legs of the seats on the plane and they couldn't unpry him!" Cove says. "He was so strong, they had to literally feed him full of drugs to get him relaxed enough so they could get him out."

Cove was later informed that the man was a pulp mill worker who'd been having mental problems. Although he'd been sedated it hadn't worked, and in mid-flight he'd attempted to throw himself out of the airplane. "We may never have found him," Cove says, "especially falling from an airplane like a Mallard. You're never quite sure where you are, so if he'd fallen through the cloud I'd have had to say, 'Search 50 square miles.'"

"Red and I sat in the coffee shop at the airport, watching policemen running in and out, and doctors running in. Red says to me, 'How are they going to get him out?' I said, 'I don't know, Red, but as long as I've got a cup of tea here – he ruined my first one – we can sit here all day.'"

Pacific Western Airlines (PWA)

In September 1970, BC Airlines was bought out by PWA, and so Cove's employer changed, as did his seniority. The "new" PWA pilots were "frozen on the Nord 262s," and not allowed to bid on any other equipment until they'd done their time. The Nord, Cove explains, is a DC-3 but high-wing with prop-jets, and carries 29-passengers, a beautiful flying airplane that the pilots loved. He flew them until the company eventually retired the aircraft.

"By this time Jack Moul was running the Herc program for PWA. The first time I ran into him I said, 'It's unbelievable how my career has gone since you first offered me a job with your airline. I finally got to fly for PWA, but in a wrong move.'"

He lasted a year with PWA, resigning from the company in July 1971.

Canadian Forest Products (CANFOR)

When CANFOR called to ask Bill Cove to join their instrument flight department, he was ready for the challenge. He worked for CANFOR from 1971 to 1976, flying their Grumman Goose G-21Amphibian, Mitsubishi MU-2B prop jet and Cessna Citation 500 Fan Jet.

But in 1975 he fell ill, resulting in the loss of his licence although he continued to be employed doing office work for the company. Cove believes that his illness, diagnosed as ulcerated colitis, was brought on by the combination of flying in pressurization aircraft, drinking too much coffee and not enough water, and becoming dehydrated. He explains that with ulcerated colitis you either had to get rid of it with radical surgery, or control it. "Mine I couldn't control."

After a six-month hiatus, Bill Cove got his licence back in 1976. "There was a period where we thought I was never going to get it back, but I still flew with a pilot in the right seat," Cove says. "Someone said, 'That's not really legal!' and I said, 'You show me in the rule book which seat the pilot has to sit in.' They looked and said, 'He's right. The captain can be designated on the flight from either seat.' As long as the copilot is licensed, and his medical is up to date, you can put anybody in the left seat. The insurance company might not have liked it, but I flew all over."

In the end, the illness was a negative that became a positive. Otherwise, he might have kept up the breakneck pace that had been his *modis operandi* throughout his life, especially during the time he spent as a corporate pilot.

Cove relates a typical day in this type of job: "You get up at 5:00 in the morning, report to the flight centre at 6:00, do your flight planning, and you're airborne at 7:00. You might fly for one hour, then spend 12 hours waiting because they get involved with dinners and luncheon meetings. This goes on, day in and day out."

As a corporate pilot, Cove was continually flying into new airports. "One night, I was getting over Chicago and air traffic control said, 'You've got lots of fuel?' 'Yes.' 'Good. Your hold is likely to be an hour-and-a-half.' So, for 90 minutes we sat in this one-minute, two-minute, racetrack pattern, over a strange airport. But, that gave me a chance to look at the approach and listen to the instructions other pilots were getting."

Cove also says that because airlines usually have large training and development budgets their pilots receive continuous training. The corporate pilot has to be regimented to study the books on his own.

He decided that the career of a corporate pilot wasn't for him. He'd often toyed with the idea of buying and selling aircraft, negotiating contracts, matching pilots to planes, supplying crews. But could he make a living doing this type of work? And where did one start?

Weldwood of Canada Limited

"One day, I got a call from Vern Roberts, area manager for Weldwood of Canada," Cove says "They were having a terrible time. Vern felt they were getting hosed with their invoices, so he called me in to have a look. It took six days, but I showed him hundreds of invoices where they'd paid too much money, and came back with a recommendation. His boss looked at what I'd discovered and said, 'Are there any consultants around here?' So right away I thought to myself, 'No, there *aren't* any aviation consultants!' And there weren't, in that day. I could perhaps specialize with small jets and prop jets, and things like that."

After the meeting, Roberts brought Cove to meet Carl Rathburn, Weldwood's General Manager of Logging and Forestry.

"He told me to find him an airplane, so I found a Beaver sitting in the mud up in Kamloops. I got that for exclusive use for $75 an hour. It would cost Rathburn money only when he used it, and I would cost him money only when he used me. We piled over 300 hours on that airplane that year."

Six months later, Rathburn made Cove an offer to come to work for Weldwood of Canada Limited. He stayed with the company for 11 years, from July 1976 to January 1987, as Aviation Manager and Chief Pilot (Fixed Wing).

B. Cove Air Ltd.

In 1976, he had also started B. Cove Air Ltd., to buy, sell and manage airplanes and personnel for various companies. "I had numerous contracts with little companies, helping them get started, hiring pilots for them, flipping airplanes."

Soon, the Coulson Group of Port Alberni became one of Cove's major clients.

Before Cove left Weldwood to go on his own he asked Coulsons if they could guarantee him work for two years. They could, based on a handshake. He was with them for four-and-one-half years, finding aircraft, doing pre-purchase inspections, and purchasing aircraft such as the Mitsubishi prop jet, the Grumman Goose and then helicopters.

The Cove family moved to Port Alberni in 1987, and Bill became Aviation Manager for Coulson Aircrane Ltd., lining up machines and people.

"I first hired Bobby Thompson, who was the best Sikorski 61 captain going for logging. I brought him here, and he brought Neil Thompson, and other guys kept coming in, the tops in the industry. We felt that the only helicopter to go logging with, at the time, was the S-61s, and those are the small ones the company has now."

Helicopter logging allows a company to go into an area and pluck out specific pieces of timber, usually large, expensive wood, and remove them from an area without doing damage to the surrounding forests or waterways.

In the normal course of operation, a chokerman will place a choker cable around a log, the helicopter will fly in dangling a 150-foot line, and the chokerman will hook the line to the cable. "The average log load weighs around 7700 pounds," Cove says, "but we've had loads of up to 13 000 pounds! If late in the day the wind is blowing hard up the mountain, and the helicopter's at the end of the 45-minute cycle [you put only enough fuel in to log for 45 minutes, to keep the weight down], you can haul higher log loads."

The helicopter usually carries one big log at a time, but sometimes takes "multiple turns" consisting of two or three smaller pieces, weighing around 7000 pounds altogether. "With the massive helicopters, they could have th :e logs dangling, each log weighing 10 000 pounds – almost 30 000 pounds of logs hanging there!" Cove says.

"Coulsons were good conventional loggers, on the ground, but they weren't really sure about helicopter logging. However, you just hire the experts . . . and they hired the best in the business."

Although Bill Cove enjoyed his work with Coulson Aircrane, again he was working backbreaking hours. "The hard time there was the 20-hour-a-day job. I bought all the fuel, organized the helicopters, I was doing everything, the desk job combined with flying," Cove says. "I was just sick with worry, and we had a serious accident just as a result of fatigue. I hit a deadhead coming out of Teekearne Arm. It flipped the airplane, a little Cessna 185 float plane, over onto a log and destroyed it. That was out of sheer fatigue, I just wasn't thinking right."

Cove recalls "running along on the step, going really fast, when BANG! we hit this thing. It hit with such an explosion that I thought the whole side of the airplane and the floats had gone. I swerved, clipped the end of the log boom and we cart-wheeled. The float picked up water, it struck on the corner of this cartwheel, flipped over and we were upside down."

He describes the images that followed. "It's pitch black under the water. I'm trying to hold my breath and get my seat belt undone. The windshield caves in and Ian gets blown out through the hole. When I finally get the seat belt unfastened, the doors won't open. Now I'm running out of air and I'm practically dead. Through sheer strength I get the door open, reach the surface and finally take a breath of air just as the boom boats come on the scene."

McDonald wasn't injured but it was a close call for Cove. He had broken a vertebrae in his back, and suffered numerous lacerations. Later, in the emergency room of Powell River Hospital, the doctor rolled him over on the operating table and what seemed like a gallon of water poured from his nose and mouth. "The nurse shrieked and the floor was flooded."

That was his worst accident, "as far as coming close to death myself, and doing damage to the airplane." He had another one, which didn't hurt him as much as it did the aircraft, when a brake locked on the Grumman Goose he was landing and it went over on its nose.

New Loads for Mister Cargo

After four-and-one-half years with Coulson's, and the accident with the 185, Bill Cove decided to retire. "I'm mending and I'm not interested in going away on a contract. What I'm looking for is just to buy and sell airplanes for people."

Then he received a phone call from the manager of Western Bus Lines in Port Alberni. He needed a driver. "'What the heck, I'll give him a hand," Cove thought – and so began another new career phase.

Mister Cargo is doing what he likes best: arranging, managing and taking an active role in a people-oriented operation. He arranges bus sightseeing tours, meets and greets the passengers, looks after them and their itineraries, and drives the bus. He has fun with his passengers, and they, in turn, have fun with him.

"But," he says, "I'll never give up buying and selling airplanes. Last year I helped Dr. Wilson here with the purchase of a King Air turbo prop and setting up a charter service."

He still receives many job offers – a six-week contract to fly a twin engine Mitsubishi for a mine in the northern Yukon Territories, a contract to ferry a Beaver to Whitehorse. Bill Cove is still fully licensed, "commercial, instrument rating, floats, you name it." He also holds a private rotary wing licence, gained when he worked for Coulsons, "that was part of the deal," and is licensed on the Bell 206. He has accumulated 65 hours on rotary wing.

When Bill Cove reflects on his career, and his 23 000 hours in the air, he acknowledges that many changes have taken place in aviation – "and all for the good, believe me." He cites increased use of helicopters over fixed wing aircraft for bush work, and new navigation and communications systems. "When I think back on the hours and the flights we made over open water with people on board! If those engines had ever coughed!"

Changes also have come about in the industries served by west coast bush pilots, such as the logging camps scattered throughout BC's forests. "In the late 1950s and the 1960s it was such a dynamic industry," Cove recalls.

But the logging industry has become ravaged by protests over wasteful and damaging clear-cut logging practices. Bill Cove saw it all, and allows that "the logging companies really did do a bad, bad service to us. This province has been just totally robbed."

Cove feels that a compromise solution must be sought, and fast. "Because the loggers went too far, now the protesters have gone too far. There's got to be a balance, and it can be done. I've seen loggers work around creeks. This is where the helicopter is so valuable."

Adventures keep happening to Bill Cove. In 1998, he flew the Beaver aircraft that was featured in the recent Harrison Ford film "Six Days, Seven Nights" to Oshkosh with its new owner. Flying first with wheels, they landed at St. Paul, Minnesota, and put on floats so Cove could instruct the owner on float-flying. They did landings and take-offs from the Mississippi River, landing beside sternwheelers and other boats. On the way back they stopped in Sturgis, South Dakota, to observe the gathering of Harley-Davidson motorcycles. "Imagine, 139 000 bikes!" Cove exclaims. "You could just smell the rich, rich pot!"

Beverley and Bill Cove at their home in Port Alberni, 1998. (S. Matheson photo).

Both the Coves' sons are pilots. "Willie is on the DC-10 with Canadian Airlines International, and Danny is on the Dash-8 with Air BC," Cove says proudly.

Bill Cove gives full credit to his wife, Bev, for keeping the home fires burning when he was so often away from home. "She has always been really supportive, to all of us," he says. Bev keeps busy and happy while her perennially energetic husband continues to seek new challenges.

The changes experienced as both an aircraft pilot and a tour bus driver excite Bill Cove. "Flying is so professional," he says, "the challenge of coming out of the clouds and finding a runway, and all that. It always pumped me up so much. With the bus, from an entertainment point of view, dealing with the people first-hand is just marvelous. I really get a kick out of it."

He readily admits to being a "people person."

"I really am. My passengers constantly say, 'We've never had a bus driver do for us the things you do!' I help them to their rooms with their bags. I always have candies. Tomorrow I'm buying five dozen donuts to take on the bus. They just love it. It's all such fun!"

The Great Escape

Barry Davidson has the least number of flying hours of any pilot featured in this book – no more than 50. But those hours changed his life dramatically and became the reason for his story, and those of his comrades, to be portrayed in an Academy Award-winning Hollywood film.

"Before you come over to visit, rent the movie, *The Great Escape*," Barry said. " James Garner played me."

When one meets Barry Anderson Davidson, it's easy to envision the handsome young man portrayed in photos, newspaper clippings and other documents that support his story. In fact, if his youthful escapades were to be depicted by one of today's actors, Brad Pitt or Leonardo diCaprio would win the role.

In his 80s, Barry's eyes retain their twinkle and his sharp humor remains as cutting as it must have been in his younger, more rebellious, years.

"I'll tell you what was real and what wasn't in that movie," Barry says, as we go over the chain of events that led to *The Great Escape*. "For starters, no Americans were there! How's that? And you saw where Steve McQueen got tossed in jail, with his ball glove and ball? They just did that for dramatic effect. The Germans wouldn't have let us keep a *pencil*! They weren't playing around."

Barry Davidson was a German prisoner of war (called a "Kriegie") for five years, from July 6, 1940 to May 5, 1945. Five years of incarceration can put a severe dent in a life plan and leave memories that linger forever. And it all came about because he wanted to fly.

Davidson was born in Calgary, Alberta, on August 12, 1914. His early career saw him working for a Calgary brokerage firm, James Richardson & Sons, Limited. There, he met Fred McCall, a World War I flying ace.

"Fred McCall talked me into learning to fly with him, Bill Smith and Howard Sandgathe. They had a flying school up at the old municipal airport in Renfrew, across from the golf course where the baseball diamonds are now," Davidson recalls.

And so, "just for fun," Davidson learned to fly. It cost very little, with air time included in the fee of $175. Starting January 12, 1937, he trained on an open cockpit deHavilland DH 82A Tiger Moth (CF-CBS) and a deHavilland DH 60A Gipsy Moth (CF-CAO). His log book indicates that Sandgathe was his instructor, and that his instruction time totaled 304 minutes, or five hours and four minutes. He received his private pilot's licence on July 25, 1937.

Davidson was excited about the potential of his new-found skill and wanted to make some use of it. Following the Japanese attack on China that year, he wrote to

General Chiang Kai-shek, the political and military leader of Nationalist China, offering his services to the Flying Tigers. The reply, dated November 1, 1937, from the Headquarters of the Generalissimo in Nanking, reads:

> *Madame Chiang Kai-shek instructs me to acknowledge receipt of your letter of September 6, asking for a position with the Chinese forces. Madame Chiang Kai-shek regrets that there are no vacancies at present and therefore has to decline your offer.*

In 1938, Davidson went to work for Prudential Life Insurance and the next year was transferred to Vancouver. But again the flying bug bit. Knowing that his Grade 10 education was not deemed sufficient to join the RCAF, and on hearing that "the RAF would take anybody," he applied to the Royal Air Force. To gain an interview he was asked to arrange his own transportation to Ottawa. He did so, via CPR cattle train. "They reimbursed my fare later when I was accepted for pilot training."

His sole reason for wanting to go into any air force was to improve his flying skills. "My log book would show that to get my licence I had only about six or eight hours flying on the Tiger Moths, so I wanted more experience."

Joining the RAF would certainly help him to increase his flying hours, and he was pleased to be accepted as a "pupil pilot" on July 24, 1939. But by then, Barry Davidson was no longer a kid. "I got in to the RAF less than a month before I turned 25. I just made it under the wire."

Davidson was first sent to Montreal for overseas posting, and in 1939 he boarded the *Antonia* for Liverpool. He was finally going to see the world!

He began as an Aircraftsman 2nd class, flying Tiger Moths from a grass strip at the training school in Desford near Nottingham. The informal setting suited Davidson's impetuous nature.

"I got in a plane with my instructor and we took off. He said, 'Now take over and see what you can do with it.' I flew the goddamned Tiger Moth better than my instructor! He said, 'You don't need me,' so we'd take our golf clubs and fly to a golf course. That was my flying training."

With around 50 flying hours under his belt, Davidson was ready for bigger things. He was told he had the knack, and "it seemed, in my flying experience, that was very true."

"Then we went to Grantham and I applied for single-engine fighter training." His Commanding Officer was Wing Commander Douglas Hamilton, whose father was Lord Hamilton. In May 1941, Rudolf Hess, Adolf Hitler's right-hand man, made a historic flight to the Hamilton estate in Scotland, where Hess attempted to persuade Great Britain to get out of World War II.

While in Grantham, Davidson trained in Hawker Hinds and Hawker Harts. In December 1939, Davidson was posted to a conversion unit for training on twin-engine aircraft where he put in some eight hours on Avro Ansons.

"In early 1940 we went from there to Norwich southeast of the Wash, up on the east coast of England where it's indented on the ocean," Davidson says. "The fall of France had happened. The Germans were developing aerodromes all over Europe so the RAF was testing us on Blenheims. I went to Oxford and I had about 12 circuits and bumps [landings] so I'd get used to twin engines and inside cockpits." In June 1940, he was sent to an aerodrome near Hastings. At this time, Davidson was granted a short service commission as Acting Pilot Officer.

Davidson recalls that the Blenheims used for training were in bad shape, and he had to do practice takeoffs in several aircraft before finally finding one he would fly. "Britain was so badly off for equipment, you wouldn't believe what they were flying. Anyhow, I got about three and three-quarters hours flying time on the Blenheim, and then I was told I was going to No. 18 (Burma) Squadron at West Raynham."

On Saturday, July 6, 1940, Davidson was late for the briefing so was assigned the longest run, a solo flight into France and Germany to pinpoint the development of advanced aerodromes.

"I had to go," Davidson says simply, "and we were the only single aircraft [RAF Blenheim R 3662]. Just three of them were kept bombed up and ready for operations. I only had a crew of two, Sergeant Gilmore as observer-navigator, and Sergeant Fiske, the wireless operator and air-gunner."

He put in one hour flying the Blenheim to test the crew before leaving on the flight at 14:47 hours. His total flying time on the aircraft before the operation was four-and-one-half hours.

"We carried a 1000 pound bomb load: one 500 and two 250s. My trip was through Belgium and down south to within 15 kilometres of Paris, looking for these four aerodromes. We crossed over to Belgium toward Paris, flying at about 3000 feet – that is, until someone shot at you and then you went down low. We got to the point where we were to turn back and we still hadn't seen anything and hadn't been fired at, believe it or not. No fighter planes, nothing.

Barry Davidson in training at Desford, England, with Tiger Moth, July 1939. Photo was titled "Ready & Willing – as we all are." (Photo: Davidson collection)

"We started back up towards England, coming back through France, and suddenly we saw this new aerodrome straight ahead of us. We flew down the runway and I dropped the 500 pound bomb on the equipment at the end of the runway – which was just to practice bombing. Then I said, 'We'll take out the buildings with the 250s.' We flew over and dropped the 250s on the building area.

"We'd just climbed to 1700 or 1800 feet when they suddenly woke up. The flak opened up and at 1800 feet we got hit."

The aircraft took a midship hit. With a Blenheim, all the controls run down the centre of the airplane, toward the floor on the right side. The shell explosion severed the elevator cables. The aircraft flipped over and went into a steep dive.

"At 1700 feet, you haven't got time to get the hell out and jump," Davidson says. "For some reason, and that's instinct again, I remembered 'when elevators are gone, try trim'. I reached down to the tail trimmers and they worked. We came out of the dive – just lucky but anyhow we came out of it. The tail trimmers were going up and down, and the compass was gyrating because of this movement."

With the compass unserviceable, it was difficult to pinpoint their exact location. Davidson's plan, if they couldn't see land, was to just "dump it in the ocean and call a May Day." But after 15 or 20 minutes, land came up to his left. Going northwest out of France, they thought that had to be England. Meanwhile, they were still in the line of fire. They were below the white cliffs, flying at 200 to 300 feet off the sea, unable to gain any height.

"My rear gunner yelled, 'It's getting hot back here!' so I said, 'Okay, down she goes.' I pulled the wheels up, because I had them down for identification. In those early war days there was no radio IFF – identification friend or foe – so you'd lower your undercarriage to identify yourself as 'friend' when returning to the coast of England, or risk being shot down by anti-aircraft batteries."

They dumped down on the beach, "no crash or nothing, we just landed. Lucky again."

At that moment, Davidson noticed an RAF Hawker Hurricane sitting on the beach, which he presumed had done the same.

"But I thought the British were firing at us because we weren't near the corridor. In those days, you had to come in a certain corridor from England because the Germans had captured so many of our planes and were using them for bombing. But anyhow, there we were.

"I was reading a map in the observer's position, trying to see where we might be in England. I'd received permission to get this girlfriend of mine from Nottingham into the station, so I was looking there. Suddenly I looked up – and Germans were swarming down from the cliffs onto the beach!"

Their location was now painfully clear. They had made a circle, and were actually heading south along the coast of France. The white cliffs, thought to be at Dover, were actually German-held French cliffs on the other side of the Channel near Calais. They had force-landed between Calais and Dunkerque, in enemy territory! Now, the Germans were coming at them, guns at the ready. They swarmed around and into the airplane.

"There's one funny part of it," Davidson says. "I had my [forward-firing machine] gun on Fire. One German guy sat in the cockpit, pressed the firing button, and the gun went off. Germans were blown all over! Didn't hit anybody, though, because the plane was more or less up-angled. But they said, 'For you, the war is over.' And it was."

The date, July 6, 1940, remains indelible in Barry Davidson's mind. The war had been going on since September 1939. He hadn't been in the air force quite a year.

"We were put in jail in Calais," Davidson says. "The next day they said they were going to fly us over to Frankfurt an der Oder." The crew was held in custody by the German troops overnight in a barn, part way between the beach and St. Omer. Then they were taken by car through St. Omer to Brussels, and flown to Munster.

But Davidson wasn't ready to accept prisoner status.

"I got together with the crew and I said, 'This is our chance to take over the plane and get out of here!' We got into the German plane okay, to find about 10 or 12 German soldiers already inside – so that was it."

They spent the night in Munster, then were taken by rail to Frankfurt Interrogation Centre.

"We ended up in a recession camp, an interrogation camp near Frankfurt an der Oder, and were there about three weeks." Here, Davidson was separated from his two crew members and was never to meet them again. He doesn't know their fate. The RAF Officers Records, Air Ministry, lists only a

Pilot Officer Barry Davidson near Frankfurt an der Oder, at German interrogation camp prior to being sent to Barth, July 8, 1940. (Photo: Davidson collection)

Map of Germany and adjacent countries, showing prisoner of war camps.

terse description of what brought the airmen to their doom: "Identified on return flight but failed to reach base."

Following three days in solitary confinement, and another 11 days at the interrogation camp, Davidson was moved up to Stalag Luft I (from Stammlager Luft - permanent camp for airmen) at Barth on the Baltic Sea. He soon discovered that, beneath the seemingly benign prison routine, a plan for escape was being carried out. "Actually, it was funny. We dug so many escape tunnels up there at our first camp – 47 in all – that the Germans were afraid to drive a truck around the camp! It was laughable."

Davidson's two-edged job involved organizing sports and developing friendly relations with the German guards and officers. He turned on the charm and got equipment for their sports events. Davidson's success in these endeavors gained him the nickname, "The Skate Man." It was later changed to "The Fox" as he became skilled in obtaining escape materials such as road maps, railroad schedules and information about the geography of the surrounding countryside.

"We were *officers*," Davidson states. "That's one thing I want to make clear. When you see the pictures of the theatre we had, the baseball and hockey, you can see how well organized we were. I called it a 'rest camp' in a sense, although it wasn't that."

The men incarcerated in the prison camps knew they had to keep busy or else go insane.

In addition to his assignments, Davidson also read hundreds of books supplied through the Red Cross and YMCA. Prisoners were allowed to send out four letters per month. Davidson used one to instruct his brokers in London on stock purchases, using accumulating back pay.

On April 10, 1942, he and other prisoners of war (POWs) from the Royal Air Force, and Dominion and Allied Air Forces, were moved down to Sagan in the north-east corner of Poland, 100 miles from Berlin, to Stalag Luft III. This supposedly "escape-proof" camp became notorious as the setting for The Great Escape. At first, Davidson was billeted in East Compound, the site of actual tunnel proceedings.

The secret escape organization was headed by South African-born RAF Officer Squadron Leader Roger Bushell, who was known as "Big X" and the man in charge of the "X" Organization committee (which handled such "nefarious" operations as escape plans, communications, security, etc.). Senior British Officer (SBO) Wing Commander H.M.A. Day, called "Wings Day," was also an important member this committee, as well as a Canadian pilot, Flying Officer Wally Floody, who was assigned to supervise all tunneling operations.

Davidson soon found his talents required, and he started organizing sports and other activities. "We even had a course in secretarial shorthand. There was gardening. And, of course, the tunnel activities. I, at times, worked on the tunneling myself."

In the film version, the Germans become suspicious about the number of avid gardeners. "These men are officers, not peasants!" say the perplexed guards.

"Well, it was because of the tunnels," Davidson explains. "We were pushing the material brought from the tunnels into the cultivated gardens, sand underneath and dirt on top. People who were on the escape committee would fill 'sausage bags' made from long underpants, with sand, inside their pant legs. Later, as they stood hoeing the garden, they would pull on a string to release the bottom of the bags and let the sand dribble out, then cover it up with garden dirt.

"I didn't work on the tunnels for too long. I guess I was too busy running the sports, that sort of thing – and scrounging." Now he became known as "The Scrounger," and this work became one of Davidson's most important roles in the secretive operations.

"I got hold of a little German named Fischer, who hated the Nazis. He was the interpreter, and he and his wife were acrobatic dancers. He was my main ally. He got us radio parts, different things such as insignias for the uniforms, printers ink, copies of passports and passes which could be used for our forgeries – everything for escape purposes: maps, compasses, train schedules, blankets and rations, travel permits, bolts of cloth, camera, timber, picks and stuff for the tunnels. It's hard for a civilian, or a person who was never in a prison camp, to know what we brought in."

There were four different compounds: East, Centre, North and South (the American compound). "Before the escape the Americans had their own hut, but they were moved to a separate compound. The Germans had purged a lot of the guys to another compound just before the escape."

When the occupants of East Compound were moved to North Compound, they knew they'd be searched "from here to breakfast." At great personal risk, Fischer volunteered to carry over all their escape equipment. Here, Davidson was confined to contact work covering Fischer.

"He would have been shot right away if he'd been caught, but he worked with me, and also another German, "Dutchy" Schultz, who was quite a nice guy and got a few things for me. They had wineries in Germany and he brought in champagne. I had to get up at six o'clock in the morning to retrieve it out of the laundry bag, that's how he brought it in. The men also made wine out of raisins, prunes, potatoes, anything. We had some homemade booze, like moonshine – there wasn't lots but there was a fair bit. We had quite a few parties. Anyhow, this went on while the tunnel was going."

Although they didn't flaunt these enterprises in front of the Germans, "you couldn't hide the still, not very easily. You could hide a radio but not a still. But, they didn't seem to mind. As one German said, 'It keeps you guys busy.'"

Davidson recalls a German security fellow named Glimnitz, who became known as the Head Ferret. His job was to look for tunnels and any escape equipment. "He was quite a character. Our job, of course, was to prevent detection by keeping track of the ferrets – every time they came or went was signaled to the others on the Escape Committee. One hut would have tailoring and be making suits and stuff out of blanket material. One hut would have mapping or surveying.

"We had people on guard to watch for the Germans at each end of every hut; you never let the Germans leave your sight. We had a signaling system set up. The person at the first hut would have a hand signal that indicated what direction the German, or Germans, were going – we couldn't make sound signals – so they were followed by every sentinel."

Actually, three main tunnels were begun on the same day in April 1943 and given the code names of Tom, Dick and Harry. Tom tunnel was from Hut 123, Dick was from Hut 122, kitty-corner from Hut 109, and Harry was from Hut 104.

It seems amazing that the plan was not discovered earlier – a definite tribute to the ingenuity of the men involved, their security system and code of silence. For the tunnel workers, a tin can containing pebbles would be rattled from ground level to give warning and the escape hatch put back to normal in two minutes.

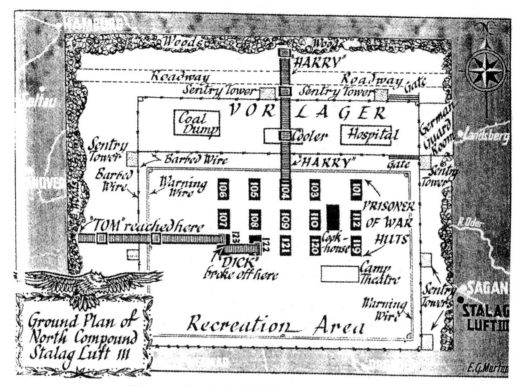

Diagram of Stalag Luft III, drawn by E.G. Morton.

Mounds of sand from the excavations was secreted in a hut located a distance away from the tunnel entrance. Davidson was housed in No. 109 barracks, and the final escape tunnel was behind No. 104.

"I tried digging in the tunnel, but I got claustrophobic," Davidson says. "The tunnel was about 350 feet long, but about 30 feet straight down – and that's a long ways down! – because the Germans had sound equipment to detect digging." It was the longest prisoner-of-war tunnel ever made.

"You've got a tunnel only big enough to squeeze through [three feet square] and you're pushing this little truck ahead of you with the sand on it. You had to lie on your stomach, or your back to get the top part. For shovels [to hack at the compacted sand] we used tin salmon cans that came with our Red Cross parcels, and we put the sand in a box on the trolley."[1]

There were three little trucks, or trolleys, one in each of the three sections of the tunnel, which were divided by two "halfway houses" named Picadilly and Leicester Square. The sand – 200 tons of it by the end – was moved by the trolleys to a sand-dispersal chamber, where it was shoveled into the sausage-bags for transportation to the next stage. Members of the "X Organization" called "penguins" would then insert a

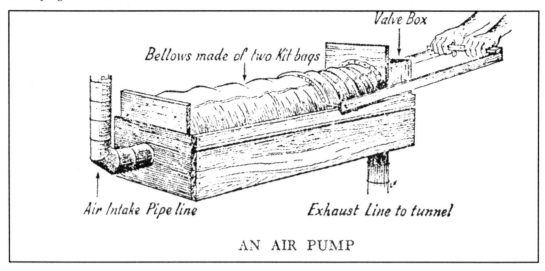

Valve Box

Bellows made of two Kit bags

Air Intake Pipe line

Exhaust Line to tunnel

AN AIR PUMP

sausage bag into each trouser leg, later releasing it into garden to be mixed with the soil. Later, Dick was abandoned and used as a sand-dump for Tom.

The tunnel walls were shored with bed-boards and sections of air pipes made from powdered milk tins fitted together. An air conditioning pump was designed with bellows made from two RAF kit bags mounted on runners. The curved pipe carried air pumped by the other bellow along the tunnel to the work-face. The box between the bellows contained a system of flapper valves made from leather. The system supplied fresh air to the underground chambers and tunnel face. Cave-ins were a constant danger. Davidson recalls that Wally Floody, the engineer in charge of tunnels, had two or three close escapes from cave-ins.

Further, the Germans were always suspicious, knowing the top priority of the prisoners was to escape, and finally, the Tom tunnel was discovered. "We had to abandon it. We couldn't do anything else when they found the damned thing! They collapsed the tunnel."

Following discovery of Tom, the POWs used the shaft of Dick to conceal additional dirt from their third tunnel, Harry. "Roger Bushell and the Escape Committee decided they'd use the other tunnel [Dick] to put the sand in, because we were running out of places to store the sand so it wasn't detected," Davidson recalls. This work went on during the winter of 1943-44.

"I'll tell you how Roger Bushell's thinking went," Davidson goes on. "He was a lawyer, and he was called Mr. X [or Big X]. When we were running out of space to store the sand from the tunnel, he suggested we take one room that was fairly close to where we were digging the Harry Tunnel. Using Red Cross parcels as a camouflage, we filled this room with sand from the tunnel! The Germans finally found it, got rid of the sand, and cut us off Red Cross parcels for a couple of weeks. But we'd got rid of all that sand by filling a whole room with it. Just think that we could get away with it! But we knew that the Germans knew we were digging tunnels, because they'd found the Tom Tunnel, and they assumed we were digging another one."

The risk was enormous: being caught could mean a death sentence. Davidson describes the philosophy behind the attempt to escape as two-fold: "To get home. And to disrupt the Germans, keep them agitated."

"Roger Bushell had hoped that 200 men might escape. To have so many of us out there would cause a hell of a state of confusion, and it would take a lot of troops to round them up. That was the purpose."

In the Hollywood film based on The Great Escape, one of the characters reiterates this conviction – they wanted to escape, yes, but also to confuse the Germans behind the lines, to drive them insane. At the same time, they realized their chances of making it to freedom were very slim.

"But, some of the guys were fairly well equipped," Davidson says. "The Poles, Czechs and people like that, spoke German. Bushell was fluent in German, and quite a few of the others were."

Davidson wasn't multi-lingual and therefore knew his chances on the outside would be somewhat reduced. "But, you've got to visualize it: Germany was full of out-side workers, Yugoslavs and whatnot, who couldn't speak English or German either. I was only going out to get the hell out of the place, I didn't have a clue what I would do." He didn't have a set of documents to aid his escape. In fact, his only aid was a uniform that had been altered by removing the wings, stripes and buttons, so it appeared to be just an airforce-blue jacket. "All I was going to do was go out. I didn't have any visions of getting back home or anything like that. And we never thought of anybody being shot."

Two weeks before the escape Walter Floody was transferred away from Stalag Luft III, along with some others who were under suspicion.

On the assigned night, March 24, 1944, the Escape Committee waited for the "dark of the moon," estimated to be 9:30 p.m. They'd planned ways to dodge the guard-box searchlights, and knew when the German patrols guarding the wire outside the camp-ground would be away from the tunnel exit out near the woods.

The tunnel fell short of the ideal place to exit in the woods, so the first person to escape lay in a tree to watch for the Germans. An "all clear" signal (a tug on a rope) was given to the next person in line, and so on. By 4:45 a.m. on March 25th, 76 officers had escaped.

"I was number 78, I think, on the list of those going out," Davidson says. "But unfor-tunately I had been seen talking to Fischer shortly before the escape. We had such a good security system that the Committee knew the Germans had seen me talking to him, so Roger Bushell asked me if I'd step back and not go out.

"Anyhow, I stepped back. I would have been just at the top of the ladder when the Germans came in and all hell broke loose. They called in SS [Secret State police - German Gestapo] troops. It really disrupted them because they didn't know how many had got out at the time, so we were mauled around. We were made to stand up outside our huts all the rest of that night."

It took a period of time for the news to filter back of the brutal murders of 50 of the officers who had escaped that night.

When Group Captain Massey (SBO) was called to the office of the camp commandant and informed that 50 men had been shot, he pointedly asked, "How many were wounded?"

The commandant's answer was abrupt. "I have no authority to say anything more."

That ended the interview, but Massey knew from those few words that the officers could not have been shot while trying to escape. If they had, some would have been wounded and returned. All 50 officers had, in fact, been murdered.

"So," Davidson says, "that was it for the escape end of things."

The travesty of shooting the escaping officers will long be remembered by all countries involved, as it totally went against ethics for handling prisoners of war.

"Hitler wanted to shoot us all. He was told about the 76 who came out, but he was talking about all of us. When you see my log book, listing the nationalities of the prisoners who were shot, you'll see that they picked men from various countries: Canada, Britain, Australia, New Zealand, South Africa, Argentina, Czechoslovakia, France, Greece, Lithuania, Norway, Poland, and South Morocco." From the list he reads the name of Flight Lieutenant Hank Birkland. "He came from Calgary, my mother knew his mother."

Only three of the 76 made successful escapes (Per Bergsland, Jens Muller and Bram van der Stok), while 17 were returned to Sagan, four sent to Sachsenhausen, and two to Colditz Castle, while 50 were murdered by the Gestapo.[2]

"The Fox" went into action, working silently and secretly with two anti-Nazi sympathizers, Fischer and Schultz, to discover the chain of events that had followed the escape. He then passed on the written information received from Schultz, unread, to Squadron Leader Walters, who had taken S/L Bushell's place as Operations Officer on the Escape Committee, as Bushell had been killed in the escape attempt. "What this written information contained I do not know," Davidson says, "but I assumed it had something to do with the people who were responsible for the killing of our men."

"The stupid thing is, I can't even remember what happened to Fischer," Davidson says. "That bugs me. I've got his name and address in my log book. Why he gave it to me I don't know. I never wrote to him. I just wanted to forget it."

The remaining Sagan prisoners of North compound erected a memorial to the assassinated officers, listing the men's names and their countries of origin, "In Memory of those officers who paid the extreme sacrifice after escape on the night of March 24, 1944. *Per Ardua Ad Astra.*" The "Unfinished Vault," designed by ex-POW F/Lt. Todd, is located in Sagan, Germany, now called Zagan and part of Poland. Inside were placed the ashes of the 50 slain Allied flyers (the urns were later removed and taken to the Old Garrison Cemetery at Poznan), with their names inscribed on granite scrolls that rise from the vault.

Was it worth it? To plan and work so hard to excavate the tunnels, and to smuggle in a multitude of supplies to facilitate the escape, to have just three successful escapes out of 76 attempts, with most of the rest slain?

"It depends on your point of view," Davidson says.

Walter Floody agrees: "I suppose the answer lies more in the instinct than the intellect," he writes in a report of his 20-year recollections. "It has to do with the desire to be free."

In 1962, film producer-director John Sturgis contacted Paul Brickhill, author of *The Great Escape* and also a member of "X Organization" at Stalag Luft III, to seek his advice on who they should hire as a technical advisor. Brickhill recommended Walter Floody.

Floody advised Sturgis and the special-effects staff, Paul Pollard and Hal Miller, art director Fernando Carrere, and prop-master Frank Agnone, on everything from the uniforms to the air bellows, the documents, even to the still designed from a trombone. All details were checked until, in Floody's words, they became "all too true for comfort."

The entertainment media must often alter the stark truth, however, as "life ain't art." Names of main characters were fictionalized (Davidson's character was called Hendley), while several characters and their duties were amalgamated. But outstanding personalities were portrayed, such as Bushell, Howes (an RAF officer who worked with Bushell on the escape plans) and others. "All the main characters showed up in the picture, played by actors," Davidson says.

The role of Barry Davidson, alias "The Fox" and "The Scrounger," was played by James Garner. Davidson retains a copy of a letter written by Garner (dated March 22, 1994) to the RCAF Prisoner of War Association in Ottawa:

"The Great Escape" is one of the highlights of my motion picture career. The fact that it recalls an event of untold courage and bravery is a source of pride to me and a tribute to you. I applaud your heroism and salute the memory of those no longer with us. My warmest personal regards to you all.

The movie concludes with a voice-over, reading names from the scroll of the 50 officers shot by Hitler's soldiers.

Through the efforts of Hollywood, the story of The Great Escape became known to a new, wide audience, to be forever etched in the memories of those living in the free world. But what happened to the remaining prisoners after the monument was inscribed, and the dead mourned? There is, indeed, another chapter to the story.

"The Germans were fairly sharp after that," Davidson recalls. "They removed the Commandant we had. He was a nice guy, he respected us as we respected him. Then they issued this warning, 'Escape is not a sport.' The Germans said they would shoot anybody who tried to escape."

That seemed to end the escape attempts. "I'm pretty sure it did. See, Roger Bushell was gone, as well as others important to the escape business."

Memorial to the 50 officers shot by the Germans March 1944, built in 1945. (Photo taken in 1991 in Sagan – Davidson collection)

Davidson reads names chipped into the memorial stone, and adds personal comments: "Flight Lieutenant M.J. Casey, assistant to Bushell; Squadron Leader I.K. Cross, the forger; Velenta, a Czech , a keen type, always down working in the tunnels; Danny Cole, who was Polish, a great tunnel boy; Kirby-Green from South Morocco, who forged documents – all were gone. Bushell had escaped two or three times before, but that was the end of it."

The POWs remained at Sagan until January 27, 1945, when the entire camp was given orders to evacuate within 30 minutes. The men's hopes were raised as they heard the sounds of war – the Russians were attacking Breslau only 30 kilometres (18 miles) away!

That night, the full camp, numbering in the thousands, with the exception of the sick, began their forced-march in -35° weather – trudging through the snow for 36 straight hours, with infrequent stops to rest in barns on beds of straw. The next day, the sounds of war became inaudible as the men moved further from the battle-sites. The decrease in sound increased their anxiety.

On the fourth night, they arrived at Mauskau, where they built sledges to push or pull their supplies along the roads. But soon the snow turned to slush, the sledges had to be abandoned and the 40- and 50-pound packs again were loaded onto the men's backs. The rest of the 18-mile march that day was torturous. Sick prisoners fell back, to be shoved along with rifle butts by the guards. One night two prisoners, an RCAF and a South African airman, were shot and wounded by guards as they attempted to cross a fence to find straw for their beds.

A poem titled "Retribution," painstakingly printed in Davidson's treasured log-book, reflects the despair.

The vaulted dome of Heaven, china blue,
that cups the gleaming of the sun
where swallows soar and swoop in silent fun,
and rainbows build an arch of brilliant hue,
calls from its boundless depths that Man should view
the miracle of flight that he has won
and guard it lest he find he has undone
the benefit and good he sought to do.

God never meant that he should desecrate
the quiet beauty of the sky with flame!
Or urge our gallant youth to dedicate
destruction to the glory of a name!
And those he spared see justice in their plight,
the pain of caged birds, observing flight.

On the fifth day they marched 20 kilometres (12 miles) to Spremburg, a rail centre, where the compounds were split up and the prisoners loaded into box cars heading for various destinations. It had been a tough ordeal and was far from over. The men's clothing was inadequate, they were not allowed to change or wash their socks and their feet suffered horribly, and they were fed meagre frozen rations. Diarrhea and stomach problems became epidemic.

When they boarded the cattle train Barry Davidson was the last one on, being so weak he needed help. Luckily, this placed him near the only ventilation, a crack in the door. They rode on the train for three days, stopping for short exercise breaks every six hours. By the time they reached Tarmstadt, Marlag – Milag Luft I – on February 5, eight members of the group had perished.

Over a thousand men arrived at Milag, exhausted and sick in heart and spirit. The camp had been recently evacuated by interned Merchant Marines, and the camp was filthy. The beds crawled with bedbugs.

They remained at Tarmstadt until April 20, then were force-marched to the outskirts of the City of Lubeck, which took 10 days. The attitude of the guards oddly became more lenient as they neared Lubeck. Could it be because of the propaganda leaflets being dropped by the Allied air forces, warning that Germany was losing the war, and those responsible for mistreatment of prisoners would be severely reprimanded?

"We finally ended up by Lubeck in the northwest corner of Germany, following the marches and train rides in cattle cars," Davidson says. The Kriegies were at the end of their endurance and, luckily, at the end of their ordeal.

When they arrived at the prison camp at Lubeck, the CO, Group Captain Wray, inspected the facilities and refused to allow the prisoners to enter. Typhus had broken out among the prisoners already there. They were taken 15 kilometres (nine miles) south-east to Trenthorst, to the estate of a former German tobacco industrialist, and were billeted in his cattle barns – a decided improvement over the prison camp facilities.

On April 20, 1945, Russian armed forces took the city of Luckenwalde, 20 kilometres (12 miles) south of Potsdam. The news on the BBC of allied victory was unbelievable to the miserable prisoners. Then, over the hill came a British scout car. A faint cheer went up. The POWs swarmed the car as the driver called headquarters: "Hello H.2. Hello H.2. X34 calling. Have just released second POW camp. Standing by." The cheers were loud and jubilant. It was really over! They were free.

"We were released on May 2nd by a Scottish Tank Regiment," Davidson says. "They

came over the hill, the Germans were gone, and from then on we were on our own.

The day before VE (Victory in Europe) Day, May 8, 1945, Allied officers arranged to transport the ex-POWs to airports and then fly them to England in Lancasters and Dakotas (DC-3s) to various "rehab" centres. At 12:00 noon on VE Day the first lorry of Kriegies arrived at the aerodrome, ready to go home.

But a further surprise awaited Barry Davidson and others. "We came back to England to find that we were still fighting Japan. The Royal Air Force were going to send us over there! Believe it or not! We got hold of our Canadian ambassador to England and told him the circumstances. Stupid!

Flight Lieutenant Barry Davidson. (Photo: Davidson collection)

Ignorant. I hadn't flown for five years, the other prisoners of war hadn't flown for at least two or three years.

"He got hold of the RCAF. They transferred us from the RAF to the RCAF, dating back from November 1944 to the time I got out in June 1945. I got as much pay then as I got the whole five years in the RAF. And they didn't make us go to Japan after five years in a Prisoner of War camp."

So, after being processed and receiving medical exams, the ex-POWs were finally sent home.

It was time for Barry Davidson to put his dreams into place, and that is what he did. He started several businesses, had a successful career in securities and insurance, and enjoyed his family of two daughters, Bryanne and Elizabeth, and one son, Barry Jr.

Barry Davidson flew just once since returning home.

"Some of us ex-POWs were invited out to the Airdrie aerodrome where they have the Harvards. A friend of mine was there and he had his little plane, so he talked me into going up and flying. But the air regulations here are for the birds! You can't do anything! I said, 'How about a loop?' 'Can't do it.' 'How about rolling it?' 'Can't. You're in an air-lane.' You have to just go up and sit and fly the bloody plane! Didn't thrill me."

Twenty-five years after his incarceration, Calgary *Herald* reporter Johnny Hopkins interviewed Barry Davidson about his thoughts and memories:

"It's a difficult thing to assess now," said Davidson. "At the time the dominant emotion was one of utter frustration . . . of simply being confined, of not being able to help my country, and of not really knowing how the war was going. Now I guess the emotion is one of regret. They were five years lost, as they were, of course, for every serviceman whether or not he was a prisoner. Time dulls the hardships and the dangers, but the memories remain even though the bitterness might subside" (Calgary *Herald*, June 1, 1965).

Barry Davidson's log book, containing sketches, watercolor paintings and poetry completed by himself and other ex-POWs, is a national treasure.[3] The drawings and poems clearly capture the emotions of men whose freedom has been snatched away – and the eternal hope to recapture that freedom.

I HOPE

I hope that I will never know, so many days that pass so slow;
So many weeks so much the same; so many months without a name.

I hope that I will never eat (when Jerrie's dust is off my feet)
Another tin of Martin's stew, or drink another Kriegie brew.

I hope my cup will overflow with all the joys I used to know,
With wine, and women to be kissed, to make up for the things I've missed.

Such hope led officer airmen from the allied countries to pit their time, talents and their mortality on a plan that almost worked – The Great Escape.

        *   *   *

NOTE: Barry Davidson died shortly after this story was completed, on October 25, 1996, at age 82. The Nanton Lancaster Society Air Museum in Nanton, Alberta, is in the process of restoring a Blenheim IV aircraft in honor of Davidson. Davidson made his ill-fated landing on the occupied coast of France near Calais on July 6, 1940, which changed his life forever. The museum hopes to have the restoration completed to the point where the markings of Barry Davidson's aircraft may be applied and the bomber dedicated in the year 2000, 60 years later.

The aircraft which will become the "Barry Davidson Memorial Blenheim."

Footnotes

[1]Details of the tunnels became known to the public with the release of detailed drawings made by Flight Lieutenant Ley Kenyon, D.F.C., one of the R.A.F. officers who shared in the escape project. His drawings had to be left behind sealed in watertight containers and hidden in the Dick tunnel when the prisoners were sent on a forced march in January, 1945. But first they flooded Dick as a precaution against the drawings and other documents being discovered by the Germans. The drawings were later recovered by a British officer who had been hospitalized at the time of evacuation. After his release by the Russians, he went down into the tunnel to discover that the floodwater had seeped away, leaving the documents undamaged in their containers.

[2]For a complete story, see: Brickhill, Paul: *The Great Escape*, Faber and Faber, 1951. A sequel (Andrews, Allen: *Exemplary Justice*, Harrap, London, 1976) chronicles the efforts made by the RAF Special Investigation Branch to track and capture the Germans responsible for the murders of the escapees. The Mirisch-Alpha Production screenplay (written by James Clavell and W.R. Burnett) was based on Brickhill's book.

[3]In October, 1995, Calgary's Glenbow Foundation mounted a display of many of the artifacts from The Great Escape, including kettles and the truck used for excavation. Included in this exhibit was Barry Davidson's priceless log book.

The Paper Bag Prince

Daniel Erskine McIvor was born in Killarney, Manitoba, on August 30, 1911, the second of six children and the only son of a Presbyterian minister and his wife, a deaconess. The McIvors moved to Souris, Manitoba, when Dan was three years old and, in 1919 when Dan was eight, to Winnipeg.

One day while at the beach with his mother a "thing" flew overhead that made a lot of noise. His mother explained that it was an airplane with two men in it and they were looking for forest fires. On his own, Dan assumed that when they found a fire they might drop some stuff out of the airplane to put it out.

When Dan's Sunday School teacher, Mrs. Mary Leach, took her class on an outing to River Park, she introduced them to her son Alf, a pilot. He allowed them to see and touch his yellow biplane. "I'll never forget putting my hand on the side of that fuselage," Dan says. "I touched it and I smelled it, and oh! That day I knew I was going to be a pilot." Alf gave each of the children a model airplane, which flew beautifully and became one of Dan's treasures.

Those experiences established Dan McIvor's two dreams: to become a pilot and to help save forests from the devastation of fire.

In 1925, the McIvor family moved to Fort William, Ontario (which later amalgamated with Port Arthur to become Thunder Bay). He left school early and went to work for the Royal Bank of Canada, where he met Isobel "Bud" Auld. When a better job that paid $110 per month came up at Parslow's wholesale company, Dan took it. "I was in clover!" Following a seven-year courtship, he and Bud were married on July 5, 1937.

Flying Fever

There was no opportunity for Dan to learn to fly, however, as lessons cost $12 an hour and he now had a family to support. But as always, the church guided his path.

"I coached a basketball team with our church, and one day I was told that a couple of fellows from Winnipeg were overhauling five engines for the flying club at the Fort William Airport. Dad and I went out to meet them. One, named Kirkaldy, who had been a Squadron Leader in the airforce, was 6'7" tall and skinny as a rake. The other, Gordy Brown, was an engineer; he was 6'4", and a basketball player. I was 6'2". We three tall men joked and got along tremendously, so Dad and I invited them home for dinner."

Gordy Brown had built a Corbin Junior Ace two-place airplane in Brandon, Manitoba, but he needed 50 more hours to get his limited commercial licence. The airplane was brought to Fort William and Gordy saw Dan often while he put in his hours, even letting him "fly" once in a while.

95

"As soon as Gordy got his licence he was hired by Al Cheesman, a famous old bush pilot who had a Fokker Super Universal and operated a flying service out of Port Arthur. His pay went up to $300 a month! I thought, 'That's it, I *am* going to be a pilot, and I'm going to build an airplane, too.'"

First, Dan bought a welding outfit and took a course. Then he purchased plans for a Corbin Junior Ace two-place, side-by-side, high-wing airplane, with the same strut arrangement for the undercarriage and wing as Charles A. Lindbergh's *Spirit of St. Louis*.

"I bought a book, *Airplane and Engine Maintenance for the Airplane Mechanic* [by Daniel J. Brimm and H. Edward Boggess, Pittman Publishing Corporation, 2nd printing 1936] that told me everything I needed to know about building and maintaining an airplane – strength of materials, how to splice control cables, weld, do woodworking, make joints, rig an airplane. I built the airplane using that book," Dan says. He made the wooden parts – ribs for the wing, spars, braces, and fairings – in the family's spare bedroom.

Dan's father, now a Member of Parliament, spoke to C.D. Howe, then-Minister of Transport, and told him his son was building an airplane. "Is there anything you can do to make sure he doesn't kill himself?" Howe asked his inspectors to go to Dan's house whenever they made a trip to Fort William and check out his progress.

The plans called for a small, French, nine-cylinder, 50-hp, radial engine. But because Gordy Brown had put in a Cirrus Mark III, 98-hp engine in his airplane, Dan did the same, with "about 10 times the strength in my engine mount as the original."

"When the inspectors saw that, they became more friendly and helpful," Dan says.

When the fuselage was complete he received permission from "Canada Car" (Canadian Car and Foundry), an airplane factory, to take his airplane into their sandblasting shop. After several hours' work, it looked fine. He planned to return the next night to oil the interior of the tubing of the fuselage and give it a coat of zinc chromate and two coats of aluminum paint. Unknown to Dan, during a slow work schedule the foreman authorized his workers to complete the preparation and painting. "He charged me just One Dollar, and that airplane was perfect!"

When World War II broke out Dan bundled up his airplane and stored it in the warehouse of his employer, as he could neither get it licensed nor buy gas. His dream was put on hold "for the duration."

Royal Canadian Air Force

One day, when Dan was in the bank, his former manager called him into his office. There, he introduced him to Squadron Leader Sellers who had come to Fort William as an RCAF recruiting officer. "Here's a man you want in the airforce," the bank manager said. "Dan is building an aircraft that you should see."

Sellers was duly impressed by Dan's workmanship, and called him later that afternoon to say that they needed a Sergeant in charge of trade testing at Niagara Falls.

Dan was interested. The next morning, however, Sellers reported that the job had been taken, but if Dan would join up as a Carpenter Rigger he could give him a B Group. This would authorize him to sign out aircraft after minor repairs and daily inspections but not after an overhaul. "You'll go direct to a squadron, you won't have to go through any training school," Sellers said.

Dan was by then 28 years old, and knew that the maximum acceptable age to become an airforce pilot was 29. He discussed the offer with his wife, Bud. Her reply was practical. "We know we have to get in that war if Hitler is to be stopped."

Dan McIvor joined the RCAF on October 19, 1939 (Service #R51516) and spent most of that first year repairing and assembling airplanes. Then he received permission to apply for remuster to pilot from his Commanding Officer, Squadron Leader F.R. Miller. When two weeks had passed and he hadn't received confirmation, Dan asked Miller if he would have a better chance for remuster if he had his private pilot's licence. When Miller replied that without it he hadn't any chance at all, Dan asked for special leave to get his licence.

He went to Kingston on Thursday, July 25, 1940, and took an hour's flying training. He went home for the weekend, returned to Kingston on Monday, and to his base on Thursday, August 7th, one week later, with his licence. His time in the air had been eight hours 30 minutes on dual, and five hours 25 minutes solo, a total of 14 hours.

"When I received my private pilot's licence, I anticipated problems with the eye examination so I memorized the eye chart and passed with no problem," Dan says. "I only needed my glasses for close work and didn't use them in the airforce ground crew." His eyesight actually improved over the years.

When Dan returned to base with his pilot's licence, S/L Miller asked for a serviceable Norseman to be brought around. Following the daily inspection, Dan accompanied Miller to the dock and stepped down to the float to help his Commanding Officer up the ladder. "No, you go first, into the left-hand seat," Miller said. "I want to see what you've learned." He then gave the young pilot an hour's instruction on flying a Norseman on floats, showing him how to hit a wave so he didn't bounce, making landing after landing. What a thrill, to fly a Norseman! When they got out, Miller offered short, but never-forgotten, words of praise. "Dan, you'll do all right."

Dan McIvor received his remuster on December 23, 1940. He trained on Tiger Moths at No. 2 Elementary Flying Training School in Fort William, and on Harvards at No. 2 Service Flying Training School in Uplands. He received his wings in June 1941, but not a commission. "That didn't bother me. I loved being a sergeant pilot, a non-commissioned officer."

He then applied for overseas, and got it. But being overseas not a good experience for Dan. He was concerned about leaving his wife, Bud, who was expecting their second baby. He also became ill, and discovered that he had a duodenal ulcer. He spent a month in the hospital in England and as a result never saw combat. "I was supposed to be on Wellington bombers. I got up in one just for a ride but then I was grounded with the ulcer." He was put on duty in a tower until being shipped back home, to Rockcliffe.

By this time, Dan's and Bud's two daughters had been born, Mary Anne on January 8, 1939, (Dan had joined the airforce in October 1939 when she was nine months old) and Wendy on March 7, 1942. "I arrived in New York from overseas, went to Dad's office in the House of Commons in Ottawa, and his secretary told me I had a baby girl."

At Rockcliffe, Dan took a refresher course. On its completion in July 1942 he was posted to No. 8 Bombing and Gunnery School at Lethbridge, Alberta, to take bomb-aimers out to the range. After a year he requested a transfer to No. 124 Ferry Squadron in Ottawa. A year later he was back in Lethbridge, where he ferried airplanes brought from repair depots to flying schools around the province. He received a commission as Pilot Officer on September 23, 1943, and was quickly promoted to Flying Officer. He remained in Ferry Squadron until receiving his discharge on January 1, 1945, with the rank of Acting Flight Lieutenant, and a total of 1733 hours 40 minutes flying time. All of the ferry flying was VFR, mainly between Lethbridge and Vancouver but often as far as the east coast.

Post-Airforce Adventures

After his discharge from the service, Dan tried a number of careers, including running a tire shop on Vancouver Island and being a fruit farmer in the Okanagan Valley.

One day he chanced to meet Dave Smith, a pilot who operated a small air service, Filby and Smith Airways, in Penticton. Smith hired Dan to take the odd trip. That led to the two pilots barnstorming on weekends up and down the Okanagan Valley, from 1946 to 1948. "At one point we dug an airstrip out of the sagebrush above the town of Keremeos and flew passengers with a three-place Super Cub," Dan recalls.

When Smith suggested that Dan get his instructor's rating and come to work for him, Dan resisted – he was going to be a fruit farmer! But Smith persisted, and flew him to Grand Forks where the inspector was giving rides for instructor rating. Dan read the book on the way down, learned the patter, and got his licence.

And so began Dan's life as a pilot instructor. "I took a Taylorcraft to Revelstoke and started a school there. I had 40 students! Imagine it!"

One day in 1948, when he stopped in Vernon for gas on his way to Revelstoke, Dick Laidman of L&M Air Services of Vernon (who later became president of Pacific Western Airlines) offered Dan a job. He jumped at the chance. "All I had to do was charter flying – we had a Stinson on floats, which I flew regularly – instructing, maintenance and looking after the books, for $200 a month!" he laughs.

Dan landed this Cessna 140 (CF-EKR) at night in Vernon, BC. (Photo: McIvor collection)

One day in 1950, Dan had taken a charter flight to Trail in a Cessna 140. He had left Trail just at grounding time, a half-hour after sunset. "I was coming home in the dark, but the weather was good and I knew the mountains. When I got to Vernon they would usually shine a car's headlights down the runway, as there were no airport lights there. I had a beat-up old Chev. Dick usually brought his own car out but this day he brought mine and if you shut my engine off the lights went out. He shut it off, then left."

Dan spotted a parked car with its lights on so he came down over it, but instead of a runway there were trees! Whoops! Wrong car! He swooped up, saw another car, but again, wrong one. He circled the hangar, alerting Normie Brown who lived across the street. He drove over and shone his lights down the runway. Dan came in and landed.

It so happened that Johnny Hatch, General Manager of Queen Charlotte Airlines, was there and had watched Dan's performance. When Dan landed, Hatch approached him. "Do you do this often? Fly around in the middle of the night in an airplane with no radio, and no lights at the airport?"

"No, only when it's necessary."

"Well, if you ever want a job with Queen Charlotte Airlines, come and see me."

Queen Charlotte Airlines

Dan went out the next week and on August 1, 1950, commenced work for Queen Charlotte Airlines. He was based at Zeballos for two years before he finally got a transfer to Vancouver. Dan stayed with Queen Charlotte Airlines for another year, then applied for a job with Russ Baker's Central BC Airways (which in 1953 became Pacific Western Airlines Ltd. (PWA) and is now part of Canadian Airlines International). Dan started working for his new employer on December 1, 1951.

Fires in the Forest

Earlier in his career, Dan had become interested in the idea of controlling and dousing forest fires. When he was with Queen Charlotte Airlines he had witnessed a fire at one of the Gibson Brothers' logging camps at Sandy Point. "They had a float camp, but the fire was on the shore. I went over on my way to Tofino and saw the cook trying to put out the fire by throwing pails of water on it. I thought, 'Gee, if I only had a tank I could put that fire out, just like that!' I went on down to Tofino and when I came back I saw the fire had got away from him. It burned the cold-deck machine and three cold-deck piles of logs, and went right to the top of the mountain. It had burned millions of dollars of wood right there, that I could have stopped."

Dan spoke to the owner, Gordon Gibson, and suggested he buy the Stranraer aircraft from Queen Charlotte Airlines, put tanks in it, and keep it sitting there ready to put out a fire whenever one started. Dan even gave him a cost estimate, including paying an engineer and a pilot, and Gibson showed definite interest. Then Dan was transferred back to Vancouver with Queen Charlotte Airlines, and the matter wasn't pursued.

But, the idea germinated in Dan's consciousness from that time on. During a five-year PWA contract with Forestry, he worked on every fire in the Vancouver Forest District, hauling crews, and pumps and hoses. He sometimes brought up the idea of putting water tanks on Beavers but no one seemed interested. It was felt that a Beaver couldn't carry enough water to make it worthwhile.

Dan worked for Pacific Western Airlines, flying Norseman and Beavers, until April, 1956.

MacMillan Bloedel Limited

When he heard that MacMillan Bloedel Limited (M&B) was looking for a pilot, Dan didn't pay much attention until Doug Taylor, the Vancouver District Forester with whom he'd been working and who was now retiring, suggested he check it out. "You'd have a much better job with M&B than with PWA, with a real future, and it will give you a chance to do something about fire fighting," Taylor urged.

In his interview with the president of MacMillan Bloedel, Harry Berryman, Dan was told that if he were hired he'd be flying the G21 Grumman Goose (CF-IOL). This amphibian aircraft was previously owned by Imperial Oil Ltd. and now by West Coast Transport, the aviation wing of M&B.

"So I took the job and the Goose was mine," Dan says. "And oh, I loved that airplane!"

The Paper Bag Prince

"Don Watts, the Fire Control Officer for M&B, and I became good friends," Dan says. "One day I heard about Ontario Forest Service trying to put out a fire with paper shopping bags filled with water. I said, 'Don, look at this! We've got a paper division here, let's get a whole bunch of paper bags . . .'"

The idea was put into play. They obtained a large supply of ordinary brown paper shopping bags and stored them in the hangar to be available at a moment's notice. Then they took 50 bags, inserted plastic liners in each and lay a piece of corrugated cardboard across the bottoms of the bags. Next, they bought set of rollers to stretch across the back of the Grumman Goose. "There's a hatch on the right-hand side. We took the hatch off and laid these rollers across. We could put five bags on the rollers at one time. Each bag held about three gallons of water."

Everything was all set when Don Watts phoned to announce, "We've got a fire over in Port Alberni! Get those bags on the airplane!" Dan had them on and ready to go in 15 minutes. Don and Dan flew over to Port Alberni, landed on the canal, and got a bucket and filled the 50 bags with water, which took an hour. Then they loaded the bags into the airplane and took off to bomb the fire.

Dan recalls one big tree burning in a small open area. "All it would have taken was a gust of wind and it would have spread to the surrounding forest. Don got five bags up on the rollers and we came in less than two feet above the tree. I wasn't going to miss it! When I knew those bags would hit, I yelled at him to 'Drop!' and he pushed out the five bags. So, five times three, 15 gallons, that hit that tree, bang!"

It was hard to tell from the moving airplane if they'd made a direct hit, so they came around and did it again with another five bags, and again. "In all, we put 50 bags in and when we were finished there was not a sign of smoke!" Dan says proudly. "The whole length of that tree had been burning, and now the fire was dead. We sent a man in that night and he reported that 98% of the bags had hit the tree. The ground was covered with wet paper. This was the first fire extinguished by an airplane in British Columbia."

The Martin Mars

MacMillan Bloedel Limited, realizing the importance of being able to control, or put out, forest fires that could destroy millions of dollars worth of timber in minutes, were very interested in McIvor's and Watts' innovations. They appointed the two men to a committee consisting of 16 logging companies plus the Forest Service, with a mandate to improve the methods of fighting forest fires.

"That was giving me a gift!" Dan beams. "Don and I went to the committee and said, 'If you would promise to use an airplane with tanks on it if you had a fire, we think we could talk one of the operators at the airport into installing a set of tanks.' Then I went to every operator, but the only one who would put tanks on an airplane was Al Michaud of West Coast Air Service [former operator of Vancouver U-Fly]. He ordered a set of tanks, and aircraft mechanic Gordon Peters installed them on top of the floats on a Beaver. They were rotating tanks so they'd dump quickly."

Dan phoned Doug Taylor and told him the tanks had arrived. "Tell Al that if he can have the tanks installed by tomorrow morning, I'll use it," Taylor replied. "We have a lightning storm at Sechelt."

Gordon Peters worked all night to get the airplane ready, and the next morning Doug Taylor chartered the Beaver to go up to Sechelt to the lightning strike. They fought it for 10 hours and put it out with one airplane. Taylor elatedly phoned Dan. "We'll never have to use a crew on a fire again! We'll use airplanes."

The next day deHavilland was sold out of tanks as every operator on the coast rushed to install tanks on their Beavers. That year there were a number of bad fires up the Fraser Valley in BC's lower mainland.

"You wouldn't believe the number of airplanes that were dropping water on fires, and we learned a lot," Dan says. "Ontario Forest Service had 80-gallon tanks, two 40s, on their Beavers, and 160 gallons on their single-engine Otters. On testing, they found the Otter with double the water was eight times as effective as the Beaver. I said, 'If that's true that doubling the water increases the effectiveness by eight times, we've got to get a big flying boat."

Dan recalled seeing a photo of a huge flying boat with 140 men standing in a line across the wing – an aircraft so large that a person could stand up straight inside a wing, where an engineer could open a hatch and service an engine while in flight. That might be worth considering. But what were they called?

One day, while driving around with Bobby Morin, a PWA mechanic with whom Dan had worked for many years, Morin said, "Oh, you must be talking about the Martin Mars. They're up for surplus bid tomorrow at Alameda, California." He gave Dan the invitation for bid, which gave him all the information he needed about the Mars.

Six Martin Mars, designated Type JRM-1 had been built by the Glenn L. Martin Company for the US Navy in 1946.[1] They were a high-wing, all-metal, four-engine flying boat whose hull featured two decks with watertight bulkheads beneath the lower one that extended nearly the full length of the 13-foot-wide cabin. They were 120 feet long, with a wingspan of 200 feet consisting of one centre section, two outer panels, two ailerons and four flaps. Wingtip floats were attached to the outer panels by a streamlined "V" brace.

These amazing aircraft, powered by four Curtiss Wright R-3350-24 radial engines rated at 2500 hp, mounted on steel tubular structures, had been designed so each engine could be removed as a unit from the nacelles. The four-bladed Curtiss Electric propellers, measuring 16 feet 8 inches in diameter, had controllable pitch and full feathering characteristics.[2]

When Dan discovered that the US Navy was getting rid of the four remaining Martin Mars, the only ones of their kind in the world, it seemed Divine Providence.

Buying the Flying Boats

To his dismay, when Dan phoned the surplus officer at Alameda he was told he was too late to enter a bid but was given the name of the purchaser, The Mars Metal Corporation. Dan hurriedly put in a proposal to his bosses at M&B and urged them to act before the aircraft were dismantled. "They could drop 6000 Imperial gallons at once!" he said excitedly. "They'd be perfect!"

Even though management initially turned down the idea, Dan persevered and finally an investigative trip to the Naval Air Base in California was approved. But no good story is without conflict, and Dan McIvor's nemesis became a man named Air-Vice Marshall Leigh Stevenson (Ret'd), a friend of H.R. Macmillan, the owner of the company.

"I went down to Alameda, California, in May 1959, with Harold Rodgers, Chief Engineer of BNP Airways, and two engineers from Fairey Aviation, and we checked the airplanes out carefully," Dan says. "They were in great shape and had been flying just seven years previous so most equipment was like new. We recommended that the four aircraft be purchased and one be converted to a water bomber on a trial basis.

"We knew what we were talking about, but then Macmillan decided that they must have Air-Vice Marshall Leigh Stevenson's okay first. We were faced with a date when the first airplane had to be moved from the Navy airport. He was told he had to go down before that date, but he kept delaying the trip."

It took a thorough report to the brass and pressure from J.V. (John Valentine) Clyne, Chairman of the Board, to get Stevenson to go to California to make his inspection.

"The next day things were in the clear and we started moving the airplanes," Dan says with a smile.

It was indeed a close call. The scrap merchant, The Mars Metal Corporation, had received orders to remove the first aircraft from the Alameda Air Naval Station within 90 days, and one each 30 days thereafter. If they were intact they could be flown out, but the work of taking the airplanes apart had already begun.

"We had hired Navy men at better than their regular salaries and told them of our concern about the delays," Dan recalls. "They took the engines out and carefully put them on the ground, all ready to reinstall. Then they took off other parts to look like as if they were demolishing them. They even put one aircraft into the water and floated it across to the San Francisco Municipal Airport and beached it there, to gain time. We gained a month there."

Just prior to the deadline to dismantle the second aircraft, the deal was done: on July 29, 1959, M&B forwarded a telegram stating their purchase agreement of $100 000 US for the four Mars. Later that year, a consortium of six BC forest companies formed a private company, Forest Industries Flying Tankers Limited (FIFT).

Ferrying the Mars to Canada

Dan McIvor spent most of July 1959 at Alameda Air Station looking after the logistics of readying the Mars for flight to their new Canadian home. Knowing they were now the sole owners in the world of Martin Mars, he also managed to buy, for a mere $3200, ninety tons of surplus Mars stores and equipment worth $3.5 million, as well as drawings and maintenance records.

According to Dan's log book, he began to ferry *Marianas* Mars (Serial 76821, civil registration CF-LYJ) to Pat Bay, Canada, on August 5, 1958, along with a US Navy pilot. Next came *Caroline* Mars (Serial 76824, CF-LYM) on August 27th, *Philippine* Mars (Serial 76820, CF-LYK) on September 5th, and *Hawaii* Mars (Serial 76823, CF-LYL) on September 12th. (The registrations were later changed to C- plus four letters, e.g. C-FLYJ).

"On the September 5th run, *Philippine* Mars was almost lost en route to Canada," Dan recalls. "An engineer in training inadvertently cut off all fuel to the engines and the aircraft descended from a cruising altitude of 10 000 feet to wave height. There was some mad scrambling to feather the engines and readjust controls to bring the engines and props back to life. Whew!" Luckily, the rest of the trip was uneventful.

On their arrival at Victoria International Airport, the big airships were set on dollies between the old wartime hangars to await their turn for conversion.[3]

Transforming the Mars to Water Bombers

"There again, Air-Vice Marshall Leigh Stevenson and I had a difference of opinion," Dan says candidly. "He said we couldn't cut a hole in the bottom of the airplane to drop water because maybe it wouldn't work and we'd want to sell them.' I said, 'The Navy tried to *give* them away, and couldn't!'

"So anyway, he had the first one drop out the side. There were four doors, two on each side, and the drop was made through those doors so it wouldn't cut up the fuselage. The bottom of the tank was flat, and I knew that the water wasn't all getting out in an effective time." Dan declared that a complete waste.

The water tanks were designed by Fairey Aviation's licensed aeronautical engineers to carry the maximum payload for that aircraft. The final payload was 60 000 pounds, equaling 6000 Imperial gallons, based on the maximum gross weight of 162 000 pounds placed on the aircraft by the Department of Transport. A considerable increase in weight was allowed by the Department of Transport because the aircraft was being loaded on the step. (In order for the airplane to come up on the step, it must be taxiing at a speed of around 60 mph).

Fairey Aviation first went to work on *Marianas* Mars, removing unnecessary seats and military equipment, and fitting the tank and water pick-up probes. With one Mars converted, they waited for a fire. None came, and therefore no positive tests for the airplane – just a series of problems. "We had unserviceability, we had props going out, engine failures, probes breaking off, you name it," says Dan.

Mars probes in the "down" position. (Photo: FIFT collection)

In the spring of 1961, the Department of Transport's chief medical officer was sent over to England for a course. His replacement, an RCAF Squadron Leader, changed the regulations about eyeglasses, to Dan's disadvantage. "You could only have a certain strength in the lens, more than that and you couldn't fly," Dan says. "My glasses were too strong, so my doctor told me I was going to lose my licence. He said, 'I can hang it up for about six weeks to give you a chance to get somebody in your place' – he knew all about the Mars – but Air-Vice Marshall Leigh Stevenson immediately chose Bud Richmond to take my place as Chief Pilot."

Dan was assigned to check out Richmond on the Mars. "In all my experience of checking out pilots on new types of aircraft, Bud Richmond was the only pilot who I checked out and felt that he was not capable of handling the Mars as a water bomber," Dan says. "During the flight he was nervous and trembling. He reached down, grabbed a rag and rubbed the sweat off his face, then dropped the rag and grabbed the control column again, hands still shaking. I reported this after the flight but was overruled by Stevenson."

Dan had no choice but to back away from flying. He now concentrated on his work with the British Columbia Forest Fire Protection Committee (Coast), and the Canadian

Forestry Association of British Columbia. In 1960 he was presented with an award for this work, and for his role as instructor in annual forest fire control courses held in Vancouver.

On June 23, 1961, *Marianas* Mars (CF-LYJ) crashed on a mountainside, killing Captain Bud Richmond and his crew: copilot Wally Wiggins and flight engineers Bobby Morin and Jack Edwards.

The crash shocked and saddened the entire aviation community, none more than Dan McIvor.

"I knew how to fight fires with airplanes, I could really do it, and I'd told them over and over, don't ever climb up to make a drop," Dan says. "If anything happens such as an engine failure you must be able to leave the fire zone going downhill. And, don't ever go into dense smoke. If you can't fight the fire without going into thick smoke, find some other way of getting at it. Even if you don't hit at it directly you can still stop it from moving.

"Anyway, Bud Richmond was put in as Chief Pilot when I had to retire because of my glasses. I heard later that he had gone on a fire in a narrow valley in the Mars, in dense smoke, couldn't see anything, and then climbed out of it. Luckily, he didn't hit the side of the valley. I had suggested one of the best pilots I ever knew, Wally Wiggins, to take my place, but Stevenson was General Manager and he put Bud Richmond in."

The fire on June 23rd was near Northwest Bay, in a valley. Dan illustrates how one should have approached this "fire in a cup," and how it was actually done.

"Instead of making his approach from above the fire, which would have allowed him to glide, he was climbing as hard as that old airplane could climb, fully loaded, barely clearing the tree-tops, trying to get up to the fire, to the high part of the valley. He did it absolutely opposite to what he should have done! He didn't drop his water. He hit the trees and killed the whole crew, and started a bigger fire than the one he was fighting.

"Oh, what an awful shock that was, from an operation that I knew was perfectly safe if you used common sense."

Shortly after the accident, Dan and Ernie Shorter, M&B's vice-president of operations, met in Nanaimo to check out the crash site at Northwest Bay.

As Dan McIvor reported in *Pioneering Aviation in the West* (Canadian Museum of Flight & Transportation and Lloyd M. Bungey; Hancock House Publishers Ltd., Surrey, BC, 1992, p. 293), "I had flown over the wreck. I had talked to people on the ground. The evidence was quite conclusive. I told Ernie, 'There was nothing wrong with that airplane. There is nothing wrong with the concept. It was pilot error, nothing else but pilot error.' Ernie agreed with my conclusion and reported back to the directors."

Within a week they had approval to get the next aircraft converted, and work started on the *Philippine* Mars, LYK. Due to the urgent need for an operative water bomber, the conversion plans for the first Mars were used with no changes.

"We established a drop area at Nanaimo Airport where we set out tomato cans over a much larger area than the drop would cover," Dan says. "The engineering department, with the help of about 50 people, ran the tests and we measured the amounts of water in each can and charted it on the map.

"On the *Philippine* Mars, LYK, with the side drops, the water came out in a large blob and then trailed a long, thin stream or spray, most of which didn't even reach the ground. We put a load on, climbed up, dropped it, and shut the doors after three seconds. We landed, went back to base, and measured the depth of the water still in the tanks. It was four to five inches. I figured with the size of the tank, we were carrying 1500 gallons that were doing no good. In order to eliminate this useless waste, a new, sloping, floor was installed in the tanks, and the load cut down 1500 gallons due to the smaller-size tanks.

"We had better performance of the airplane, but less water. For this reason I decided, with the full agreement of the engineers, to go through the bottom of the aircraft where we could have all of the water out in three seconds. The improvement in performance was noticeable by the pilots."

In the aftermath of the accident with *Marianas* Mars, Stevenson was no longer General Manager although he still retained his directorship. The DOT medical officer returned from England, the change regarding eyeglass lens strength was canceled, and Dan was reissued his licence and his job, becoming General Manager of FIFT.

The *Caroline* Mars (CF-LYM) came with an illustrious history. The aircraft had set a passenger-carrying record on March 4, 1949, for carrying 307 persons on a US Navy flight from San Diego to San Francisco; in August 1949 it set a new world seaplane distance record by flying nonstop Honolulu to Chicago (4748 miles) in 24 hours and 12 minutes.

Caroline Mars sadly became the next aircraft to bite the dust – on the taxiway at Fairey Aviation in Victoria during Hurricane Freida, on the night of October 12, 1962, when one of the 1/2-inch steel cables pulled out of the clamps and the hawsers snapped. *Caroline* Mars was salvaged of all usable components, which were added to the "spare parts pile," and the rest went to Capitol Iron Ltd. of Victoria, for scrap.

The blow was severe to the Martin Mars program, but the company still kept its faith in the project. Now that Dan had his licence back and was again in charge of the program, he continued with the conversion of *Philippine* Mars, CF-LYK.

Convincing logging companies to call the Mars as soon as possible after spotting a fire became Dan's priority. He was adamant that it would take these big flying boats less time and money in the long run than piddling around with myriad smaller aircraft and ground equipment.

"The question came to be, how could we get the logging managers, who would be responsible for calling us, to call in time and not wait because of fear of the cost until it was too late?" Dan felt that nothing short of his Mars could put out a fire before it went raging over hundreds of acres.

"Then we got a fire at Cowichan Lake, which Bill Waddington and I put out in six drops," Dan says. "We went in for a seventh load, came back and there was no fire, no smoke. The fire had been way off in the bush on a steep hillside and they told me it would have taken them a week to get a crew into it, let alone fight the fire. We stopped it dead in its tracks and had pictures showing how each drop put part of it out. It was fantastic."

Several days later another fire erupted at the head of Ramsay Arm on Bute Inlet, opposite Campbell River on the mainland, which covered about 10 acres of over-mature cedar. "The cedar was burning like mad and we put it out in 22 drops in a little over three hours," Dan says. "We picked up water going away from the fire, did a U-turn, came back and dropped as we came in so the water could get in under the canopy at about 100 feet."

Dan flips forward to the present, to tell of the long-term effects of dousing this Ramsay Arm fire. "Bill, my son-in-law, and I needed some white pine logs. I phoned MacMillan Bloedel's log supply people because I had dealt with them for so many years. I said, 'My name is Dan McIvor. I used to work for M&B, you don't know me, but I need some white pine.' He said, 'Dan McIvor?? You saved my ass!' Apparently, this fellow was working on the Ramsay Arm fire in that great, big, cedar forest. He had crawled in under logs and over logs and into the fire and was fighting it all by himself, on his feet, the only way they could get into it. There was no way you could get a Cat or a hose or a pump in there. He said, 'I'd had it. I was surrounded by fire and it was *hot*.'"

The man explained that moments after he'd gone into this fire it had started flaring. Dan came in about 100 feet off the ground, half-way up the huge, 200-foot-tall trees, which measured 14 feet in diameter. They were reportedly five windfalls deep, making 50 to 60 feet of great logs piled throughout the valley.

"You came along and put a drop of water right on top of me," the man said. "Right now, that fire was out!'

Dan says that the water drop wouldn't have hurt the fellow at all – in fact, to seriously injure or kill a person with a water drop you'd have to drop it at very low altitude of less than 100 feet.

Dan and his son-in-law got their white pine logs.

Dan has high praise for the system now employed by Forest Industries Flying Tankers in their use of the Martin Mars. They send out helicopters with GPS (global positioning system) where there's a report of a lightning storm. If they see a fire they immediately head for the nearest water, and en route they alert the Mars. They pick up a bucketful of water, take it back and dump it on the fire. If it's a tiny fire maybe that will put it out, or knock it down so they can get it the next time. If they can handle it, they'll cancel the Mars so it costs very little; if they can't handle it, the Mars is there quickly.

New Directions

Still supportive of the project in spite of its setbacks, in December 1963 the FIFT directors authorized the fourth aircraft, *Hawaii* Mars, to be refurbished. By July 1964 the work was completed.

"By this point, the Mars operation was gaining notoriety around the country as an efficient and effective means of fighting forest fires. Word also spread about the rescue of these massive World War Two bombers and their reincarnation as weapons to stop fire destruction. Vintage aircraft lovers and the general public alike began to get caught up in the awe and wonder of the project."

But differences of opinion regarding management of the Mars began to surface. For Dan, the Mars operation was a passion. "I knew every aspect of it, intimately," he says. "Years of flying over the vast forests of BC strengthened my resolve to preserve them. You have to walk through the ashes of a forest after a fire to understand the desolation . . . the stillness . . . the smell . . . the greyness. It is the ultimate clear-cut. To think that a water bomber could prevent or stop this was magical.

"I had worked many seven-day weeks for a number of years because I believed in the project. I had proved that it worked. I decided to go home."

In 1966, Dan resigned from his job as General Manager of the Forest Industries Flying Tankers Ltd.

Over 30 years later, Dan can look back on his work in pioneering the use of the Martin Mars as flying tankers with pride and also with some regret.

Dan McIvor, hale and hearty at 87, at his home in Richmond, BC, June 1998. (Photo S. Matheson)

Although he did some more flying, his log book records his last flight with *Philippine Mars*, LYK, on October 1, 1966.

Following his termination with FIFT, Dan got a job with PWA, which he held until he retired. His last flight was recorded on July 30, 1967, flying a Beaver to Prince George.

Dan McIvor took early retirement at age 62, which he insists is the perfect age. "You'll last four years longer than if you retire at 65. You're ready for retirement at 62, your body is ready for it, and you can have so much fun. Look at me – at 87! [in 1998]– going strong, because I retired at 62!"

There's no denying that Dan McIvor is fit as a fiddle, still straight and tall, with a feisty spirit and sharp mind. His hours in the air total 12 000, accident-free, flying everywhere in everything, and often with the flames of Hell flaring beneath his wings. He was qualified on single and multi-engine, with VFR/IFR ratings, on wheels, skis, floats – even operating float planes on snow surfaces – and on amphibians and flying boats.

Reflecting on Mars

Dan keeps aware of events concerning his beloved flying boats, *Hawaii* Mars and *Philippine* Mars. "Tom Irving, the General Manager of FIFT at Sproat Lake near Port Alberni, tells me it costs them about $2 million a year to keep them serviced and crewed and everything, but that's nothing when you consider the cost of fires. In 1994 they had that terrible fire in Penticton. In 1998, fires by Swan Hills in Alberta cost around $80 million."

The Penticton fire started at a number of points at the base of a 200-foot vertical drop canyon. Soon, the fire reached the top of the canyon where it raged for five days, moving rapidly toward the city limits. Dan's energy heats up as he recalls that situation. At its peak, the Penticton fire employed over 700 people from local fire departments, and an aerial assault fleet including three Firecats, one L88, four CL-215s out of Ontario, two Martin Mars from BC (at a cost per unit of $30 000 per hour), one DC-6, nine helicopters and numerous Bird Dog aircraft, as well as bulldozers, excavators, skidders, watertrucks, low-beds, buses and first aid vehicles. But 3000 people had to be evacuated, 18 homes were lost and 13 475 acres of land burnt.

"All they needed to have was a helicopter, but any airplane would do, and go on patrols – they know where the lightning strikes are – and put a drop of water on *immediately*. But few of them do it. The only people who do it right is Forest Industries Flying Tankers, and they are the only people in the world who don't have any fires getting away from them."

Tom Irving would seem to agree. "The idea of putting the most amount of water or foam on a fire in the shortest possible time, in a direct assault, has served very well through all these years, and it's a philosophy that remains valid today."

The Mars are a unique aircraft that provide a singular service. "There's nothing in the world that comes close to dropping 6000 Imperial gallons [7200 US gallons] on a fire in a whack, and doing it every seven-and-a-half minutes thereafter with the two of them working in tandem," Irving says.

At a fire in June 1998 for instance, the turnaround times of each aircraft was 11 or 12 minutes. "So, every six minutes we'll say that fire got 6000 gallons of water and foam, first from one airplane then another."

But, the cost of the Mars at $2 million per year, whether or not there are any fires that year, is a regular and high expense and the bottom line is always a concern. "In the past we've always been operated as a Fire Department, so it was a simple cost centre," Irving says. "Recently, financial and economic situations being what they are, our owners have indicated to us that they want us to dilute those costs. The only way we can do that is by marketing, so for the last year or so we've been making quite an effort to promote our services through trade shows, the Internet and advertising.

Among new ventures is an attempt to negotiate a contract to lease one Mars to the County of Los Angeles Fire Department for fire operations beginning in September of each year when fire hazards are on the wane in BC.

It seems odd that the Mars, originally from California and then sold to a BC company, could be going home, even though they would be operating from Los Angeles rather than their original base in San Francisco.

As we look out from the FIFT offices at Sproat Lake, we see the remaining two red-and-white Mars, the largest operational flying boats in the world (with some dimen-

Philippine Mars C-FLYK dropping during the 1998 Salmon Arm fire. (Photo: FIFT collection)

sions comparable in size to the Boeing 747), bobbing gently on the waves as they wait for a fire alarm. *Hawaii* Mars, like a dowager queen prepared for a dramatic stage entrance, has received a cosmetic facelift for the California demonstration flights.

"That's precisely what we did in that exercise," Irving says. "It's purely a marketing endeavor and we sure hope it will eventually meet with success. Although we aimed at one Southern California customer we tried to high-profile ourselves down there so others also know we're available."

Other marketing efforts have had considerable success this past fire season. The FIFT flew a lot of Mars hours on fires for the BC Ministry of Forests and the State of Washington Department of Natural Resources. Early in 1998 one Mars was sent to Atlin in northern BC for eight days on a detached operation for the BC Ministry of Forests. Later in the summer both Mars were hired to fight the big Salmon Arm fire. "We had the Mars there on detached 'ops' for over two weeks for that one," Irving says. "It was good for us and good for the Ministry.

"The Mars performed beautifully," Irving adds with a great deal of pride. "They flew for 118 hours on that job, never missed a sortie, and only had a handful of minor snags. Mind you, we did an awful lot of maintenance at night to keep them ready for daytime 'ops'. If you give them a lot of TLC, they pay you back in spades."

Even though the airplanes are getting older, Dan McIvor and Tom Irving insist that they are in better mechanical condition now than they ever were. "The people who maintain our aircraft also fly them, so there's a lot of incentive to do the work well," Irving notes. When a magazine article states that perhaps 1998 would be the last year for the old Mars, Dan scoffs. "I'll bet that was written by the competition!"

Tom Irving and his crew are unconcerned about the age of their airplanes, placing their trust in the better-than-average construction and maintenance of the Mars.

"Certain decisions were made when the Mars came into service with the United States Navy that benefit us today," Irving says. "For one, the Mars were designed as unpressurized aircraft in spite of the fact that the Navy wanted them pressurized. But because they were unpressurized they had to fly in weather turbulence, they couldn't get above the weather, and so the wings were redesigned for weather. Well, most of our fires have turbulence so that's a benefit we gained. Structurally, the aircraft are built like bridges."

He cautions that this doesn't mean there are no problems – but the FIFT strives to keep ahead of the problems. "We've got a maintenance program that is outstanding. We know several years ahead of time what we're going to be needing to keep these things in first-class condition."

Inside the Mars

Pilot Hugh Fraser offers to take the author on a tour of *Hawaii* Mars. We walk out past the waiting Bell LongRanger helicopter (one each is stationed in Campbell River, Sproat Lake, Ladysmith and Powell River), past where the Grumman Goose "Bird Dog" sits poised for flight, and into the little boat to motor out to the mammoth Mars. Fraser explains that the Mars are fueled in the water from tanks on shore,

The Grumman Goose "Bird Dog" sits poised for flight, Sproat Lake, BC, June 1998. (Photo: S. Matheson)

connected by a pipeline that runs along the bottom of the lake to emerge at a fuel buoy.

As we approach the great airship, we see workers climbing about with paint buckets and tools, splashing on shiny red-and-white paint, applying varnish, doing finishing touches to the newly-upholstered red seats. But, those are only the surface improvements. Fraser emphasizes that the Mars is in top condition throughout, and it goes without saying that these aircraft undergo continual, high-quality, maintenance.

"There is no 'killer' component, or weak link in the chain, that if one thing goes the whole airplane cannot be repaired," Fraser says. "When we thought we might be short of props we bought some from a Constellation which have the same configuration. We kept the props and sold the rest. We have 12 rebuilt engines."

The flight deck is as unique as the rest of the aircraft, which is best described as "maneuvered by the pilot and operated by the flight engineer." The pilot has the normal complement of flight and trim controls and flight instruments, but only basic engine indicators. Although the pilot has a set of throttles, most of the throttle work is done by the flight engineer on voice command from the pilot.

The Flight Engineer station, located 30 feet behind the pilot, has a vast array of engine monitoring instruments, throttles, mixture controls, and basic flight instruments as well as fuel and propeller management controls. "It's kept simple up front for the pilot because we're concentrating to look through smoke, wind and low viz," Fraser explains. "We don't want an unnecessarily elongated checklist. Both pilot and engineer have checklists. There's a crew of four on each aircraft: pilot, first officer, and two flight engineers."

This aircraft also has a "recording accelerometer," which monitors gust forces, shock and turbulence on the airplane.

We proceed through the interior of the Mars, with Fraser pointing out unique attributes: the aft section behind the wings holds three tanks of foam (installed in 1987); the forward section (cargo area) holds 6000 Imperial gallons of water in a fiberglass and Douglas-fir plywood tank (some fuel tanks were replaced by water tanks in a later conversion). It's explained that a pickup, using probes that are slightly larger than a man's hand, scoops up 6000 gallons – 30 tons – of water in 22 seconds at speeds of 140 mph. The water can be released from one side or the other on *Phillipine* (LYK), and from the bottom on *Hawaii* (LYL), but usually it's dumped all at once. A foaming agent is added to the water to provide deep soaking and cooling of the fire area. The Mars can fly for five-and-one-half hours nonstop, or longer if necessary, making it quickly accessible to most remote BC forests along the west coast.

We walk upright inside a wing, and stick our heads out through a door that leads, for in-flight emergency servicing, to the four 18-cylinder Wright Cyclone engines, each with a takeoff power of 2500 hp. The aircraft has 26 doors in total, leading into and out of myriad rooms, galleys and storage areas.

We scramble from the lower deck to the flight deck via a long circular staircase, climb ladders and pop up through a hatch on the wing. Fraser nimbly jumps out and trots across the wing surface. "Come on!" but the author is too chicken. The aircraft sits so high, the water is so far below – so she stands, head poking up like a prairie gopher, clearly overwhelmed by the 200-foot wingspan that seems to stretch to the perspective point and the Moby Dick tail flipping behind, 50 feet above the water.

A Day in Life on Mars

All fire calls are received by Dispatch. Normally the problem will be identified and Dispatch will notify the hangar to put the crews on alert. "If we're 'Low Hazard' and haven't done a warm-up, we'll warm up at least one Mars. If we're in the high range of 'Moderate,' or in 'High Hazard' or 'Extreme,' we would have done a warm-up already so the crews and aircraft are ready to go," Tom Irving explains.

The warm-up usually includes a taxi run on the Taylor Arm of Sproat Lake.

"If the logging division calls back and says, 'Yes, we want the Mars,' the Dispatcher hits the siren and it's just a matter of getting out to the aircraft on the crew boats. It usually takes about 10 minutes and we're in the air. Meantime, the Bird Dog, the Grumman Goose which is an 'amphib', has already entered the water via the ramp and departed. It flies slower than the Mars so that bit of head start is beneficial, and it reports back by radio what's going on. In essence it's the eyes and brains of the operations."

The Bird Dog, flown by experienced pilots, relays messages advising the Mars where to make the drops, and organizes the procedures.

"The instructions are a collective decision made by the Bird Dog and the Fire Boss on the ground," Irving says. "Once they've established what they want, the Bird Dog will radio information and instructions to the Mars when it's finished its pickup and is headed for the fire. Then, just prior to entering the airspace for drop, the Bird Dog will cut in front of the Mars and lead him in. The Bird Dog is always flown by a Mars captain; they rotate between flying the Bird Dog and the Mars, so the Mars crew coming in

Philippine Mars C-FLYK dropping on a pulp mill fire. (Photo: FIFT collection)

has confidence in this fellow who's leading them into the fire because he knows the capabilities of the Mars."

For all its size, the Mars is highly maneuverable, although somewhat slow to respond to the controls, "but that's how you learn how to fly them. You have to remember that." With all four engines running, the throttles are advanced and the Mars gathers momentum, engines thunder, water-spray fogs out behind. It speeds along the water and up onto the step, causing water to spew in a reactive wave as the big flying boat roars into the sky overtop the mountains – Mars, the God of War, on a mission.

The pilot's instruction with regard to a fire is, basically, "not to do anything stupid," Irving says with a laugh, although his statement is serious and reiterates Dan McIvor's advice. "No, they don't have to receive any instructions," Irving elaborates. "They know the decision to operate or not operate is theirs alone, and they'll never be criticized for not operating on a fire because of any hazardous conditions, whether it's smoke, wind or whatever. You don't go into heavy smoke, and you fly fairly low. Some of the drops are at 100 feet above the fire. We have trees out here 200 feet high."

There are always dangers, of course, such as snags called "widow makers" that reach up above the canopy, leafless, nearly invisible and treacherous. "That's why you have a Bird Dog. He shoots approaches," Irving says. "While the Mars is doing its first pickup and he's talked it over with the Fire Boss, then the Bird Dog approaches onto the target so he's identified any hazards that might be there. Power wires, snags, you never know."

Two fires still discussed with awe, and some regret, remain the only two that have ever got away in the Mars' 38 years of operation and attending hundreds of fires.

The Taylor River Fire, a few miles up Sproat Lake, occurred in 1967 and burned thousands of acres. "It was one of those fire storms that just blew up on them," Irving says. "They're pretty rare here. I can't envision it, but apparently the whole side of one hill just exploded. I think they had a lightning strike and the lightning went down the two guy wires of a pole or something that a BC Hydro crew was installing. Then they had a fire on their hands, with no fire-fighting equipment. I heard they were running down to the creek filling their hard hats, trying to put this out, and in no time flat things blew up."

The second fire that "got away," known as the Moriarity Canyon fire, occurred in 1978, flaring deep in a box canyon. It was hopeless to try to get in and out as the aircraft would have had to fly "right into the box." No action could be taken until it had burned out of the box area into an area safe to fly.

By the end of 1998, records show that the Mars had dropped nearly 50 million gallons of water or foam over an average of 20 forest fires per year.

The job of the FIFT is to "suppress" fires rather than put them out, Irving says. "We suppress them, then we let the ground crews do the mop-up and that's when we use our helicopters to a large extent. They're really valuable in the mop-up operation."

The Bell LongRanger helicopters are used for medical airlifts, timber cruising, aerial fire detection, and suppression of spot fires and clean-up operations. Their 120-gallon "Bambi" buckets allow the helicopters to attack and suppress small fires, sparing the Mars for the big jobs.

The FIFT has four Mars pilots, all of whom must have at least 7000 hours, preferably mountain and coastal, flying time. One pilot will have his days off while there is one on each Mars and one on the Bird Dog. There are a specified number of hours that each can fly until being replaced by a fresh crew. "On a normal sortie they are fueled to go for up to six hours," Irving says. "If they're needed back at the fire they'll come in, have something to eat while they're refueling and refoaming the aircraft, and then go back out again." The Mars each may accumulate 100 hours annual flying time. Therefore, the pilots, while not building a great number of hours, are content with the knowledge that they are performing specialized, high-calibre work.

Dan McIvor's philosophies on flying, aviation in general and the forest-fire business can be encompassed in his terse statement, "Cut the bureaucracy and get at the fires immediately!"

His vision of using the Mars to fight forest fires is steadily gaining respect throughout British Columbia and in fact throughout the world. At the BC Aviation Council's 60th anniversary conference in Penticton on October 16, 1998, Dan was presented with the Lifetime Achievement Award in Aviation by the Council. Appropriately, FIFT sent *Hawaii* Mars to Penticton to do a flying demonstration as a salute to Dan in honor of his award.

With the acknowledged help of his "Friend up there," Dan has become familiar with every aspect of the west coast wilderness, in all seasons. Through his farsightedness – obviously overcoming the problems incurred by his strong corrective lenses – Dan McIvor and his idea has saved millions of acres of forest from destruction by fire.

"For us to put a forest fire out with paper bags, it's laughable, isn't it?" he says. He leans forward in his chair, bright, lithe and energetic at age 87.

Then he sits back to reflect on this daft notion. "And yet, we did it."

Footnotes

[1]*Caroline* Mars, with more power from Pratt & Whitney 3000 hp engines, was a JRM-2, the only one ever built.

[2]Statistics quoted in an article titled "Martin Mars Flying Boat" by Ron Edwards, published in *Giant Flying Boats*, Vol. 2, 1989 p. 36, give rise to visual comparisons: the Martin Mars aircraft contains 7.5 miles of wiring; three million rivets, 60 000 pounds of aluminum, 25 000 pounds of steel, 1.9 miles of conduit and piping, 800 square feet of plywood, 750 pounds of rubber, 800 pounds of plastic, 650 square yards of fabric, 2000 pounds of copper, tin, zinc, and other metals. It takes 300 gallons of paint to cover each Mars.
While in service with US Navy Air Transport Squadron Two (VR-2), the Mars fleet established distance and weight-lifting records (68 327 pounds), and together the five logged some 87 000 accident-free hours. Other records were established, such as numbers of people carried on flights, which was unequaled until the advent of the Boeing 747.
These Martin Mars, originally meant to be used as long-range, high-altitude patrol bombers but actually put into service as transport planes – carrying everything from personnel and heavy equipment, to exotic loads such as radioactive marine life from the Bikini atom bomb tests, hatching eggs to rejuvenate Guam's poultry population, and a load of 160 pet monkeys from the Philippines – were declared obsolete in 1956,

and replaced with faster jet aircraft.

"Documents maintained by the Naval Air Transport Service during the JRM's first 18 000 hours of flight operations show that the overall cost (direct & indirect) on a plane-mile basis was $4.04 per airplane mile. Considering its weight-carrying and speed capacity, the cost per ton-mile on some test flights came to just over 44 cents.

"In recognition of their role as transport aircraft in the South Pacific, the Mars were christened after the islands they were to visit and serve: *Marianas, Philippine, Hawaii, Caroline,* and *Marshall* (Serial 76822, lost in service, April 5, 1950, off Honolulu after an in-flight fire)."

[3]The conversion design and engineering was done by George Grover, who had been an engineer on the Avro Arrow project. He still does the engineering work on the Mars 40 years later.

Fur Traders and Voyageurs

Independent fur trader Alex Robertson celebrated his 70th birthday on September 6, 1998, and shows no signs of quitting the business he's been involved in since his youth. Robertson Trading Company in La Ronge, Saskatchewan, continually hums with a friendly old-days atmosphere, directed behind-the-scenes by modern business acumen.

On seniors' pension day, people sit on benches outside the store, chatting in the sun, or wait in trucks in the store's parking lot before starting their day's commerce. Across the road on Lac La Ronge, engines of float-equipped bush planes emit high-pitched whines. Then they take off across the water, transporting people and cargo – often expedited through Robertson Trading Company – throughout the vast northern sector of the province.

Residents of nearby native reserves and also those in town have come to depend on Robertson's over the last 30 years. Some have their monthly cheques sent directly to the store and come in to clear debts, get some cash and buy merchandise. Alex Robertson knows his customers, and chats amiably in English or Cree about everything from the weather to the last, or projected, fur catch, also taking time to inquire about their personal health and social welfare.

"They don't trust banks and they lose post office keys," Alex notes, "so when their cheques arrive here I tape them to their accounts. Then we go over it together."

Alex Robertson is a trim, compactly built individual with thick grey hair, glasses and a serious but pleasant and unlined face. He dresses in a similar style to his cus-

Alex Robertson at his "desk" at the back of the store, Robertson Trading Co., doing business as usual (June, 1997). (Photo: S. Matheson.)

tomers in plaid flannel shirt, grey denim jeans and beaded belt, to which is attached a leather sheath holding a jackknife, and soft shoes.

An elderly native man approaches the long counter, known as "Alex's desk", at the back of the store. "How much is your rent?" Alex asks the man. "$250? Okay, we'll take that out." He carefully counts out the cash, shows the customer and seals $250 in an envelope to send to the man's landlord. A young native boy approaches the counter, eyes shining. "Can I have a free banana?" "Of course. Say please and thank you." The boy utters the required manners and scampers off to claim his prize. A shy, elderly woman pushes a shoe box toward Alex. It is filled to the brim with fresh blueberries. "I picked them, south, by Pine House. For your family," she says.

The Fur Trader

Alex Robertson was born, and spent his formative years, in Calgary. "During the second world war, my dad was offered a training school in Medicine Hat for airframe mechanics and engineers," Alex recalls. "After the war he was transferred to Grande Prairie to open trade schools for returned servicemen."

Alex began his career as a fur trader while still in high school, working for the Hudson's Bay Company store in their raw fur department – one of 12 stores throughout Canada that concentrated on fur alone.

When the trade schools closed in Grande Prairie the Robertson family moved to Edmonton. Alex finished Grade 12 while continuing to work part time for the Bay's raw fur department there, and they later employed him on a permanent basis to continue his apprenticeship as a fur buyer.

Alex Robertson's first Hudson's Bay posting was to Prince Albert, Saskatchewan, where he again met people who lived off the land, although here were more native trappers. Sensing the potential of its young apprentice, the Hudson's Bay Company sent Alex to Montreal for an advanced fur-training program.

Back in Prince Albert, his education continued at a fast pace, and he worked his way up to manager with the company. He temporarily managed 20 or 30 different stores over the years where he "learned directly from Northern people." He learned to speak some Chipewyan and to "become passable" in Cree

"I learned how to get along with people and to have respect for others' lifestyles, just thinking of them as normal, everyday citizens who lived in the bush," Alex says. "I spent a lot of time out in canoes and boats, besides running the store." Alex's respect for the older generation and their way of life has remained one of his principle trademarks.

While Alex was running these stores he became acquainted with the coming influence of the airplane on Northern lifestyles. "It was all airplane. People were constantly flying. There were no roads in those days." There is no doubt in Alex's mind that aviation opened up the North. "It introduced these people to the world. You couldn't hide in the bush anymore. Changes, of course, were inevitable."

He married Phyllis Emma Couttie, who joined Alex where he was managing a store in Fort Smith. Soon a family of four children came along, and together they travelled to the various posts – Stony Rapids, Beauval, Ile a la Crosse, La Loche – to be introduced to the North and to the people who populated the life of a fur trader. "Because of that, our kids, three boys and a girl, grew up to love the North," Alex says with quiet pride.[1]

When Alex's boss was transferred to Edmonton, he was appointed manager of the raw freight department in Prince Albert. But in 1965 the fur business took a drastic tumble. Dissatisfied with the money he was making with the Hudson's Bay, Alex quit in 1967. He bought La Ronge Grocery store from Stan Kowalski, and moved his family to La Ronge, 150 miles north of Prince Albert.

"I left a great big house, a great big job I loved and people I liked, and I came up to La Ronge, to a little dingy store with a wife and four kids, and an old '59 Oldsmobile that I'd picked up. We went from living in a fancy house to a tent for two months, then moved into a little chicken-shit store that you wouldn't even believe existed on this property."

He chose La Ronge for several reasons, none based on solid business rationale. "It was an exciting spot for me, I just loved it up here," Alex says. "I didn't come necessarily for the fur business, that was incidental. It was a small store and I knew it had a number of loyal customers. I felt I could build it up but it would take a long time."

They'd left a three-story house overlooking the city of Prince Albert, with four bedrooms, a fireplace, and a little waterfall in the back yard. When they moved into the back of the store in La Ronge, they learned to cope with an old oil-fired barrel in the basement for heat, and no running water. "We had a big pot for the bathroom and the rottenest kid that day had to empty out the toilets. Really primitive! It makes a traumatic experience to move to a place like that," Alex says, in an understatement.

He admits the move was difficult. "We were outsiders and every day that first year there were fights, both with native and white kids."

Alex' wife, Phyllis, seemed to take it all in stride. "The challenge seemed to make her perk up," Alex says. "She just blossomed and matured."

The Last of the Free Fur Traders

Now that Alex was sovereign of his own domain, the training he'd received with the Bay stood him in good stead. He could grade every type of fur, with his eyes closed, winning competitions hands-down.

One of the business aspects of Robertson Trading Company is to sponsor, or outfit, trappers and miners and expedite their supplies, mostly by air, to the trapline or camp site. "We do a lot of that," Alex says. "One year we were carrying a lot of mining companies and trappers and buying a lot of fur, so I went to the bank and asked to borrow a million dollars. I told them we were handling some very, very large mining accounts and doing it out of a very small store, but we were providing a service, outfitting for groceries and dry goods. We'd tell the companies, 'If we haven't got it, we'll go and get it for you. We'll pick it up and whatever we pay for it, that's your cost, we won't charge you for gas or time.' We wanted to provide good service, and we've kept it up to this day, 30 years later."

He didn't get his requested million dollars from the bank, but he came close with a line of credit for $975 000. The store, in turn, sends out the goods and then waits to be paid by the companies or individuals. There could be risk, but Alex knows his people.

For a short time Alex and a friend, Lynn Riese, owned an airplane, a Cessna 185. "We were building a cabin up at Hepburn Lake, north of Otter Rapids, and we thought it would be a good idea. Lynn is one heck of a bush pilot, one of the best, but now he's into other things such as the wild rice business. He had a tourist camp in the Territories. He used the 185 to fly people up there, and we used it when we were building the cabin."

The cabin got built – still retained by the Robertson family – the tourist camp went belly-up, and the airplane was sold.

Although Alex has flown with numerous pilots throughout the North, he followed his own advice to "stick to what he knows best." He uses local flying services to expedite his goods to far-flung Northern customers.

"La Ronge Aviation and Athabaska Airlines have been here for many, many, years, and they supply a tremendous service to the North. They've opened up this country. But like everything else today, it's getting to be a tough business. Costs are escalating, and as roads go further north that cuts into their flying operations. But, we use these services to outfit and fly out most of our trappers, fellows who deal with me."

The fur season usually opens the 5th of November and, in the old days, the trappers would not return to town until Christmas when they brought in their fall catch. Now they come in frequently, aided by snow machines and aircraft, sometimes flying back and forth several times during that period.

"The trappers now have power plants, and radios and television sets. They know what's going on in the news," Alex says. "They may have to fly in and fly out of their home territory but they're right up to date with modern equipment. They can educate their family without any schools, through correspondence courses and watching t.v."

When the trappers whom he outfits return with their catch, most sell to Robertson Trading although there's no obligation to do so. "They just have enough integrity to give us their business," Alex says, "and in the 30 years that we've been here, very few have given us a licking. I helped them, and they still come by and see me, even the third generation now. Even today it grabs my heart, this feeling of nostalgia."

In 1997 when Robertson Trading Company celebrated its 30th year in business, the La Ronge newspaper, *The Northerner*, ran a feature page containing dozens of congratulatory ads and testimonials. "Listening to Alex talk about furs is like listening to a pianist play a rhapsody," states the reporter. A more down-to-earth statement is made by Doug McLeod, executive director of the Lac La Ronge Indian Band. "Robertson Trading represents something that aboriginal people have almost lost: a business that treats them with respect and understanding. Established customers can get credit for groceries or cash if they are going out to the trapline for a few weeks, or pay off their bills with furs once they get back."

"Over the years you get to know the good guys and the bad guys," Alex says philosophically. "You get to know their idiosyncrasies."

He fondly recalls the day an old trapper, Amos Rat, came into the store, and asked Alex to outfit him to go back to the bush one last time.

"Amos Rat had been a tremendous trapper in his day. I mean, he was built like a little grizzly bear," Alex recalls. "But he was old when I came here, and he retired in 1972 or '73. Then one day he came to me, in his old moccasins and fancy pink hat and red scarf, and said he wanted to go out trapping again. I said, 'Amos, no damned way. You're too old!' Amos just smiled. 'How old are you, 73?' Amos nodded happily. 'There's no way I'm going to let you go trapping, Amos, and that's it, so I'm off the hook.' He didn't like it, but he went away."

The pestering continued over the next few years, and when Amos turned 76 Alex finally relented. "Why not?" he said to himself "He's not going to live much longer, he's a tough old guy, he might even come back, and he won't be happy until he goes. This may be a dumb mistake but if that's what he wants to do, I'm going to let him go."

Robertson Trading Company staked Amos Rat with groceries and supplies, and paid to fly him to his trapline about 100 miles north of La Ronge.

There was no radio communication in those days, and no messages came as to how Amos was faring. No one, it seemed, had heard from him or seen him. Alex became worried. He felt responsible.

Then one day just before Christmas Alex went to the bank and when he returned to the store, there was Amos Rat. He had no fur with him, but his red scarf was still there and his fancy pink hat was perched jauntily on his head. He was puffing on an old pipe and looking very fit, "just a real tough-looking bush man."

"*Nuh muggeegway saggweesoo*?" Alex said in Cree. "No mink?"

Amos laughed, "Ah, ha ha!" Then he kicked his foot toward a little wooden box.

"What's in that? Your tea pail and stuff?"

Amos just smiled. Alex busied himself doing a few things about the store and continued to make small talk with the old trapper. He was glad to see him, really glad, because he liked him, and here he was, safe, even though he had no furs. Finally, Amos stooped down and removed the lid from the wooden box. Then he stood back and looked at Alex, his dark eyes dancing. The box was full of mink! Close to 100 of them!

"Amos Rat turned out to be the best trapper in the whole of the North that winter, for mink," Alex says. "He brought them in, paid off his debt, and was a happy man. And so was I. He showed himself, me, and the community that he could still do it. He was still the best mink trapper in the North! And proud!"

Alex sentimentally recalls the scene. "Amos Rat never returned to the trapline, but he showed me a thing or two and I've never forgotten his story. It grabbed my heart, and even though it happened long ago, I've never forgotten it."

Alex then repeated the gesture with Amos's brother, Noah. "Noah's wife still looks back on those trapping days as the best days of their lives. Well, they all do."

There are other stories, too. "There are guys who go in for two or three years and never do come out," Alex says. "Nobody knows what happened to them. And then I've had customers dealing with me for 10 years or more and I've never even seen them!"

When orders are received for groceries and other supplies, Robertson Trading Company packs and sends the order out by air, and the trappers send in their fur the same way. Sometimes they sign over and send in their pension or wage cheques to pay for supplies that the store air-freights to their traplines, or to fishing, tourist or mining camps all over the North.

In Alex Robertson's many years of dealing with the people who live off the land, he's seen a slow progression, an upgrading of lifestyles, "just like in the old homestead days." Alex gives aviation due credit for aiding this progression.

"At one time, when I used to fly in to different places, the arrival of an airplane was a big occasion. Everyone would come down to help unload. A lot of native kids wanted to be pilots, and some actually have, because they know they can't make a living in the old ways anymore."

Alex considers how these changes have affected his customers. "Fishing is a tough way to make a living today because of the expense of flying fish in or out. The price they get for them is not equal to their expenses of boats and motors and air freight rates. And trapping? There's no reason anybody should go trapping anymore because it's not economically viable, it's a stupid business. The native people, and a lot of white people today, love to go out on the traplines, it's a challenge, it's exciting, but if it comes to dollars and cents, forget it.

"I know trappers who fly into the Northwest Territories," Alex continues. "It costs them $3000 to fly in, $3000 to fly out, and they might make four or five trips per year. Two or three of those trappers might make $50 000 or $60 000, maybe as high as $80 000, a year, but the net return is not that great."

Simon Eninew ship-ping out his fish the modern way – by air-craft. (Photo: Robertson collection)

One of Alex's customers showed him his bills: $2600 to fly him to his trapline in the Northwest Territories in a Twin Otter. "Those things are expensive, and it's not a sked flight. They go out to the middle of nowhere and land on ice or snow. Gas up there is $5 or $6 a gallon. And then they have their food, and supplies, and usually a snowmobile and gas for that. They like to talk about dogs but most use snow machines."

A tour through Robertson Trading company shows how the past and the present can converge in harmony. Alex looks around the store with a great sense of satisfaction. "Though I think I know everything about a fur when I first see it, I still take the time to grade it properly," he says. "I've been in this business 50 years – 30 years on my own in the private fur business, and 20 years when I was with the Hudson's Bay Company. And it's still exciting."

Pilot, Engineer and New-Age Voyageur

With aircraft buzzing on and off the lake in front of the store, and Robertson Trading Company's dependence on air transport for expediting supplies, it seemed fitting that at least one of the Robertson children would become involved in aviation. That role fell to Ivan. Not only has he fixed and flown aircraft over most of Canada's north country, but he has also travelled its waterways by canoe. He's paddled from northern Saskatchewan across the Northwest Territories to the Hudson's Bay, and also to the Arctic Ocean, in sojourns of up to eight weeks.

Ivan, who is Alex and Phyllis's eldest son, was born in Prince Albert in 1956 and was 11 years old when the family moved to La Ronge. He remembers the town being a quite different place in 1967 from what it is today. "There were Otters and Beavers taking off and everybody was busy. There was Athabaska Airways, La Ronge Aviation, Norcanair. It was easy to get into aviation at that time."

When he was 16, Ivan began loading and off-loading airplanes for Athabaska Airways, whose base was locally run by Bill Jackson, and La Ronge Aviation, owned and operated by the Campling family. He quickly found a mentor in Pat Campling, who had also been young and inexperienced but full of ambition when he became involved in the business. Campling's uncle, John Stanley "Red" Boardman, had started a tourist business called Red's Camps in La Ronge. With his uncle's death in 1956, Pat, at age 21, had found himself a business owner.

He began by flying in his customers via Athabaska Aviation, but in 1961 Pat and his wife Shirley joined forces with pilot Russ Aronec to form La Ronge Aviation. They started with a Cessna 180, and soon the company acquired more Cessnas, a Norseman, Beavers, and two Twin Beeches. In 1966 they bought out Dolphin Airways of Lynn Lake, Manitoba, and began to serve the expanding mining activity in that area. In 1969 the Camplings bought out Aronec, sold Red's Camps, and by 1973 La Ronge Aviation had acquired Northwest Territorial's water base in Yellowknife, NWT. It was a grand little company for Ivan to encounter, and the admiration was mutual.

"Our families were fairly close," Ivan says. "When the Camplings moved to Edmonton in 1976, Pat gave me the opportunity to go with them and train for my commercial pilot's licence through the Edmonton Flying Club. He supported me throughout, and gave me a job after I got my licence in 1977."

Ivan returned to La Ronge to work for La Ronge Aviation as a dockhand, and flew whenever he could as a swamper, helping to load and unload the Twin Otter.

"I consider my real initiation into aviation came when La Ronge Aviation got a contract to move fuel drums with the F-27, from a small lake called Camp 10 in the Northwest Territories," Ivan recalls.

A Cat had been used to keep the ice strip open, so he and a work-group flew north out of Lynn Lake in early spring, landing the Twin Otter on the "mostly frozen" lake. They stepped out of the airplane to be greeted by howling cold winds and the sight of fuel drums floating in water around the reefs where the ice had just thawed. Two tents, their sole accommodation, were barely standing and in disrepair.

The work over the next two weeks was arduous. The men took turns wading into the water to retrieve the fuel drums and load them into the Twin Otter for delivery to various locations around the Territories. "At first, we pulled the drums out with a rope, and then a helicopter showed up and drum movement got faster. But someone still had to wade into that icy water to hook the drums to the helicopter."

Although Ivan was a swamper, he was daily gaining knowledge on what one could do with an aircraft on floats or skis. He loved it. "I've always said, 'If you can't put it on skis or floats, it's not worth flying!'" he laughs.

Ivan is a shy person with sandy hair, blue-grey eyes, a well-modulated voice and animated gestures. He laughs easily, and becomes passionate when talking about his interests: his family, fixing and flying airplanes, and exploring the North by canoe.

Ivan's next job took him to Otter Lake, 50 miles north of La Ronge, to work on the dock for Shirley Campling's brother, Garry Thompson, who operated Nipawin Air Services Ltd. "Working for Nipawin Air meant you did everything, dockhand as well as maintenance duties," Ivan recalls. "At first I spent a lot of time inside Beaver and Otter floats, helping with repairs and tightening leakers, mainly because I could fit."

After attending Southern Alberta Institute of Technology (SAIT) in Calgary where he received a diploma in aircraft maintenance, his dockhand duties lessened.

Garry Thompson's company bought and sold various aircraft, such as the first 300 h.p. Cessna 185 to operate in Saskatchewan, and a Norseman (CF-SAM) that's now displayed in the Western Development Museum in Moose Jaw. A string of Single and Twin Otters came and went. When Thompson purchased the Norcanair base in Uranium City, Ivan was sent there, but still doing maintenance and not flying. He was working on his engineer's licence, however, and getting loads of experience.

"I sort of went through the transition with Nipawin Air. Great Shield Air took over the base from Garry but they went into receivership. La Ronge Aviation ran Great Shield Air for the receiver. Eventually Garry got his company back, so I'm not sure who was running what, when. But in that three or four year period, between '81 and '83, I got my engineer's licence and was sent to Uranium City as an apprentice engineer – still not flying but gaining experience."

There he worked with respected engineers such as Lorne Andrews, John Finch, Ernie Onofrychuk, John Rodgers and Don Snur, and considers his time spent in "U-City" memorable. When Uranium City shut down, Ivan moved to Stony Rapids to work for Ben Siemens of Aero North.

"It's difficult to mention Aero North without also mentioning John Campbell, Ben's right-hand-man," Ivan says. "Together, they ran Aero North and I thoroughly enjoyed working for those two characters. It was Ben who got me flying. He said, 'I don't really have enough work for a full-time engineer and I don't have enough work to hire a full-time pilot, so how would you like to become a pilot-engineer?' Then I really started flying. It was busy!"

His trips were mostly for medical purposes, or caribou hunts, especially with the natives from Black Lake. When hired by these native hunters, Ivan would fly them and their rifles around in a Cessna 185 until they found a herd of caribou. This was not a difficult task as the animals were never more than 30 miles north of Stony Rapids.

"The procedure is, if it's not too windy and conditions permit, to approach downwind, then pull the mixture control just before touchdown," Ivan explains. "The caribou stop and the aircraft glides in a lot closer than you'd get if you let the engine run. They can't see distances very well and our shapes confuse them. There's no noise to scare

Pilot Ivan Robertson is employed to take hunters out. Here, the aircraft is packed to the rafters with the results of "a good hunt." (Photo: Ivan Robertson collection)

them and being downwind they will not get our scent. The hunters hurry out of the aircraft and start to shoot.

"I've seen some hunters wait until two caribou are lined up and then shoot through both of them," Ivan continues. "They will shoot seven or so and then I'll haul the hunters and some of the choice parts of the meat back to Black Lake, where the work of preparing the meat is left up to the women. Then I'll take some more guys out, and keep repeating the scenario."

Because there isn't room in a Cessna 185 for seven caribou plus three people, they usually cut up the meat and pile it on the ice, leaving the hide on to keep the ravens from getting at it. Left there overnight, the meat will bleed. The pilot and a couple of helpers return for it later.

"It's not a standard practice to haul wet meat in the aircraft," Ivan says. "The blood gets into the belly of the aircraft and corrodes the cables. Also, it's hard to clean. One time, when [engineer] Lorne Andrews and I pulled the tail cone off a Beaver to check the trim actuator cable, we found the tail cone full of frozen caribou blood. So, we promoted the idea of taking the hunters back and returning later for the meat. Although it didn't work all the time, most hunters complied."

"The Dene are interesting people," Ivan adds. "You should see their faces light up as we drop in on a group of caribou. But, the hunters need to be reminded not to load their guns in the aircraft. Another precaution for shutting down the engine on short final is to be sure the engine has stopped before the hunters get out. This avoids any over-enthusiastic hunters getting near the prop when it's moving. All the hunters want to be ready and get a jump on the shooting."

On one occasion, Ivan was chartered to fly a man and his dog team to Wollaston Post so he could enter the team in the local winter carnival. "The Cessna I had been flying was filthy, the interior covered in frozen caribou blood, hair, and small chunks of meat," Ivan says. "There was blood on the ceiling, and even in the back where the survival kit was kept. This aircraft was a meat wagon!"

Usually, Ivan says, when transporting dogs someone would sit in the back with a club to stop them from killing each other while being in such close quarters, as once they start to fight it's hard to get them to stop. But on this trip to Wollaston the dogs were quiet. After unloading, Ivan discovered the reason for their good behavior. The ceiling, floor, and the aircraft interior right to the back were spotless. The dogs had eaten off every speck of frozen blood! "I thought 'Mr. Clean' had done a commercial back there!" Ivan laughs.

"I could always tell when my next trip was a special charter," he adds. "John Campbell would show up with a couple of pails of soap and water. We'd wash the caribou blood and hair from the aircraft to make it more presentable for some of our fussier passengers."

An occasion where aviation became a lifesaver occurred one cold winter day in Stony Rapids. The temperature that morning was 42° below zero. They discussed the risk of taking a medical trip to Uranium City when the weather was colder than the cut-off temperature of 40° below zero. Both Ben Siemens and Ivan agreed that a trip that day shouldn't be a problem.

Ivan was about to leave when he was approached by the wife of his friend, Joe Hanson, who ran the taxi business in Stony and also did some work for Midwest Drilling. "Joe didn't come home last night," she said anxiously. "Will you look along the river?"

Ivan took off and flew low-level over the river, following the swamp-buggy tracks. Joe's last job had been to dismantle the Midwest Drilling camp at Pine Channel. There, Ivan spotted the sleigh full of stuff, and a hole where the swamp-buggy had disappeared through the ice.

"It was a bad scene," Ivan says. "I had to gain some altitude to talk on the radio to call our dispatcher, John Campbell. Then, while I was talking to John, I noticed some smoke from a nearby trappers' cabin. I flew over there and saw two guys waving at me.

"I landed on the swamp-buggy tracks, and picked up Joe and the fellow who had been working with him. On the way back to Stony, Joe told me that when they'd gone under the ice he had managed to grab the other guy's parka hood and pull him from the icy water. When they tried to start a fire they couldn't even hold a match because they'd lost all dexterity in their fingers from the extreme cold. They had to use the full box of matches to get a fire going."

Although Joe had saved his companion's life – and Ivan had saved them both – the other fellow was in bad shape and had to be flown out on a medevac.

Ivan has first aid training, which he considers essential knowledge for someone who spends a lot of time in the wilderness. "There are all kinds of stories where pilots are hauling pregnant ladies, and wondering if the babies will be delivered on the aircraft. I recall pilot Randy Capstick saying he once filled out his log book showing he'd departed with three people and arrived with four!"

Ivan moved around for a few more years before taking a job as a heavy-duty mechanic at Rabbit Lake uranium mine near Wollaston Post. He'd made up his mind to leave the flying business for something more steady. Before he left, however, Ben Siemens made a statement that later proved correct. "Bush flying is like a disease – once you're bit there's no cure. You'll be back."

Diane Smood had been working as a laboratory technician at the uranium mine for 13 years when Ivan arrived. Love bloomed and they married three years later.

"We both had good jobs there, but I missed flying," Ivan says. "I sometimes kick myself for leaving the mine, but I decided to take a job with Dawn Air at Southend. Then I went to work for Wayne Woods of Wollaston Air Services at Wollaston Post, both flying and fixing. At that time it was hard to separate the two professions."

He and Diane eventually left the North for Calgary, where Diane attended university while Ivan found work with a helicopter company, Western Rotorcraft Ltd. But Saskatchewan's North country called again and Ivan returned to take a job as pilot-engineer for Floyd Glass's company, Athabaska Airways, based in Points North. Diane stayed in Calgary and Ivan came home as often as possible.

He then spent a season at George Fleming's Hatchet Lake Lodge in the Athabasca region. The famous lodge, complete with its own airstrip, is one of the largest outfitting camps in Saskatchewan. It serves approximately 700 tourists during its three-and-one-half month summer operation and employs 50 people.[2]

The flying field remained unsteady, however, and Ivan and Diane never knew what outlying point should be called home. When their first child, Kimberly, was born, the choice was made to give up flying for a steady job where Ivan would have a permanent base.

He found a job in Calgary as maintenance engineer for Canadian Regional Airlines. "From flying a Single Otter to doing maintenance on a high-tech Dash-8 proved to be a challenge," Ivan recalls, "but I had a very good time working with those people. They made the transition easier, from flying in the North to life in the city and working for an airline."

But, a few years later the North beckoned again, and this time the entire family returned to La Ronge when Ivan was offered a job in aircraft maintenance for Northern Air Operations. "Work-wise, moving back to La Ronge was a real step backwards – but, it's closer to the North and to my family, where I want to be," he says philosophically.

Ivan has about 3000 hours flying time, and still misses the joys of being employed as a pilot. "I still believe the Otter and Beaver to be old friends."

Ivan's love of the North was born in the blood, as part of his heritage. "I think a lot of it has to do with the closeness of the Northern communities and its characters," he says. "I used to look forward to all the folks returning North in summer for another season – guides as well as fishing lodge, exploration and forest-fire-fighting people."

In recent years, however, the fond memories of flying have been balanced by a passion for exploring the northern rivers by canoe.

His excursions have involved 800-mile wilderness trips with canoeing partner Jim Murphy from Fargo, North Dakota, who he met on the Thelon River in 1987. The men usually meet in La Ronge, and drive or fly to their point of embarkation. Ivan's wife and three young children stay home for now. "My wife is very supportive of my canoe-tripping addiction," Ivan laughs.

What is the main difference between flying and paddling across the country?

"Flying is like window shopping – you can look at the wilderness but you can't experience it," Ivan says. "When you're down there in a canoe you get to touch it, you're there!"

He notes specific adventures, such as "becoming part of a caribou herd."

"It's great when you fly over a herd of caribou, especially if they have a full rack of horns, and even better if the tundra is in its fall splendor. But the best is when you are standing among a herd of caribou and they divide to go around you," Ivan says. "Or when you're standing on a hill, holding your arms straight up, hands fanned out to look like horns. The caribou, having poor eyesight, will walk right up to you. That's the experience I like the best." Ivan pauses as he recollects the vast aloneness of the tundra. "There's that feeling of staggering insignificance one gets after traveling the river day after day, and realizing just how big the North is."

Sadly, on his trips into pristine wilderness Ivan has noticed a problem directly attributable to

his second love, aviation. "There's nothing more irritating than paddling along and coming across a bunch of fuel drums that have been left behind, or an exploration camp that hasn't been cleaned up properly," he states. "A cache of fuel drums has been at Tulemalu Lake for years. Some of the drums are full and lay half-buried in the moss. The fuel is all time-expired and nobody is going to use it, but it's still there."

Like his father, Ivan is thoughtful about the changes they've witnessed in the North. He has known both the old and the new ways, from childhood memories and stories, from first-hand friendships with people who frequent Robertson's Trading Company, and from his own outlook from air and water ways.

"I would certainly like to see clean-ups policed," he says, "and it can be done. After crossing a height-of-land near Mosquito Lake we came across one camp that was recommendable. All that was left of the camp were images of the tent walls that still remained in the moss and lichens. If we hadn't spotted a pile of rocks we wouldn't have found the camp at all.

Ivan Robertson with canoe (Akaitcho III) on Dubawnt Lake, NWT, July 1987. He notes that explorer J.B. Tyrell met with similar ice considions on Dubawnt in 1893. (Photo: Ivan Robertson collection.)

"But, without aviation, this area would still be in the stone-age," Ivan reasons. "You had to have aviation to open up the North, and you've got to think positive. By exposing more tourists to the North, they get to experience our pristine wilderness. Only then will people realize how valuable it is, how fast it is deteriorating, and how important to attain that elusive balance between commerce and tradition."

Ivan feels that more people should come up North, to paddle, fish, and enjoy the wilderness. "I don't know many Canadians who canoe tundra rivers, but there are a lot of people from the United States who do. You may not be an Arctic explorer from old, but the view from the canoe is the same."

For now Ivan is back home in Saskatchewan, employed in air transport maintenance. He fits in, to both the town and the industries that helped to make the area – the fur trade and aviation. His children, like he was, will be raised in La Ronge where the Robertsons are known to everyone, and that's a good feeling.

Ivan's brother Scott runs the Robertson Trading Company store, along with his father Alex. His brother Tim also lives and works in the area. His sister Heather Lori and her husband, too, work north of '60. The North has been good to the Robertsons, and they to it.

Scott Robertson, now managing the store, stands among the souvenirs of 30 years of collections. (Photo: S. Matheson)

Ivan readily acknowledges that he and his family have been blessed. "Yeah, well, we have, and we realize it. I figured that after living in Calgary for eight years and still wanting to come back to the North, I'd better go. And stay."

The Legend and the Legacy

The legacy of Robertson Trading Company is that all customers are to leave with smiles on their faces. They *do* look happy – whether buying merchandise, bringing their furs to one of Canada's last free traders, arranging for supplies to be expedited to their camps up North, or just sitting and chatting outside the store on sun-warmed benches. The float planes roar like sea-lions as they leave or land on the lake, connecting La Ronge with the territory beyond the roads. The Robertson family is at the centre of that action, and hope to remain there for many, many years.

Customers happily wait on benches outside the store, soaking up the sun. L. to R.: James McIver Ratt, Moses L. Ratt, Miles Ratt. (Photo: Robertson collection)

Footnotes

[1]Their first child was Ivan. "He wasn't too interested in the fur trade, but he became an excellent engineer and a pilot. And he explores the North by canoe."

Second son Scott took a business degree from the University of Saskatchewan. Scott now manages Robertson Trading, overseeing their 30 to 35 employees. Scott, taller than his father, is a hardworking young man, attired in modern dress. Like his father, Scott has come to know the customers, and converses with them in their native languages.

Third son Tim attended the University of Saskatchewan and holds undergraduate degrees in Education, Arts (Native Studies) and Honors (Native Studies). He works in the North with Young Offenders for Social Services.

The Robertsons' daughter, Heather Lori, is a Registered Nurse. "She took a special course at Dalhousie University to train as an outpost nurse, and has worked throughout northern Saskatchewan and other northern areas of Canada. She met Dr. James Stempien on Baffin Island and they married in 1990. They have traveled and worked in various parts of the world. While living in Victoria, Heather completed her degree in nursing at the University of Victoria."

"And so," Alex concludes proudly, but modestly, "they've all done fairly well."

[2]The lodge is a landmark in the North, confirmed by the authors of *Wings Beyond Road's End*, "Airplanes Over Saskatchewan's North," Saskatchewan Education, Northern Division, La Ronge, Saskatchewan, 1992.

"Fleming's Hatchet Lake Lodge, which generates valuable business for the air companies and provides seasonal employment for many northerners, demonstrates that aviation still has a viable and flourishing role in areas of the north without road access" (p. 128).

Watching the Arctic

Pete Jess wouldn't call himself a gambler, but challenging and beating the odds have directed his life from his earliest years.

Pete was born in Montreal on February 2, 1953, and grew up on a farm in the Eastern Townships 50 miles south of the city. Life on the Quebec farm was busy. The Jess family milked 100 head of Jersey cows with the help of farm hands, and put up silage and hay. They also had a sugar bush and hand-tapped 2000 trees every spring.

Pete's interest in flying was fueled by stories told by his father, Ed, who had been a Lieutenant Commander in the British Fleet Air Arm for six years during World War II.

"On an aircraft carrier in the British Fleet Air Arm, the Captain of the Ship looked after the boat and the Lieutenant Commander looked after the airplanes," Pete explains. "Dad saw action all through the Atlantic, in Malta for a year and in the Pacific. He had about 6000 hours on the Swordfish and Grumman Avengers, flying off aircraft carriers, and in combat during WWII. He was awarded the Distinguished Service Cross for sinking thousands of tons of enemy ships with torpedo bombers. A number of his Fleet Air Arm navy buddies would come to visit us and I'd hear all their stories."

Ed Jess was also an avid photographer and had built up an excellent collection of black-and-white photographs documenting the war from his perspective as a navigator and observer.

But Pete had no real appreciation for what his father and his comrades did until he himself started to fly helicopters years later. "We didn't have GPS [global positioning system] when I started to fly," Pete says. "We had to map-read, and there was just the odd beacon to follow. The weather was often lousy and we had a limited amount of fuel. But all that paled in comparison to my father's stories of lifting off an aircraft carrier at night in a single-engine piston airplane. They'd fly 100 miles or so away from their ship to find target ships – who were also trying to shoot at them – by dead-reckoning, lining up, flying 20 feet above the waves, dropping a torpedo, and then trying to find their way back to their own ship, which was blacked out!"

"And so," Pete concludes, "a person might hear all these hairy-chested bush pilot stories, but the flying we did [in northern Canada] was really like being at war with no bullets. In other words, it was fun. I don't think the other was fun."

Growing Up Challenged

Pete was thus schooled in aviation through stories of his father and his friends, and also by building model airplanes. "I started out with little hand-controlled Cox 049 engines, building and gluing these things together and then crashing them. I had subscriptions to flying magazines, and knew the insides of the different Cessna airplanes intimately from pictures."

But Ed Jess never encouraged his children, and especially Pete, to seek careers in aviation. "My parents were totally against that. They thought I should go to school, and then maybe find work in one of the local factories. I had as much interest in working in a factory as jumping off a high bridge with no water under it! Every day, on my way to school, I'd pass by the local factories to see the guys hanging out the windows trying to grab some fresh air."

It may seem odd that Ed Jess, considering his and his family's achievements, would recommend that Pete stay in school or find work in a factory. But, as Pete rationalizes, "he was very much from the old school. He'd been to war, had two engineering degrees, and was of the opinion that unless you got a university degree, you were dead. Chance of success without one was nil." And Pete didn't do well in school, hence factory-work seemed a viable option.

Pete's poor school performance, as it turns out, was a hand-eye coordination problem, and he was fortunately enrolled in a remedial program at McGill University's learning centre.

The Call of the North

After a few years working at various jobs, Pete realized he had a hankering to fly. During one winter when he'd worked at Sunshine Village in Banff, he had met Roy Anderson, nicknamed "the Viking," who worked as a helicopter pilot up North in the summer and as a ski instructor in Banff during the winter. He advised Pete to seek work in a Northern oil or mining camp, where he could make some good money and also save because the jobs included room and board.

Following a brief stint with Brewster's Rocky Mountain Adventure Tours, where he met his future wife, Judy Szombathy, Pete went on to see what new job he could scare up.

"I spent about two weeks pounding the pavement in Edmonton. No joy. I was getting pretty desperate and was looking through the Calgary phone book when I spotted the name Panarctic Oils. Hey, with a name like that they *had* to work up North! So I phoned Calgary and spoke to the receptionist, Beryl Jamieson. I said, 'My name is Pete Jess and I'm looking for work.' She said, 'Do you mean that radio operating job that's open?' Without any hesitation I replied, 'Yeah! That one!' She said, 'Just a minute, I'll put you in touch with the head of the radio operators.'"

Pete had some experience operating radios on boats, and he hoped that would get him in the door for an interview. The man came on the phone: "Yeah, we're looking for a radio operator. Where are you?" Pete told him he was in Edmonton. "Well, go out to the airport, get on the airbus, come down to Calgary, take a cab to our office, and come in for an interview. Keep all the receipts and we'll refund the money."

Wow! He'd never been treated like that before! But, there was still the interview to go through. When asked where he'd operated radios in the past, Pete told him honestly that he'd worked on a boat in Hawaii, and on one in Ireland one summer. Then he added that he also had aspirations to fly. "Well, if you're a radio operator you have to be a weather man, too. That's essential knowledge for a flying career." Pete responded immediately, "I'm willing to learn."

"Good, you're hired – $850 a month plus an isolation bonus. You'll be working two weeks on with one week off. Your training starts when you get there."

Pete was told to fly back to Edmonton and the next afternoon be at the WestCan terminal at Edmonton International Airport ready to fly North. He hadn't time to buy, or even think about, suitable Northern attire, so he threw his mountain apparel and climbing boots into a packsack, and jumped on the company's Lockheed Electra to fly to Rea Point, south of King Point on the east coast of Melville Island.

It was the first week of September 1973, and the Arctic was starting to cool off –Pete noted the puddles had ice on them – although there was still daylight nearly 'round the clock. There had been some heavy rains at Rea Point and the strip was not in good enough condition for the Electra to land, so they went on to land at Resolute Bay. The company then sent over two Twin Otters to pick up the people and freight and take them back to Rea Point.

Pete was starry-eyed as he watched the men unloading and reloading, and observed the local people and the terrain. He especially noticed one of the Twin Otter pilots, "looking extremely confident about everything." Everyone seemed to know him, and he chatted amiably to the crews. Pete walked up to him. "Excuse me, I'm really interested in flying. Is there any chance I could ride up front with you?" "Sure! Go around the other side and hop right up there." In those days they didn't fly with copilots on Twin Otters, so here was his chance to sit beside the pilot, observing the Arctic for the first time from the cockpit.

The pilot's name was Gary Hanson and as they flew he explained what was involved in being a Twin Otter pilot for Panarctic Oils. Pete was jubilant: "I hadn't been in the Arctic for 20 minutes and there I was, sitting in the right seat of a Twin Otter, leaving Resolute Bay for the 200 mile trip across Bathurst Island and along the Viscount Melville Sound to Rea Point. There were a bunch of oil guys sitting back in the passenger seats, looking very glum because they were going back to work, and I was on Cloud Nine. He let me steer the airplane and he told me stories about the Arctic. That trip had a profound effect on my future."

When they arrived at Rea Point, Pete was greeted by Barry Craig, a radio operator with a "gruff, dry sense of humor" who had been given the task of training the neophyte. Even though Craig had a well-deserved reputation for being curt and matter-of-fact, Pete reveled in learning the job and became extremely thankful for Craig's knowledge. "He helped me out tremendously," Pete recalls. "He taught me radio operating and weather, all the stuff I needed to know."

Pete spent two weeks training at Rea Point, then flew south to Calgary on the company's Electra. During his week off, he found an apartment in Penthouse Towers in downtown Calgary – 1000 square feet, fully furnished, for $115 a month! – which he shared with another Panarctic employee who was on the opposite shift. This economy would help him save money for future flying lessons.

By now Pete was getting to know all the Electra pilots, and on each trip in and out they let him sit in the jump seat where he'd talk aviation and "yak their ears off." All were willing to share their knowledge with the enthusiastic young operator, and Pete vowed, in turn, that when they asked him for information he'd ensure it was thorough and accurate.

By the time Pete returned to Rea Point on his second trip in, he felt like an oldtimer – until Barry Craig informed him of his new job assignment: to go out to a rig site to radio operate on a "Herc move" (using a Lockheed C-130 Hercules, a medium-lift military transport plane).

"A Herc move was a big deal for everybody," Pete says, "not only for the crew who had to tear the rig apart but also for the radio operators stationed at the two ends of the move. It could take 100 to 120 Herc loads to move a rig from one spot to another. The weather was atrocious, and you just didn't screw around on Herc moves. I was a brand-new, green radio operator and weather man, and my first job was a Herc move by myself on one end!"

The rig manager (drilling foreman) was Lawrence Jones. "I hope you don't get stuck with Lawrence Jones, he's the worst!" everyone had warned Pete. The drilling foremen were the top guns, and one negative word could result in a lowly employee being sent home on the airplane and banished from the oilpatch, forever.

Jones came in, looked Pete over, and sat down. "So you're the new radio operator."

"Yes."

"Well, we've got a job to do here and you'd better not mess up. I don't know why I got stuck with a green operator."

"I'll try my very best. I'll do whatever I can and if I don't know, I'll ask," Pete said.

"Well, it sounds like you're trying to start off on the right foot anyway," Jones responded gruffly.

Pete didn't "mess up," and Lawrence Jones became his mentor. "I worked my butt off for him, and in turn, he helped me to understand the weather systems and get to know everybody all over the Arctic, and all the radio procedures, which are second-nature to me today."

Meanwhile, Pete and Judy were still communicating. When she gained her degree in education, she found a teaching job in Calgary so they could be together when Pete had time off.

But, after 18 months as a radio operator, Pete concluded that the best job to earn really big bucks was as a heavy equipment operator. He applied to Don Connelly, a construction foreman for Panarctic, and with Lawrence Jones's personal reference, Pete was given the chance to learn this trade.

He had returned to Calgary for his week off, before beginning his new job as heavy equipment operator, when the phone rang early on Halloween morning, 1974. Judy took the call, and Pete heard her say, "He's right here. He came home yesterday." He took the receiver to hear the caller respond, "I'm glad to hear that, because Panarctic's Lockheed Electra, Papa Alpha Bravo [CF-PAB], crashed last night, killing 32 people."

It was a horrific story. After Pete and the other passengers had disembarked, the aircraft had done a quick turnaround and picked up the opposite crew in Edmonton. It crashed on the approach to Rea Point in Bayam Channel, about a mile offshore, and two miles short of the company-owned landing strip. The accident occurred the night of October 30, 1974, and its cause was seemingly undetermined.

Pete recalls that the ice had lately formed, and was about 18 inches thick when "the aircraft came in, and pancaked on the ocean ice. The cockpit and a couple of the engines broke off. Some of the material that was inside, strapped down on pallets, broke loose and skidded a few hundred yards ahead on the ice. The fuselage of the airplane, the whole body where all the passengers were, crunched and went in and underneath the ice. Some people had survived the crash and floated around in the water for a while before they died." Parts of the aircraft that went through the ice came to rest 100 feet below on the channel floor.

Pete's younger brother, Bob, was also working at Rea Point. Len Storvold, the Arctic Superintendent, sent up a Twin Otter to evaluate the situation. They spotted fires on the ice from two miles away. On site, Len and Bob threw a Skidoo into the back of a pickup truck, drove to the beach, and headed out onto the ice on the snow machine. Another foreman put together a search party and followed them on foot.

Some bodies were still floating in the hole in the ice, surrounded by fires from spilled oil and fuel. The flight engineer, Gary Weyman, and the copilot, David Hatton, had escaped from the cockpit, but the captain, Brian Thomson, did not survive. The flight engineer, in pursuit of help, began to walk back to the camp over the ice and snow; the copilot was found leaning up against one of the engines in a quasi-conscious state.

"It was an absolutely unbelievable scene," Pete says. "Fuel on the ice, on fire, and the engines on fire. My brother came home and related the story before I left to start work as a heavy equipment operator. But I, myself, have a vivid memory of landing at Rea Point, looking out the window of the airplane, another Electra, and seeing the broken-up cockpit that had been recovered from under the ice sitting on the ramp."

Within hours, Pacific Western Airlines sent in a mercy flight via Rea Point which itself had to fight blowing snow, thin sea ice, darkness and extreme cold to pick up the survivors. (The Calgary *Herald* reported that the wind chill factor had dropped at times to 100 Fahrenheit degrees below zero).

"I knew most of the people on the airplane, and everybody died except for the copilot and the flight engineer," Pete says. "And that wonderful lady, the receptionist at Panarctic, Beryl Jamieson, who I'd gotten to know over the years, her son had just been hired on as a radio operator. He died in that crash on his first trip north."

Company president Charles Hetherington stated that the 32 men killed were from nine different contracting companies. "The fine men we lost were pioneers," he said in a statement to the Calgary *Herald* (Nov. 10/74), "just [like] the men who in the past ventured into remote areas to carry forth the development of Canada."

Panarctic Oils engaged the services of five divers, using television cameras, to locate the remains of the downed aircraft, and to assist coroner Walter England of Yellowknife in carrying out his investigations.

The accident had an effect on Pete's life that he wouldn't realize for some time because of people he met, such as Phil Nuytten, the owner of Can Dive Services in Vancouver and of Nuytco Research Ltd. "Phil came up to do the recovery of the aircraft cockpit and the bodies," Pete says. "Then I encountered Phil again a year-and-a-half later when I was driving the big machines. He was putting in a floe line, the very first under-ice gas pipeline to be installed in the world."

Pete's new job involved driving Foremost Delta 3s, great flat-deck machines used to move heavy pieces of rigs across the ice, and he enjoyed this work. He recalls his three-and-a-half years spent with Panarctic Oils, as radio and heavy equipment operator, as being far more beneficial than any time he could have spent in university. "It was a period of incredible learning for me. I was making friends, making money for the first time, I had all kinds of brand new experiences and I had freedom. I was just 20 years old."

Flying on His Own

During the weeks Pete had off, he would fly south to Calgary to spend time with his two loves: Judy and flying. As they made plans to spend their lives together, he related to Judy that the machine he really wanted to fly was the helicopter.

He'd flown in one at the Columbia Icefields, with an Alpine Helicopters pilot whose job it was to replace propane bottles on generators located on mountains-tops. "We'd get out of the helicopter and move around a couple of 100-pound propane bottles and lash them down. Then he would pick the little Bell 47 up into a hover and dive it off a cliff that was about 2000 feet straight down. I was hooked, right there."

Now, Pete made a visit to Klondike (later Kenting) Helicopters in Calgary, where he was told that the training course for a rotary-wing licence would set him back $13 500 – a huge amount of money even for a guy making Northern wages.

To increase his knowledge of flying, Pete decided to start with a private pilot's licence. He began his training on fixed-wing aircraft with the Calgary Flying Club at Springbank general aviation airport located 20 miles west of Calgary, with instructor Gordy Blake. Judy would come out to the airport and stand at the side of the runway to watch Pete do touch-and-gos as he trained on the club's Cessna 150.

He recalls the day his instructor announced it was time for him to do a solo circuit. "I'm not ready," Pete protested. "I can't do this." "Yes you can, away you go," Gordy Blake replied. He went up, "and it was really cool, being by myself in an airplane." He got his private pilot's licence in 1975.

He chose not to get his instrument rating, however. "I had no aspirations to fly fixed-wing, none at all. I wanted to fly helicopters and that's what I'd been saving my money towards. Judy had been teaching school so we were living on her salary and banking my money from the North."

In November 1975, a year after the fatal crash of the Electra, Pete quit his job with Panarctic and came south for what he thought might be the last time. "I went out to Klondike's hangar beside where Kenn Borek Air Ltd. is today, plunked my $13 500 down on the desk and said, 'Here I am.'"

There he met Chris Reynolds, chief instructor for Klondike Helicopters, and Keith Ostertag (called KO), their chief pilot. "Two of the guys who played a role in my training at that time were KO, a terrific guy, and Phil Love, another instructor there. Chris Reynolds was also going to play a role in the formation of me as a pilot, and also as a mentor who I still call regularly for advice," Pete says.

"Chris is very much a no-nonsense guy, and I believe he is the best helicopter instructor this country has ever seen. A number of things that Chris was to teach me over that winter would eventually save my life. I attribute my being here to his teaching, and I say that with absolute certainty."

Pete felt proud that he had spent time in the North and had earned good money. He had radio procedures, weather and theory of flight down pat, and now he just wanted stick time. But, even with this background and experience, flying a helicopter didn't come easy.

"When you first learn to fly helicopters it's quite frustrating because you just can't do it, period. You hear stories about people taking over from the pilot who's had a heart attack. If you're flying a Cessna 172 or a Bonanza, it's probable that you could get down in one piece. If you were required to take over a helicopter's flight controls and you'd never had any helicopter training, you would *not* get down in one piece. When learning to fly a helicopter, you wonder, 'What is wrong with me? Why can I not do this?' It's a coordination exercise that you are required to learn."

By his third week of training, Pete felt he was a hopeless case. "I went home to Judy and said, 'The guy treats me like I'm a moron! He tells me that I'm trying to kill him – and me! I mean, who's the customer here, anyway?' She told me to shut up because she recognized the guy was a great educator, and I should feel privileged to be learning from someone like him. So I did, and shortly thereafter I was thankful that I'd never said anything. By then I realized the guy was brilliant, and I'd better get my stupid little ego out of the way, and forget about having spent three years saving money and being proud of that, and being a little bit infatuated with learning to fly and all this, and I did.

"Then, one day it clicks and you sort of giggle to yourself, you find you can hover and so forth, and your instructor looks over and goes, 'Hmmph, so you're not an imbecile.'"

Finally the time came when KO took him out in the Bell 47 to a dried-up slough bed near Chestermere Lake to do circuits. When they landed, KO stepped out of the helicopter and said, "You go around, now." Pete experienced the same sinking feeling as he had when Gordy Blake said those words at Springbank airport, but this was much worse. He was not ready to do this with a helicopter! But when KO pointed at him and said, "Go!" away he went. He circled around and came in for a landing, amazed that he'd got it back safely on the ground. KO got in and said, "See? *Now* we're going to teach you how to fly!"

For the rest of the winter, Pete's lessons were taught mainly by Chris Reynolds and Phil Love. The primary lesson concentrated on how to do auto-rotation in the event of an engine failure. "All pilots learn that, they have to," Pete says. "If it's done properly a helicopter is a much safer place to be, under an engine failure, than a fixed-wing airplane, because you can land in a much smaller place with no forward speed. Chris taught me to be totally aware of my surroundings.

"You don't have to fly every mile anticipating the engine's going to fail but subconsciously you register places, as they're going by between your feet, where you could land. I wouldn't be here today if he hadn't drilled that into my head. He also taught me that if you're the pilot in command, until you hand the control over to somebody else, nobody monkeys around in your cockpit."

In April 1976, after 100 hours of training, Pete completed his written exam. When the Ministry of Transport examiner, Harry Fallis, arrived from Edmonton to supervise his practical exam, Chris and Phil both seemed a bit tense. Harry was known to be a tough examiner.

Harry's first instructions were, "Go out and do a walk-around the helicopter." He did. Then Harry said, "Okay, let's go out to Chestermere Lake and do some circuits."

As they took off, Harry reached down and fiddled with the carb heat. Pete reached over, grabbed his examiner's hand, and said, "Don't touch that." Harry looked over at Pete, and the young pilot thought, 'I've just told Harry Fallis to take his hand off the carb heat. I've blown my ride!" But Harry seemed to take no offense, explaining that some things could be done one way or another.

On arriving at Chestermere Lake, they did some circuits and auto-rotations. "Do you smoke?" Harry asked. "Yes." "Well, shut down the helicopter, let's have a break." Pete landed, shut off the machine, and they had a smoke break, sitting out in the field. Finally Harry said to Pete, "We'll return to the hangar now. Do you mind if I fly back?" "No, not at all." "That's good," Harry said, then added, "You know, in this examining stuff I don't get to fly that much any more. This will be kind of fun."

Pete was sure then that he'd blown his ride, but there was nothing he could do but ride back to the hangar as a passenger. "Okay, you tie 'er down and come on inside," Harry said.

As Pete tied down the helicopter, he was worried sick about his instructor's reaction. "Chris is going to kill me. This is awful." But as he entered the hangar he saw Phil and Chris wearing big grins. Harry motioned Pete to the inner office. "I don't know if this has ever happened before in a Canadian practical helicopter test," Harry Fallis said, "but I'm going to award you 100 marks out of 100 on your practical exam. You deserve it."

The award had a double meaning for Pete. Not only had he pleased himself and his excellent instructors at Klondike Helicopters, but he recalled those painful years when he'd had to attend a special school in Montreal to relearn how to crawl. It seemed like a long time ago, yet only yesterday – the humiliation, the challenge, the perseverance and finally the reward.

"I was the kid who couldn't chew gum and walk, and couldn't bounce a basketball, and had to do all those exercises; who sat in the corner as a dunce and got his desk pushed out in the hallway, and was considered a lost cause," Pete says. "And I later found out that some 'expert' educators in Montreal had given my parents the advice that I should *never* fly because I would be a disappointment to them and to everybody else. That's why my dad had been standoffish about my flying. He'd been advised by these so-called experts that I didn't have, quote, 'the right stuff.'"

The practical exam was given in the morning, and in the afternoon, Keith 'KO' Ostertag, the chief pilot, offered Pete a job. "Every helicopter pilot's nightmare is that he won't find work after he's spent all this money and taken the training," Pete says, "but this was boom-time. And imagine, they were going to pay *me* and I'd be going up, not in a Bell 47, but a Hiller FH-1100 and a Bell Model 206 JetRanger with a turbine engine!"

His first job was a summer contract to fly out of Resolute Bay in the Arctic for a company called Polar Gas. On a Sunday morning in mid-May 1976, Pete "with his Five-Star sleeping bag" waved good-bye to Judy as he lifted off from Calgary International Airport to fly a helicopter, on his own, up to Resolute Bay. The trip took 10 days.

"I got held up between Yellowknife and Cambridge Bay," Pete recalls. "It was breakup and it was very foggy, with low clouds, and in those days there were no navigation aids. We didn't have GPS or anything, so I had to map-read my way across the Barrens. I had nothing but this needle-ball airspeed, an ADF that picked up a beacon 20 or 30 miles away, and a little HF radio."

The pilot was expected to dead-reckon off the ADF from Yellowknife, then would lose the signal until picking up the next one at Contwoyto Lake (the beacon maintained by Pacific Western Airlines for their air routes to Cambridge Bay and Resolute, and also used by Panarctic Oils). The next beacon was at Cambridge Bay.

The procedure Pete followed for loading was to fill the helicopter's fuel tanks, then fill plastic five-gallon jerry cans and place them on the back seat, on the floor, and on the racks on the side. The loaded machine would stagger into the air to fly north, away from Yellowknife's beacon. Then he'd be his own navigator.

"I was flying along at 200 or 300 feet above the ground, because I couldn't fly in the clouds and there was this little space between the ground and the clouds," Pete says. "It's much easier to read a map when you're high up, but when you have to fly so low it can be difficult. I made mistakes reading the map, I'm sure that's what happened, and I ended up way out, to the point of what we call 'no return'. This happened several times. I had to find a place to land, fill up the fuel tanks from the jerry cans, and get into the air again. If I didn't have the beacon ahead, I'd fly back in a southerly direction until I picked it up and then go back to Yellowknife. So, in this way I eventually made it to Resolute."

There, he received his instructions, "to take rock, bird, and plant doctors to different spots along the proposed Polar Gas pipeline route so they could do studies."

Although Pete wasn't aware of it, the company had sold his services as a 1500- to 2000-hour pilot. He arrived in Resolute with 130 hours total flying time, based on 100 hours of training, another 10 hours of instruction in that aircraft, and 20 hours getting to Resolute. He came home at the end of that first season with 450 added hours. In those days, pilots could fly for 10 or 11 straight hours because of the 24 hour daylight, "Nobody cared," Pete says, and they had great weather that summer.

His assigned aircraft was a Hiller FH-1100, a five-passenger, turbine engine helicopter comparable to a small JetRanger – "a nice little machine except it had a nasty reputation of throwing off the main blade." Judy found out about this idiosyncrasy after Pete had left, when someone remarked, "Oh, Peter went North. I hear he's flying that 'widow-maker.'"

With Pete's first assignment came his first challenge as he prepared to take a group of scientists over to Beechey Island (the burial site of three Franklin Expedition crew members). Located 75 miles east of Resolute Bay, on the southwest corner of Devon Island at the entrance to Wellington Channel off Lancaster Sound, the small one-mile-wide island forms a noticeable landmark with cliffs rising to a 600-foot-high plateau.

"These great, big, burly guys came out, put a Zodiac boat on one rack, and a five-gallon can of gas and a 10 horsepower outboard motor on the other rack," Pete says.

"Then they piled in with all their gear, so you could barely close the doors. I looked at all this, thinking, 'This is no good.' Then came Chris's advice, 'If it doesn't feel right, don't do it. But, in the interest of customer relations, explain why.'

He could have lifted off, but it would have totally over-torqued the helicopter, been over gross weight, and illegal.

"I've always been a learner by demonstration, so I thought I'd *show* these guys how it wouldn't work," Pete continues. "I fired up the helicopter and, in an attempt to lift, I pulled 100 percent torque on the gauge. It didn't move off the ground. I took the power off and said, 'I'm sorry, we're going to have to get rid of some of this stuff. It won't lift off.' Then I got the big response, 'What do you mean, it won't lift off?? We chartered this helicopter for the summer and the salesman in Calgary said it would carry this much for this far . . .'"

Pete figured the salesman might have said it would carry 1000 pounds for 1000 miles or something equally ridiculous, but as the pilot he had to explain that while it *could* carry 1000 pounds, that maximum load could only be carried for 20 miles because that was all the fuel you could carry, grossed out. He explained that while they hadn't necessarily misinterpreted it, perhaps nobody had explained the situation clearly. If they wanted to carry all that gear for 200 miles he could do it, but it would take several trips – at extra cost. And if they wanted to take that drum of fuel along, well, that would be a trip by itself.

Finally they said, "Well, okay," unloaded supplies that weren't absolutely necessary, and off they flew to Beechey Island. They made a number of trips over several weeks, flying at 100 knots, about top speed for that helicopter, at 100 feet of altitude. The scientists tabulated animal life along the ice-edge where the water of Lancaster Sound meets the ice of Wellington Channel. "Two seals, three guillemots, four seagulls, one walrus," the scientists would call out as they made a run. Then they'd turn out over the sea ice, a mile further back from the ice edge, and do exactly the same thing, comparing the daily counts over a two-week period.

One morning as they were preparing to go out, a strong wind came blowing from the west. Pete didn't feel right about travelling downwind that far away from the ice at such a low altitude. If something should happen, such as the engine quitting, he would want to turn into the wind to land. He suggested they go a little higher – or perhaps down over the ice and then back up into the wind – but the scientists were adamant that to make the survey correct it must be continued in exactly the same pattern. Again, Chris's voice echoed from Pete's training days: "Be careful. Be aware of what's going on." But, this time, the customers' wish prevailed.

They were 500 feet away from the ice edge, out over the water, and Pete had just pulled up the nose at the end of the run, when the engine quit. "I auto-rotated toward the ice and was able to turn it quickly into the wind and stretch it out," Pete says, "but as we landed I turned to the scientist, Kerry Finlay. 'Suck it down,' I yelled, "we're going in.' I don't remember what I did, except that I did it right. And that was simply train-ing, training, training.

"I couldn't get it all the way into the wind because it was coming from my tail, but I managed to land cross-wind on the ice. I got out and paced off the distance from the tail rotor to the water – 20 feet. We had *just* made it on. Although we had floats on, the wind would have blown us right out into Lancaster Sound. The helicopter would prob-ably have sunk."

Pete discovered that a little vacuum line on the governor had loosened, causing the engine to fail. A "bush repair" was possible, but the ice floe on which they'd landed was unstable. Even as they watched, pieces broke off, bringing them even closer to the edge. They could walk away, up the channel, and would have to if the ice floe broke off com-pletely. They would likely be rescued, but the helicopter would be gone. He had to move it, but how? It would be impossible to drag.

He radioed Resolute to report the situation, but they were an hour away and the ice was not going to last. Pete found some electrical tape to fix the broken line. Then they all climbed aboard, and he picked the machine up into a hover. At a height of six feet off the ice he flew it up-channel, away from the open water, hover-taxiing at 10 mph. Then they flew towards Cornwallis Island over the ice.

When he reached the island their rescue helicopter had arrived, bringing a mechan-ic. The faulty tube was replaced and they continued on their way. From then on, pilot and scientists had a mutually-respectful working relationship. "That's where your rep-utation starts to build – you're either okay or you're a jerk, there's no in between, so I started to develop the reputation that I was okay," Pete laughs.

Flying for Kenting Helicopters on the Polar Gas Project, July 1976. Polar Bear Pass on Bathurst Island. (This is the helicopter the polar bear inves-tigated). (Photo: Jess collec-tion)

His superior position was almost destroyed, however, when he unexpectedly met one of the native inhabitants of Beechey Island.

Pete continued to fly the scientists from Resolute Bay to Beechey Island. They would get into their little Zodiac boat to do tests out in the water while Pete waited in the helicopter parked on the beach. This day, it was bright and sunny, 60 degrees Fahrenheit, with just a three mph wind. To take advantage of the breeze, and to keep the cockpit from turning into a hothouse in the sun, Pete 'pinned' open both doors by wedging in paperback books. Then he went around and stretched out in the passenger's front seat where there were no pedals or stick. He lay back and soon fell asleep.

"I woke up a half-hour or so later," says Pete, "and the hair on the back of my head was standing right up. Then I heard this noise: click! click! click! and suddenly the helicopter, which was on floats but resting on the gravel beach, moved. A polar bear had come up the other side and was standing on the float, with his chin over the pilot's seat.

"A helicopter is very loose on the floats, and as he'd stood up he'd got his head stuck in the door. He was looking me over. He'd turn his head to one side, then the other, like a puppy dog. I was just freaking out!"

Pete closed his eyes and quickly assessed his situation. His gun was in the boot at the back of the helicopter. Both doors were propped wide open. He couldn't do a thing, so, what became important to his survival, he *didn't* do anything.

"I finally decided to make some noise, but not from my mouth, to surprise him and hopefully make him go away or at least get him to back out of the helicopter. His nose and mouth were just 18 inches away. His breath stank. I was sitting there trying not to do anything to upset him, assuming that anything I did at this point could be wrong. And if I did something wrong, I was going to die."

Pete reached over and very slowly pushed the book out from the edge of the passenger door. As he'd hoped, the breeze started the door swinging toward him. Pete watched for the bear's reaction as he lifted up his hand, and, with the door slowly closing, he managed to grab the handle and yank it closed, hoping it would make a loud enough noise to surprise the bear.

"You're not supposed to slam the door of a helicopter or any airplane, but I pulled that door closed as hard as I could, ready to pop it open again and jump out if he came at me. What happened was, the little window above the sliding window of the passenger's door popped out, flew across the cockpit and bonked the bear on the nose. He reeled back, withdrawing his head from the helicopter, and stood two feet away from the float. I reached over and pushed out the book holding open the pilot's door. The book fell onto the gravel, and the bear actually looked down at it as the door swung closed. But I mean, we're talking about little aluminum and Plexiglas door, not much between us!"

At this point, Pete breathed easier. He could make a getaway. But something else came into play: the desire for revenge.

"When a human being has something happen that you don't understand, or you can't control, you usually have one of two reactions," Pete says philosophically. "You get very angry, or you get very scared. I'd just been through the 'very scared' phase and as I began to think I had the upper hand, I got angry. And so I did a series of things that you should never do.

"I didn't want to rustle around in the helicopter, maybe he'd jump for it and smash the door or something, so I reached over from the passenger's to the pilot's seat, and pushed the starter button. You should *never* start a helicopter when not sitting in the pilot's seat. But anyway, I induced fuel to the helicopter and lit the turbine off, and as the rotor blades started going around the bear backed off a further 20 feet. Then I scrambled over into the pilot's seat and quickly got everything spooled up, until the thing was running at full power. The rotor was going, everything was ready to go. The bear was over on the beach. He hadn't moved away. That's when I thought, 'I'm going to get you!'"

The second "wrong" thing he did was spontaneous: he lifted the helicopter into the air and started flying down the beach after the bear, who turned and galloped away. "Now we're going downwind, down the beach," Pete says. "I've got him running, he's going flat out, maybe 40 mph, he's really scared.

"Then he jumped into the water off this little cliff, and started swimming as fast as he could out to sea. I'm chasing him with the helicopter, causing the rotor wash to blow the water all around him. Now I think I've got the upper hand. This is a real sign of immaturity, remember, this is going way back.

"Well, as soon as you start thinking it's all together, complacency sets in, and that's the point I'm at. I'm hovering over him, lifting the helicopter up and then going down low on top of him, roarr!! and lifting it up again. He'd roll over onto his side in the water and I could see he was panicking. He's at the stage I was at – in fear of his life – five minutes ago. Now I think I've got the upper hand. I pick the helicopter up and just as I lift up this time, *he* gets angry. He reaches up and takes a swing at the helicopter with his giant forearm and paw – just missing the float.

"*I'm* now back to quaking in my boots, realizing I've just about caused my own demise. If he'd touched that float I'd have been upside down in the water, 500 feet offshore, in the ocean with a pissed-off polar bear. With the strength of the bear – they can weigh 1000 pounds – it would have flipped the helicopter upside down. I'd have gone right over with the floats sideways. He probably would have kept swimming away if the rotor blade hadn't hit him or something, but I would have been far away from the shore, upside down, in the water.

"I would have died, I'm sure – if not in the crash, later from exposure, because it was another five hours before the guys came back in the boat. I never could have swum to shore, no way I'd have made it in that cold water.

"I quickly moved the helicopter back over, set it down on the beach, and breathed a sigh of relief. Ooh! Never, ever, would I let that happen again. That was a big lesson for me."

The Discovery

Another incident that had a deep effect on Pete's life also occurred that summer. A new survey was being conducted along the Boothia Peninsula toward Spence Bay, and he didn't know that area very well. He was flying along in the fog, looking for a fuel cache he had been told was located at Cape Anne on the northwest shore of Somerset Island. As he followed the shoreline in the helicopter, very slowly at 50 feet, he suddenly found himself out over open water. Had he made a wrong turn? He couldn't see a thing in the dense fog except for blue water where, just moments ago, there was water and shoreline.

"I thought I'd gone out over the ocean," Pete says, "but then I saw all these white things in the water and realized they were hundreds and hundreds of whales! I'm trying to concentrate, I'm petrified that I've flown out over the water, I don't know where I am, yet these whales are preoccupying my mind. Wow! Then all of a sudden there's the shoreline again. I flew along, eventually came to my fuel cache at Cape Anne, and set down. Whew, got away with that one! As I'm pumping the fuel in I'm wondering what had happened, and where that was that I'd spotted the whales."

When the weather cleared up further west, Pete picked up the helicopter and flew to their camp down on the Boothia. Three days later in clear, sunny conditions he came back along the same route to solve the mystery. He found that he'd flown across the

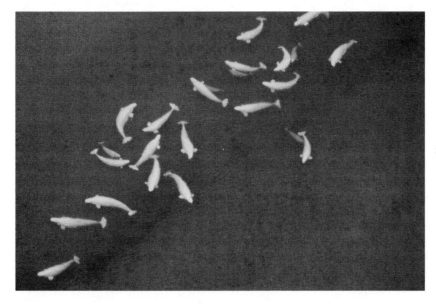

Beluga whales at Cunningham Inlet. They come in with their calves, and also shed their skins in the shallow water. (Photo: Jess collection)

mouth of Cunningham Inlet, from Gifford Point to Cape Anne. It was in the inlet that he'd seen the whales.

He took one of the scientists back with him and they sat for an hour, transfixed, watching the belugas swimming around, seeming to smile as they lifted their heads and arched their flukes to rub old dead skin against the limestone gravel, shedding it in floppy ribbons. They were small compared to other whales, between eight and 16 feet in length and weighing about a ton, with the females a bit smaller. The charcoal-grey calves huddled close to their mothers, nudging to nurse. It was easy to understand why these white whales were sometimes called "the canaries of the sea," because of their melodious, symphonic, trumpet calls mingled with high warbles and pops and trills.

"I was thinking, 'Boy, would Judy ever be thrilled to see this!'" Pete recalls. "I kept that place in mind, and went back many times during the summers of 1976 and '77."

During his first summer spent flying in the Arctic, Pete added hundreds of hours to his log book, to now total nearly 600, and made great money. He had no accidents, although he did have one more engine failure. The same piece of equipment had packed up a month later when he was 200 feet in the air with a net full of groceries slung underneath. He'd punched the groceries off and then set the helicopter down beside the eggs and milk, now splattered across the tundra.

The company had promised he could come home during the long weekend at the end of August, for a valid reason: to attend his wedding. Judy made all the arrangements with her family in Saskatoon and Pete's family coming from Quebec. But 10 days before the wedding date, Pete knew he wouldn't be able to get away – there was no one to replace him. Enduring the wrath of in-laws before they actually became related was not how Pete and Judy wanted to start their marriage, but they had to postpone the date to Thanksgiving weekend, October 9, 1976. Even then, to keep that date Pete had to quit his job. "I basically resigned and they sent up another guy to replace me. I was bushed, I'd had a whole summer there, it was great to get home."

There wasn't much helicopter flying during the Northern winters in the time of darkness and cold, so Pete took short-term radio operating contract jobs with Panarctic Oils. Then in February 1977, he received a call from Bow Helicopters. They had a job for him, flying a JetRanger on contract for Panarctic Oils. The helicopter was already up there. "It was sort of wintertime flying, after it got light," Pete says. "I flew surveyors and seismic guys around on the islands, all that spring up to summer."

Then it came time for the delayed honeymoon. He and Judy took their first holiday, driving her Volkswagen Beetle to Nova Scotia and back.

Logistics

In the fall, Gordon Hood, Chief Engineer for Panarctic Oils, offered Pete a job as an Engineering Technician, to look after logistics dealing with ice roads, airstrips, surveying and helicopter use. It was extremely good money, although the work would be different from anything he'd yet done. He discussed it with Judy. He'd never had a flying accident, he had a good reputation so far with about 1200 hours built up, not a high time but all of it in the Arctic. In fact, the only trees he'd ever seen while flying were when he'd ferried a machine to or from the North.

It was decided that he should at least try the new job. If it didn't work out he could always go back to flying. And so he did, staying with Panarctic Oils for almost three years to look after contractors as they surveyed the company's ice roads, ice airstrips and drilling platforms. They also did ice-blasting experiments and ice-motion surveys for positioning drilling rigs, which involved hiring large, twin-engine 212s from Bow Helicopters for night IFR slinging, done even during 24-hour darkness at 40 degrees below zero or colder.

After the ice had frozen in December, Pete and his flight crew, Bill Kipke and Marty Voss, would go out in helicopters, using night-vision goggles and armed with navigation instruments to aid VLF (very low frequency) transmissions. This was the first night civilian IFR slinging operation done in Canada.

Meanwhile, another Calgary company, Dome Petroleum, was becoming active in the Beaufort Sea and needed to learn about ice movement, structure, engineering and physics. Pete was hired by Gordon Harrison, a vice-president of Dome Petroleum in their ice research department, and was specifically employed by CANMAR (Canadian Marine Drilling) operating out of Tuktoyaktuk. He worked with this company for almost four years, providing logistic support for their ice research work.

There was very little restriction on expenditure during those halcyon days, and Pete had helicopters, airplanes, machinery and crews working for him. "I had a wonderful, wonderful time at Dome."

The night of March 18, 1982, stands out in Pete Jess's life. Tim Parsons, a flight service station manager at Tuktoyaktuk, became concerned when a JetRanger helicopter, owned by Quasar Helicopters and working on the Polar Shelf project, had not returned to base. When an aircraft flying over the same route reported picking up an emergency signal, he alerted a crew to the need to mount a rescue mission.

Pete Jess, Dome Petroleum's senior field technician, two Dome pilots, captains Bill Kipke and Marty Voss, nurse Wynne Dobbs and Tim Parsons set out at 9:00 p.m. in heavy snow and the pitch darkness of an Arctic night. Because the Dome helicopter had no direction finder, Pete used a hand-held model. They had to touch down several times so he could walk away from the helicopter to gain an accurate reading. They eventually found the downed helicopter 120 km northeast of Tuk. The Calgary *Herald* (March 14, 1984) reported the scene that greeted the rescuers:

> *They found the pilot, Lloyd Cummings, sitting on a sleeping bag in the snow. He didn't even turn to look at his rescuers as they approached. Cummings was close to death, with frostbite and broken legs. When he had regained consciousness after the crash he had*

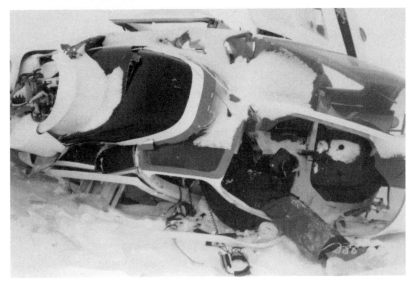

March 18, 1982, JetRanger helicopter, "presumed missing" near Tuktoyaktuk. Found crashed on Beaufort Sea ice. Dome rescue crew was awarded Certificates of Bravery & Letters of Commendation signed by Transport Minister Lloyd Axworthy. (Photo: Jess collection)

managed to struggle out of the helicopter, but his hands were too cold to open his sleeping bag so he had sat there, helpless, for up to five hours. He was put on a stretcher and flown back to base.

Engineer Bill Andrechuk was nowhere to be seen. He had wandered off in a daze and later dug himself into a hole in the snow for the night. He was rescued by another [Dome] helicopter the following day as he tried to return to the scene of the crash, followed by three Arctic wolves.

Two years later, the six people responsible for the rescue of Cummings and Andrechuk were awarded certificates of bravery and letters of commendation signed by federal Transport Minister Lloyd Axworthy. The Dome company's newsletter praised the work of all six: "Search and rescue is dramatic enough anytime, but Bill and Marty and their superb ability were brought to focus because of the extremely bad weather. The success of the rescue depended a great deal on Peter's constant manning of the locator, and Wynne's emergency medical training and Arctic expertise." Tim Parsons, then on a six-month assignment in Tuktoyaktuk from his usual employment at Calgary International Airport, was also highly praised for his heroism and quick action on that grim night.

That same year, Pete was flying a Kenting-chartered Aerospatiale Twin Star helicopter for Dome Petroleum. One night, while flying from Tuktoyaktuk base to McKinley Bay on the Tuk peninsula at 1000 feet altitude with copilot Andy Andruluk, the aircraft suddenly yawed, hard, in cruise flight. Andy had been dozing but he came awake with a start. "Don't do that again!" he grumbled. Pete's voice was quiet. "I didn't do anything." It came again, a sudden jerk. "Don't try to scare me," Andy said, his voice now carrying a tremor. Pete immediately put the aircraft into auto-rotation and turned the controls over to Andy who made a very soft run-on landing on the ice.

When the rotor blades stopped turning they got out to discover the vertical stabilizer on the aircraft tail had broken off. It was hanging by the wire that sends power to the strobe light on the top of the tail. "We counted ourselves lucky because if this piece had departed the aircraft in flight, the results probably would have been disastrous," Pete says. It was another time that Lady Luck smiled on Northern pilots.

The Breadalbane Project

In 1982, Joe MacInnis, a Canadian medical doctor who specialized in underwater (diving) medicine, approached Dome Petroleum for support, announcing his discovery of what he believed to be the world's most northerly known shipwreck. *The Breadalbane* was a supply ship that had been sent by Queen Victoria to search for the lost Franklin Expedition, and it had sunk in August 1853, in a storm off Beechey Island. There had been no loss of life. When the boat became caught and crushed in the ice, everybody had disembarked and taken refuge for the winter on a sister ship. *The Breadalbane*, MacInnis said, was a perfectly preserved shipwreck, with everything intact but sails and ropes.

"Dr. MacInnis was gathering support to do a dive on the shipwreck for *National Geographic* magazine," Pete recalls. "Dome's way of supporting the project was to give him the services of me and my department, for a year."

There, Pete saw underwater robots in use for the first time. The concept of using them fascinated Pete, and his first reaction was, "I could build one of those!"

"My scientist friends at Dome had for years struggled to observe things under the ice," Pete recalls, "and they always had to bring in Phil Nuytten's diving crews from Vancouver and great huge planeloads of stuff, and make holes in the ice and all the rest

Phil Nuytten emerging from submersible after his first dive on the Breadalbane (April 1983). (Photo: Jess collection)

of it. So I was just fascinated by this underwater robot system. The robot was supplied by a company in the States, and the technician, Martin Bowen, had come up to service it. With me being a helicopter pilot and him being a robot technician, we both actually 'flew' this robot on the shipwreck for the movie."

Pete explains that a robot is "flown" from a surface position. The operator views objects below the surface through a television screen, and uses a joystick, similar to that of a helicopter, to move the robot around – which in this case was 350 feet below surface, connected by a cable. The robot could be made to travel in various directions, pick things up, take pictures, and perform a number of tasks. Similar operations were shown in the 1997 film, *Titanic*.[2]

The robot used on the *Breadalbane* project was huge, "the size of a Lazy-Boy chair," causing Pete to think, "That's too big. We've got to have something we can put down through a little hole in the ice." Back at Dome, Pete could talk of nothing but underwater robots. They were, he stated to everyone who would listen, the new technology.

Meanwhile, on the home front, Judy had continued teaching school until the children were born, and had become used to saying bye-bye to her husband whenever the job called for him to travel North. Sometimes he'd be away for a few days, or even from two to six weeks. Their sons Matthew and Ted were born in 1981 and 1984, respectively.

Jessco Logistics Ltd. and Sea Scan Technology

At the beginning of 1984, the winds of change came whipping through Dome Petroleum, and Pete began to think about going on his own, in the Arctic.

"I was really keen on building these robots even though I didn't know how I was going to do it," he says, "but Judy and I sat down and figured out financially where we were. Then I approached the company about early retirement and 'took the package.' I cashed in my shares and started Jessco Logistics Ltd., an Arctic supply, logistics and service company for expeditions and that sort of thing.

The new company started with "a shingle in Resolute," which is a very expensive place to operate. Then they advertised the company's services in Calgary and things began to happen.

At the same time, Pete and Judy started a company called Sea Scan Technology, for the purpose of designing and building the world's smallest remotely-controlled underwater robots. The company was relatively successful, designing, building and selling 32 robots, but "went under" when a new partner was prosecuted for some funds that went missing.

Jessco Logistics was still operating, however, so Pete and Judy decided to take their work North. What they really wanted to do was build a lodge. In 1991 they applied to lease some property through the federal government's Land Lease Process at Cunningham Inlet where Pete had first seen the beluga whales.

"We had no idea that Nunavut Territory [comprising the eastern Arctic] was about to be formed, and that there was a cut-off deadline where all leases and everything else would be frozen until Nunavut settlement negotiations were over and the territory formed in 1999," Pete says. "We put our application in at the end of June and they cut it off in July. There were people who thought we had insider knowledge, but we did not. We'd poked around all spring, thinking we had all kinds of time, then put in the application and started the process.

"To make a long story short, we ended up with a 30-year renewable federal crown lease on Cunningham Inlet for our lodge, which we own today. It's on the northern shore of Somerset Island, 50 miles south of Resolute Bay in the newly-created territory of Nunavut."

Arctic Watch

Arctic Watch was advertised as "an adventure for the mind, a journey for the soul."[3] Tours would expose visitors to the sights of 2000 migrating beluga whales, spectacular wildlife (musk ox, belugas and narwhals, polar bears, seals and Arctic foxes), as well as 375 000 birds of every hue and description found at the world's most northerly bird sanctuary on Prince Leopold Island. Tourists could also view graves of sailors on lonely Beechey Island who had been caught in the ill-fated Franklin Expedition of 1845-47 during their search for the Northwest Passage. They could come to know ancient Thule and Inuit cultures, and basically enjoy unforgettable Arctic experiences. The company emphasized its dedication to the preservation and conservation of the Arctic's natural and human history.

The first summer, Judy and Pete spent two weeks camping on the beach in tents, and planning the logistics of providing room and board for their visitors. Judy fell in love with the place, and personally chose the spot for the Arctic Watch lodge.

The next year, 1992, Pete went up in early June to supervise the movement of goods for their camp, which arrived in Resolute in two Boeing 727s and one Hercules. Then he chartered a Twin Otter from Kenn Borek Air, piloted by Bill Leschasin, to transport these supplies from Resolute to the Arctic Watch beach camp at Cunningham Inlet. During the first week the work necessitated 60 round trips.

"We ended up with a giant pile of stuff on the beach," Pete says. "If you can imagine two 727s and a Herc load in one pile, that's what we had. We were also helped by two Calgary businesses, Sprung Instant Structures Ltd., who constructs the buildings we use, and Kenn Borek Air Ltd., who very kindly helped us by deferring the cost of renting the airplanes."

Jess family in the summer of 1996. Kenn Borek Air Twin Otter at Arctic Watch, Somerset Island. (Photo: Jess collection)

By that summer, Arctic Watch lodge consisted of 26 Sprung buildings (constructed from aluminum I-beams and a translucent composite skin) including little cabins called Qarmaks and a main building that could accommodate 50 people. It was not necessary to have lighting, as the lodge would be open only during the summer when there was 24-hour daylight in the Arctic.

Tours were booked to accommodate scientific studies, hiking trips and whale watching, with Matt and Ted acting as guides. "We also hired four to six Inuit students from Resolute for the summer because there's work beforehand, building up to when tourists arrive, then after they leave in shutting it down.

"We didn't use boats at the lodge because the whales come into the inlet with their babies, and are very sensitive to any disturbance in the water. You can stand on the gravel bars and watch them swim in extremely shallow water, from as close as three feet away," Pete says. "They bring their babies with them into the fresh water estuary, the Cunningham River, and they squeak and pop, and roll in the gravel and molt their skin right in front of you."

Pete and Judy had aspirations of building up a bigger tourism operation, as Jessco, the supply, logistics and service company, was still doing well. Then they were approached by some people who expressed interest in becoming partners to help build up Arctic Watch. "In a nutshell, the partnership was not a success," Pete states flatly.

Then the ever-ready smile returns to his face as he looks forward, rather than back. "The good news is that Judy and I still have the land and we built a new facility in Resolute Bay, from where we'll be supporting new activities at Arctic Watch."

Deep Expeditions

Pete Jess's enthusiasm is contagious. "You're going to see some incredible things in the next few years, really exciting," he says. "My friend Phil Nuytten and I have put together a company called Deep Expeditions. He just finished building the second of two brand-new manned submersibles. And starting in February 2000, our first location is the *Breadalbane* shipwreck that he and I did together so long ago!"

Do the adventures ever end? Not likely, and to say that the moon's the limit is to put a restrictive parameter on Pete Jess's ideas.

The plans hold excitement for Jessco Logistics and the entire Jess family, as it is scheduled that both Matt and Ted will be trained as submarine pilots. Matt, at 17, took training for a private pilot's licence in preparation for qualifying for a commercial flying licence as soon as he reaches 18. Matt states that he is "very, very, aware of safety." Pete and Judy couldn't be happier when they hear those words.

Ted will follow the same pattern if he's interested. Then they can both go for their submariner's tickets, and be aircraft as well as submarine pilots.

"What I'm trying to do for them is expand their horizons," Pete says. "They've been exposed to incredible mechanical-aviation-marine situations. By the time they're finished university, my biggest ambition is for them to be able to do whatever they choose and be happy. They'll have a fairly varied menu to choose from."

Pete looks back on his own childhood, and his current efforts to be a role-model dad. He admits that his own father still finds his accomplishments hard to understand.

His brothers and sisters, however, think it's terrific.

"I just set out to do interesting things, because I love people and I love machinery, and I love the combination of both."

Pete readily acknowledges that Judy is "the key to the whole thing."

"I could never have done this without Judy's support," he says. "We laugh about it sometimes, and say, 'Could we ever have imagined that we'd do the things that we've done together, and with the two young men who are our sons?' No, we never could have, and it just gets better."

Footnotes

[1]Two of Pete's brothers also fly. "John is a successful and highly-regarded contract helicopter pilot who specializes in long-lining and high-altitude slinging, setting steel and pulling logs off mountains," Pete says. "He's got probably 20 000 hours. He lives in Whistler, flies heli-skiing and logging, and does special steel-setting jobs. Companies hire him to put air conditioners and satellite dishes on top of tall buildings and that sort of thing.

"My other brother, Jim, flies out of Saskatoon for Points North."

A third brother, Bob, is in business in Calgary.

Pete's two sisters, Kerry and Wendy, are involved in environmental occupations.

[2]The *Titanic*, a British steamer of the White Star line, struck an iceberg and sunk the night of April 14-15, 1912, about 1600 miles northeast of New York City. Of the 2200 passengers, only 705 survived. A blockbuster film was released in 1997 depicting the incident, and using a robot, "Jason Jr.," to investigate the wreck.

Pete explains that, "The technician on the *Breadalbane* project, Martin Bowen, was also Jason Jr.'s pilot. He flew Jason inside the *Titanic* when they discovered it. He has flown it inside the *Bismarck* [a German battleship sunk by the British on May 26, 1941, about 400 miles off the coast of France], and on the *Lusitania* [a passenger ship of the Cunard Line that sank off the coast of Ireland on May 7, 1915, after it was torpedoed by a German submarine. 1198 lives were lost of the 1924 persons aboard, and the incident propelled the U.S. into WWI]."

[3]Some of the videos produced about the Beluga Whales of the Arctic, and Arctic Watch, include:

A 47-minute video, "Symphony in the Shallows – the Beluga Whales of the High Arctic", (Carey-Mac Productions), featuring the work of scientists David St. Aubin and Thomas Smith.

A 54-minute video, "Arctic Kingdom - Life at the Edge," produced by National Geographic Television, April, 1995, which opens with the approach of a big polar bear, and a poetic introduction: "The sun's rays touch the ice and like a living thing, [the Arctic] responds. As the ice surrenders to the rising sun it becomes a world in motion, full of danger, and drama"

A 52-minute video, "Arctic Watch - Whale Tagging," which has been produced as a pilot for a television series.

"TAKE A LOOK IN THE BACK ... I THINK OUR LOADS SHIFTED."

The Flying Physician

William Bernard, MD, learned to fly upon his return from US Army service in 1947. In 1998, at 85 years of age, he began his 52nd year as a licensed pilot. He continues to fly his Cessna 210-E purchased in 1966, and is proud to be a charter member of The Flying Physicians Association.

The Early Years

William Reisch Bernard was born in Springfield, Illinois, USA., on March 16, 1913. His father was a physician, and established the path that his son decided to follow. In the fall of 1931, William entered the University of Notre Dame, Indiana, where he graduated with honors in 1935 with a Bachelor of Science degree in Pre-Med. His medical degree was obtained in 1939 from Washington University, St. Louis, Missouri. Post graduate work followed in St. Louis at De Paul and St. Louis Maternity hospitals, where he specialized in obstetrics and family medicine. But just prior to commencing a residency in obstetrics and gynecology he was asked to come home and act as *locum tenens* for his father, who had become ill.

Before he could return to his promised residency, the United States entered the war following the Japanese attack on Pearl Harbor on December 7, 1941, and William entered military service as a physician in the US Army. There his new degree was put to work as "Battalion Surgeon," working as obstetrician, surgeon, and anesthetist for military personnel and their families, and later with German prisoners of war.

Dr. Bernard was discharged from the army after four years of service, in February 1946, with the rank of Captain of the Medical Corps.

"I arrived home to my parents' house in Springfield with a wife and three-month-old baby son, and a massive debt," he says. He set about rebuilding a practice with his father and a year later the young family moved into their own home.

The Urge to Fly

In June 1947, Dr. Bernard's younger brother Jack told him that he might qualify for help with further education. "Why don't you come with me and learn to fly?" he asked. "You're eligible under the US Veterans' Bill of Rights!"

Dr. Bernard thus began his flight training June 30, 1947, and received his private pilot's licence on August 21st.

"Most of my training took place at a very small field with a runway maximum length of 1800 feet," he recalls. "All my preliminary training up to and including solo and cross-country was done on a Luscombe. After about 20 hours I was signed off to fly a Piper J3 Cub and also a PA-19. After receiving my private licence I was permitted to fly several of the former military trainers, including the Ryan PT [Primary Trainer] 22, the Boeing Stearman PT 26 and the BT 13."

His first forced landing occurred on his second solo flight when the engine ceased on takeoff from lack of oil. "The mechanic who'd changed the oil just before I flew the Luscombe had forgotten to 'safety' the nut from the oil pan," Dr. Bernard says. "It loosened and all four quarts of oil drained out during taxi and run-up. I was just about ready to turn cross-wind when the engine quit. I landed straight ahead in a cornfield with minor damage to the plane and none to me." Shortly after he received his private pilot's licence, the school and airfield he'd been using was forced to close.

Soon another school opened with Cessna 120s and 140s as training planes. He acquired his commercial certificate October 1, 1949, multi-engine rating in 1952, instrument in 1959, and seaplane in 1960.

In the early 1950s, Dr. Bernard bought one of the first Cessna 170-B aircraft ever made, which he flew for 200 hours before upgrading to one of the first Cessna 180s sold in Illinois. "I gained considerable cross-country experience in this airplane, traveling as far west as Wyoming, north to Minneapolis, east to Dayton, Ohio, and south to several points in Florida," he says. A Cessna 195 with a 330 h.p. Jacobs engine was purchased next, which he used to commute between central Michigan and Springfield, but his children didn't like it because they couldn't see out the windows.

The Flying Physician

In June 1954, Dr. Bernard became a charter member of The Flying Physicians Association (FPA). Its formation was first discussed at the 1954 Philadelphia Jaycee Transcontinental Air Race, and the first meeting held June 5, 1955, during the American Medical Association's annual convention. Dr. H.D. Vickers of Little Falls, New York, was elected president.

In October 1955, the association was incorporated under the laws of New York state as a not-for-profit society to promote safety, education and science-oriented research and human interest projects related to aviation.[1]

Soon there were 795 members from across the USA., and now members are represented from 17 different countries of the world, including Canada. They have no formal contact with any other medical group. Even though at times the FPA might be confused with Australia's "Flying Doctors," the difference is that in the Australian organization the doctors are not pilots, but accompany pilots to make emergency medical calls.

In the early 1950s, the Illinois Department of Aeronautics had noticed that very few Fixed Base Operations (FBOs) were offering ground school along with their flight training programs. As well, there was a scarcity of qualified instructors. They began to offer a free ground school. Some of the questions asked on the Federal Aviation Agency's written exam pertained to health, so Dr. Bernard was invited to participate and deliver health-oriented lectures. He did this for 10 years, travelling to various parts of the state on a weekly basis.

"While it was not the original intent of the department to aid in the advancement of more than student pilots, these ground school classes actually gave a goodly portion of the information needed for both the commercial and instrument ratings," Dr. Bernard says. "As soon as the FBOs found out they could make money doing this, they forced the closure of this type of instruction and so I lost my job. I was still invited, however, to partake in some of the annual safety courses given by both the state and federal departments of transportation."

Welcoming Alaska to the Union

The idea for the Flying Physicians to undertake a "massive civil defence exercise" was instigated in 1959 by then-executive secretary, Mark Degroff, a manufacturer of medical equipment for physical therapy in Tulsa, Oklahoma, and owner of an early twin-engine Cessna 310. He sent out queries to all members, advertised the idea in medical journals and received a positive response.

On June 14, 1959, 78 aircraft carrying 210 occupants signed up to fly north to Alaska from the "lower 48." Their purpose was to welcome the 49th state, which had become part of the United States of America on January 3, 1959, by a proclamation issued by US President Dwight D. Eisenhower. Alaska was the first new state to join the Union in 47 years, and the only state separated from the continental US by another country. (Hawaii became the 50th state on August 21, 1959). Another reason for the trip was to test the feasibility of transporting large numbers of people safely over vast distances in light aircraft.

Accompanying Dr. William Bernard was his wife and another couple, flying in his 1956 Cessna 182 (purchased after trading in the Cessna 195), along with the restricted amount of 40 pounds of luggage. Their "survival gear" included two Ford Motor Company-supplied disposable tents, four disposable sleeping bags, a rifle and a shotgun, ammunition, fishing gear, subsistence gear and extra water.

"My 182 was a little better equipped than most of the single-engine light planes at that time," Dr. Bernard says. "Instrument rating was still an uncommon achievement. I had two Narco [National Radio Company] radios, with both voice communication and navigation. Each radio had 12 frequencies divided into two groups. There were only about 24 frequencies at that time, so I was covered."

"I also had an ADF [Automatic Direction Finder] with both the needle and the oncourse tone abilities. These were the days of A&N radio ranges; ADF was used to follow original A&N courses and could 'home in' on a radio station. This was a great aid in both Canada and Alaska, since there was not the volume of VORs [very high frequency omni range] that are present today."

The group rendezvoused in Great Falls, Montana, on June 14, 1959, for an inspection of all aircraft by the then-Civil Aeronautics Administration (CAA - now absorbed by the Federal Aviation Agency - FAA) and the military, and a briefing on the proposed flight north. For fun, it was decided to hold a handicapped efficiency race to Edmonton using total elapsed time, with fuel stops and customs clearance in Calgary.

"Winds and weather were thoroughly investigated, with special attention paid to winds aloft," Dr. Bernard recalls. "My copilot was a World War Two B-24 bomber captain and he suggested we stay as low as possible, enjoy the bumps and not sacrifice a lot of ground speed for smooth ride. We took off in eighth position and eventually landed in Edmonton five minutes ahead of the others, including those in the Cessna 310 and the Bonanzas which were considerably faster." They won the $500 pot.

A stay-over in Edmonton prepared them for the trek North, where they received briefings from the Canadian Department of Transport and the military. From Edmonton they would be landing at Grande Prairie, Alberta, and at airstrips along the old Northwest Staging Route that paralleled the Alaska Highway: Fort St. John and Fort Nelson, BC, Watson Lake and Whitehorse, Yukon, to their destination of Anchorage, Alaska.

"We were cautioned to follow the Alaska Highway, and were told that one of the Department of Transport's DC-3s would monitor our progress, but would attempt no searches 10 miles either side of the highway. Therefore we were limited to a very narrow corridor."

Because none of the aircraft was equipped with long-range tanks, their maximum range was four hours. To be on the safe side, they were instructed to land every three-and-one-half hours.

Dense fog at Edmonton delayed departure for several days. "Many of us started our tour toward Dawson Creek and Fort St. John, but were forced to return to await another day. During this time an interesting and humorous event occurred that could have been tragic."

One of the tour members from southeastern Illinois had his private pilot's licence for one week and his new Piper Tripacer for only two days when he left for the trip. "He apparently had no real problems until leaving Edmonton," Dr. Bernard says. "There we were all assigned a 'buddy' to fly with so that in the event of an accident or incident, help could be almost instantaneous.

"Our illustrious Tripacer pilot became separated from his buddy, found he could not make it to Fort St. John, and began to return to Edmonton. He was unfamiliar with radius of action, and as a result spent considerably longer on the outbound flight than he should have. As we approached Edmonton on our return and came in contact with approach Control, and with fuel not really critical but low, we heard Tripacer 4433 Charley also on the frequency."

The pilot declared that he was lost, about out of fuel, and needed help. He did not know for sure but thought he was somewhere north of Edmonton.

"Suddenly he announced that he *was* out of fuel, the engine had stopped, and he was going to land on the runway in front of him! Approach told us to stand clear while they spent some time trying to contact the Tripacer. Finally the Controller became very upset and in no uncertain terms said, '33 Charley, where the hell are you?'" No answer.

"By now our fuel was lower so we were permitted to land. Unbeknown to us, 33 Charley was safely on the ground, without damage or injury, at what was then a very secret military airport," Dr. Bernard says. "He reported being met by three Jeep-loads of heavily-armed guards. They were very demanding, and refused to permit him to be towed from the runway. Finally they gave him enough fuel to get to Edmonton airport, pointed him in the right direction, and forced him to depart on the runway remaining, which was obviously adequate."

In November 1954, Canada and the US had agreed to the construction of a Distant Early Warning (DEW) Line along the Arctic coast from Alaska to Baffin Island. This early warning radar line helped to solve the common problem of North American air defence, and was completed in 1957. But its inauguration required flight plans that would reflect at most a 15-minute difference between estimated and actual arrival, to be made from the ground prior to anyone entering the area. As a result, the group was required to make their first stop at Fort St. John, re-file, and give as accurate an estimate as possible.

"One of the Bonanzas was flying very low coming in to Fort St. John," Dr. Bernard recalls. "He flew below the tops of two groups of trees and failed to see a wire in his path. He carried the wire with him to the landing, and discovered he had destroyed all the telephone communication for several hundred miles, besides badly lacerating his propeller spinner and putting some serious nicks in one blade."

An engineer in Fort St. John did an inspection, used tin-snips and a file to clean the damaged spinner, then carefully measured the deep gouge in the propeller blade. He smoothed it out and, taking another measurement, filed a similar notch in the other blade.

"He accepted his fee and signed off the aircraft as airworthy," Dr. Bernard says. "The pilot continued the trip with no more problem than increased noise and the requirement to keep the cowl flaps open to avoid heating the engine. But when he arrived back in Great Falls after our trip, the CAA immediately grounded the plane until the new spinner and propeller could be procured!"

The next leg of the trip took them to Fort Nelson. "This, too, was a military base that could now be used by civilian aircraft, but our arrival was a surprise. The hotel we were assigned to had burned to the ground the day before, so there were no real facilities to house us. The military came through with cots and blankets and bedded us down on the hangar floor. Not plush, but adequate." The townspeople came out with a potluck supper and also supplied breakfast to see their visitors off to their next stop at Watson Lake, Yukon.

Near Watson Lake, one of the Cessna 170s experienced engine failure because of carburetor ice. The pilot made the required forced landing but in so doing stalled 10 feet up. "The plane landed rather firmly to say the least, and crimped the fuselage badly enough so that the elevator and rudder would not work properly." In due time, help arrived. The engineer shortened the elevator and rudder cables, again with an airworthy pronouncement, and sent the somewhat disgruntled 'flying physician' on his way. "Finding that the plane flew reasonably well and he had full control, he too continued the trip, only to be grounded for very major repairs on landing back at Great Falls."

On leaving Watson Lake for Whitehorse, they followed the Alaska Highway and its adjoining river, to pass over a required reporting point of Teslin. "Reporting in, the lonesome communicator invited us to stop for coffee. We landed at a gravel strip nearby, walked to his office, had a very enjoyable visit, then off to Whitehorse."

On leaving Teslin, the station manager suggested that they follow the Teslin river canyon which paralleled the highway rather than the highway itself. "He said that the canyon was wide, unencumbered by obstruction, and that we should stay low so we could see some of the animals in the area. This was perhaps the most beautiful and exciting portion of the trip."

They knew they were getting close to Whitehorse when they could hear the tower communicator clearly, but they could not find the field. "He suggested we turn on our landing lights so he could spot us. We did, and he informed us we were about two miles on final, and to climb until we could see the runway. This was the first and the last time that I've ever climbed rather than descended for landing!"

They spent a couple of days in Whitehorse, taking side trips to Skagway and back on the narrow gauge railway, and also purchased a case of "medicinal whiskey for snakebite." While there, the group took time to discuss the country over which they'd flown, and agreed that "the trip from Fort St. John to Whitehorse contained some of the most beautiful and desolate country we had ever seen. We were always below the tops of the mountains. Our VHF communication was line of sight, so, of necessity, we had to be fairly close to whoever was to receive our communication."

At Northway, the entrance to Alaska, they were told that the airstrip, used during the war as a transfer point for Lend Lease aircraft being flown from the USA to Russia, was supposedly paved with gold-bearing ore. Not so exciting was the American Customs officials, "much more difficult than the very pleasant Canadian Customs people had been." At first, the officers were not going to permit them to bring in their "medicinal spirits," but the doctors insisted it was for personal use so were finally allowed to bring it along "for a small fee – on top of the much larger fee we were charged for the privilege of re-entering the US."

Their route from Northway was to be direct to Anchorage, but they decided to divert to Fairbanks. "We were somewhat lucky in doing this," Dr. Bernard reports. "There were a lot of forest fires around and visibility forward was almost nil. The controller was stationed at the military base at the time, and he had radar. After a few preliminaries he was able to vector us directly to the Fairbanks airport.

"Fairbanks then was a relatively small town with very few paved streets, no public transportation or traffic signals, many non-plumbed toilet facilities, and a huge population of sled dogs. We wandered around and saw most of the town that night."

The next afternoon the group was off to Anchorage, where they spent five days. "One of the people we met there was bush pilot Bob Reeve. Among the aircraft he owned and used at that time was an old, former military DC-6, which had been configured to hold about 60 people. A group of us chartered this aircraft with its crew for an all-day flight from Anchorage to Nome and to Kotzebue, with part of the flight bordering the Russian Diomede Island."

They found Nome to be even smaller and more primitive than Fairbanks, with buildings constructed on pilings driven into the ice, a sight "most unusual to us from the lower 48." There, they watched the first unloading that year of a freighter in the harbor.

At Kotzebue they were welcomed by the native Indian and Eskimo (Inuit) population. Although the passengers were treated well, they soon discovered that their crew was being ignored. "Wien Airways was operative in this area and Reeve's aircraft were not always welcome," Dr. Bernard says. "It wasn't until after we began the trip back to Anchorage that we were informed why the crew did not leave the airplane. Also, fuel was refused but since the captain had refueled at Nome, there was adequate to return to Anchorage."[2]

During the Flying Physicians' trip back from their tour of Alaska with Reeve they viewed, while airborne, both the setting and the rising of the sun and also flew around Mount McKinley, the highest peak in the United States at 20320 feet above sea level.

The day before the Flying Physicians started for home in their own aircraft, the DC-6 in which they'd toured, along with its crew, was lost in the Aleutians (Bob Reeve was not on board). The shock and sadness of the accident was the only negative memory of a wonderful trip.

"We had been well received by all communities we visited," Dr. Bernard recalls, "and everyone marveled at the fact that so many planes could safely fly such distances with so many people. We definitely proved to the Civil Defence executives that the feasibility of such an endeavor was for real." Also while there, the group had met with local physicians and visited several hospitals, exchanging notes.

Of the people who flew on that first trip in 1959, just four remain active in FPA. "Some have dropped membership, but many have passed to their reward," Dr. Bernard says.

Can Doctors Fly?

Several years ago, one of the associated medical officers for the Federal Aviation Agency (FAA) wrote a much-discussed article about the general lack of safety of flying physicians. Dr. Bernard refutes that statement. "It has since been proven that our safety record is actually no worse, but may also be slightly better, than other groups of studied pilots, i.e., lawyers, accountants, morticians, etc.," he says. "However, I do know that many physicians have much more on their minds than just flying the airplane."

Is there a definitive difference in personalities of those who become doctors and those who become pilots? And do doctors, with their typically 'Type A' high-achiever personalities, make conscientious pilots?

Dr. Douglas W. Johnson, chief of Radiation Oncology at Baptist Regional Cancer Institute in Jacksonville, Florida, and also a Colonel in the US Air Force reserves, refers to this question on his website.[3] He states that, "In fact, personality and achievement profiles as measured by the Armstrong USAF Aeronautical Laboratory in San Antonio have found that pilots and physicians are virtually indistinguishable. Perhaps this is why physicians fly – they get the same sense of satisfaction from a flight well performed as from a surgical procedure well executed or a diagnosis accurately made."

Dr. Johnson goes on to say, however, that at one time accident statistics did reveal that a number of physicians were becoming involved in aircraft accidents due to over-confidence, inadequate training, lack of time to take special courses such as instrument rating, purchasing too complex an aircraft for the pilot's skill level and determination to get to a destination whatever the weather conditions.

The FPA has therefore emphasized safety, education and research projects in aviation to offset these disturbing statistics. It offers check-ride programs in which qualified members ride with others less qualified to monitor their techniques and to help increase others' aviation knowledge. This mandate was followed by the FPA when developing courses, using volunteer lecturers, in subjects such as aviation physiology, crash survivability with shoulder harness installation, survival kit organization and proper flight training.

During the "Cold War" era of the 1960s, the FPA also developed an Emergency Mobilization Plan to complement the programs of the military, Civil Air Patrol and Red Cross. An aerial medical armada was formed consisting of up to 1500 airplanes and medical personnel who were prepared to fly into remote strips in case of disasters.

Humanitarian efforts also rate high on the list of FPA goals, with tours of duty organized to bring medical services to needy areas in various countries.

"... the FPA embodies what we as physicians value most," states Dr. Johnson on his website, "service to community, promotion of health and safety of the community and of ourselves, the sanctity of the individual, the celebration of a challenge well met and the collegiality of those willing to take the less-travelled road."

Dr. Bernard's Personal Path

Dr. William Bernard continued to build his general family practice, periodically updating his knowledge with graduate courses. In total, he spent 55 years in solo general and family practice, and was the last physician on his hospital staff to have privileges in all branches of medicine but nose and throat. During his career, he delivered nearly 5000 babies, performed most of his own surgery, assisted in neuro- and thoracic surgery, cared for tubercular mothers, and was one of the first doctors in the area to use Tomoxifan in the experimental treatment of breast cancer – as well as one of the last doctors to make house calls.

He also intensely loved flying. Once, the Cessna 182 blew an engine shortly after its annual check, resulting in Dr. Bernard making a forced landing with two of his children as passengers.

"The spot for landing was not perfect and the plane struck a ditch, tore off the nose gear and went over on its back and was destroyed," he says. "None of us received more than very minor injuries." The accident did not have negative effects on his boys, however, as both became pilots. Robert is a captain with Northwest Airlines and William Jr.

The flying Bernard family: left to right, Dad, Bill Jr., Robert, Patricia (all pilots), 1975. (Photo: Bernard collection)

flies a home-built Mustang 2. Dr. Bernard's daughter Patricia also got a private pilot's licence at age 17.

Soon after the crash of the 182, Dr. Bernard purchased a 1959 Cessna Skylane, followed by a Cessna 205 and finally a Cessna 210-E, which he still owns. During the 32 years he has owned this aircraft he has flown it over 4000 hours, covering 45 of the lower 48 states, Alaska, Canada and the Caribbean. "After almost 51 years of flying I've accumulated over 7000 hours of fun flying with about 1000 hours of actual instrument besides all of the simulated," he states proudly. "Cross-country time exceeds 5000 hours. For someone who has never been employed in aviation, I think this is quite a record."

Following that seminal trip to Alaska, Dr. Bernard has flown North six times. Once, instead of following the highway, the Flying Physicians flew straight north to Inuvik, then on to the Arctic Ocean, and followed the coastline to Windy Pass down to Fairbanks, passing through several time zones (there is a time zone change between Fairbanks and Anchorage). Dr. Bernard has flown, in his Cessna 182 and then in the 210-E, on each of The Flying Physicians' 10-year anniversary cruises: 1969 (10th), 1979 (20th) and 1989 (30th). Each trip has covered more than 5000 miles and just over 50 hours flying time.

Dr. Bernard in Whitehorse, sometime in the 1980s. (Photo: Bernard collection)

"On the 20th anniversary trip about 44 hours was IFR," he says. "It was the most difficult and probably the poorest for sightseeing. One year we flew following a rather lengthy period of serious forest fires, many of which were still burning."

He plans to follow that record with the 40th anniversary trip in 1999 to Victoria, BC, at "a young 86" years of age.

"I'm still current and capable on instruments, and will continue to take my annual refresher courses," Dr. Bernard vows, "so I should not have much trouble."

In 1960, at the request of the FAA Surgeon General, Dr. Bernard was accepted as an Aviation Medical Examiner (AME). In 1963 he became a senior AME, permitted to examine all classes of pilots and also to make some decisions on whether or not each person was physically fit to fly. He retired from this position in 1994.

During his aviation career, Dr. Bernard set some personal and professional records. He was the first native-born physician in Sangamon County, Illinois, to become not only a pilot with his own aircraft, but also to be rated ELS Mel Commercial, Instrument (single and multi-engines, and single engine sea). The honor did not come without some challenges.

"All the medical personnel here deemed me to be just a little bit odd, and some even thought I was crazy," he writes. "For about 18 years I was the only 'crazy' flying doctor in central Illinois. Now there are several, some with experience in the military and a couple who own and fly their own jet aircraft. No one calls us crazy anymore, and especially so when we are able to do things they can't, and go places in relative safety and in a relatively short time.

"At the time I learned to fly in 1947, it was not a popular hobby or occupation," he adds. "It was also considered dangerous, and most insurance companies would increase the premiums, especially for life, health and accident insurance. Some would not even sell insurance to you if they found out you were flying."

Dr. Bernard was one of three members of his college graduation class to learn to fly, and the only one to fly himself to 10 consecutive class reunions. He also was the first person at Notre Dame to pilot his own aircraft to his 60th reunion, bringing a member of the 50-year golden anniversary class – his younger brother – with him.

For many years he worked with the Division of Aeronautics' safety program discussing medical problems as they concerned "man, the machine and the environment." For this work he became the first physician in Illinois (and perhaps in the USA) to be inducted into the Illinois Aviation Hall of Fame.

He is also proud of his membership in the United Flying Octogenarians (UFOs), who have over 300 members in the USA, Canada and the UK. Dr. Bernard explains that the UFOs are a group of active pilots who have reached the age of 80. The organization is sponsored by the Aircraft Owners & Pilots Association (AOPA) and in 1998 the oldest active member was 99. "At 85, I'm one of the 'junior' members," Dr. Bernard states. The group has annual meetings in conjunction with AOPA, and publishes a monthly newsletter.

"Our president, John Smith, began flying in his teens and flew everything from Jennies to Jets before retiring as a United Airlines pilot. He is 90, and was one of the founders of the organization. He now lives in Poughkeepsie, New York, and flies a Bonanza and a pressurized Baron."

Bill and Ann Bernard, early spring 1997. Aircraft with present paint scheme and modifications done Feb. 1996. (Photo: Bernard collection)

The fact that Dr. Bernard himself was 85 years old in 1998 did not deter him from planning a number of special flights, including trips around the States, plus the Great Lakes FPA chapter meeting in Winnipeg, Manitoba, in September, and the AOPA convention in Palm Springs, California. And then there is the FPA meeting in Victoria, BC, in 1999, to be followed by a flight up the coast to Juneau and Anchorage, Alaska.

"At the time of this writing, April 17, 1998, I have just been released to fly by the eye surgeon who gave me two new eyes (cataract removal and lens replacement), and the vascular surgeon who repaired an injured and thrombosed artery in my left leg, both surgeries done in March 1998," Dr. Bernard writes. With his vision back to 20/20 on both sides, and "just a little gimpy" in one leg, he's doing fine.

While he has never used his membership with The Flying Physicians Association to directly benefit his medical practice, Dr. Bernard found it valuable as a source of medical information, which comprises a portion of all their meetings. It also helped him to become an Aviation Medical Examiner (AME), wherein he examined all three classes of pilots (Class I, private; Class II, commercial; Class III; airline) and to learn of the problems of those working in aviation. "I also gained much useful information for my own personal practice of medicine, especially when there was a discussion of new procedures or medications not generally available to most practices. For example, because of the material I was able to bring home from some of our meetings, our local hospital became the first in central Illinois to have telemetry [patient monitoring system]."

Over the years Dr. Bernard has served on the FPA's Board of Directors as president, secretary and chairman of various committees. He is past-president, and a charter and life member, of the FPA. His affiliation with the group has involved tours throughout the US and Canada as well as the Caribbean.

"Aviation and flying have been the most rewarding part of my life," Dr. Bernard writes. "Hopefully, I will be able to continue until 2003, which is the centennial anniversary of the Wright brothers' first controlled flight."

As the first draft of this story was being written in the summer of 1998, Dr. Bernard suffered a medical setback when he had to have his left leg amputated above the knee. "Needless to say, this has slowed him up a bit, but likely only temporarily," writes his son, William Jr. "He is already planning to fly his plane again, although it may not be until the first of the year."

Indeed, by 1999 Dr. Bernard was wearing a prosthesis and "getting along well using a cane to help in ambulation." And he began to take flying lessons all over again – just like when he first started back in 1947.

"I must learn to taxi, which is very difficult with one working leg," he writes. "I must alternate my right foot from the right to the left pedal. Later, I will learn the process of taking off and landing. Am looking forward to the challenge."

Considering the fact that he turned 86 years of age on March 16, 1999, and is bothered by osteo-arthritis in his knee and ankle, the challenge is quite understandable.

"I'm now awaiting permission from the US Federal Aviation Agency . . . to regain my pilot's licence, which I automatically lost because of my disability," Dr. Bernard continues. "I have 90 days from the date of the letter to accomplish this."

He signs off, anxious to continue his lessons, regain his licence, and fly off to the next reunion of the flying physicians.

Footnotes

[1]The objectives of The Flying Physicians Association read:
"As physicians, with knowledge in the effects of flying (physical, mental and emotional), we strive to increase safety and to preserve health by providing basic information through example and teaching to the medical profession, to aircrews, and to the public at large, influencing members of the medical profession to fly and to develop expertise in the effects of flying, which will result in better utilization of aircraft for emergency services, better cooperation with state and federal aviation agencies, better qualified aviation medical examiners, and more significant research."
(source: Flying Physicians Association, Inc., Box 677427, Orlando, Florida 32867, USA).

[2]According to Archie Satterfield's book, *The Alaska Airlines Story*, (Alaska Northwest Publishing Company, Anchorage, Alaska, 1981), Bob Reeve, founder of Reeve Aleutian Airways, had known Noel Wien and Nat Brown of Wien Airways for some time, when Reeve and Brown had flown in South America. They hadn't gotten along in South America, and they didn't like each other any better in Alaska. Unknowingly, the Flying Physicians had stepped into this tenuous situation.

They couldn't have hired a more daring and capable bush pilot than Bob Reeve, however. During World War Two, when other Alaskan airlines capitalized on the war to secure important contracts and charters, Reeve was able to grab a charter to serve the Aleutians, mainly because nobody else wanted it. According to Satterfield, "It was a place where few other pilots wanted to go under any circumstances, and certainly not on a regular basis. Reeve flew where no military pilots could go, and he did it every day" (p. 81). Reeve's career was capped by having one of the top records of flying hours in the North country, most of them flown under spectacular conditions. Bob Reeve was one of the outstanding old-time bush pilots, with an ability to "survive and flourish where others failed" (Satterfield, p. 43).

[3]Dr. Douglas W. Johnson is chief of Radiation Oncology at Baptist Regional Cancer Institute in Jacksonville, Florida, and also a Colonel in the US Air Force reserves. His website is: http://www.jaxmed.com/dcms/jax-medicine/october97/flyingphysicians.htm.
(Permission received from FPA to use logo.)

From Northern Snow to Kona Wind

Dawn Dawson's mother says that the first word her baby girl ever spoke was 'fly.' Dawn believes that to be true, for she wanted to be a pilot even before she went to school. "During the war, I built model airplanes and read magazines on flying. Even in grades four or five, when bored with the teacher, I'd draw Spitfires and Hurricanes."

Dawn Dawson was born in Penticton, BC, on February 25, 1932, and grew up in the southern Okanagan village of Osoyoos. Although airplanes weren't common to the dry, hilly area where the main economy was agriculture and fruit orchards, and neither her two sisters nor her brother expressed interest in aviation, Dawn longed to fly.

When she was 13, her mother drove Dawn and a girlfriend to the Okanogan area of Washington state where the girls went for their first airplane ride with a barnstormer. The die was cast.

Dawn got used to being considered an oddity. "Oh, yes," she laughs. "In grade 10 they sent everyone to see the guidance counselor. She'd say, 'You've got to know what you're going to be, and to program your schooling accordingly.' I kept telling her, 'I *know* what I'm going to be. A pilot.' But she had me take tests and concluded I should be a nurse."

Dawn studied geography through a correspondence course when she thought it might help her planned career. Then, she heard that McGill University in Montreal offered university courses that included a flying program. "Perfect," she thought, but her request to apply was denied. "Sorry, this program is for males only." It became obvious that her chosen path would be a rough one. Fine. She wouldn't go to university. She'd just "learn to fly."

The summer Dawn was to enter Grade 12, she and her mother travelled to Vancouver so Dawn could check out the flying schools. She struck her first positive response at Vancouver U-Fly. Sure, they'd teach her to fly, but when she announced she wanted to become a bush pilot the instructors gently suggested she start by going for a private pilot's licence.

"No, I don't want a private licence, I want a commercial licence!" she said determinedly.

She was finally persuaded to sign up initially for a private licence, but she made it known, very plainly, that it would be just a first step toward becoming a commercial pilot.

Dawn Dawson at Oliver, BC, airport, November, 1950. Logging time for her commercial licence in a Cessna 140. (Photo: Bartsh collection)

Learning to Fly

The Michaud brothers, Lloyd and Al, who ran Vancouver U-Fly, gave their new student all the encouragement she needed. "I couldn't have picked a better flying school," Dawn says. "They were very, very cooperative."

The Michauds were also practical. "They knew I couldn't be a bush pilot, that no one would hire a woman, so they geared their instruction to my becoming a flight instructor, although they didn't tell me that *per se*. But when I wanted to do my cross-country and my solo, instead of just going across to Vancouver Island we went through the mountains to Oliver and Penticton."

Dawn's lessons started the first of September 1950, and by November she had her private pilot's licence. To build time to begin her commercial, the Michauds let her use their Cessna 140 on less-busy days. At 18 years of age, she was blithely flying over the mountains to Penticton, Cranbrook or Kamloops – challenging areas with steep hills and winds.

She next joined a class of 10 students – as the only female – to take instruction for instrument rating. The other students had taken ground school together, but Dawn was put in with this group as she continued to pursue her commercial licence so all would start and finish instrument training at the same time. "You didn't *have* to have an instrument rating then but I wanted to take as many things as I could, because they had conveyed to me that I was maybe going to have a hard time getting a job."

One day the students were informed that Canadian Pacific Airlines (CPA) had plans to hire from this graduating class. On completion of their instrument training, the students were lined up to take their rides with Department of Transport (DOT) inspector Bill Lavery. One by one Lavery went up with each student. Then he came to Dawn.

"She's a girl!" he said, pointing at her. "Where is she ever going to use an instrument rating? Nobody's going to hire her! I'm not wasting my time." He turned and stamped into the office, with Dawn at his heels.

Dawn recalls Lavery as being a big, rough man who didn't mince words. "No way am I giving some *blankety-blank* girl a ride!" he said. The argument became so heated that Al Michaud motioned for Lavery to go out to the parking lot with him, where their words still carried. "You *have* to give her a ride," Michaud said. "She's a good student, and she's graduated like the rest." "Nobody tells me what to do," was the inspector's stubborn response.

Finally, Michaud won. Lavery came marching back to the office. "I'll take you up for a ride, but that doesn't say I have to *blankety-blank* pass you," he snarled to the young student. "Let's go."

Dawn clearly recalls her feelings of that moment. "Normally I don't get mad, but if I do, I get mad internally and don't show it. Fortunately he made me mad and that over-ruled my nervousness at taking the test. When we went up I was determined that whatever he told me, I was going to do – perfectly."

The test involved several categories, all under the hood: radio range, approaches, steep turns and stalls, both with full instrument panel and limited panel. The limited panel involved the use of primary instruments only, such as Turn-and-Bank Indicator (needle ball), Airspeed Indicator and Magnetic Compass, but nothing else – just the minimum aids to stay right-side-up.

Dawn took the DOT inspector through all the requisite steep turns and everything else he could think of. Then came his order to do the radio range and a let-down over the airport, with just needle ball and airspeed indicators as aids. Dawn made her first approach. "Hmmph, okay," was Lavery's comment. Following her second approach, Lavery turned to her. "That's not bad, you know." Then came the third, on which she landed. The red face was now on the inspector. "You've done very well," he admitted.

She taxied in and they disembarked. Lavery came around the airplane, put his arm around his first-ever female instrument-rated student and offered congratulations.

"Well?" said Al Michaud nervously, as they walked in to the office.

Lavery looked at him. "There was no *blankety-blank* way I *could* have failed Miss Dawson," was his reply.

Now, in the spring of 1951, at age 18, Dawn Dawson had her instrument rating and the distinction of being one of the first women in Canada to be so licensed. Her battles were far from over.

When Al Michaud forwarded the marks of the 10 students to Canadian Pacific Airlines he naturally sent in Dawn's as well. CPA replied that they wished to hire every one. "So I got hired – on paper," Dawn recalls.

The students were then called in for personal interviews with Herbert Hollick-Kenyon, CPA's first chief pilot, whose career is enshrined in Canada's aviation history.

"There sat the great man, looking down at some papers. Then he looked up and kind of frowned. I said, 'I am Dawn Dawson, and I'm here for an interview.'"

Herbert Hollick-Kenyon cleared his throat and rearranged his papers. Finally he said, "We don't hire women pilots."

"Why not?"

Another throat clearing. "It wouldn't be compatible in the cockpit."

"Why not?"

"Well, humph! humph! We can't hire women because the pilots have to share the same room when they overnight. And we can't afford single rooms."

"Do you have stewardesses?"

"Yes, we do."

"Then why couldn't I share a room with the stewardess?"

He turned to stare out the window for a moment. "No, no, that just wouldn't work. However – and we're making a big concession here – we will waive the RN [Registered Nurse] requirement for a stewardess, because you do have a commercial licence, and we'll hire you on immediately as a stewardess."

Dawn left the office feeling deeply disheartened. They were hiring the nine guys with whom she'd taken the course, but not her. She went back to U-Fly. "Don't worry," Lloyd Michaud said. "You'll have a career in aviation, but maybe now you *should* consider being an instructor.

"I don't want to be an instructor."

But the Michauds persisted. "You won't have any trouble getting hired as an instructor, you won't even require additional training. Just study the criteria – there's no handbook – and take a ride with Len Milne of the DOT."

"Go through that again! Oh, no!"

Prince Rupert Aero Club

Dawn's mother had by then moved to Prince Rupert, BC, where she learned that the local flying club was advertising for an instructor. Dawn applied.

"They couldn't get anybody else to go, so they hired me," Dawn says. "I went up there even though I didn't have an instructor's rating or a float endorsement."

The club's only airplane was a Taylorcraft on floats. Bob Kelsey, president of the Prince Rupert Aero Club, gave her a couple of circuits in the Taylorcraft and she was on her own. "I took the airplane and flew around and around, taking off and landing on the water in the bay, until I had enough time to get my float endorsement. Then Len Milne came to give me a ride, first for floats and then for instructor's rating. I got both, so I spent the summer of 1951 instructing on floats for the Prince Rupert Aero Club."

The local newspaper ran a feature on the new flying instructor, describing Miss Dawn Dawson as "a little slip of a girl, nothing over five feet tall, with a bobbed haircut and laughing grey eyes." Bob Kelsey added that having "Miss Pilot" as an instructor was sure to boost the club's current membership drive.

By October, the weather turned bad and the lessons ended. The club couldn't afford to pay a non-working instructor over the winter so Dawn was out of a job. She headed south to Vancouver where she heard of an instructor's job in Port Alberni. She was hired by Bob Gayer, General Manager for Associated Air Taxi in Vancouver, and went over to Vancouver Island to work for their newly-acquired company, Port Alberni Airways.

Island Flying

There, Dawn worked for Jack Moul, instructing, dispatching and even fueling airplanes. She enjoyed it all. Pilot Slim Crosson took her out in the Waco and showed her how to maneuver on floats in the busy canal, to jump out the front window of the airplane to push off log booms, to spot and avoid any cables that might run between a boat and a boom, and to carry fuel down the ramp in five-gallon pails from barrels cached up on the bank. She was learning, and was intent on showing that she was as game, and could be every bit as capable a pilot, as the guys.

Dawn came to admire the dexterity and skill of such pilots as Jack Moul, Ron Connelly and Slim Crosson, who were flying up and down the west coast of Vancouver Island. Sometimes they'd take her on a flight to teach her survival lessons for flying in such conditions.

"It was very difficult flying. The rules and regulations weren't in place then as they were later. We'd go up and down the Alberni canal and there would be fog, so we'd have to fly lower and lower until we were taxiing right on the water. If we could see, we'd taxi on the step. Often we'd come upon tugboats hauling or pushing log booms. We'd be going along, suddenly see a cable, and know we were in between the boat and the boom."

By the following summer of 1952 work for the flying school had dwindled, and the company had to consider either selling or closing down.

Mainland Adventures

Dawn soon found another job instructing, this time for Ralph Hermanson at the Chilliwack Flying Club, for the air cadet season. There again, she encountered the "gender problem" – but this time it came from another woman!

"The flying school did some charters into the interior," Dawn says. "A man had booked a trip and the flying club assigned me as the pilot. On the day of departure the passenger drove up with his wife, a very pretty blonde woman. He said, 'Where's the pilot?' I said, 'I am.' 'Oh, okay,' But when I went to take his briefcase, his wife jumped out of the car. 'You're the pilot?? Oh, no! My husband isn't going off with any damned woman pilot!'"

"So," Dawn laughs, "that was the end of that."

During her employment with the Chilliwack Flying Club she met Jerry Pringle, a member of their board of directors. He informed her that a first-ever instructor's school was being planned, and they were seeking candidates from aero clubs across the country. Some senior level, along with junior level, instructors would partake in discussions and flying sessions and then write a manual to be used by instructors across Canada. Dawn applied and was accepted.

The two-week school, sponsored by the Department of Transport, was held in Lethbridge, Alberta, to make use of the ex-air force barracks to house the participants, and also to utilize the Fleet Canucks from Lethbridge Flying School.

Seminars were held in the mornings, and in the afternoons participants would put their discussions into actual flight practice. For Dawn Dawson it was a wonderful chance to meet women flyers from all over the country. There was Vera Strodl Dowling, who'd enjoyed a distinguished flying career with the Air Transport Auxiliary during the war, and had recently emigrated from England to become an instructor at the Lethbridge Flying Club. There was Helen Harrison Bristol from Vancouver, the first female in the British Empire to qualify for seaplane rating and who, in 1937, had been the first Canadian woman to receive her instructor's, multi-engine and instrument ratings, and the first woman in the world to hold a commercial licence in four countries. From Merritt, BC, came Phyllis Drysdale Lindsay, who had earned her private, commercial and instructor's licenses at the Victoria Flying Club. These were the only women out of about 50 men taking the instructor's course and Dawn, being the youngest, felt well-protected among her more seasoned peers.

By attending the Instructor's Refresher Course in Lethbridge, Dawn, at 20 years of age, came to know Canada's aviation "movers and shakers."

"The major DOT inspectors were there – 'Mac' Willson, the chief Instructor-Inspector from Ottawa who was in charge of the course, Len Milne from the DOT's western division and Moe Louch from the eastern division. I was, of course, looking for a job. Moe knew of an opening at the Calgary Flying Club so, prior to the end of the school session, he flew me to Calgary and introduced me to the manager, Bill Smith. Through his recommendation Bill hired me. It was really a miracle because I was a woman, and a young one, and the Calgary Flying Club had a fine reputation. Anyway, Moe backed me, and that's how I got my job."

Dawn stayed with the club for two years, and while there fate stepped in to change her life's course. On her second day of work she met Gordon Bartsch. "I was standing behind the counter and this chap walked in, came over – and asked me out! I stood there, kind of blinking because I didn't even know him, then he said, 'We'll go to the stock car races.' That appealed to me so I said, 'Okay.'"

"It was the only thing I could think of," Gordon says.

They began to date, in a group, as friends.

Gordon Bartsch was born in Lethbridge but had grown up in Calgary. He was now 21 years of age, and had been working during the summers on construction, running heavy equipment, Cat-skinning, and running a drag-line and shovel. He had spent the past winter working for the Hudson's Bay Company, hanging draperies.

Then one of his friends, Dennis Bonham, who was taking his commercial flying lessons, offered to take Gordon for a ride. "Gee, can you really make a living doing this?" Gordon asked. "This is so much fun, this is for me!" During the winter of 1951-52 he was at the Calgary Flying Club every weekend, washing airplanes and sweeping the hangar floor to earn some free hours of instruction.

"When Foothills Aviation needed a hangar tender, I took that job," Gordon recalls. "It didn't pay much but they gave me a room under the then-control tower in the corner of Number One [Foothills Aviation] hangar, so I fixed that up and I lived there. I virtually lived at the airport."

He got his private pilot's licence in the spring of '52, and started working on his commercial. One day, Frank Fielder, of Boyd & Fielder aircraft refuelers, informed him that Hal O'Keefe, aviation manager for Mannix Construction, was looking for a copilot on the Lockheed Lodestars.

"I'm not qualified to do that!" Gordon protested. "I only have 95 hours." He thought no more about it until three days later when Fielder approached him again. "Why haven't you been over to see Hal?" he demanded. "Get over there!"

On July 1, 1952, Gordon Bartsch, with much trepidation, went to see Hal O'Keefe. He was greeted warmly. "If you can have your commercial licence by the end of July, you've got the job of copilot on the Lodestar," he said.

Boy, that was really something. Gordon's boss at Foothills Aviation was totally encouraging. "You can live here and work part time, but you're relieved of all duties." He then went to see Bill Smith at the Calgary Flying Club, who called out instructor Bill Place. "Bill, this is your student for the month. You get him through."

"So, all that happened," Gordon says. "I had to write my commercial exams in Edmonton. I passed them, fortunately, came back to Calgary, took my commercial ride at the end of July and got my licence. So, I got my job as copilot on the Lodestar.

"Bill Lavery came from the Department of Transport and gave me my twin engine endorsement. I just sat in the seat with my hands on the control column. Hal O'Keefe was in the left seat and he was actually doing the flying with the rudders and that sort of thing, so it was kind of a shoo-in. I had my twin engine endorsement and my commercial licence and the whole thing in 30 days. And my first flying job, for $300 a month."

His first trip was a flight from Calgary to New York as copilot with Hal O'Keefe, who told the young pilot to "just sit on your hands so you don't get into any trouble." He'd never used radios because the Calgary Flying Club aircraft didn't have any, but living under the control tower had familiarized him with "all the radio chatter."

One rainy, drizzly morning in the middle of September 1952, Gordon had just returned from a two-week trip in the Lodestar. Part of the copilots' job following a trip was to return to the hangar the next morning to clean the airplane and sweep the hangar floor. The "news" was that a *girl* was working as an instructor over at the flying club!

"I went marching over there, sloshing through the rain," Gordon says. "I remember it like it was yesterday. I opened the door, looked across the room and saw this girl behind the counter – and that was it. Love at first sight, pretty much."

They made plans to go to the stock car races, but there was a glitch. "Another fellow, Bob Millott, thought he had a date with her that night, so when I went to pick her up we both arrived at her door at the same time." Gordon laughs when recalling the scene. "We pulled up together, but my car broke down right there, so we decided to all go out together, Bob and Dawn and I, to the stock car races, which we joked about for years."

"It was fine with me," Dawn says nonchalantly. "I was friends with both of them."

Dawn and Gordon continued dating until after Christmas when Gordon received a transfer to Toronto. He was away for about five months, but continued to see her on his return trips to Calgary. In the fall of 1953, Dawn and Gordon began to study together for their airline transport (then called senior commercial) licenses.

"As soon as we had enough time, which I think was 1000 hours, we went to Edmonton and stayed at my grandmother's place, and wrote off our senior commercial."

Again, fate stepped in to give their lives a twist. That fall, Dawn's niece passed away and Dawn asked her boss, Bill Smith, for time off to attend the funeral. He offered her the use of the club's Stinson to go back to BC. As Dawn flew over the mountains toward Oliver she suddenly felt a sharp stab of pain in her side, which quickly worsened. By the time she landed she was doubled over and barely able to get out of the airplane. Her aunt had come to take her home to Osoyoos until the funeral the next day, but on the way, Dawn fainted. The doctor diagnosed that her appendix had ruptured in flight!

During the 10-day recuperation, Dawn stayed with her aunt, then went to visit her mother who was now living in Kamloops with Dawn's younger brother. Over Christmas, she received a visit from Ron Connelly, who she had dated and worked with in Port Alberni. He had also come to see her when she was working in Chilliwack and a few times since she'd moved to Calgary. Now he was on his way to Ontario, where he was flying out of Red Lake. "For a Christmas present, he gave me an engagement ring," Dawn says.

Gordon Bartsch was devastated when Dawn returned to Calgary wearing a ring.

"I had a whole year to try to talk her out of it," he says. "I tried, oh you bet! but it didn't work. I was away an awful lot with Mannix, but I said, 'Don't marry him – marry me!' She did not change her mind."

Dawn Dawson and Ron Connelly were married in December 1954.

"I was not very happy at that point," Gordon recalls. "In the spring of 1955 I went with Canadian Pacific Airlines. I liked my job with Mannix, but when I told Hal that CPA was hiring and asked 'What should I do?' he said, 'If you don't go I'll fire you for being stupid.' Hal knew that the future, in aviation, was with a major airline, so I went out there and was with them until 1960, based in Montreal and flying the Montreal-Madrid, and Montreal-Mexico City routes."

In 1956, Gordon married a Trans Canada Airlines stewardess, Melba Misselbrook. They had one son, Russell, followed by daughters Melene and Leslie.

The Connelly's Northern Adventures

In the meantime, Dawn and Ron Connelly moved to Red Lake, Ontario, where Ron was flying Norsemen for Barney Lamb of Ontario Central Airways. Dawn got checked out in their Super Cruiser and made one trip for them, but nothing else was offered. In the spring they heard that Pacific Western Airlines (PWA) was forming. The company was looking for pilots and also for an instructor to take over the flying school in Whitehorse, Yukon. Dawn and Ron sent in their credentials and were offered a combination job: Ron to fly charters out of Whitehorse and Dawn to run the flying school.

And so, in the spring of 1955, Dawn started her new life in Whitehorse, instructing students in a Cessna 140 and a Fleet Canuck. "A lot of young people there wanted to be pilots. I had students right from private through to commercial, who then were signed on by the airlines. I had the ground school at night, as well as the flying to do. I ran it all on my own."

What many of Dawn's students lacked in formal schooling they made up for in enthusiasm, as they bravely tackled courses necessary for the written exams such as air regulations, the theory of flight, weather and navigation. Thus, Dawn and Ron were soon introduced to "the characters of the north," and they fit right in.

A number of Dawn's students were local trappers, miners or prospectors.

"One interesting person was Moe Grant. He loved airplanes and does still. He already had his licence, but he'd had it taken away from him when he'd crashed in a

Tiger Moth. He'd walked out, but froze his feet and as a result had to have amputations just above the knee. He wanted to get his licence back so I said, 'Well then, let's do it. There's no reason why not.' We started with skis because there wouldn't be the problem of working the brakes. It took quite a few letters of persuasion before the DOT said they'd allow this, but they finally came up and gave him a ride, so he got his licence back, on skis.

"Then come summer we said, 'Why can't you fly on floats? There are no brakes on them either.' So, they allowed him to fly on floats. Then it was just a matter of time until he got a regular private licence. He has owned his own aircraft since then, and 'lives to fly'."

One summer, PWA's southern base needed the Beaver from Whitehorse, and in trade offered a Junkers. Ron and Dawn flew the Beaver to Prince Rupert, picked up the Junkers and took it back. "Nobody wanted to fly the Junkers so it was given to Ron, being the junior man," Dawn says. "It took a lot of muscle. I couldn't sit to fly it, I couldn't reach the rudder pedals, so I put couple of pillows under and behind me. I was actually standing up."

Although a lot of pressure was needed on the pedals, the airplane handled fine, but heavy. Also, the attractive and unique corrugated metal cover made the Junkers unsuitable for the northern climate. "We didn't like it in the fall, when we were clearing the ice and freezing rain off the wings," Dawn says. The chore involved carrying ropes and brooms on board. "If you got a little frost you had to take the rope up and down each groove, back and forth. It was hard work." They flew it back to the southern base before the weather became too cold.

One time Dawn was hired to take out a prospector in the Super Cub, on floats. As they left Whitehorse her passenger leaned over and said, "The last time I flew with a woman, it was snowing and we crashed. So I'm sure glad the weather's good." He pointed to the patch worn over the eye he had lost in that accident. Dawn smiled, nodded and kept flying. But as they crossed over to the far side of the mountains it started to snow. She had never landed on the lake they were going to, but Ron had warned her, "You can only go in one way and take off that same way. Be *sure* you do that."

The weather was right down, so Dawn literally crawled up a creek looking for the lake. When she saw the large body of water she touched down, off-loaded her passenger, then took off the opposite way to which she'd come. When she told Ron how she'd gone in and out, he became very upset. "*I told you,* you have to go in and come back the same way!"

"Well, I couldn't see any other way to do it," Dawn said quietly, "and it turned out all right."

The next time she flew over the area she checked it out, and said a quick prayer. The lake was a bowl surrounded on three sides by cliffs. The trick was to come in over the top and down so you had a go-around if needed. She'd been saved by the fact that she'd

Dawn Dawson on snowshoes with axe, going to get branches to put under skis. Whitehorse, Yukon, 1957. (Photo: Bartsch collection)

come "just crawling" over the creek and popped down as soon as she saw the water. "I wouldn't be going around anyway because I was slow enough to be able to just sit down. But," she adds, "that's the way you *shouldn't* do these things."

Her flying experience now included floats, skis and wheels, flying over ocean and mountain, in sleet, fog, snow, and in the extreme cold and isolation of the North.

"The second year we were there – and I was doing the odd charter then – PWA pilots were joining CALPA, the Canadian Airline Pilots Association," Dawn recalls. "In order to join, a pilot had to be with a major or a regional carrier. PWA was trying to become the regional carrier when they amalgamated the different airlines. All the pilots were put on a seniority list according to when we were hired, and I had a number one less than Ron's because I'd actually started work before he did – I think I was number 11 and he was 12."

Things looked great.

"But when they finished negotiations and the final seniority list came out, my name wasn't even on it!" Dawn continues. "I called the Vancouver office. Gordy Moul, Jack's brother, was on the committee and I asked him why I wasn't on the list. I was told it came down to the fact that CALPA would accept PWA only so long as they did not have a female on the seniority list."

Dawn still doesn't know the true reasons behind such a decision, but her name was detrimentally removed from the list. "The pilots in Vancouver who were doing this wouldn't even discuss it. I was pretty upset. When Shirley Render was writing her book about women pilots, *No Place for a Lady*, I was talking to Ron, reminding him how upset I had been. He said, "Upset! You were so *mad*!"

Even years later, when Dawn discusses the subject with people who were in the drivers' seats at the time, there is a defensiveness. "Yes, there still is, because they knew they were wrong. Oh, they came back with some excuse – they said they had to take me off because I was a flying instructor and that did not include flying instructors – which was *not* the case at the time."

Dawson City

This situation precipitated a move that Dawn and Ron had been considering for some time: to go on their own. When a flying service in Dawson City became available they bought it and went into private business. "Ron wasn't set on airline work anyway, but he enjoyed the flying he was doing so that's what we did. But then, I couldn't fly because I couldn't get into CALPA, so we quit PWA and bought out Pat Callison's Flying Service in Dawson City." [The history of Pat Callison and his aviation experience have been chronicled in his self-published book, *Pack Dogs to Helicopters*].

Callison's Flying Service owned one Beaver and two Cessna 180s. To swing the deal, Dawn and Ron brought in Dawn's father, Crae Dawson, as a third partner. "We called our company Connelly-Dawson Airways. Everybody thought it was because our name was Connelly and we lived in Dawson City, which wasn't it at all. It was because of my father, Crae Dawson."

Ron Connelly, 1960.

At first, Dawn concentrated on office duties and expediting work, but soon was flying both the Cessnas and the Beaver.

"The Clinton Creek Mine hadn't yet been developed, so I used to fly out the grubstakers who were doing the preliminary work, and land on a little strip there.

"We flew supplies in for the Cat-trains that were hauling oil industry supplies, machinery parts, groceries, mail or personnel, over to the Peel Plateau. We'd land as near as possible, throw a tent over the engine to keep it warm, unload and get out before the engine got cold. At our little airstrip at the home base, we'd drain the oil from the engines every night and take it into a shed," Dawn recalls. "Then in the morning we'd put the Herman-Nelsons on to heat it up."

They also did mail runs up and down the rivers to various isolated spots, landing on skis in the winter and on floats on the rivers in the summer. They got contracts for government departments such as Water Resources, testing the ice and the water in different places, and occasionally did emergency Medevac flights.

"The cold and remoteness made it harder work, but it was really, really enjoyable. I loved going out to these places and seeing these people. Our arrivals always made them happy because we were bringing them things and they were happy to see and talk to people, to find out what was going on."

But it was still the wilderness, where life or death could hang by a hair. "When we first went up there, they didn't have much mapping done," Dawn says. "The maps were blank – unmapped, uncharted. Beyond the Ogilvie Mountains they'd show a big white spot, and so as we flew we would note distinctive marks of rivers, creeks and hills; so we developed our own maps."

Weather communication was handled by the Army Signal Corps based in Dawson City. "They had a land line to Whitehorse for Morse Code only," Dawn says, "no voice."

When Dawn reflects on her career, she acknowledges that although she was operating in a man's world, the other pilots were good to her. "They didn't have to treat me as an equal, but they did. Sometimes people would come through and say, 'Oh, gosh, a girl, I'm going to write something on you,' but I wouldn't want that because I wasn't doing anything that the men weren't doing. I felt very fortunate, and I didn't think I should be put in the limelight, as a woman, for doing identical things that they did, every day, and got no credit for."

Sometimes the men would offer to help, and did. But sometimes there was no help available and Dawn either had to do the work or sit there. Once she was on a fuel haul in the Cessna 180 while the two Beavers were being flown by other pilots; each were hauling six, 12.5-gallon drums. When she got to the lake nobody else was there, so she unloaded the barrels and rolled them up onto the bank. "It was hard work," she states frankly. "They each weighed 80 or 90 pounds."

But Dawn, at five feet, four and three-quarters inches in height, and weighing approximately 120 pounds, was determined to do the work the same as the men. "After the third day I was getting pretty tired but I wasn't going to tell them that!" she laughs.

Meanwhile, the Bartsch family had kept in touch with the Connellys.

In 1959 the Bartschs moved to Vancouver where Gordon flew DC-6s for CPA on the Vancouver-Amsterdam and Vancouver-Honolulu routes. But he was becoming frustrated with the seniority system of the big airline. He had been checked out with CPA as a captain on DC-3s, then put back as first officer, then second officer. The airline was shrinking and lay-offs were a direct possibility.

Some of Gordon's flights began to take him on the Whitehorse and Dawson City run. During a visit, Gordon, Dawn and Ron discussed the feasibility of bringing up a DC-3. The oil industry was rapidly developing and Connelly-Dawson Airways needed a large aircraft to haul fuel to caches for helicopters that were doing seismic work in remote areas.

Gordon evaluated his position: he had lots of time, he was familiar with the DC-3, he had an airline transport licence, and they were short of pilots for the construction of the DEW Line. The three started "crunching numbers" and decided that Gordon would leave CPA, move to Dawson City, join the company and they would buy a DC-3. So in 1960, Gordon Bartsch bought in to Connelly-Dawson Airways and moved North. They bought their DC-3 (CF-CPY) from CPA (the airplane is now on the pedestal at Whitehorse airport), and Gordon Bartsch became the first person in Western Canada to use the DC-3 as a bush aircraft on a commercial basis.

Dawn also was checked out on the DC-3 for her twin endorsement, but not without a fight. She had to convince the DOT inspector that, as a woman, she was strong enough to capably fly the DC-3 if it lost an engine on take-off, fully loaded.

The following winter brought much flying in the Yukon, the Northwest Territories and up to the Arctic Islands. They decided to use the DC-3 on their scheduled mail run rather than the Beavers because the increased payload made it more economical.

"There weren't radio aids or anything, so we would go charging up these valleys in the DC-3 just like we were flying a Beaver. We'd go into lakes with a couple of feet of snow, on wheels," Dawn says.

"Oh, we scared the hell out of ourselves a couple of times," Gordon adds.

Dawn recalls when they first got the DC-3 and took it, in the fall, to Old Crow. Because there were only sandbars to land on, they asked the local RCMP constable to check their condition for landing. "If you can drive a car down there at 60 mph, it will be okay," Gordon explained.

First landing of a DC-3 (or any large aircraft) on a sandbar in Old Crow, Yukon, 1960. (Photo: Bartsch collection)

They came in, circled, saw the sandbar, lined up and made their approach. The entire population of Old Crow was down below, watching. This was really something, a big airplane landing right at the edge of the village! There the people stood, smiling and waving at the end of the sandbar, and beyond them was the river.

The pilots' first shock was the roughness. The second was that the people were standing in the way! Surely the RCMP hadn't driven a car there for a long, long, time because the sandbar was incredibly rough. The airplane bounced crazily over stones, "and you can't brake when you're bouncing," Gordon notes.

"We were trying to stop it and these people kept coming closer and closer as we were rushing toward them," Dawn says. "When we finally got stopped we sat in the cockpit looking right down at them. I snapped a picture of these people all smiling up at us. Boy, they had a lot more faith in us than we did! That was the end of the strip. They figured that's where the airplane had to stop, so they'd stood there! They didn't realize that we *just managed* to stop there!"

The photo was so impressive that the company sent it out on their Christmas cards, commemorating the first landing of a DC-3 at Old Crow.

Connelly-Dawson Airways was a profitable venture that paid the bills and made a decent living for its owners and employees.

So, what happened?

Gordon considers the chain of events. He had arrived to fly the DC-3 in April 1960. "By winter, I realized this wasn't going to work. My feelings were too strong. I told Dawn after Christmas that I wasn't able to handle it and I was going to have to leave. We talked about it and she decided she felt the same way. That's when decisions were made."

Gordon and Dawn left for Montreal, together, in April 1961.

New Trails

Gordon's wife and children, who had been living in Vancouver, moved to Calgary. A reconciliation attempt was made by both couples, but it was no use. By the spring of 1962 divorce actions were served.

With the passing of time, the situation has righted itself. "It turned out well, other than that short period of bruising," Gordon says, "but it was a very traumatic time in our lives. It was a very, very hard time for all of us."

Gordon soon found work with Field Aviation of Calgary, a salvage and maintenance company. Chuck McAvoy of Yellowknife had salvaged a Pacific Western Airlines DC-3 (CF-PWF) from Great Slave Lake, which had sunk when the pilot had landed on rotten ice. While it still rested on its belly on the ice, Chuck had stuffed it full of empty oil drums, so when the ice melted the airplane floated to the surface. He then towed it across the lake, got it to Yellowknife, cleaned it up, and put new engines on it. Gordon went up with Field Aviation and flew it out – complete with dead fish inside the wings. The airplane, re-registered as CF-JWP, was then rebuilt in Calgary.

Gordon's next job was flying a DC-3 as copilot with Bob Lundberg for Peter Bawden's oil company, which was drilling in Melville Island in the Arctic. Gordon welcomed the opportunity as he had never been beyond the DEW Line.

It wasn't exactly the type of trip he'd hoped for. They loaded up in Yellowknife and took on fuel. On February 2, 1962, Gordon and Bob "Crazy Legs" Lundberg, a tall, gangly fellow with a great sense of humor, crossed the DEW Line in the DC-3 (CF-CAR) and headed out to the Arctic Islands.

The beacon they were homing in on had blown a circuit breaker while the attendants were watching a movie and they hadn't reset it, so the pilots couldn't find the rig. "The winds were such that we were farther north than we thought," Gordon says. "We turned around and cranked back, but by the time we found out where we were we didn't have enough gas to get to the DEW Line. The engines quit and down we went, in the dark. We slid to a stop and busted up the airplane about four miles from the strip."

Luckily, no one was hurt. They walked to the DEW Line site and a crew from Calgary eventually came to pick them up. They brought another DC-3 back to finish the three-month job.

Gordon's next job was flying for "Can-Tung" (Canadian Tungsten Mine) north of Watson Lake, making a total of 265 trips into the mine during one summer. Dawn, meanwhile, had gone south to do some float trips out of Cassidy airport at Nanaimo. When Gordon heard that Cassidair planned to set up a satellite flying school for the summer at Watson Lake, he called Dawn and she came up to run the school.

Dawn had 12 students – "very interesting gentlemen, all different" – to put through in the two summer months.

Gordon and Dawn made a number of Can-Tung trips together in the DC-3, as both were qualified. And when BC Yukon Airways found themselves short a pilot, especially during hunting season, Dawn took their clients out in the 180s.

They returned to Calgary that fall of 1962 and were married at Christmas. Gordon continued to find work flying Chuck McAvoy's DC-3 (CF-JWP). "Chuck was a real help to us. He knew we were trying to get started again and he gave us a real break."

The next spring, Dawn and Gordon were awarded a contract to haul fish out of Hay River for Willy Lazarich. "The strip's ready at Keller Lake, 300 miles northwest of Hay River," they were informed. "Come on up." When they attempted to land, however, they found the strip in such poor shape that they almost got stuck. "We put some frozen whitefish in the back to keep the tail down and went back to Hay River. Three days later they called again. 'Oh, it's good now, you can come back in.' So we went in and promptly *did* get stuck. We were there for seven days."

They tried shoveling a path out for the DC-3, 700 or 800 feet in length and the width of each main wheel, but the snow was two feet deep. With the temperature at 30° below zero, every few hours they had to run the engines to keep them warm.

Finally, after hours of shoveling, they got into the airplane and started the engines. Then they both sat looking out at the two little paths they'd dug, with banks of snow on either side. "It doesn't look good," Gordon thought. "If we veer for just an instant and catch a wheel in that snow, it's going to ground-loop us."

Suddenly Dawn spoke. "You know, if we catch a wheel, it's going to ground-loop us."

Gordon put his hand on the mixtures to cut the engines, resigning himself to the fact they were stuck until they could figure out what to do. His hand rested on the top of hers. Dawn had come to the same conclusion at the same moment.

Without saying another word, together they pulled the mixtures closed.

They had survival gear with them, but were saved from having to camp in the aircraft by an invitation from a group of nine fishermen to bunk with them in their shack.

They might have been better off in the airplane.

The snow around the shack was stained yellow, offering an indication of the general hygiene. Inside was a dirt floor, crude tables, chairs and bunks, and a heater of sorts. For supper, they were offered meat of some kind, and vegetables – carrots, potatoes and onions – procured from a pit in the floor.

They were told that a German man lived further down, in a nice little cabin in the trees. The fishermen lent Gordon and Dawn their snowmobile so they could pay the man a visit. In the dark, as it always is during winter in the North, Gordon gave the snowmobile full throttle and ran straight into a pile of snow – which in fact turned out to be a stack of frozen whitefish covered over with snow. "The engine quit and we lay there on our backs with whitefish all over us, just killing ourselves laughing," Dawn says.

The German man invited them to come for dinner the next night, which would offer a relief from the Spartan fare of their main hosts. Alas, his offerings were even more plain: homemade head cheese and potatoes. It was also very warm in his cabin. "It had a dirt floor too, and was very small, one room, so our feet were freezing while our heads were in 95° air.

"We ate there several times with him," Dawn says, "until I just couldn't eat any more head cheese."

The sleeping arrangements at the home shack with nine roommates proved awkward. The cabin was divided into two rooms separated by an open archway. In one room were the bunks, and in the other the kitchen and sitting area. The only place where Dawn and Gordon could lay out their sleeping bags was in the kitchen.

"They had a table and bench seats, so Gordon lay on one bench and I lay on the other against the log wall that separated the two rooms," Dawn says. "One night I felt a hand come through the log wall. I whispered the problem to Gordon so we quietly switched places. That ended the groping."

Dawn and Gordon were finally able to make their escape by shoveling a strip in the snow, 40 feet wide by 1500 feet long, beveled at the end of the strip. "That took six days," Dawn recalls. "The snow was two-and-a-half feet deep and we'd throw it as far as we could, then go over it again, so we moved each shovel-full three times."

"Now we were behind financially," Gordon says. "The DC-3 could carry 6000 pounds so we put 10 000 on it. When it's 40° below zero the airplane climbs just fine. We did the takeoff and ran right down the 1500 feet and up the bevel, doing about 60 mph. You're supposed to keep it on the ground until you're going about 90, and then if the engine quits you have enough rudder control to keep it straight. At 60 you don't, but if an engine had quit we'd have just pulled the power and landed."

As they roared down to the end of the strip and up the bevel, Dawn reached down and upped the gear. Gordon pinned it, and they continued their takeoff run with the gear coming up, actually flying.

They unloaded at Hay River and went back again for another load. Fortunately the wind hadn't blown in the strip. They made 10 trips.

"The DC-3 has a complicated setup," Gordon explains. "There are two levers. You have to pull up one and then the other to raise the gear. Dawn, being short, sat on a pillow so she was higher and so had to lean down even more. Usually her forehead would hit my knee when she reached down to do this. On about the eighth trip, three days later, we were doing a takeoff when I heard this mumbling. I said, 'What did you say?' and she said, 'There's *got* to be an easier way to make a living than this!'

"We really had a laugh. It seemed so funny."

Range Airways

The next stage of their careers came about through another person's misfortune.

"A young chap owned Viking Air Service in Calgary," Gordon says. "He had an Apache but when he was having some work done on it he leased another one to do a trip. He unfortunately had an accident and killed himself. So this airplane was sitting there, available, with the charter and the licence and everything, but no owner."

Dawn picks up the story: "After a time, we went to see the company that held the mortgage on the airplane. We said, 'We can put up $5000 or something, take it over and make payments.' So the deal was made and we changed the name to Range Airways."

The new company shared a desk with Rudy Strick from Mannix Construction, who said they could get their own phone and camp there to keep their overhead low. And so Range Airways came into being in 1963, with one airplane and two people. Dawn ran the office while Gordon went downtown knocking on doors. Then they would trade off, alternating on trips, working it any way they could to make a buck.

They began by peppering local business offices with cards and visits, focusing on Alberta Gas Trunk. "We were desperate for their work," Gordon says, "and I had been down there so often that they wouldn't even let me in the office any more. The secretary, Marie Gee – who eventually came to work for us – was shielding Mike Haverland, who was the man I needed to see.

"One day in July, Dawn and I were at the Calgary Stampede when we came upon an artist doing charcoal cartoons. Well, we got an idea. We cut a picture of Mike out of their company magazine, went back to the fairgrounds, and asked the artist to draw a picture of Mike's head coming out of the Apache, going over a pipeline that had squirts of oil coming out of it and bandages and that. Mike had a big cigar in his mouth, and was holding his cowboy hat, which he wore all the time, over his bald head. Then we had written across the cartoon: MIKE, BE A RANGE-RIDER!

"We took it down to the office, rolled in a tube. Marie gave it to her boss. A little while later she heard a guffaw of laughter coming from his office.

"We got a phone call from Mike Haverland that Sunday morning. 'I need a trip right now.' 'Yes, sir!' That got us into Alberta Gas Trunk with a pipeline patrol contract, and we never looked back."

By the end of 1963, Range Airways had grown from one to two Apaches, plus a Comanche, and they had hired pilot George Gledhill.

When they got a contract to do high altitude photography, they formed Range Aerial Surveys with photogrammetrist John McMurchy. Photogrammetry is the process of making a survey or a map with the help of photographs taken, especially from the air. "From 25 000 feet you can measure the height of a sidewalk curb," Gordon explains. "Engineering companies use that sort of stuff."

"We converted one of the Piper Apaches to hold a hatch for a big camera," Dawn adds, "and I did the flying for two summers. We also had a camera operator, and sometimes a navigator, including Molly Reilly on the northern Alberta section, depending on the job we were doing. We covered areas across the North up to Hay River, Grande Prairie and Fort Nelson. I also spent one summer in The Pas, Manitoba, where the country was unmapped – or poorly mapped – which was really interesting."

One of Dawn's flying jobs with Range Airways that summer was in Churchill. There were no fuel stops between The Pas and Churchill, and the Apache could hold just enough gas to make it. Because the weather had to be perfect for aerial photography, Dawn would get up at five o'clock each morning to do a weather check, but it was never good enough and she just wasn't getting in. This went on all summer. One morning she checked and decided, "This just *has* to be it." She got the crew out of bed, flew into Churchill, landed and fueled, did the required work along the Hudson's Bay, came back, fueled, and returned to The Pas. Wow! Time for celebration!

It was also quite a feat to use a turbo Apache at altitudes of 18 000 to 25 000 feet. "Normally you can't get over 12 000," Gordon says, "but we'd put turbo-chargers on the engines so were able to get up high."

"And we were on oxygen all the time," Dawn says. "With those modifications we were able to get up to that altitude."

"I was flying out of Edmonton one time, at 23 000 feet," she adds. "We had arranged to have a block of line that actually belonged to one of the present airways. I could hear Air Canada take off with the DC-8, but they, of course, deviated and went around. When one captain asked the air traffic controller why he had to deviate, he was told that we were doing some photography in the area. Then they called me to get my position. The Air Canada captain heard a female voice on the air and asked, quite incredulous, 'Are you a *girl*?' I said, 'Yes, sir.' 'What are you flying?' 'An Apache.' He comes back, 'No, no, they'll never believe this. A *girl* in an Apache, at 23 000, and *I have to go around her*!'"

Gordon and Dawn Bartsch at Whitehorse, Yukon, Great Northern Airways, 1965. (Photo: Bartsch collection)

Great Northern Airways

In the meantime, Dawn's personal situation had also improved. Her father had disowned her following her marriage breakup and she had not seen him since. But when her brother got married and Dawn and Gordon attended the wedding, fences were mended, and about six months later he phoned. "I want to talk to you kids."

He informed them that Connelly-Dawson Airways was running into some trouble and perhaps they could help. The principals of the two companies met in 1965 – Crae Dawson and Ron Connelly, with Dawn and Gordon Bartsch. It was decided to join Range and Connelly-Dawson airways, and form a new company called Great Northern Airways (GNA).

"So now we were back in business with Ron and his new wife, Carol, and Dawn and I, and her dad," Gordon says. "We brought in a fourth partner, Norm Keglovic.

Great Northern Airways started with bases in Whitehorse, Dawson City, Inuvik, Mayo, Ross River, and Calgary. Then, in 1967, when Herman Peterson of Atlin, BC, wanted to retire, they also bought his base and airplane. The company grew to 24 airplanes and 160 employees. Dawn had instructed at least four of the company's pilots.

"We took over the scheduled service from CPA, the Whitehorse-Mayo-Dawson run that they had operated for years, and extended it on to Ross River and Old Crow in the Yukon, and the Northwest Territories base of Inuvik, and Sachs Harbour in the Arctic Islands, using DC-3s. We used an Aztec for the Whitehorse-Ross River run," Gordon says. In 1968, the company received permission to add Clinton Creek, Yukon, site of a new Cassiar Asbestos mine, and Tuktoyaktuk, NWT, a DEW Line base.

Soon, they acquired five DC-3s, then a Fairchild F-27 turboprop that could carry up to 40 passengers or 10000 pounds of freight or a combination. When the company absorbed Banff Oil's aviation division, they were operating two F-27s, then added a DC-4 for Panarctic Oils contracts in the Arctic Islands.

Contracts came in every variety: The Glenbow Foundation of Alberta hired them, with help from Heiland Explorations and Panarctic Oils, to bring the historic cart of explorer Sir Francis McClintock from Melville Island to Calgary. The Prudhoe Bay oil discovery on the North Slope of Alaska added business, as did Pan American Petroleums, who hired one of their F-27s three times a week for crew changes and northern freight haul operations. The company also advertised northern oil tour flights – "Nose around the North with GNA" – to allow American and Canadian business executives to view "on-site" action. The tours took them to Whitehorse, Inuvik, Prudhoe Bay, Sagwon, Fairbanks and Anchorage.

The road to success had a few bumps and "hard landings," however. They lost two F-27s, "one where we parked it on a hill outside of Resolute Bay, and the other was a very minor-looking accident, but it was cheaper to chop up the airplane than repair it," Dawn says. There was no loss of life in these accidents.

"In all of our flying we had three fatalities, in one accident with Great Northern," Gord says. "A 180 went through Lake Laberge in a whiteout where you couldn't blame anyone. The pilot and two passengers were killed."

Dawn and Gordon bought out Ron and Carol Connelly and Norm Keglovic, while Crae Dawson remained part-owner of the company.

Then they took another daring step. They personally went to Ottawa and to Washington, DC, to apply for a Class One licence to do international charters with large aircraft. "We walked in and did this all on our own," Dawn says. "They asked, 'Where is your lawyer?' and we said, 'We don't have one.' 'Everyone uses lawyers for this!' 'Do we really need one?' They laughed and said, 'No, I guess not. Not if you can type.' So we managed to get all our licenses ourselves."

They now added recreational charters to the United States, and promoted ski weekends at Aspen, Colorado and Whitefish, Montana.

Gordon picks up the story. "We had a very valuable set of licenses, and that's what a competitor wanted. He wanted to do international work and we had the licenses and he couldn't get them. . . . Then one Friday afternoon the bank pulled our operating loan, which was a demand note for a half-million-dollar overdraft. We were out of business in a week. It bankrupted the company."

Their licenses were all transferred over to their competitor. "Then that person backed out and everybody in the North got left hanging," Dawn adds.

"Suddenly Dawn and I were on the outside. And then they started selling our equipment at 20 cents on the dollar – Beavers on floats for $25 000! Two hundred thousand dollars worth of F-27 parts for $20 000."

The Bartschs helplessly watched their dreams die.

"Not only were we broke, we owed the bank $50 000 in personal guarantees – and they came after us. We ended up having to pay it out of [a later business] the restaurants in Hawaii."

The final analysis was that Great Northern Airways was no more, and Gordon and Dawn Bartsch, now approaching their forties, had no choice but to start again. It still smarts to recall the situation.

"A trustee in the bankruptcy claim went through everything," Gord says. "He looked for all sorts of illegal things that management might do and couldn't find anything. He called me at the end of this and said, 'You know, Gordon, if they had left you alone you had it made. There was no need for this bankruptcy.'"

The day Great Northern Airways died, a strange drama took place in Whitehorse.

"On the last day that Great Northern was in existence, the DC-3 that Dawn and I bought, CF-CPY, was taking off from Whitehorse when the engine quit. Captain Joe Langlois aborted the takeoff and stopped the airplane on the runway, and it never flew again. So the airplane started with us, and the last day we were in operation, it quit too," Gordon says.

Dawn picks up the story. "Northward Aviation [Ltd., of Edmonton] got it after Great Northern was no longer in existence, but they never restored it or changed the engines so it sat on the side of the tarmac in Whitehorse for years. The old pilots would come and look at it, and it bothered them to see this airplane sit idle."

One of the pilots who'd flown it was John Goodkey, who had served in the RCAF, then enjoyed a long career as a captain with Pacific Western Airlines before joining Great Northern Airways in 1965 as its chief pilot. "When he died," Dawn continues, "John's wife had a little DC-3 engraved on his gravestone marked CF-CPY, because he liked that airplane so much.

"Then Joe Muff, partner in Alcan Air and a prior GNA employee, managed to buy it for a dollar. 'We should restore it,' he said, and he got the local flying club interested, with Bobby Cameron leading the campaign. They did that, then got a local fellow to

DC-3 (CF-CPY) on pedestal at Whitehorse airport. (Photo: Bartsch collection)

design a pedestal so it became a wind-vane. It's the only pedestal in the world designed that way."

Dawn and Gordon made a trip to Whitehorse just as the restoration work was starting. The airplane was sitting on the tarmac, and Bobby said to Dawn, "We're going to strip it. I think you and Gordon should go in and take anything you want off it first." They took out the throttle quadrant and the big trim tab, and when Dawn got back to their home in Kona she built a lamp out of it. Just before the airplane went up on the pedestal, the little stainless steel tag sporting its serial number was also removed and sent to the Bartschs.

A few years later, Dawn and Gordon went up to Whitehorse to have a look at the faithful old DC-3. "As we were driving in, the airplane kept turning, following us. I got a real chilly feeling," Gordon says. "It turned again and followed us as we drove out."

Aloha!

After the collapse of their company, Gordon and Dawn sat down to consider what they might do next. Gordon's sister, as well as Dawn's mother and stepfather, were living in Hawaii. Why not take a holiday there, and think things over?

Their next venture was so far removed from anything they'd known before that it gave them exactly the lift they needed. In 1972, they opened a Pottery Steakhouse on Oahu, at Kaimuki, a section of Honolulu behind Diamond Head.

Intrigued by once seeing potters in Holland working at delft, Gordon broached the idea of integrating such an enterprise into a restaurant business. "We got a kiln and a potter's wheel, Dawn took courses in Honolulu, and with a book in one hand we began to make our dishes." Gordon, meanwhile, researched the existing steakhouse business in Honolulu.

"The Gods were smiling on us," Gordon says, "because everything turned out well."

They found a location in a rundown nightclub building in Kaimuki near Diamond Head, cleaned it out, and began making plates on which to serve future guests. Then, they were fortunate in hiring Sam Uyehara, an experienced Island chef and also a potter.

"He stayed with us to the very end," Gordon says. "The only arguments I had with him was trying to give him a raise and take time off."

The first week The Pottery Steakhouse was open, the local food editor came in. When her rave review appeared on the front page of the newspaper's "Dining Out" section, the business took off. The 125-seat dining room was soon expanded. Eighteen months later, in 1974, they opened another restaurant in Kailua-Kona on the Big Island of Hawaii, and moved there to live.

Gordon and Dawn ran the restaurants for 10 years, then sold them to develop three acres of land in Kona into an office complex called Pottery Terrace. As residents, they became integral members of the community. Gordon served a term as president of the Kona Coast Chamber of Commerce and Dawn managed the Ceramic Laboratory, while Dawn's mother, Florence Collins, managed the Pottery Steak House.

Seeing the World

Throughout this time, flying was never far from their field of action. They used a Cessna Skyknight, "essentially a 310," to commute between the two restaurants. Although they sold the airplane shortly after selling the restaurants, they never lost the desire to fly. Dawn's 9000 hours of flying time, and Gordon's 11 000 hours attested to their experience and knowledge. How could they build on that, and have some fun?

It came time to reassess, once again, what they wanted to do. They'd made up their earlier losses from Great Northern Airways and had become successful in a new business. A certain dream had never been far from their thoughts: to buy an airplane and fly around the world.

Research indicated that a Cessna 421B Golden Eagle should be adequate. Gordon thought they might buy the airplane in 1992 and make the round-the-world trip in 1993. But at Christmas of 1991, Dawn had a surprise.

"A friend of mine, Bob Ambrose, called on Christmas Eve," Dawn says. "'Hey, have you heard about this rally going around the world through Russia?' No, I hadn't. Then he said, 'You've always wanted to go to Russia, haven't you?'"

He faxed the information and Dawn showed it to Gordon. Although Gordon felt it might be too soon – "We didn't even have an airplane yet!" – Dawn decided to at least ask for information. The First Round-the-World Air Rally would be leaving from Santa Monica on July 1st. Again she mentioned it to Gordon, and again he shrugged off the idea as being premature. "Then he went off to work and I signed us up even though we didn't have an airplane," Dawn says.

The cost of entering the air race was not modest: $10 000 per aircraft, $10 000 per pilot (minimum of two), plus approximately $20 000 for fuel.

The plan was to retrace the flight plan of four Douglas bi-wing airplanes that had gone around the world 50 years earlier, departing from Santa Monica. This trip, leaving from the same area in 1992, had been completely plotted out by a Paris group as to rendezvous points, accommodation and fuel stops. Twelve entries signed up, none of whom had met before the rally.

The Bartschs scurried over to the mainland and bought a 1974 Cessna 421B, which they named *Kona Wind*. Then, to prepare for the race and update their skills and licenses, they virtually had to learn to fly all over again as it was 20 years since they'd flown instruments. "And by that time, 1992, we hadn't flown for four years, period," Dawn adds.

They began training at Flight Safety flying school in Long Beach, California.

"It was kind of funny," Gordon says. "The instructor was talking to us at the first meeting and he said something about an HSI. 'What's an HSI?' we asked. He just rolled his eyes." They soon learned that an HSI was a Horizontal Situation Indicator, "with a whole bunch of moving parts that work wonderfully well. Once you get used to it you can't live without one, but we had never flown with one," Gordon says.

Gordon and Dawn Bartsch with Kona Wind in 1992. (Photo: Bartsch collection)

Two assignments were imminent: within two weeks they had to rewrite their exams for instrument ratings in the United States and Canada because their licenses had lapsed, and they had to go through the "421 course" at Flight Safety on the simulator. They did both at once, combining home-study in Hawaii with practice at Long Beach.

When they took their new airplane to Flight Safety to have it checked out they found it had radio problems, among others. They had to virtually rebuild it.

"The instructor said, 'Look, you can't even take your flight test here because the radio is so poor,'" Dawn recalls, "so we jumped into the airplane and managed to get through LAX [Los Angeles airport] traffic. We came up to Calgary and met with people who used to work for us and now had their own businesses. We said, 'Here's our airplane and here's what we want to do,' and they were great. They fixed and installed new radios and gave the aircraft a complete going-over."

They also added extra fuel tanks to give them a range of 1600 miles. The *Kona Wind* now sported nine tanks (two tips, two auxiliary, two nacelle [saddles], two lockers and a nose tank), for a total capacity of 348 gallons. It was equipped with a global position satellite tracking system that, when hooked to the auto pilot and HIS, gave them automatic tracking on auto-pilot.

"When we left to go on this race I only had six hours on the airplane and that was when we flew up to Calgary!" Dawn recalls "And I did all the flying on the trip because I'd always wanted to go through Russia and around the world."

"Dawn flew the whole way," Gord acknowledges, "and I did the navigating and radio work."

It was a never-to-be-forgotten trip. During the 20 days they had 16 stopovers in six countries.[1]

There were several dicey moments on this rally caused by weather. One was on the way in to Novosibirsk in Russia. "The winds were a lot stronger than forecast and everyone was running low on gas," Gordon says. "We got there at midnight and I thought for sure three of the group were going to run out of fuel."

"A couple of them, before they got there, had to go into long-range emergency cruise," Dawn recalls. "It was the middle of the night and you don't have any radio aids or radar. The only thing we were all on was GPS [global positioning system]."

Another moment of concern occurred in Magadan. "When we took off it was only 100 feet," Dawn says. "Nobody wants to go but nobody will say 'no.' You *have* to go, you're on an itinerary."

The Bartschs proffered goodwill from their two home places, Canada and Hawaii. Flying in their Canadian-registered airplane sporting the name *Kona Wind*, at each stopover they played Hawaiian music over loudspeakers and greeted hosts with gifts of Kona coffee and macadamia nuts – "spreading Aloha! across Russia," as the *West Hawaii Today* newspaper reported (November 9, 1992).

The 1992 Around the World Through Russia rally was so successful that when another was announced for 1994, Race Around the World - Lower Latitude, they signed up. This one started on May 1st from St. Hubert airport near Montreal, and was sanctioned and sponsored by ICAO (International Civil Aviation Organization) in celebration of the organization's 50th anniversary.[2] It involved 100 hours of flying in 24 days. The Bartschs scored fourth out of five aircraft in Class II (turbo-charged piston engine). Winning wasn't expected because of the handicapping system used to help balance out the different aircraft sizes.

Two more air races followed: in 1996 Dawn and Gordon entered the Race Around South America event. They started from New York, flew through the Caribbean, down the east side to the tip of Cape Horn, then up the west side, stopping over at Santiago and Lima, into Mexico, Oxaca to New Orleans, and back to New York.

The Bartschs rebuilt their airplane, complete with new engines, so were more than ready, in September 1997, to enter the "Big Daddy" of air races, a spectacular long-distance race held in Turkey as part of the first World Air Games. Staged as the Olympics of Aviation, and organized by the Turkish Aeronautical Association under the auspices of the Fédération Aéronautique Internationale (FAI), it was heralded as the fourth largest sporting event after the Olympics, World Cup Soccer and European Cup Soccer. The 4000 competitors from 75 countries were judged in 17 different aeronautical categories. Open to single and multi-engine piston aircraft, turboprops and light jets, 19 airplanes from 12 countries participated in the race. They left from Reykjavik, Iceland, at different altitudes and different speeds, in 10-minute intervals.[3]

A "handicap against maximum cruising speed" was established for this race, Gordon explains. "Because all manner of airplanes are competing, they take your best speed, at the ultimate altitude for the plane, at 75% power. You go faster with altitude to a point. Our best speed is 228 knots at 25 000 feet, at 75% power, so that's 100%. If you get a tail-wind you'll be going at 105%, with a head-wind you'll do 80%, sort of thing, so you're competing on a percentage.

"The aircraft with the highest percent wins, so you're not racing to be the first guy across the line. We can't do 228 knots in this airplane, it's unrealistic, so they worked out a complicated formula and we were 92% of our reference speed. It worked out real well because we had a close competition with two other airplanes that also had adjusted reference speeds."

"The US won gold at 93.62%, Italy won silver at 93.60%, and we won bronze for Canada at 93.00%. That's how close it was," Dawn adds.

A serious glitch occurred when an air traffic controller became confused over which plane was which, resulting in four minutes being inadvertently added to the Bartchs' time. The second place winner, the Italian airplane, beat them by two minutes.

The same aircraft, *Kona Wind*, has been used for all four races. "We have a very good engineer in Calgary, Marvin Peterson. He's just a whiz," Gordon says. "When he says that airplane is ready to go in the race, it's ready."

The next race is scheduled for 2001. Will the Bartchs participate? Hopefully. They're just getting the hang of it now.

New Runways

In 1997, this energetic couple entered another project. They are part of a group that on December 31, 1997, bought the airport in Airdrie, Alberta, 20 miles north of Calgary, from the Conroy family, with plans to turn it into a general aviation airport.

"We've worked with the Calgary Airport Authority and Nav Canada," Gordon says. "There won't be any air traffic control at that level, but you'll be able to make an instrument approach on Calgary, and then break off and land there if you want." The company, Airdrie Airpark Inc., plans to rebuild Runway 10/28, extend and repave it, sell lots so people can build their own hangars, and install an aircraft servicing facility.

Although the Bartschs reside in Hawaii, their aircraft had been stored in Calgary until changes in hangar ownership doubled their rent. "I think we bought into this airport just so we could have a place to store our airplane," Gordon smiles. They plan to "do six and six," living part of the year in Kona and part in Calgary, quite possible with their dual citizenship.

"When we bought the airplane Gordon said, 'We'll keep it two years and sell it,'" Dawn laughs. "When we did the rally in '94 he said, 'Okay, maybe two years longer.' When the '96 one came along, he said, "I think we should go again this time,' and the same with this last one in 1997."

Gordon is pleased with the way they've come back into aviation through the rallies and races. "It's so much fun, and it gives a purpose for the airplane . . . and now we're involved with Airdrie."

"Gordon's 66 and I'm 65, you know," Dawn says, "and all our friends who were with airlines and whatnot have retired at 60. They keep saying, 'What on earth are you doing??' But, we're having fun."

Dawn and Gordon often reflect on their careers, how they started, where life took them, where they are now. "For me, being a woman, I think I'm very, very lucky that I was able to get into aviation at that time," Dawn says "When the space age started I wished I had been born a little later because I would have loved to go to space. But when I first started flying, I wished I could have got in sooner because then I could have been a ferry command pilot, and I thought that would have been great, too.

"The North is a lot of it because of the trips we did, the people we met," Dawn continues. "I could have the president of an oil company in my airplane, and the next day I'd have a lonely prospector going somewhere."

Although their lives have not lacked conflict, that's ultimately what makes a story, what creates action and suspense and drama.

"That's right," Dawn says quietly.

"That's right," Gordon agrees. "I could be selling neckties for the Hudson's Bay Company."

Footnotes

[1] 1992 First Round the World Air Rally:
"We started from Santa Monica," Dawn says, "then flew to Oklahoma City and to Bangor, Maine; up to Goose Bay, Labrador; to Reykjavik, Iceland; from there to Southend, just south of London; then from London to Helsinki. We had seven stops in Russia: Moscow, Syktyvkar, Novosibirsk, Irkutsk, Yakutsk in northern Siberia, down to Magadan, a big nuclear submarine base in Russia; and to Anadyr. From there we flew over to Anchorage, Alaska; down to Vancouver, and back to Santa Monica."

[2] 1994, Race Around the World - Lower Latitude:
From Montreal the 30 participants –the Bartschs being the only Canadian entry – flew to St. Johns, Newfoundland, then across the Atlantic, through the Azores, Morocco, into Turkey, down to Dubai (where they waited for six hours to clear customs, in searing heat of 38° and higher), to Agra [northern India] where they had a reception at the Taj Mahal. From there they enjoyed a layover in Vietnam in Ho Chi Min City, then flew up through Japan, and into Petropavlovsk in the Kamchatka Peninsula in Russia. From Siberia they crossed the Bering Sea to Anchorage, Alaska. Calgary was the second last stop, and then they returned to Montreal.

[3] 1997, Olympics of Aviation:
The 7000-mile, 12-day race included stopovers in Strasbourg (France), Seville (Spain), Rome (Italy) – "where, for some obscure rea-

son, it took the Italian refuelers one hour to decide to do the job, then three hours to complete it" – to Tel Aviv (Israel) – where they landed for protection at Sid Dov, a military airport, rather than at Ben Gurion International – Amman (Jordan) – greeted here by King Hussein's son, Prince Feisal, himself a private pilot – and Trabzon and finally Adana (Turkey) – the end of the line.

Steve Villers and the Fort Nelson Airport Debacle

Steve Villers opens an interview session by speaking his mind, especially about something as near and dear to him as the Fort Nelson (BC) Airport, his aviation home for 40 years. At issue is the mandate of Transport Canada to get out of the business of running airports, leaving the decisions on who will take them over, and how, with local councils or airport authorities.

Villers' annoyance heats up as he lists the moves made by Transport Canada and the town – uniquely integrated with the Fort Nelson-Liard (changed as of March 26, 1999 to Northern Rockies) Regional District, whose town mayor and district chair are the same person, and seven directors, four of whom serve as town councilors – to the disadvantage, he feels, of his home airport.

A promotional news supplement, the Fort Nelson *Update* (April 8, 1998) advertises "Resource-Full Fort Nelson" as the Transportation Centre of the Far Northeast of the Province of British Columbia. The town is served by the Alaska Highway, BC Rail and daily scheduled flights by Canadian Regional Airlines. Villers Air Services Ltd. is the main fixed-wing airline operating out of Fort Nelson, with another smaller service operated by Glen Gullackson. Villers does not operate a scheduled service, relying on individual charters from oil and lumber companies and other private concerns, and taking out hunters in the fall. The airline is also called upon from time to time by the Ministry of Health to do Medevacs.

The upkeep of transportation avenues has always been a costly and labor-intensive process in the North, with small regional populations responsible for huge territories. The Northern Rockies district was previously serviced by airports built in the 1940s during construction of the Alaska Highway, which runs through the centre of the town of Fort Nelson (located at Mile 300, measured from Mile "0" at Dawson Creek).

The major issue distressing Fort Nelson residents was what to do when Transport Canada announced that it was selling its airports. Each community was responsible for determining its own system of local authority to operate and maintain the local airport to safe standards. This question split the Fort Nelson community, resulting in a series of private discussions, public meetings and referendums. Steve Villers, former owner of the largest air service in Fort Nelson, set himself squarely in the middle of the debate.

The Boy from Britain

John A. "Steve" Villers was raised far from the Canadian North. He was born to Gwendolen and Arthur Villers in Caterham, Surrey, England, on the 2nd of April, 1925.

He has two 2.5 siblings, being sisters Margaret and Joan, and a half-brother, Christopher (whose father was killed in World War I).

Steve's interest in aviation began when he saw airplanes flying overhead from nearby Kenley airfield, located close to the regional London airport at Croydon, and he attended airforce shows whenever possible. When war broke out, Steve left school at the age of 15, in 1940, and found a job as a messenger boy (dispatch rider) for the Air Raid Precaution (ARP).

He remained in that job for three years, until July 6, 1943, when he was 18 and eligible to join the Royal Air Force. On an earlier interview, he had been designated as a Pilot-Navigator or Bomb Aimer (PNB). Following three weeks in London at the initial receiving centre, he went to New Quay in Cornwall for ground training, navigation and Morse, engines, aircraft recognition and other sundry courses.

Next came a grading school at Cliff Pippard near Swindon west of London, where he received 12 hours of flight training in an open cockpit deHavilland Tiger Moth with an inverted Gypsy engine.

"I really enjoyed that!" Villers recalls. "Usually, if you soloed in 10 hours you would get a pilot designation. If you didn't, you could be designated either as a navigator or a bomb aimer, depending on your marks from the ground school. I soloed in seven hours, so I made pilot designation and that's what I wanted to be."

Following temporary postings to various bomber stations to assist ground crews, Villers' group received news that they would either be posted to Canada or to South Africa for further training through the British Commonwealth Air Training Plan. Steve Villers got Canada.

He boarded a large French ship, the *Isle de France*, landing in New York. In Moncton, New Brunswick, he receive his posting to No. 26 Elementary Flying Training School (EFTS) at Neepawa, Manitoba. Because that school was about to close, after two weeks he was sent to No. 32 EFTS in Bowden, Alberta, to fly Cornells. From there he attended

No. 18 Service Flying Training School (SFTS) at Gimli, Manitoba, to fly Ansons. He received his wings in March 1945.

At Boundary Bay, BC, near Abbotsford, Villers put in 75 hours flying Mitchell B-25s, then larger four-engine

Formation flying at Boundary Bay, B-25 Mitchell, July 1945. (Photo: Villers collection)

B-24 Liberator long-range bombers. Although he was destined for the long-range bomber group in Burma, his training was still incomplete when the U.S. dropped the atom bomb and it was all over. Back he went to England.

The chance of getting a flying job was almost nil. "At the receiving centre in England there were something like 23 000 pilots waiting for postings," Villers recalls. "There had only been four of us from SFTS sent to Boundary Bay and Abbotsford, the rest had gone back to England. They were all there at Harrogate in Yorkshire, 23 000 pilots, and they greeted us with the news that our flying was finished."

Villers got leave and went home for the first time in over two years – to be recalled to a posting! Because of his previous training he was ordered to take a Transport Supply Conversion Course on Dakota DC-3s, to practice supply-dropping, glider-towing and glider-snatching, again for the purpose of going to Burma.

"They were flying supplies to troops back in the jungle and had made 600-foot strips for the large Horsa gliders to land on. After landing, they'd back the glider up to the end of the runway. Then they'd attach a long nylon rope to it, which was laid zig-zag in front of the glider, with a final loop strung between two posts on either side. We were to fly over in the DC-3 with a hook hanging below, snatch up the rope and pull the glider into the air," Villers explains.

"But, instead of Burma they sent us straight to Transport Squadron in Egypt, so I never did any actual glider-towing except during the training. And I didn't do any bombing either, so I got lucky all the way around."

Villers was posted to 216 Squadron at Almaza near Cairo. From there, he flew as copilot in a DC-3 ("It was a requirement to have a minimum of 250 hours on the Dakota before becoming a Captain in Transport Command") on such trips as south to Wadi-Halfa, to Khartoum (the capital of the Sudan) and on to Asmara, Ethiopia. Other trips took him further, to Aden, Ryan and Salala on the Southern Arabian coast and to Masirah Island. They also ran flights east to an airstrip on an oil pipeline (called H3) where they would refuel and fly on to Habbaniya, Shaibah and Bahrain.

"The war had ended by that time, so it was just like airline flying. We were moving out airforce people when they'd finished a tour and also bringing in their replacements," Villers recalls. "At Asmara there were a lot of Italian people, and we occasionally took their families in or out."

Flight Sergeant Villers received his discharge from the Royal Air Force at the end of 1946, and, with his airforce wings, went back to run the farm at Caterham and contemplate his future. Still wanting to fly, he joined No. 15 Reserve Flying School "just down the road" at Red Hill near Gatwick, and there he flew deHavilland 82 Tiger Moths and later, Chipmunks.

"I flew them for fun, and for instrument flying," Villers says. "We did two weeks continuous training in the air and so I got my instrument ratings. During the year we could go there almost any time and take an airplane and fly around. They didn't charge us because we were keeping up our flying. I liked doing aerobatics, especially with the Tiger Moth. It was a beautiful airplane in which to do loops and rolls, roll off the top, spins, things like that. I still like doing aerobatics."

Every year following, Steve Villers put in another two weeks continuous training to renew his instrument rating. By the time the reserve wound up around 1954, he had decided to emigrate to Canada. There were no flying jobs in England at all, and it didn't look like there would be for some time. Perhaps in Canada he could achieve his goal of flying full time.

In the meantime, Steve had met Patricia Oborne, and they were married on September 5, 1951. "I don't know if she was willing to come to Canada, but she did anyway!" he laughs. They had no children yet, so this was his chance to make the big move. It was decided that he would come first, on a reconnaissance trip.

Coming to Canada

At age 26, Steve Villers arrived in Winnipeg where he knew one person, a Canadian Army doctor named Ian Maclean who had been stationed near the Villers' farm in England in 1940. Dr. Maclean had, in fact, married an Irish nurse who had been living with Steve's family, so perhaps the doctor and his wife could help him get established in Canada.

"That was not a very successful idea," Villers recalls. "I got to Winnipeg and Dr. Maclean met me at the station. I'd left England with only 20 pounds, which was about $80 at that time, and I'd spent some on the ship coming over so I wasn't very flush with money. When he met me he said, 'I'm sorry but we're having another baby and we have a nurse living in the house. I can't put you up, so I've booked you into a hotel.' But he'd put me into a *very* expensive hotel so I was left with $5 after the first night!

"I went to the Unemployment Office and they didn't have anything, so I took out the paper and got a job selling Elna sewing machines door to door," Villers continues. "I'm not a salesman but after about four days I did sell a machine so I had enough money to rent a small basement apartment for about $5 a week, and buy some bread and jam."

One day, he got talking with a fellow who was going to Calgary and who convinced Steve that there would be a good chance of getting a job there. The offer of a free trip settled the deal. Steve immediately found work in Calgary, cleaning windows. After three weeks, he found a job in the parts department of Ford Transport Motor Company which paid twice as much as window cleaning. He was rich!

When he learned that he would have to make up 10 more flying hours to get his Canadian commercial pilots' licence, he contacted the Calgary Flying Club. Villers received his commercial licence, with 1000 hours flying time, in 1955 and took the first job offered, with Aklavik Air Service owned by Mike Zubko and based in Aklavik, North West Territories.

With all indications of a good life in the new country, he sent for Pat – but how could he take her up North where he had no idea of the conditions? Again he left her behind, this time in Calgary, until he could size up the situation and find a suitable house in Aklavik.

Pat was quickly realizing how much fun it was to be married to a pilot. She had more good times in store. When Steve began flying out of Tuktoyaktuk, Pat came up for a real "northern" Christmas and New Year, staying in a vacant Hudson's Bay house.

During her first winter in Aklavik, 1956, after Steve had found them a more permanent residence, Pat learned to buy fresh drinking water by the ton, which had been cut from the frozen river in 50-pound blocks of ice and hauled by a Cat and stoneboat. Then she melted it as needed, a block at a time, in a barrel inside the house. To make matters even more interesting, Pat was soon expecting their first baby. Luckily there was a doctor in Aklavik, and daughter Ann was born there in 1957.

Mike Zubko had a contract flying for the DEW (Distant Early Warning) Line, and he sent Steve to the Site 4 base in Tuktoyaktuk, flying Cessna 170s and one of the company's two 195s. Villers describes a typical day at his new job:

"We were taking plumbers, electricians and inspectors from one DEW Line site to another, and transporting food, parts for vehicles and other essentials. Every time we landed there was somebody or something waiting, so we never really shut the airplane down, just stayed long enough to unload and load up again."

He might fly west from Tuk (Site 4) to a mainland point just south of Herschel Island (Site 1), and east to Cape Parry (Site 8). The DEW Line radar stations were about 50 miles apart. He quickly became grateful for the amount of instrument flying he'd done when he encountered the brutal and potentially fatal white-out conditions that often prevailed in the North, or the blackness of winter. He says that VFR rules were never enforced.

Steve's flying work was interesting, and he began to feel like a Northern pioneer. "They were just starting to build Inuvik, called East-3, about 30 miles east of Aklavik. I was the first pilot to land in Inuvik, flying the Cessna 170. They cleared a airstrip about 100 feet wide by 900 feet long so I could take in a load of liquor," he laughs. "The following week they cleared the other half, to 200 feet wide."

At that time, a person had to have a permit in order to buy liquor. "We'd go into Aklavik and with my permit, my wife's and some of the other pilots' permits, we'd buy liquor. This was not a bootlegging operation. We'd take it up to Tuk and everyone would party – the RCMP, the nurses, everybody."

The Villers continued to become acquainted with the North, its climate and its people. Pat kept the home-fires burning in Aklavik while Steve flew to "hot-spots" such as Old Crow, Reindeer Station, Fort McPherson and Arctic Red River – from DEW Line sites to trappers' bush camps, meeting all sorts of people who had chosen the North for various reasons.

He stayed with Mike Zubko's Aklavik Air Service until the end of 1957.

"I'd had enough of the North, really, I wanted to change, and I thought I'd be able to get a job further south. Jim Burroughs had been flying there too, but he and Mike didn't see eye to eye so he was leaving. When my wife and I planned on going back to England for a holiday, I said to Jim before I left, 'If you hear of a job, give me a call.' To my surprise, in January I got a call in England. Jim was starting a flying service in Fort Nelson with Bob Kirk and they needed another pilot. Would I come? I said I would, and that's how I came to Fort Nelson."

Private Business

Their company was initially called Fort Nelson Flying Service. Its owner, Bob Kirk, was a successful but somewhat eccentric prospector who'd made money as one of four major shareholders in the Cassiar asbestos mine. He now resided at Lower Post, just off Mile 620 of the Alaska Highway, and approximately 25 miles east of Watson Lake.

"Jim and I started working for Bob Kirk and that wasn't very successful," Villers says. "We were flying two Cessna 180s and started building up quite a few clients, but by the end of three months we didn't have any pay! The gas credit was cut off and the airplanes were seized, so that was the end of it."

Jim Burroughs and Steve Villers decided to go on their own, and started up Northern Air Service. They applied for a charter licence out of Fort Nelson, got the licence in 1959, and bought one Cessna 180 and leased another, with Jim and Steve both flying. The company's business came mainly from flying crews for geological and mapping surveys, and geophysical exploration. They also flew supplies and people to seismic and oil rigs, transported Health and Forestry department personnel, and secured

the mail delivery contract to Fort Liard, NWT, giving its residents a new and valued service – regular monthly mail delivery! Two or three years later the company also got a contract to take the mail into Fort Ware once a month. And, as usual with northern air services, they

Steve Villers, Doug Ward, Pat Villers and Ann Villers on their dock on the Nelson River in 1961. (Photo: Villers collection)

flew hunting and fishing parties into remote lakes, such as Tuchodi, Kluachise and Trout.

In 1960 they bought a Norseman from Alaska Airlines but soon wrote it off when Steve lost power after takeoff, right at the Fort Nelson Airport, and went into the trees. The wreck ended up at the dump. They purchased a second Norseman from Alaska Airlines. One day Jim was flying it over Lac la Biche, Alberta, on a forest fire, and lost power at 5000 feet. He landed in muskeg, on floats, with no injuries to his passengers or to the aircraft. The little airline pressed on and remained quite busy.

Pat and Steve's son, Peter, was born in 1960, symbolically at the Fort Nelson Airport, the location of the hospital at that time.

When Jim Burroughs decided to start his own company in Fort St. John, he and Steve split up their partnership, and Steve stayed in Fort Nelson. It wasn't an easy go.

"There was quite a bit of competition here at that time with companies such as Gateway Aviation. But I kind of gained passengers and they lost some, so I managed to get a large part of the business," Steve says. "I had a Super Cub, then switched to 185s with the bigger engine. After three or four years I added an Apache, so I had one twin-engine. Then I brought a Britten Norman Islander, a short-field airplane which was very suitable for the work here, particularly for hunters because there was lots of room for their gear and you get into some fairly short strips that the hunting guides were using."

In 1971, Villers received an offer from a local entrepreneur, Bob Keen of Keen Industries, to buy him out. "He was trying to get his company to go public and wanted my outfit, Northern Air Service, to do that. I named a price and he came up with it."

Villers Air Services dock at Fort Nelson, BC. (Photo: Villers collection)

So there he was, with a fistful of dollars and no company. He flew for a while as a relief pilot for Pacific Petroleums, and actually stayed with the company for the next four years.

"Then Keen got into financial difficulties. He wanted me to buy back the charter, but he'd put it into the ground by that time. He had all the wrong type of aircraft and everything, he'd ruined most of the clients, so I thought I'd apply for my own licence again. I did that and got it. Another outfit, Simpson Air, bought Keen's licence."

Villers Air Service Ltd. started with a Seneca One, a twin-engine Piper. When Peter Villers got his private pilot's licence at age 16, the company bought a Citabria, a single-engine aircraft similar to a Super Cub. (In due course, both these aircraft were replaced).

A large part of their business came from flying hunters for local guides such as the late Gary Powell (now Barry Tompkins' outfit), and for the late Don Peck, including two of Peck's clients described as "New York Mafia people."

"Don Peck was quite a character, and he razzed these guys something terrible," Villers recalls. "He'd say all kinds of things, but these guys liked him. They said it was the best holiday they'd ever had. They were just ordinary people, really, but they didn't hesitate to let us know they were known as 'enforcers.'"

In 1993, after 50 years and close to 20 000 hours of flying, Steve retired. He recently self-published his autobiography, titled *Sky Above, Land Below.*

Steve's and Pat's son, Peter, took over the company and now has 11 400 flying hours.

"I rarely go out to the airport anymore, although I still have an interest in it and flying in general," Steve says. "I have been working with the Airport Committee to try and solve the problems of the Town taking it over."

The Airport Debacle

With all his years of flying in the North, and 40 years based out of Fort Nelson, Steve Villers counts the town, and the airport, his home. That is why, when Transport Canada announced its intention to turn

Peter and Steve Villers, Fort Nelson, standing before Piper Seneca and Britten Norman Islander. (Photo: Villers collection.)

its airports over to local authorities, the issue had great impact on Steve and Peter Villers.

"I agree that the airport would be far better run locally, but the town is too small to take the cost, and they haven't done any study on what those costs will be," Steve says carefully, noting that the airport has run at a considerable deficit in the past. "They have no idea what they'll be letting themselves in for."

As of December 1998, Fort Nelson was one of several communities in BC that could find no straightforward solution to the dilemma. The main issue was cost, and the revenue received at the Fort Nelson airport from tenants' leases, fuel and landing fees would come nowhere near to paying for the annual maintenance of the airport.

Villers recalls that the provincial government allowed the town a 30-year lease for the land, at One Dollar per year. "But prospective tenants can't get bank loans to build on leased property. So, there's no hope of getting any more revenue there because nobody can build."

Consultation with other areas revealed that some municipally-owned airports had managed to sell off lots or spaces, an option that is not viable on leased land.

One prime example of a BC community that has moved ahead positively since retaining ownership of its airport is Nanaimo. The Nanaimo Airport Commission quickly became resourceful at finding new businesses to bring in needed revenue. The commission leased out a portion of its land for a nine-hole golf course (Cottonwood), negotiated for a 150-unit pet resort, signed a long-term lease to Timberline Air for an above-ground fuel facility, and encouraged income from use of its terminal building by carriers, land leases, and parking. As well, ideas were broached such as expanding a gift shop and lounge, establishing a "continental clearance" customs office, bringing in more flights from Seattle, Calgary and other airports, and becoming certified as a Global Positioning Satellite (GPS) approach to assist in foul weather landings.

When the airport received a $1.6 million grant from Transport Canada's Airport Capital Assistance program in 1997 for runway paving and construction, with the Nanaimo Airport Commission obligated to pay 10% of the costs, Airport Manager Curtis Grad acknowledged that coming up with that 10% was "going to be a test, but we can do it." In fact, Nanaimo Airport Commission won the Templeton Trophy for 1997 for "outstanding initiative and achievement in the successful development of a community airport."

On the dark side of the ledger, the Nanaimo (Cassidy) airport lost a court challenge in 1997, and was forced to pay $300 000 in provincial property tax on its land and holdings. But, the Airport Commission pressed on, becoming landlords involved in myriad new ventures, and also hosting the 1999 BC Aviation Council conference.

Meanwhile, back in Fort Nelson, doom and gloom was the operative mood.

"Potentially, the town has very little revenue from the airport," Viller states. "Peter's got the only hangar there for fixed-wing, and it's not a big hangar. There are a couple of smaller hangars for helicopters."

Patricia A. Bailey, then-Director of Administration Services, Fort Nelson-Liard Regional District (now administrator, Northern Rockies Regional District) noted in a discussion with the author in June 1998 that Transport Canada's announcement about selling its airports was thoroughly discussed at a meeting of the Union of British Columbia Municipalities (UBCM). It was decided there to form a "Municipal Airport Common Front," consisting of 29 municipalities and municipal districts to deal collectively with the issue rather than fall prey to the "divide and conquer" scenario. At that time, Fort Nelson came under Transport Canada's Western Region (Edmonton), but in 1997 was transferred to the Pacific Region (Vancouver). The choice was left with local councils: if a town did not want to assume responsibility for management of its airport, they could appoint, and pay for, a private sector or society to do the work.

The catch? This was an option primarily open to airports that made money. Fort Nelson, unfortunately, did not, and had been losing an average of one-half million dollars per year. It therefore had to be super-creative in seeking opportunities for land use – but what were their choices?

The solution seemed to rest on the unpopular move of increasing airport user fees, as well as municipal taxes on commercial and family housing, to cover airport costs. But Villers emphasizes that Fort Nelson already has high airline ticket prices, with a return trip from Fort Nelson to Vancouver or Calgary costing around $1000 (with no advance booking reductions).

The problem, in his view, was that Fort Nelson simply could not operate the airport and make any money, or break even, while still keeping airfares affordable. "There's a limit to what people will pay to fly," Steve reasons, "and less and less people are going to fly. The larger, commercial, airlines won't have enough business to come in here with a regular service. And then it follows, all the way down."

In November 1998, Nav Canada, the non-profit corporation that took over air traffic control systems from Transport Canada, began charging fees for general aviation, again increasing costs for users of the facilities. A pilot for North Cariboo Air Service in Fort St. John was quoted an extra $87 in Nav Canada fees to fly his 206, a single-engine airplane, return from Fort St. John to Fort Nelson. "There's such a lot of argument about these increases!" Villers says, perplexed and unhappy over what is happening to his industry.

With such increases in outside costs, the local expenses for maintaining the airport would make its operation simply unaffordable.

"The town, and the airport, is too small but it still has to be maintained," Steve says. "You've got to have employees to take care of general maintenance, look after the runways, tar cracks and everything else, clear snow and sand, maintain runway and taxi lights. All that is expensive.

"The town has contacted private airport authorities who take on airport operation, but they only take on airports that are profitable," Steve explains. "They're not interested in places like Fort Nelson or Port Hardy. They were interested in Fort St. John because it's got enough traffic, but no private company is interested in this one."

Watson Lake, at Mile 632 on the Alaska Highway, is fortunate in being just north of the BC border in the Yukon Territories. Its airport will continue to be run by the feds, one of nine airports in the Northwest Territories and three in the Yukon blessed by being "north of 60." "In fact," says Steve, "they've just spent $8 Million on the Watson Lake Airport! We're below the 60th parallel, so we're on our own. Everything above is looked after by the federal government."

So there sits Fort Nelson, like poor cousins, below the 60th but still in the North, out of the hands of Big Daddy, small and unprofitable, wanted by no one but eminently necessary.

"Both federal and provincial governments take a tremendous amount of money out of this part of the country," Villers says. "Even in fuel tax – 50% of aviation fuel costs go to the federal government. Now, if you stop aircraft coming in here, think of all the fuel that is used, they're going to lose at least $2 million per year, minimum. So I think we've got a very good negotiating point, if we knew the facts."

In 1997, KPMG Consulting Services of Vancouver was retained by the Regional District to examine the airport budget and to prepare a business plan for its future. Their report forecast a $400 000 annual deficit if the Regional District continued to run the airport in the same way as had Transport Canada.

The accountants' report on potential revenue for Fort Nelson Airport was so far off base, says Steve, that he is amazed they would release it. "I don't think they got all the information," he says, cautiously. "I mean, in their report they stated that the town could get $5 million or something out of the sale of timber at the airport, on the leased land. When the Airport Committee went over it, they estimated that it would be lucky if we could get $700 000 – even if we could sell it. And the cost of [taking timber off] a small area like that would make it almost worthless, so they were $4 1/2 million out, right off the bat."

Mayor Don Edwards, in an article in the November 26, 1997, Fort Nelson *News*, acknowledged that although the timber had been cruised and stumpage would be paid by the municipality, the "price of land was rather nebulous at this point and forestry is cyclical."

The local Fort Nelson *News* had a field day trying to cover the views of the two factions, for or against the town taking over the airport. Letters to the editor filled many pages, as well as comments from the town's lawyer and negotiator, Donald Lidstone, and articles written by reporters trying to get a handle on this important issue and convey a solid position to the public.

A referendum was scheduled, and on November 12, 1997, the paper simply printed the details concerning the referendum question and a synopsis of Bylaw No. 91. They further printed a "quick and dirty" calculation of what the airport was likely to cost each business and residence through taxes, and beside it a more detailed, "to the penny" calculation. The KPMG financial report offered a thumbnail sketch of financial issues, stating basically that if the referendum were approved, the Regional Board would levy a property tax throughout the town and regional district to raise $250 000, and install an "Airport Passenger Ticket Tax" of $15 per ticket to hopefully raise another $200 000. The report notes that "anyone who flies in BC is already familiar with ticket taxes implemented by other airport operators."

In return, Transport Canada would transfer ownership of all buildings, infrastructure and equipment to the Regional District for One Dollar. All lease and other revenues currently collected by Transport Canada would continue to be collected by the Regional District, except for the federal aviation fuel tax. Transport Canada would also offer, payable in the year 2000, an "operating and major maintenance subsidy" of $920 000 to provide a financial cushion to help with the adjustment. A note in the announcement adds that this offer should be considered generous, as The Town of Smithers, BC, received only $200 000.

On November 26th, however, a newspaper article on the airport seemed to suggest that the $920 000 transfer money was burning a hole in the pocket of the town council, and that a referendum had been hurriedly called so that the money could be accessed immediately rather than having to wait until the year 2000.

It was also mentioned that the airport lands were owned by the Province of BC and only leased to Transport Canada. The Regional District had also negotiated with Crown Lands to obtain a 30-year lease for One Dollar per year.

In the same edition (Nov. 26/97), readers learned that the municipality had agreed to take over responsibility for several permanent federal employees who had been working at the airport, and who would then join the town's unionized (CUPE) workforce complete with their seniority and benefits.

The government's National Airports Policy (NAP) plan was explained to citizens in a "Just the Facts" column published in the *News* on December 19, 1997. "The federal government will NOT continue to maintain the airport after 2000. The National Airports Policy states, '... [the federal government] will be withdrawing from any ownership or financial/operational involvement in [regional/local] airports during the five years beginning April 1, 1995. Between April 1995 and March 2000, federal funding declines gradually and on March 31, 2000, federal funding for regional/local airports will cease.'"

As of November 19, 1997, nineteen BC communities had completed negotiations with Transport Canada to own and operate their airports, with five nearly completed.

The First Referendum

The first referendum for a vote on the Northern Rockies Regional District's Airport Service Establishment Bylaw No. 91, held in December 1997, was defeated.

Fully 62 percent of the 1254 voters were against transferring the airport's operation to the town, being afraid of a huge increase in their taxes. "Our nose is NOT out of joint over this," the December 10th Fort Nelson *News* quoted the mayor as saying. "We're thrilled that a group is organizing to take the issue forward . . . The Town and Regional District will provide whatever support and assistance they can."

"Fort Nelson-Liard [the former name of Northern Rockies] is the only community in British Columbia to vote down an airport initiative," the reporter states. "Some problems are anticipated in the efforts to negotiate a private sector agreement, because Fort Nelson's airport lands are actually owned by the province and not the federal government. A 'simple' transfer is not possible and separate arrangements will have to be made with BC."

On February 25, 1998, the *News* reported that "after the defeat of the airport referendum, members of council and the regional board voted to remove themselves from further negotiations."

An *ad hoc* committee was quickly formed to "informally" work on keeping negotiations moving ahead. Then, in a further motion, the municipality agreed to work on the airport takeover, to take in two members of the *ad hoc* committee and examine their findings. One discovery clearly showed a discrepancy in the evaluation of marketable timber on the airport. "The lands branch estimated the amount of timber available in the 'provincial package' as only about $500 000 compared to several millions estimated by KPMG [the Vancouver accounting firm hired to assess the financial projections for the Fort Nelson Airport]. This was because older maps were used," quoted the *News* (Feb. 25/98). Further discrepancies were found in the value of gravel on site.

When Transport Canada issued a deadline for a contract to be signed by December 1, 1998, or the airport would be closed, tempers flared.

"Well, that was nonsense!" Steve Villers says, his voice rising with anger and indignation. "Then a gag order was put on discussions. The council never told anybody about the negotiations until they'd got the thing approved [in private], and then they had to go to the public to approve it.

"And I don't understand the Chamber of Commerce," Villers adds. "They put up a notice, 'SAY YES.' Yet we were told that they'd be increasing the taxes here if they did this. It would put some people out of business, and certainly no new businesses are going to come in with huge taxes. So, it works 100% against the future development of the town."

Steve Villers moves from the focal point of the situation hounding the Fort Nelson Airport to general care of airports by Transport Canada. He applauds the new safety and communication systems, such as the Global Positioning System (GPS), that make flying so much safer, allowing pilots to know exactly where they are at all times. Also, there are many good airstrips around the country, not like in the old days.

But, he also says that there have been "one series of blunders after another" since Transport Canada took over the Fort Nelson airport after the Air Force left in 1958.

"We had a good hangar here, 200 feet long and 120 feet wide by 30 feet high. It was built in the 1940s when this airport was first started during construction of the Alaska Highway. But, they wouldn't rent it out to anybody unless it was aviation-related and, because it was a wooden hangar, it was almost impossible to insure it to hold a $15 million airplane – and that's what they're worth now. So as a result, the big hangar sat empty for a period of time, even though there was revenue potential from other companies to store trucks and things. In 1993, they spent about a million dollars to destroy it."

He then cites Transport Canada's move to decommission various runways.

"They closed down Runway 07/25 here in Fort Nelson, the only runway that is into wind, leaving just 03/21 operating. This very nearly caused a major accident a while ago when our daily airline came in during a more than 40-knot cross-wind, 90° to the runway. A gust hit just as it landed, and one wingtip came within one foot of hitting the ground."

The option of having two operative runways is necessary in Fort Nelson, Villers says, because of local wind conditions. "Fort Nelson is fortunate in that it does not have a lot of high winds, but when it does blow hard it usually comes from the southwest, blowing 90 degrees across the main runway."

Some pilots continue to use the defunct runway anyway, including, at times, Steve's son, Peter, who now runs Villers Air Services Ltd. "They ignore Transport Canada and use it, for safety reasons. Pilots say 'Go ahead, write it up, and give me a ticket,' or whatever. But, they don't."

Although Runway 07/25 hasn't been maintained since its closure on December 1, 1997, Villers feels it's still basically safe to use, and certainly safer than trying to fight the wind by coming in on 03/21. "They said they were two cracks in it, but I taxied over it and never noticed any bumps. They probably could have filled those two cracks for a couple of hundred dollars, they're nothing major." He sits back, shaking his head. "Now, they've just done that, but instead of fixing the cracks completely, right across the runway, they've fixed just two-thirds, leaving about 15 feet on either side, why I don't know! It would have cost absolutely nothing to have done the extra 15 feet."

Knowing that Runway 07/25 was still being used during strong wind conditions, Transport Canada's next step to promote its disuse was to nail into the tarmac large plywood crosses, a third of the way from each end of the runway. "Now, those are coming off in the wind," Villers says, "and nails are sticking up three inches."

Then the windsocks were removed on 07/25, an action repeated on various, unmanned, emergency strips along the Alaska Highway. "They took a welding torch and cut down all the windsock poles!" Villers says. "I mean, this is a complete disregard for safety! I just don't understand."

Transport Canada has rendered useless a number of old emergency-use airstrips located at remote points such as the Sikanni Chief, Prophet and Liard rivers, which Villers describes as all good, 5000-foot-long by 200-foot-wide airstrips built in the 1940s during construction of the Alaska Highway. Until recently, these airstrips were equipped with windsocks, important aids for pilots when making emergency landings.

The point is, of course, that Transport Canada doesn't want aircraft landing on these old airstrips, because of safety issues regarding their use as they are no longer being maintained. But Villers feels this shows a complete disregard for safety.

North Peace MLA Richard Neufeld has been made painfully aware of this situation. Because of their generous dimensions these old airstrips could accommodate large aircraft, and were regularly used by the Ministry of Forests to store fuel and as landing strips for both fixed-wing and helicopters during fire-fighting season. The Department of Health also used them for Medevacs. But after years of doing basic maintenance such as grading to keep down second-growth trees so airplanes could still land, Transport Canada formally "decommissioned" a number of emergency strips along the Alaska Highway. Large white "x"s were painted, and in some cases ditches dug across the runways.

"When you're talking about 200 to 300 miles between hospitals in the North," says Neufeld, "it's kind of handy to be able to land an aircraft beside the highway to pick up people that have been hurt, or be able to go to fires that are very close by – you can control them quickly."

In a *Canadian Aviation News* article (Aug. 17/98) the Minister of Forests, David Zirnhelt, states that part of the reason the federal government wanted to extricate itself from these old airports was liability issues, although to his knowledge that had not been a problem. In fact, ditches dug across airstrips might introduce accidents that the feds were trying to avoid.

"There are a tremendous number of American pilots who fly small planes from the 'lower 48' to Alaska," says Zirnhelt. "They do VFR [visual flight rules] and they fly the highway. If they get into trouble they can land at these airstrips.

Steve Villers next item of complaint concerns environmental cleanup work being undertaken at the Fort Nelson airport. One-half million dollars were spent to dig up materials considered to be hazardous that were left behind 50 years ago by the airforce.

In Villers' opinion, they should be left alone, unless deemed to be causing a problem. The soil considered to be contaminated from oil and chemicals such as those used for de-icing was simply piled on the grass.

"They dug it up and put it in a big pile all covered with plastic, so there's a real mess down there now!" Villers says. "Now, how did that help anything? They're supposed to spend another $10 million doing cleanup. They could have run the airport for the next 30 years on that money!"

The Airport Committee

Steve Villers became a member of the *ad hoc* Airport Committee formed in Fort Nelson to hopefully gain more knowledge about the situation. The committee's aim was to also seek out any government aid that might help the town make the transition toward owning and operating its airport.

"First of all," Steve says, "we had to get information – s what our revenues were, how much it was going to cost us, and how much we were going to lose. If it was found that we'd be $150 000 or $200 000 short, we'd have to seek help. But they couldn't put all the costs on the taxpayers."

A difficulty for citizens voting on the referendums was the "gag order" imposed on the negotiations by Transport Canada. According to Mayor Edwards, while negotiations weren't public, neither were they secret, but the citizens felt they were being kept in the dark.

Finally, a management proposal outlining a plan for the Fort Nelson Airport was received in June 1998, from Mel Feddersen, Director of Canadian Operations, YVR Airport Services Ltd. This subsidiary company of Vancouver International Airport Authority, located in Richmond, BC, manages 12 airports worldwide (four in Dominican Republic, one each in Bermuda, Santiago (Chile) and Wellington (New Zealand) as well as Canadian airports in Hamilton (Ontario), Moncton (New Brunswick) and three in British Columbia – Fort St. John, Kamloops and Cranbrook.

The company had initially expressed no interest in taking on the Fort Nelson Airport. "When we looked at the Fort Nelson airport from the perspective of making money, or breaking even, we saw that it couldn't," says Mel Feddersen in a telephone conversation with the author on May 7, 1999. "And we didn't want to get into a situation where we were taking fees from the local taxpayers yet not making any money for them from this operation."

"They have a lot of experience in airports," Villers says, "and the two they did not initially want because of the deficits were Fort Nelson and Port Hardy. Because of the gag order, however, the details of their proposal could not immediately be released to concerned citizens and a shroud of secrecy was observed."

The Airport Committee's minutes of the meetings were also considered confidential, and members were not allowed to discuss the situation outside of the meeting room.

"I read the proposal and felt that the town would be crazy to accept it," Villers says. "It would cost an initial sum of $250 000 to hire these people to manage the airport, and that didn't cover any expenses. That was just management fees. So we'd be looking at the same costs that we'd have anyway, plus another $250 000. I gather that they'd put an airport manager on, a part-time one who would come up once or twice a week and look after things."

Fort St. John Airport had taken the company's offer, but the Fort Nelson scene was different. For one thing, Fort St. John is a much busier airport, with around 90 000 landings compared to Fort Nelson's 18 000. Also, they had much more revenue coming in from leasing property to fixed-base operations (FBOs) on the airport.

The Fort Nelson Airport Committee, whose president was also one of two members on both the Airport Committee and the town's financial committee, engaged in negotiations with the provincial government to try to find a solution. Steve Villers was not a member of this group. "I wasn't asked to be a negotiator," he says bluntly. "I think the town wants to take it over without anybody criticizing anything, so I'm a thorn, there's no doubt about it."

Steve Villers researched methods of collecting fees other than increasing user costs. Instead of paying individual landing fees the larger airlines might pay the town an annual sum, making less paperwork. "Years ago we paid landing fees, so much per aircraft for landing. Then we'd get regular bills from these airports where we'd landed. But Transport Canada found it was costing them $13.80 to collect a $1.50 landing fee! Perhaps the same thing would happen here if they had to hire a person to tabulate every landing, then do billings. Another answer might be to put it on the fuel purchases made here, but the government says that's *their* revenue."

Because there isn't a large amount of fuel being sold at the Fort Nelson Airport, Villers figured that perhaps large users such as airlines could pay an annual fee, and casual, or smaller users, pay a five-cent or so tax on fuel. "That's what we pay right now, a five-cent fuel tax," Villers says, "but they're taking that off when the airport is taken over because the government says that's their revenue, it doesn't go towards the town."

Any subsidy offered to the town by Transport Canada would be part of the forthcoming negotiations, with a National Airports Policy (NAP) to be completed in 1998-99.[1]

But resolving the Fort Nelson airport debacle was slow going, with much innuendo and misunderstanding permeating the community. On April 22, 1998, the Fort Nelson *News* again ran a "Questions and Answers" column, noting that many letters and petitions had been forwarded to Transport Canada from local residents and political allies.[2]

It had been confirmed that "there are no funds from Transport Canada to keep the airport operating after March 31, 2000." With nothing to be gained by delay, the citizens were urged to get on with a resolution, based on a sound business plan.

"Fort Nelson is one of three municipalities in BC that has not completed negotiations," confirmed Patricia Bailey in June 1998, "and we've heard there are several more across Canada." It was indeed a difficult situation, with no solution in sight.

The Worst Case Scenario

The ultimate fear was, of course, that the airport could be shut down. Villers feels that the government losses – aside from local losses in service and revenue – would be tremendous. "I worked it out. If aircraft weren't coming in here, the federal government would lose between $400 000 and $500 000 per year, on just fuel tax. As far as I know, all the present landing fees and aviation fuel tax goes to the federal government."

The provincial Ministry of Forests has a tanker base in Fort Nelson, owned by the ministry and leased from the federal government, and employs Conair to fight fires in the area. "One day this year six water bombers worked for about six hours on 15-minute round trips to contain a fire," Villers notes. "This fire would have got out of control if they had been operating out of Fort St. John or Watson Lake. Not only would the fire have likely got away, but also it would have cost them another $15 000 to $20 000. That's in one day! I've seen fires around here where they've brought in fixed-wing aircraft, helicopters, 100-men crews and their groceries and so on, spending up to $100 000 a day. The provincial government couldn't afford to not have this airport."

Some of the oil and mineral companies have their own area airstrips. Petro-Canada has an airstrip at Sierra near Fort Nelson, but they also have personnel who come in to Fort Nelson for meetings and site visits. Other such companies would likewise be affected.

Dennis Erickson, Canadian Regional Airlines' Manager of Corporate Communications in Calgary, confirms that his airline operates a daily "sked" service (except Saturday) out of Calgary through Grande Prairie and Fort St. John into Fort Nelson. He is confident that a suitable agreement can be reached for private ownership and management of the airport.

In a telephone conversation with the author on February 16, 1999, Erickson said that Canadian Regional Airlines plans to continue serving Fort Nelson, and he feels positive about moving forward to privatization, turning airports over to local authorities. The company does like to know, of course, who the landlord is, and hope that rents won't become exorbitant for Canadian Regional's office and ticket counter located on the airport, and landing fees.

"It's really a matter of time until we see consolidation of landing fees and rentals," Erickson says. "We don't want to be subsidizing airports through expensive AIF's [airport improvement fees]. The landlord must be fiscally responsible, and amalgamate use of personnel and machinery with town and airport use to keep costs reasonable. We are always going to be tenants of airports, never landlords. So, if the rates – the AIFs – skyrocket, then, we'd have to find a new airport."

Canadian Aviation News (August 17, 1998) published a feature article on "Northern Airport Abandonment" and quoted Richard Neufeld, MLA for the North Peace District, on his efforts to help with negotiations to enable the Fort Nelson Airport to remain open.

"I think it behooves all ministries and government to look seriously at that airport," Neufeld said, at a meeting held in the Legislative Building in Victoria during the summer of 1998. "The biggest problem is that the population there is so small. We're talking about 6000 or 7000 people being able to maintain an airport . . . and it just becomes unmanageable." Neufeld expressed hope that the minister, along with other ministries, would be able to meet with the Fort Nelson residents "fairly soon" and work out a business plan to deal with the issue.

By February of 1999, the situation remained unsolved and the people were becoming weary. A poorly-attended meeting was held at a local theatre, with more airport committee members present than townspeople. Those who attended were treated to an energetic display of rhetoric, however, duly reported in the local *News* on February 17th.

> *Mr. [Donald] Lidstone [the town's lawyer who has handled most of the negotiations] spoke bitterly about the way the federal government had dumped the airports into the laps of the local taxpayers. It was not, he said, a negotiation but a unilateral decision to unload the responsibility on to the provinces, who in turn handed it down to the municipalities. It was, he said, 'a dastardly nefarious, one-sided, airport policy.'*

The Resolution

A second referendum was held March 6, 1999, with the result that the regional district *would* take over the airport, with YVR Airport Services Ltd. managing it for an interim two-month contract "to start the process off."

Still, some "glitches" prevailed, such as confusion over the leasing arrangements. Transport Canada leased the airport from the provincial government, and the town is unable to secure a lease from the provincial government until the federal government gives it up.

Mel Feddersen of YVR Airport Services Ltd. said they were trying to negotiate a better deal with the provincial government, to obtain clear, or some form of reasonable, title to the land. He was hopeful that a solution would be reached to allow the Fort Nelson airport to become a viable entity.

But was the worst of it over? In early March 1999, Steve heard a radio broadcast on which a representative from YVR Airport Services Ltd. stated that one of their first mandates would be to close down Runway 07/25, as it wasn't needed. Steve's investigations on their reasoning produced more anxiety, a seemingly ongoing malady in this little town at Mile 300 of the historic Alaska Highway.

The environmental issue at the airport, noted earlier by Steve Villers, was of particular concern when making final arrangements with Transport Canada and the BC Ministry of the Environment, because of potential long-term liability and clean-up costs. Finally, as a result of "hard negotiating and 11th hour assistance from the BC Ministry of Environment," Transport Canada signed an "environmental side letter" accepting full responsibility for clean-up activities including for leased lands.

The townspeople were mostly relieved that the haggling seemed to be over. "The community demonstrated a positive forward-looking intention and once the arguments were presented properly they got the message and gave their blessing to the process that will lead to the ownership of the airport by the community," states the editor of the Fort Nelson *News* on March 10, 1999. "This expensive process to change the minds of those who had voted 2-1 against the same proposal is a salutary lesson in how not to treat the voters. They must be a part of the discussion process if they are going to make the right positive decisions . . . A win is a win, but in this case the win is an endorsement for those on the airport committee who have worked to bring the best deal they could to Fort Nelson."

The Airport Committee was not consulted about the arrangements, a point that angered some and caused others to agree that the committee had no true legal status so had no right to be included in negotiations.

A more permanent arrangement for airport management was put out to tender, with bids closing April 22, 1999. Three were received: from YVR Airport Services Ltd., ATCO Airports Ltd. (formerly Frontec) and Airport Performance Group. On May 10th the successful bidder, ATCO Airports Ltd., was selected to take over operations as of June 1, 1999, on a five-year contract.

ATCO Airports Ltd. is a western-Canada based company that manages, operates and maintains airports including aviation facilities throughout Canada and the United States, e.g., Dawson Creek and Castlegar, BC; Portage La Prairie, Manitoba; and North Bay, Ontario.

"Administrator Pat Bailey led the regional district's negotiating team in the final talks with Transport Canada,' reports the (newly-named) Northern Rockies Regional District Municipal Bulletin (Vol. 1, Issue 1, April 14, 1999). "'It was pretty hectic,' she said, 'but we're confident we did a good job for the community.'"

Mayor Harry Clarke noted, "We chose ATCO because they have extensive Northern experience and interests, and because they proposed to have an experienced manager on-site, and because they offered the best price."

Asked bluntly, if the airport shut down what would it do to Villers Air Service, Steve Villers seriously considers the question. "I'm sure Peter would quit. He could get a job with anyone. It's difficult to do anything now, from hiring good pilots to getting check rides. You've got to have a check ride on each aircraft, and if Transport Canada won't come up here, from Vancouver, to do a check ride for several months from the time you need one, how can you hire a new pilot?"

Steve Villers (Photo: Shirlee Matheson)

And so, if negotiations were to fail and a "CLOSED" sign appear on the Fort Nelson Airport, alongside the severed windsock poles and plywood crosses, Villers Air Service might cease to exist and Peter leave to seek work as a pilot for someone else's airline. It's not the heritage that Steve hoped to pass on, and he's still "fighting City Hall" to determine a solution – along with other BC communities left staring at dark runways that may revert to wilderness moose pastures.

"I decided to write a list of all the stupid things that the 'professionals' had done to the airport since Transport Canada had taken it over in 1958," Steve says, "but it's not for publication."

For the present, simply recording the annals of history pertaining to his second home, the Fort Nelson Airport, is Steve Villers' personal therapy.

Footnotes

[1]The National Airports Policy (NAP) provides that regional local airports be offered first to the provincial or territorial government where they are located.
According to The Honourable David M. Collenette, P.C., MP, in a letter printed in *Canadian Aviation News* (June 15, 1998), to ensure fairness for all airports affected by the NAP, any funding made available to a new airport operator is based on each airport's budget for the fiscal years ending on March 31, 2000. Any funds used by

Transport Canada to operate the airport during this period are not included in the contribution agreement signed with a new airport operator.

Collenette goes on to explain that in 1995, the government introduced new measures to increase the viability of regional/local airports by reducing to variance between costs and revenues at the individual sites, which will affect the amount of money available in each case.

"In answer to some additional questions by Fort Nelson residents," Collenette says, "there is no agreement in place between the United States and Canada that obliges Canada to operate the airport in Fort Nelson and there is no other source of federal funding to assist with the operating costs for an airport. Federal taxes on fuel sold at airports will not be turned over to the airport operators. Any fee levied on aviation fuel through a lease with a fuel company will accrue to the landlord after the lease is assigned to the new operators."

Collenette concludes by saying that it is recognized that Fort Nelson is an important transportation link, with the Alaska Highway and the airport providing the main modes of transportation available in the area. "Transport Canada is pursuing other venues for the airport, and will be working to effect the transfer to a local group before March 31, 2000."

[2]Lorne Pennycock, Manager of the National Airports Policy (NAP) Implementation for Regional/Local and Small Airports, responded to questions directed by Susan Munro, a member of the Airport Committee. One by one, Pennycock refutes Munro's arguments, from giving Fort Nelson special consideration because of its contribution to the economic well-being of the area, to its being designated as a Remote Airport that provides the only reliable, year-round, transportation to an isolated community, thereby requiring continuing federal support.

"Clearly that is not the case for Fort Nelson," writes Pennycock, in his letter published in the Fort Nelson *News* (April 22/98) and reproduced in *Canadian Aviation News* (June 15/98), "therefore it will not be reclassified as a Remote Airport. We also discussed the possibility of Fort Nelson being declared an Arctic Airport, which would be included in the lump transfer of all Yukon and Northwest Territories airports to the respective territorial governments through a formula funding agreement between the federal and territorial governments." But with Fort Nelson located in British Columbia, this was not viable. "In the case of Fort Nelson, the airport, along with all others in BC, was offered to the provincial government. As you know, the government of BC declined," Pennycock writes.

He further refers to the defeated referendum and its repercussions on a timely settlement. "I contacted Mr. Cliff Rhodes, Transfer Manager [Transport Canada] in Vancouver, who informed me that a local referendum had rejected the idea that the Regional District could take over the airport. Transport Canada is concerned about entering into an agreement to negotiate with an organization [Airport Committee] that does not have the authority to conclude an agreement." He states that a Letter of Intent could be initiated and signed, however, to promote discussion, which he would forward to the Regional District.

Although the Regional District could apply for a federal grant, administered under the Airports Capital Assistance Program (ACAP), for funding toward airport capital projects related to safety, asset protection and operating cost reduction, the hitch is that they were eligible to apply *only* if they were the owner and operator of the airport. And would an ACAP grant help Fort Nelson? Or, might it be "too little, too late?"

The Adventures of Tundra Wolfe

"I can't recall how or why I first became interested in aviation," says Wally Wolfe. "It must have been the influence of the movie matinees that I went to, for 10 cents a shot, most Saturday afternoons. I think I saw every aviation-oriented movie ever made at that time."

Walter "Wally" Albert Wolfe was born in the small railroad town of Melville, Saskatchewan, on July 6, 1937, to parents Robert and Bertha Wolfe. He has two sisters, Doreen now living in Saskatoon, and Eileen in Vancouver, and one brother, Wayne, in La Crete, Alberta. Fortunately for the aviation-enthusiast, in 1950 the opportunity arose to move to Edmonton and he was able to begin his aviation career in earnest.

In 1953, at age 16, he joined 395 Air Cadet Squadron, based in a hangar on Kingsway Avenue at the Edmonton Municipal Airport. Because he lacked personal finances to pay for a regular course he hoped to obtain his private pilot's licence through an Air Cadet sponsorship. His efforts were successful.

Wally Wolfe's first recorded flight took place on July 2, 1956, in a Fleet 80 Canuck (CF-DYY) when he commenced flying lessons through the Edmonton Flying Club. He soloed in 7:45 hours, and received his private pilot's licence on August 9, 1956. Soon after, he took a friend to Cooking Lake southeast of Edmonton, flying in the Fleet 80 Canuck, which he laughingly called an "F-80" or a "Fleeterschmidt."

Wally Wolfe in the Royal Canadian Air Cadets, 1953-1956. (Photo: Wolfe collection)

"Well, feeling that I was the greatest thing since sliced bread because I was now a glorified pilot, I began strafing another friend's cabin," Wolfe relates, still amazed at his youthful foolishness. "After a few passes and successfully 'shooting up' the place, I returned to home base. As I taxied in to the Edmonton Flying Club's gas pumps and shut down, I noticed the club manager, Maury Fallow, waiting for me."

Apparently, another cabin owner at Cooking Lake had not appreciated Wolfe's dive-bombing expertise, had noted the registration of the Canuck and called the RCMP, who notified the club manager. Wolfe was grounded for a month. "That was very reasonable punishment, considering that they'd entertained the thought of taking my licence away altogether!" Wolfe notes.

By 1956, when he finished with the Air Cadets, he had attained the rank of Warrant Officer, 1st Class.

In 1954 Wolfe had joined the City of Edmonton Squadron, 418 RCAF Auxiliary, which had served in World War II flying Mosquitos. There, he received training as an Aero Engine Technician and worked on Mitchell B-25 light bombers.

"It was commonplace for the bombers to do practice bombing runs at Bittern Lake near Wetaskiwin, south of Edmonton," Wolfe recalls. "On one particular exercise, I went with them. My station during the flight was behind the flight crew in front of the bomb bay. The aircraft did its usual bombing run, dropping all of its bombs except one. The bomb bay had an inspection panel on top, and I was instructed to have a look inside and assess the situation."

The bombs usually hung by two hooks. In this case, he found that one hook had let go and the bomb was still hanging by the other one. The crew did two more bombing runs in an attempt to loosen the remaining bomb, to no avail. The bomb bay doors closed and the flight returned to Edmonton.

"If it had let go while we were on our way back, it could have left a nasty hole in the bottom of the airplane, not to mention what it could have done to me," Wolfe says. "After landing and parking at the hangar, the Armorers put a mattress down on the tarmac under the bomb bay doors. Then they opened the doors. The bomb didn't fall, so it was removed successfully. Phew!"

Wally Wolfe soon attained the rank of Leading Aircraftsman (LAC) with the squadron and travelled with them as a member of the ground crew to maintain the aircraft engines during various exercises ("war games"). They practiced bombing runs, fighter intercepts and such at Abbotsford (BC), Winnipeg (MB), and Summerside (PEI). A highlight for Wally was being in charge of a flight that received a trophy for the most points in achievement.

Following completion of high school, and after his association with 418 Squadron in 1957, Wolfe found work as "general joe boy" at the Edmonton Flying Club. "This meant moving and gassing aircraft, cleaning hangar floors and helping with the maintenance of the flying club's aircraft." That year he also began an apprenticeship for Aircraft Mainte-nance Engineer, while taking training for a Commercial Pilot's Licence. A job perk was being able to use the club's aircraft at the employee's reduced rental rate.

The young pilot, still full of spunk, was of the opinion that aerobatics weren't all that difficult and one day decided to try them, again in his pseudo-warplane the "F-80."

"I went up to 5000 feet and dove to attain the necessary airspeed to get me over the top," Wolfe recalls. "Unfortunately, I didn't maintain the proper 'pull' on the stick, nor did I have enough airspeed. When I got to the top, the aircraft was barely making it over. With not enough airspeed the plane stalled upside down, at the top, and scared the living . . . out of me! I leveled out, checked everything within visual range, and gingerly returned to the hangar where I did a more thorough check of the aircraft.

"Some days later I was talking to Bill King, one of the instructors, about my 'expertise' in aerobatics. He offered to take me up and show me how to do it properly, which he did."

Wolfe received his Commercial Pilot's Licence on March 25, 1959, and also acquired his Aircraft Maintenance Engineer's Licence the same year. "Now I could get any job I wanted. Dream on!" he laughs.

The only position offered was at the Edmonton Flying Club as a flying instructor — *if* he could get his Instructor's rating. He received a Category III rating on May 15, 1960, with 323:40 hours flying time, and instructed all that summer and fall. By winter, when activity slowed, the club offered to keep him on at his current salary *if* he promised to stay one more year. Wolfe considered the offer and turned it down. He had sent out a number of letters of application, and felt sure that something wonderful would turn up.

He had worked at the Edmonton Flying Club from May 1960 to January 15, 1961 as a flying instructor. Now, after completing a number of courses through the club, and accumulating 765:05 flying hours, he was ready to begin a real flying career.

At this time Wally's friend Dave Dorosh, also an Aircraft Maintenance Engineer, informed him that he'd bought a Canso (CF-NJL) which was sitting at Vulcan, Alberta, *sans* engines. Wolfe and Dorosh built up the overhauled engines in a hangar at Edmonton Municipal Airport, adding generators, fuel and hydraulic pumps, and various accessories before taking them to Vulcan for installation. Meanwhile, Wolfe continued to send off letters inquiring about jobs as a pilot or pilot/engineer, or a flight engineer on larger aircraft.

When both engines were finished, on a cold day in February, Wolfe and Dorosh took them out to Vulcan. Canadian Pacific Airlines towed the Canso out of the hangar, then Dorosh and Wolfe tied it down and began putting the trailing edge on the wings. At first the weather was sunny and calm — ideal! — but the next day high winds and cold temperatures prohibited further work. It took several weeks to complete the engine installations and hang the props.

In March, Wolfe obtained a Multi-Engine Rating through the Calgary Flying Club, and on March 23, 1961, he flew up to Edmonton for his check ride with the Department of Transport inspector. He received his endorsement, necessary for him to fly copilot on the Canso to Ottawa. "There was a bit of a panic because we were leaving for Ottawa within a week," Wolfe says.

On Good Friday, March 31, 1961, with Pete Mahoney from Ottawa as pilot and Wolfe as copilot, they flew the Canso from Vulcan to McCall Field (Calgary Airport), with plans to take it to Ottawa the following day. "The Canso is the first large aircraft I've ever flown," Wolfe records in his journal. "I am quite excited about the whole affair!"

It took seven hours and 20 minutes to fly from Calgary to the Lakehead. "We had a little trouble map-reading from Winnipeg to the Lakehead due to the amount of lakes and dense brush in the area," reports the prairie pilot. "However, that didn't prove too much of an obstacle." They encountered a low stratus area between North Bay and Killaloe, but arrived safely in Ottawa.

"My first impression of Ottawa — and also my last — regarding aviation opportunities was very disappointing and below my expectations," Wolfe records. "Since the Canso's future is undecided and there are no other possible flying jobs at present, I'll be leaving Ottawa today by TCA's DC-8."

The thrill of high-flying is also noted. "The trip back to Edmonton was fantastic! We flew at 35 000 feet, cruising at 550 mph! And the return trip took *only three hours*."

That April he found his first flying job with Smith Airways in Swift Current, Saskatchewan, instructing, and flying charter and power-line patrols in a Cessna 172 Skyhawk, a Cessna 150 and a Piper Super Cub. He learned that wind conditions in southern Saskatchewan were to be respected, especially in the afternoons. During the peak time, small airplanes and novice pilots stayed safely on the ground.

Wolfe made himself useful in the maintenance shop, but it wasn't the career he'd planned. "The situation here is somewhat discouraging," he notes in his journal. "Instead of doing plenty of flying as anticipated, I'm spending most of my time in the shop on maintenance."

He later discovered that if he had stayed in Ottawa one more day he would have been offered a two-and-a-half-month job flying copilot on Spartan Air Service's DC-3. What a disappointment!

The flying work he did for Smith Airways often involved doing power-line patrols in the Super Cub, which Wolfe describes as "a marvelous little performer." He got a kick out of landing in fields behind towns and then strolling over to the local café for coffee. He was doing a little bit of everything but not much of anything: instructing, power line patrols, crop-spraying and some unexpected night flying in an aircraft "not equipped with any lights whatsoever, landing on an unlighted strip at 10:30 p.m. with the fuel gauge reading slightly below zero."

When he heard that Bob McNeil at Western Propeller in Edmonton might be looking for a flying instructor, he applied and received a job offer. A fact-finding trip showed Wolfe that the company "wasn't too organized," but he was intent on leaving Swift Current. He got his Float Endorsement in June 1961 and commenced float instruction at Cooking Lake. He further buoyed his spirits by taking gliding lessons.

"The only word to describe gliding is 'different,'" he writes in his journal on June 18th. "You have much coarser control movements and, once you're airborne, you hear only the wind whistling by the canopy."

Float flying also had immediate appeal. "I will agree with anyone when they say you haven't flown until you've flown floats," he writes.

On July 13, 1961 he reached the magical "1000-hour mark."

Survair's aerial survey aircraft, an Apache, at Uranium City, SK. Wally Wolfe was Aircraft Maintenance Engineer on this contract, 1962. (Photo: Wolfe collection)

With the addition of a float endorsement to his skill set, he began to think of the adventures he might have in the North. He wrote to Alaska Airlines asking about a job as pilot or flight engineer, and to Survair in Ottawa about an engineer's job in Uranium City looking after their Apache (CF-MGC). Survair hired him on June 1, 1962, and also gave him a check ride in the Apache.

Again, the job involved mechanics rather than flying. "I'm still no closer to flying with Survair than I ever was," he writes in August, "and, judging from conversation passing among the crews, I doubt whether things will improve by next summer."

He applied to take a helicopter-flying course with Niagara Helicopters, and continued to write letters inquiring about jobs.

Although he was seeing various parts of the country, including Uranium City, Saskatchewan, and various points in Quebec, it was as an Aircraft Maintenance Engineer, not a pilot. "Flying for this company, for me, is a lost cause," he writes disconsolately the following April. He quit Survair in September 1963, but with nothing else, and "to prevent starvation," he went to work over the winter for Northwest Industries Ltd. in Edmonton, overhauling Cansos from Alaska Coastal-Ellis.

The following June he jubilantly writes that he'd "finally latched onto a half-decent job," flying for Pacific Western Airlines' (PWA) VFR Division. In July he was to fly the company's Cessna 180 (CF-ING) on floats from Cooking Lake to Frontier Fishing Lodge near Snowdrift, then on to Yellowknife.

The famous northern bush pilot, Stan McMillan, then Operations Manager for PWA's VFR/bush operation and who had hired Wolfe, would accompany him from Cooking Lake to Yellowknife. Then Wolfe would take "ING" solo from Yellowknife to Inuvik via Norman Wells.

"The trip to Inuvik from Cooking Lake was on floats," Wolfe recalls. "But to get to Cooking Lake from the Edmonton Industrial [now Municipal] Airport [where floats were installed] I had to take off from the airport runway on a 'dolly', a frame on four wheels on which the float plane rested. I lined myself up on the runway and started the takeoff run. I had to make *sure* I had the speed for takeoff *before* I lifted off the 'dolly.' If I didn't, I'd be in trouble. I might leave the dolly okay, but then I could settle back onto the runway . . . on floats!"

Once he attained proper takeoff speed and left the dolly, the dolly's brakes would lock and stop it right there on the runway. Then the flight would continue on.

"In theory, these dollies were supposed to stop straight ahead on the runway," Wolfe states. "The brake handle on the dolly was tied to the spreader bar on the floats with a small cord, strong enough to pull the brake handle on but weak enough for it to break when the aircraft left the dolly. Unfortunately, in a lot of cases, the brakes on the rear wheels did not apply at the same strength, so often the dolly would head off the runway somewhere, and even cartwheel upside-down because of its speed."

This takeoff was, fortunately, successful.

"I only did one dolly-takeoff after that," Wolfe adds, "and that was with Gateway Aviation's Beaver a few years later."

From July 1964 to the summer of 1966, Wolfe flew "skeds" and charters to places such as Fairbanks and Ketchikan (Alaska); Dawson City and Whitehorse (Yukon), Sachs Harbor on Banks Island, various DEW Line sites, and south to Vancouver (BC), to name just a few.

During his two-year tenure in Inuvik, Wolfe was initially employed by PWA's VFR Division flying their Cessna 180 (CF-ING) on floats and wheel skis. When the company dropped its VFR operations, he went with Mike Zubko's Aklavik Flying Service, also based in Inuvik. In May 1965 he began flying Zubko's Beech 18 (CF-OME) and Cessna 185 (CF-OGR) on floats and straight skis. He left there to get his instrument rating and try for something bigger and better. No such luck. Back he went to Inuvik to work for Northward Aviation flying their Beech 18 (CF-SRE) on floats and their Single Otter DHC-3 (CF-JFH) on floats and wheel skis, and he continued to do the odd trip for Aklavik Flying Service.

"It's nice flying in this area in the summer although the winter is another matter," he notes in his ever-present journal. "The coldest weather I've flown in was 70 degrees below zero." Flying on floats, skis or wheel-skis became "old-hat" as Wolfe landed on the Mackenzie, Peel and Arctic Red rivers, and nameless lakes, to service remote exploration camps and oil-drilling sites throughout the Western Arctic. He was discovering the North.

Wally Wolfe passed his Instrument Rating, Class II, in April 1966, which was added to his existing Senior Commercial Pilot's Licence endorsed for single and multi-engine, land and sea. The next step would be to go for a Class I Instrument rating, write some exams and achieve an Airline Transport licence — the top.

One day, Wolfe was flying Aklavik Flying Service's Beech 18 (CF-OME) with a load of passengers en route to Sachs Harbour. "When you checked the weather for Sachs you had to be aware of how close the dew-point and temperature readings were," Wolfe says. "If they were too close there was a good chance you wouldn't make it, the problem being that if the two came together you had fog. Since it took over three hours to get there from Inuvik, if it got fogged in just before you arrived you'd have to return to Inuvik, or to Tuktoyaktuk as your alternate — a lot of wasted time and gas.

"If, given the weather report, it looked like we might encounter fog by the time we got to Sachs Harbour, and the charter people insisted on taking the chance, we would ask the person or company to cover the total cost if we had to turn back to Inuvik. If the pilot chose to take the chance, then Aklavik Flying Services would lose if the flight couldn't make it in."

This day, by the time they reached Sachs Harbour the weather was fogging in below VFR limits. "I did an IFR [instrument flight rules] approach to the runway and got in before it socked right in," Wolfe recalls. "I didn't know at the time that they were working on the runway and had dug a trench across it. They'd filled it with dirt but it was still soft. Fortunately, when I landed the full weight of the aircraft wasn't on the wheels yet, so I rolled right over the trench."

The next problem was getting off. The trench was located two-thirds of the way down the runway and his aircraft was on the short, one-third, end, not enough length for takeoff even with an empty aircraft.

"I taxied to the end of the short part, held on the brakes, gave it full power, and released the brakes," Wolfe says. "There wasn't enough room for takeoff but the idea was to get the aircraft to a speed where I could yank back on the control column and it would jump the trench. This was successful — so I had the good two-thirds of the runway for an empty-

Wally Wolfe installing engine covers on Beech 18 (CF-OME) for Mike Zubko's Aklavik Flying Service on an ice runway, Sachs Harbour, Banks Island.
(Photo: Wolfe collection)

weight takeoff back to Inuvik." (CF-OME is now housed at the Reynolds-Alberta Museum in Wetaskiwin, Alberta.)

By mid-1965 Wolfe's flying hours had built to 2000, flying people and supplies on charters and skeds throughout the Western Arctic and to some Arctic Islands. Flying for Mike Zubko provided numerous adventures and misadventures.

One time, Wolfe had a charter to take the Inuvik Lions Club to Ketchikan, Alaska, in the Beech 18. The weather forecast was acceptable for the trip, although the only weather stations were Inuvik and Whitehorse, with nothing in between. After a few hours in the air they encountered marginal weather, just as his radio quit. Since the forecast for Whitehorse was good, he decided to press on, flying IFR. The only navigational aid he had was ADF, not very reliable under those conditions. It was low frequency and the static electricity in the clouds caused it to wander back and forth. The only thing he could do was to continue to fly his compass heading.

"In the meantime, one of the passengers, a 'DOT' type, took my radios out of the panel to try to find out what was wrong," Wolfe recalls. "At the same time, I was constantly tuning the ADF back and forth, trying to pick up a strong signal. The cockpit became a bit jammed with three people — one trying to fix the radio, a passenger, and myself. Being in the clouds and over mountains, I knew I couldn't descend without having visual contact with the ground. We were just past four hours in the air and had probably one hour of fuel left."

When Wolfe finally received a signal on the ADF, he identified it as Smith River (now abandoned) from his Canada Air Pilot book, zeroed the needle, and headed for that airport. The weather was improving and the clouds were breaking so he could see the ground. The "DOT guy" had found a short in the radio and reinstalled it after a makeshift fix, so Wolfe began calling Smith River on their VHF (very high frequency).

"Not only had we lost our way in cloud over the mountains, but we had encountered a crosswind that had blown us off course to the southeast, nowhere near Whitehorse, which was to be our first stop," Wolfe says. "I asked them to contact Whitehorse to let them know where we were and we landed, with some pretty pale passengers, to refuel and continue on to Whitehorse and Ketchikan."

Wolfe analyzes the trip by stating that "just about anything that could go wrong, did." He had lost communication, the only navigation aid he had was useless, they were getting short of fuel, he couldn't see the ground because of bad weather and they were way off course. He was also in the area commonly known as "The Valley of Lost Planes," where some northern pilots claim that more aircraft have gone down than ships in the Bermuda Triangle. (The US Army-Airforce's four B-26 Marauder bombers, which went down in the valley in January 1942, also caused it to be called "Uncle Sam's Million Dollar Valley.")

Wally Wolfe's first, and only, serious accident occurred when he crashed Northward Aviation's Otter DHC-3 (CF-JFH) on takeoff at Nodwell Lake, west of Fort McPherson.

"I had two choices for a limited takeoff run," Wolfe recalls. "Take a slightly longer run with a crosswind, or a shorter run directly into wind. I elected to take off directly into wind, but to compensate for the short run I didn't take a full load, just three passengers and some cargo.

"The takeoff run was normal. I did get off the water just before the shoreline. However, once over the shoreline there was a gradual upward slope. The wind was blowing down the slope, creating a downdraft situation. I started to lose what little altitude I had until the aircraft floats touched the ground. The slope was grassy and relatively smooth so I kept going, hoping that if I could get to the ridge just ahead I could go off the ridge into the air and be airborne.

"Unfortunately there was a small creek that wasn't very visible until I hit it with the front end of the floats. The floats tore off and the engine section hit the opposite bank, breaking a fuel line. This, of course, stopped us cold."

The fuel from the broken line caught fire in the engine compartment and Wolfe immediately ordered everyone to exit the aircraft. He considered grabbing the fire extinguisher and trying to put out the fire himself, but he didn't know how far it had spread underneath. The fuel tanks in the Otter are in the fuselage, with the forward tank fairly close to the front. Deciding that "discretion is the better part of valor," he escaped from the aircraft as well.

"Due to the 'happy' relationship between me and my employers as a result of me putting their Otter to rest, I decided to leave Northward Aviation on August 12 after checking out on the Norseman (CF-INN) before leaving Inuvik," Wolfe notes in his journal.

Jobless once again, he continued to track down leads. He found nothing until November 1966, when he was called to Chicago for an interview with a Mr. B. Vinsen, chief pilot for International Minerals and Chemicals Corporation. They immediately hired him to fly a Cessna 180 based out of High Level, Alberta, and transport mud engineers to oil rigs. While in Calgary on his return from Chicago, however, he was offered a job to fly a Beech 18 (CF-RSX – now at the Alberta Aviation Museum in Edmonton) for Lethbridge Air Services.

He took the Lethbridge job because "flying a twin-engine Beech 18 was more practical, experience-wise, than flying a single-engine Cessna," and began a new type of flying in a different terrain. He was building hours by flying skeds, basically "running a taxi service," between Lethbridge and Calgary. He soon quit. "I was never one for routine," Wolfe notes.

While living in Inuvik, Wally Wolfe had met a young nurse, Gail Saunders, who was working at her first job after graduating from a three-year diploma course from

Kingston General Hospital in Ontario. Gail had become intrigued by the idea of nursing in the North after hearing stories from one of her patients, who had augmented her daring tales with newspaper clippings depicting life in Canada's North. Gail applied, and was offered a nursing position in the Inuvik General Hospital. Meeting a strong, handsome bush pilot completed the adventurous dream. When Wolfe left Inuvik, they kept in touch, allowing the romance to continue through phone calls and letters.

Eastern Canada

In June 1967, Wally Wolfe received a job offer from Geoterrex in Ottawa flying aerial mineral surveys. "The survey equipment consisted of three systems for detecting mineral deposits in the ground: magnetometer, electro-magnetometer (EM) and scintilometer," he writes in his journal.

His assigned aircraft, a Single Otter DHC-3 (CF-IUZ), was leased from Wheeler Northland Airways Ltd. based in St. Jean, Quebec. The contracts took him to various points throughout Labrador, Quebec, New Brunswick, Ontario, Manitoba and Saskatchewan as well as south to Minnesota and Virginia.

"I had an incident flying to Ottawa from Labrador," Wolfe recalls. "I had to land at Sept-Isles, Quebec, for gas. On final approach I was throttling back on power when the throttle stuck. I was coming in too fast for a proper landing, so I first shut off one magneto, and sometimes both, to cut my power for landing. It must have sounded strange to the uninitiated to hear the engine lose a little power, then return to normal, then shut right off, then back on. I had to taxi in this way as well, until I got to the dock."

Soon Wolfe's flying hours totaled 3000, then 4000, as he flew daily over hill and dale. "The crew was myself as pilot, a navigator — necessary because when flying so low you don't have time to map-read and safely fly the aircraft — and an equipment operator in the back of the aircraft. The flying is done at 150 feet above ground level, contouring, following the terrain up and down," Wolfe explains. "Needless to say, it gets to you after a while."

On one aerial mineral survey job he was flying the Single Otter in Charlottesville, Virginia. "During one of the runs over hilly country, the engine quit. The old cliché, 'you don't have time to think, just to react,' proved true," he recalls. "I automatically switched to another fuel tank, put the fuel booster pump on, and hoped for the best. At the same time I headed downhill to give me more time. We had about 10 seconds before hitting the trees when the engine caught."

He headed back to the airport to check things out and discovered that the rear tank fuel gauge was reading higher than it should have. Anxiety turned to humor when a group of Americans crowded around them, obviously surprised to see this aircraft actually flying. To them, it belonged in a museum! Wolfe decided to play to this attitude, and a few days later put a plan into motion.

"The airport consisted of one long runway, and one short one that wasn't often used because of its length. One day, as the usual group of spectators gathered, before I gassed up — therefore keeping the aircraft weight down — I taxied out to the end of the short runway. Then I put on the brakes, went to almost full power and released the brakes. The Otter took off, with plenty of runway to spare! I made a circuit and did a very short landing.

"After this little demonstration I never had anyone kid me about my old aircraft anymore. They just couldn't believe how that Otter performed!"

Gail and Wally married in Ottawa, while he was working for Geoterrex. Their first son, Kevin, was born there on November 13, 1968, while Wally was on his way to Virginia to do some more aerial mineral survey work. "I had waited two weeks in Ottawa for him to arrive, then had to leave," Wolfe says. "I got the call in Scranton, Pennsylvania, where we were overnighting due to bad weather." (Kevin Wolfe is currently based with the Canadian Armed Forces, Air Force, in Greenwood, Nova Scotia.)

But Wolfe soon tired of this work, which often necessitated being away from home for seven or eight months of the year. After completing a job in Uranium City, he returned to Ottawa, supposedly to proceed to Frobisher Bay after a few days off. While in the city, he decided to leave the company.

Great Bear Lodge

The North! Who can ever forget it once it's in the blood? In July 1969, Wolfe came back to Edmonton to fly a Beech 18 (CF-GXI) and a Norseman (CF-LZO) for Great Bear Lodge at Sawmill Bay. The lodge was situated on the west coast of Great Bear Lake, NWT — the largest lake lying entirely in Canada, and the eighth largest lake in the world.

He would pick up fishermen from Yellowknife, where they came in by airlines, and fly them to the lodge to fish for Arctic Char (a trout related to both an American species, the Sunapee trout, and the European Char). This fish, which makes for excellent

Wally Wolfe with Beech 18 (CF-GXI) at Great Bear Lake, 1969. (Photo: Wolfe collection)

eating, is found north of the Hudson's Bay, and also at Tree River on the Arctic coast north of Yellowknife and Minto Inlet, north of Holman.

Old-time bush pilot Ernie Boffa was also working at the lodge. The tour plan called for Wolfe to fly fishermen from Great Bear Lodge to a char outpost camp north of Holman Island (a distance of 350 miles) with the Beech 18. At this time, the airstrip came right through the centre of the town of Holman. Boffa would take the passengers on in the Norseman to an outpost camp north of Holman Island to the fishing grounds. But, one "glitch" confused the plan.

"Although we had a schedule to carry out these transfers at Holman, we did not have any radio contact with each other," Wolfe explains. "Therefore, if for some reason one of us was delayed, the other didn't know what was happening. If Ernie wasn't there when I got to Holman I'd sit and wait, not knowing if he was delayed because of weather or aircraft problems, or whether he'd show at all. The same could happen if he got to Holman and I wasn't there."

After some frustrating episodes resulting in unhappy passengers, the lodge gave up on this "package tour." The Northern conditions were too unpredictable.

The sights that Wally Wolfe viewed daily from the cockpit became indelible: orange sunsets swathed over vast barren lands, indigenous people and animals at work and play, and the ease with which all adapted to their often harsh surroundings. These scenes reawakened Wolfe's artistic interests. He wanted to capture the images by drawing and painting them from photos, from memory, from imagination.

"Contrary to popular belief, this country is not 'barren,'" Wolfe says. "I came across grizzlies running uphill, and black bears — one punched a hole in my tent at Little Chicago one night when I was sleeping. His claws were about 24 inches from my head. I just lay there and didn't make a sound until he eventually moved on.

"I saw caribou herds and bird life such as snowy owls, bald eagles, ducks and geese. Oddly enough," he adds, "I never actually saw a polar bear or a musk-ox. But, viewing all this flora and fauna and the natural beauty of the landscape instilled many mental pictures for future paintings."

Wolfe recalls always being interested in drawing and, as a child, "messing around" with pencils and crayons. He had always known that his two passions were aviation and art. By chance, he just happened to get into the flying end of things first. But why not combine them?

The Artist's View

At the completion of the summer of 1969, he enrolled as an art student at Alberta College of Art and Design in Calgary (at that time part of Southern Alberta Institute of Technology). Although he looked forward to learning a new profession, he emphasizes

As a Pilot-Engineer, Wally Wolfe was responsible for doing routine inspection on the Beaver (CF-JOF), Little Doctor Lake, NWT, 1970. (Photo: Wolfe collection.)

in his journals that "my new role as an artist does not mean that I'm going to give up my flying permanently."

The art program covered four years, with summers off, giving Wolfe the time to fly on contracts for Gateway Aviation in Edmonton. That first summer, 1970, Wolfe checked-out on a Beaver (CF-JOF) and departed on June 1st from Cooking Lake for Fort Simpson via High Level, where he met Arnold Gorveatt, the party chief for Mobil Oil. During the summer he landed on small northern lakes, such as Footner near High Level on the way up, and Little Doctor Lake west of Fort Simpson. Other lakes with which he became familiar were Sundog, Bluefish, Bell Heather, Camsell Bend, Trench, Iverson and Slim. He also landed on the South Nahanni River in the infamous "Deadman's Valley," and on rivers at Fort Nelson and Wrigley, Fort Good Hope and Norman Wells.

"The summer was successful for everyone concerned," he writes. "The only incident occurred when a bear — grizzly suspected from clues — broke the Bell helicopter bubble one night. We also had visits from moose and from wolves during our stay at Iverson Lake."

Gail and Wally's second son, Todd, was born in Calgary on November 14, 1970. (Todd is now living and working in Japan.)

During the summer of 1971 Wolfe again flew a Beaver (CF-VKH) for Gateway Aviation, on contract with the Geological Survey of Canada and reporting to party chief Owen Hughes. He worked his way along the Mackenzie River area from Norman Wells, south to Fort Norman, north to San Sault Rapids, to the ramparts to Fort Good Hope; then to Little Chicago, to Arctic Red River, west to Fort McPherson and north to Inuvik, clocking 350 hours on the Beaver.

He noted that his old "home town" of Inuvik had changed some during his five-year absence. Development in the oil industry had slowed considerably, and Inuvik's population had dwindled from 5000 to 3500. Before, when he'd landed at a community, people would come out and meet the aircraft to see who had come with it and to help unload it. He was disappointed at the new lackadaisical attitude with which aircraft arrivals were regarded by local people.

"I think people had come to accept the aircraft, even though it still was the only form of transportation other than boats, and take it for granted, much like people in the south take roads, trains and airlines for granted," he notes.

He flew for Gateway Aviation for a third summer in 1972, again with the Geological Survey of Canada, throughout the Yukon and western Northwest Territories, terminating once again at Inuvik. One accident marred an otherwise perfect summer when a passenger had his arm broken by a windmilling propeller while assisting with docking procedures at Margaret Lake. He was flown to Inuvik General Hospital and made a full recovery.

This beautiful summer flying season saw an end to Wally Wolfe's career as a pilot or pilot-engineer, except for occasional recreational-flying. With 5500 flying hours and many good memories, he turned to art as a means of enjoyment and, hopefully, to "achieve fame if not fortune."

The third Wolfe son, Brett, was born in Calgary on January 27, 1973. (Brett is presently living and working in Yellowknife.)

Memories

Wally Wolfe feels that a highlight of his flying career was meeting some of the "legends" of the Northern flying fraternity. He names among them Stan McMillan, Punch Dickins, Ernie Boffa, Max Ward and aircraft engineer Rex Terpening.

He also recalls the unique challenges that faced him as well as others who pursued the nebulous career of a northern bush pilot — such as being pushed away from the dock on a river before you're ready.

"In one case, I was getting into the aircraft, doing up my seat belt, when the fellow at the dock who was holding the Beaver by the main strut let me go. Sometimes radial engines can be temperamental at startup, and when you're let go into the current of a river before you have your engines running it puts you in a very awkward position," Wolfe says. "You have to get the engine going immediately for control before the current takes you into some kind of obstruction or riverbank, where you could damage your floats or the aircraft. On a lake there's no problem because you'd just sit there, unless the wind was blowing."

Another tense situation comes in the spring and early summer when water levels are high. The rivers pick up driftwood from the banks, which cascades downstream and forces the float pilot to check carefully before landing. "There is always some area that is debris-free due to current flow so you land there," Wolfe says. "But, once you're on the water and have to go to the opposite shore, debris will likely be floating between you and your destination. You have to taxi through this flowing debris at the same speed that it's going to prevent float damage." Tricky, but a common challenge.

In winter, when working on straight skis, pilots learn to quickly place spruce boughs or branches beneath the skis after landing to prevent them from freezing to the surface overnight. "When you taxi on skis, there is enough friction underneath to cause some melting of the snow, just enough to freeze your skis to the surface," Wolfe explains. "Sometimes it's worse than others, depending on conditions."

Another winter challenge is determining from the air what the snow conditions are for landing. How deep is it? How large are the drifts? If the weather is dull, you have no shadow from the sun to use as a guide. "You just have to use your best judgment, based on past experience," Wolfe says philosophically.

And of course, engines must be warmed in the frigid Northern weather conditions. If you're staying somewhere for only a few hours, the engine can be warmed periodically to ensure that it will start when needed. If the stay is overnight, out comes the blow-pot. "It did the trick, but if it was too cold to stand waiting outside you had to get under the engine tent with the blow-pot and put up with the stink as long as possible," Wolfe says. "In later years, if you could plug into an electrical outlet, some aircraft were equipped with a permanently-mounted electric heater inside the engine cowling. Heaven!"

The wind is a constant factor that dictates flying conditions, especially on floats. Wolf recalls one incident that called for a special technique while coming to the dock at the Inuvik float base in the Otter. "The dock was located halfway up the lake. One day, when landing into a brisk wind, the landing run took me by the dock, which required turning around to come back. The Otter, however, has a very large fin/rudder area. As soon as I tried to turn the aircraft out of the wind it would weather-cock because of the fin/rudder, and turn back into wind like a weather vane. Sometimes even using power to try to turn didn't work. The only option was to shut down the engine, put down full flap, and 'sail' backwards. Once I'd sailed past the dock, I'd restart the engine and taxi straight ahead for docking."

Wolfe recalls a hair-raising incident at Arctic Red River, when a Cessna 180 came into the dock a bit too fast. A man standing on the dock grabbed hold of the main strut, a normal procedure, but couldn't stop the Cessna because of its speed. He found himself going with the aircraft past the dock, and hanging on for dear life. He managed to get onto the float. The Cessna started up, came back to the dock, and made the docking without further incident.

"Coming into a dock requires some practice and good judgment," Wolfe concludes. "You have no brakes so you have to judge the distance, river current and speed, so you

" CAME INTO THE DOCK JUST A TAD
TOO FAST......!!"

just make the dock, or beach, without banging up your floats."

His commercial flying days might be over, but not his interest in flying, and his knowledge of the industry would surely add detail and accuracy to his art-work. Now that he had a Diploma of Applied Arts, majoring in advertising art, Wolfe hoped to combine his vocation and avocation. But how?

He applied for a job at the Provincial Museum of Alberta in Edmonton, and was hired as Exhibit Designer.

"As I've pointed out, I've never been interested in routine, getting up at a certain time every day and going to work, coming home, going to bed, then starting the whole thing over again the next day," Wolfe says. "It was a real struggle, after flying, when I didn't know where or when I would be going somewhere, to have regular hours every day."

The attraction at the Museum, albeit an eight-to-five job, was the variety — "a key word." He not only did drawing and design, but also silk-screening, photo-mounting and layout. He drafted scale plans, painted exhibit panels, made mini- and full-scale dioramas and did carpentry work.

Curator of Exhibits

After working at the Provincial Museum of Alberta for three years, Wally Wolfe spotted an ad in the Edmonton *Journal* for a Curator of Exhibits for a new museum being built in Yellowknife. Both Wally and Gail had enjoyed the North, so he applied.

The museum building was only partly-constructed, but the Department of Culture, Northwest Territories, was anxious to find a suitable staff and put them to work. The director at the time, Robert Janes (now President and CEO of Glenbow Museum in Calgary), came to Edmonton to interview Wolfe.

Exhibit honoring Canada's northern bush pilots, Prince of Wales Northern Heritage Centre, Yellowknife, where Wally Wolfe was employed as its first Curator of Exhibits. (Photo: Wolfe collection)

Wolfe found Janes to be "a very down-to-earth and amiable fellow," and was happy to be awarded the job. He started as Curator of Exhibits of the new Prince of Wales Northern Heritage Centre in Yellowknife, doing similar work as at the Provincial Museum.

In 1985, the Fox Moth Society was formed by a group of local people and the government in Yellowknife. Their goal was to restore a deHavilland Fox Moth, an aircraft commonly used in the North for mineral exploration and general charters.

"The Fox Moth in the museum collection was restored from parts of three other Moth wrecks," Wolfe states. "Registration of the museum's moth is CF-BNI, from an aircraft that once flew in the Yellowknife area."

But once the restoration was complete, the Northern Heritage Centre had no space for it. The aircraft was sent to the Western Canada Aviation Museum in Winnipeg and displayed there for two years. In the meantime, "Operation Fox Moth" was formed in Yellowknife. Through the generosity of local contractors, a "Wings of Change" aviation gallery was added to the Northern Heritage Centre. It depicts the history of aviation in the Northwest Territories from the arrival of Imperial Oil's German Junkers 13 in 1921 to the present day aviation stories, and houses the Fox Moth.

"The Fox Moth was dismantled in Winnipeg, put on an airforce Hercules that was on a training flight to Yellowknife, then reassembled in the new Aviation Gallery," Wolfe says proudly.

Wally Wolfe has enjoyed a varied career in both aviation and art, and in the combination of the two fields. He has self-produced a number of coloring/activity books to teach and encourage young people's interest in aviation (including the *Fly by Nite* series by "Tom Turbo"). He plans to produce illustrated comic books that will portray such Northern adventure stories as *The Mad Trapper of Rat River*. This work will call upon his artistic skills as well as his knowledge of aviation, and the flora and fauna of the North, to augment stories of mystery, adventure and intrigue, as well as to draw the fascinating characters who resided "north of 60." His cartoons (collected in *The Best of Tundra Wolfe* and *North of 60 – the Funny Side*) have individually appeared in newsletters, newspapers and various publications.

Most of his recent artwork has been done with acrylics, although he has worked with water-colors as well. "The majority of my artwork has been on a commission basis," Wolfe says. "Therefore, there were few occasions when a print run would be made for sale in art galleries. Some have been done, however, and are for sale through the Aurora Art Gallery and Visual Effects in Yellowknife."

Conclusions

"The challenge in flying in the North was 'the unknown, " Wolfe says. "'Where will I be going tomorrow?' 'What will it be like there?' I often wonder if I had gotten an airline job, whether I would have really enjoyed it . . . the same route, same time, same places. In the North, as mentioned before, the people really depended on the aircraft and still do.

"I don't have any deep regrets about the past," he says, in conclusion. "I was fortunate enough to accomplish the two things I've always been interested in, aviation and art. I have flown over this country from the Pacific to Atlantic oceans, and from the Arctic Islands to the United States."

He has a family to be proud of, who also came to know and love the North. Wally Wolfe, artist and aviator, has captured, through living it and then painting it, a history that is rapidly changing. Wally Wolfe has always been, and still is, a free man.

The Merger of the Masters

Farm boys seem to have an edge on becoming good aircraft pilots and engineers. This could arise from their attraction to machinery plus an ability, learned first-hand on the farm, to "make things work." In aviation, making things work through approved methods can be achieved – under perfect conditions. But when you're a thousand miles from the parts stockroom or a hangar and it's 50° below zero, anything might do, from baling wire to "100-mile-per-hour tape," to get the machine and the people back home.

Chuck MacLaren and Gordon Cannam are both farm boys who have enjoyed successful careers "making things work." Chuck was born on July 23, 1917, at Viking, Alberta, and Gordon on September 16th of the same year, on a farm at Kenaston, Saskatchewan. Although both men are now in their eighties, they work full time at Edmonton's Alberta Aviation Museum restoring vintage airplanes – the same machines they used to fly and fix back in their salad days.

The Players

Chuck MacLaren was brought up to know more about horses than airplanes. But Viking was a natural gas camp site, with a Northwest Utilities' camp located three miles from the MacLaren farm. "It was a big deal in those days, in the '30s, to land a job there. Compared to farm work they paid *real big* money – like 40 cents an hour," MacLaren laughs. When a local welder filled MacLaren's head with stories of fairly easy work and good pay – and proved it by showing his pay slips – MacLaren decided to take up welding. "I learned to arc-weld through Northwest Utilities but as it turned out, I never did work for them."

MacLaren's knowledge of welding led him to a job in Edmonton in 1939 with Aircraft Repair Limited, established to repair and maintain Canada's military aircraft during World War II. This company was managed by Leigh Brintnell, owner of Mackenzie Air Service, which based its business on bush-flying from Edmonton to various points North and down the Mackenzie River. MacLaren stayed with the company until after it was acquired by Canadian Pacific Airlines (CPA) in 1942, for whom he worked until 1948.

One of the largest bush planes that MacLaren worked on was the big Bellanca 66-75 Aircruiser (CF-BTW). One day, a call came in saying that one of CPA's Bellancas had been involved in an accident at Mathews Lake close to Echo Bay Mines. Apparently, the undercarriage had been knocked off one side.

None of the five-man crew looked forward to the trip, knowing what would be involved. It was April and while the snow was melting in Edmonton, temperatures in that northern area were hovering around 30° Fahrenheit below zero. But they packed tents, layers of warm clothing, boots and food, and off they went.

Even setting up their tent was a formidable task. "There were no trees so we couldn't tie it down," MacLaren recalls. "We chopped holes in the ice, then melted snow and poured water over the ropes. When it froze, the ropes were secured so our tent didn't blow away."

They slept on furs, and ate what they'd brought plus a few locally-supplied caribou steaks.

The Bellanca was in sad shape. "They'd broke off the undercarriage. The main landing gear had torn out as the plane continued forward; the landing gear went back and tore out the tail ski. It took five days of welding with a five-man crew, and a lot of fabric work. We put the fabric on with water, and it froze and stuck. Once we got home of course it all fell off as it warmed up, so we did it again with dope."

Working for CPA during its acquisition of other smaller airlines presented some challenges for the employees. "One night we had 15 different makes of airplanes in the hangar!" MacLaren recalls.

In 1948, Chuck MacLaren shifted over to the next hangar to work for Eldorado Aviation servicing their Norsemen and DC-3s. The parent company was Eldorado Nuclear Ltd., a uranium mining company with properties in Saskatchewan and Ontario.

"Eldorado Aviation was a pretty good company," MacLaren recalls. "The aviation department supplied all the boat camps like Hay River, Norman Wells, Bear River Rapids, Inuvik and Tuktoyaktuk. The company would fly that route once a week in the summer, and the rest of the time we serviced the mine. We hauled all the uranium south by aircraft to Edmonton with DC-3s and DC-4s."

But the long hours of work caused MacLaren, now married to Iola Empey and with three young sons, to seek new employers. He went to work for Aero Engineering, affiliated with Associated Airways, for four years servicing bush planes, and from there to Gunnar Nesbitt Aviation.

"We hauled ore and freight for Gunnar Mines from Uranium City [located 30 miles south of the Saskatchewan-NWT boundary, just east of the Saskatchewan-Alberta boundary] for 10 years. When that was mined out they said, `Good-bye, boys!' and sold the airplane, so I moved back to Eldorado Aviation for 17 years."

By this time, MacLaren's "M" (maintenance engineer's) licence permitted him to work on aircraft up to the Boeing 737s. "I was never unemployed," MacLaren says proudly. "I was never out of work five minutes in my life. I could have gone to work at a half a dozen places at any one time."

Although based in Edmonton with Eldorado, he would sometimes be temporarily sent to remote locations such as Fort Smith, Great Bear Lake or Yellowknife, "wherever a plane needed repairing." There was lots of work, and MacLaren enjoyed it.

Investigations carried out by the Calgary *Herald*, however, have uncovered a negative side to employment in the uranium fields. "Uranium Mine Left Deadly Legacy," reads a story headline on April 12, 1998, citing deaths by cancer of at least 100 miners, pilots and other workers at Port Radium (Echo Bay) NWT uranium mine.

"Well, I handled uranium every day for 35 years and I'm still alive," MacLaren states. "It was in barrels. When I worked for Gunnar, we hauled a load of uranium south every day for shipping by rail to Port Hope, Ontario, for further refining."

Everyone has favorite and not-so-favorite aircraft to work on. MacLaren lists Pipers in the latter category. "They're not too rugged but they perform, they did a lot of work in the North. But Pipers have so much super-structure and stuff to hold fabric that it takes longer to repair than the mainframe. They've got little channels welded all over them to hold fabric, while other airplanes aren't like that. It's all stuff that there's no rhyme or reason to. It gives them a shape but no structural value." Then he shrugs and smiles. "Oh, they're all the same to me, really."

L. to R.: Quentin Carsell and Chuck MacLaren removing prop from a DC-3 (CF-DGJ) before changing blown engine. The nose art is a depiction of the first atomic bomb made from uranium. Port Radium, Eldorado Mining & Refining Ltd., 1949. (Photo: MacLaren collection)

His favorite airplane? "I suppose a Douglas DC-3. When I worked for Gunnar Nesbitt Aviation, we changed 30 engines – all full-time with 1100 hours on each of them – in one DC-3," MacLaren says. "Its call letters were CF-GHX, I'll never forget them. That airplane flew from Edmonton to Uranium City, 365 trips a year, for 10 years!"

MacLaren reflects on adventures with the famous old DC-3. "We used to land on the ice on Lake Athabasca where Gunnar Mines was, until we got the runway built. On the last landing of the season, the 24th of May, one wheel went through the ice and it ended up on its wing, putting a three-inch bend in the wing. We called for help. With the aid of 50 guys from the mine we picked it up out of the ice and rolled it about 10 feet onto some planks on good ice. Then the pilots flew it home, with the bend in the wing and everything. The big, gradual bend didn't seem to bother it any. It flew pretty straight.

"Our job when we got home was to re-skin the top of the wing because the pressure had made little wrinkles between the rivets."

And so the "bush repair" stories come into play. Were they supposed to fly an airplane that's been cranked around like that?

MacLaren laughs. "Well, you don't tell everything!"

Another favorite bush plane was the all-purpose Noorduyn Norseman. Designed by R.B.C. (Bob) Noorduyn in 1934-35 specifically for use in the North country, and engineered by Walter Clayton, this Canadian airplane became known as the workhorse of the North. The splendid birds, heavy, ungainly, short-but-hard-landing, cold and generally uncomfortable, were also durable, hardy and needed. The aircraft was adaptable to floats, skis or wheels, capable of carrying a good payload as well as convertible to passenger aircraft, and offered good visibility from the cockpit.

"When I was first with Eldorado they had two Norsemen," MacLaren recalls. "A fellow by the name of Johnny Nesbitt, who was well-known in those days, was flying one (CF-BZW) to take a geologist into the Uranium City area. There was supposed to be seven inches of ice on the lake they were to land on, which was lots for a Norseman, but he landed and there were only two inches.

"The airplane went skidding along with the wings on top of the ice and the engine underneath. The ice curled up on the windshield like before a snowplow until slowed up, and then the aircraft flipped over onto its back. The ice was so thin we couldn't get any equipment out to retrieve it so it simply had to sit there. When the ice finally got thicker, the Chief Engineer for Eldorado, Ernie Bjorge, engineer Will Thorson, and the pilot, Johnny Nesbitt, went in to get it."

The rescue attempt proved more bizarre than the accident:

"They had a Herman Nelson heater stuffed in the wingtip because the leading edge of the wing was frozen in and laying upside-down. When the two mechanics went for dinner, Nesbitt stayed behind and stretched out on the wing, sun-tanning, because it was nice and warm. But eventually he decided it was time to put some more gas in the Herman Nelson heater, so he walked over to where the gas barrels were – and at that exact moment the gas tank in the Norseman exploded. It blew out of the wing, and the whole airplane burnt!

"So that was the end of that Norseman. About the only thing we got off it was the landing gear that was up in the air."

Another story involving a Norseman took place at Fort McMurray on the snye (backwater forming a bay). "Cameron Exploration had a Norseman that was painted black – the only black Norseman I've ever seen. `Pappy' Hawthorne was the pilot and Alf Taylor the engineer. They were coming in to land at dusk.

"When you dropped down into the river valley near dark, it was like pulling a blanket over your head. When they set down they were so close that part of their wing reached out over the dock. Edgar Jones, a photographer, had his Stinson tied to the dock, first in line in front of the black Norseman, and then came CPA's Norseman [CF-BHV]."

The wing of the landing Norseman went over top of Jones' Stinson, taking off his wing tip, and then over top of the wing of CPA's Norseman, damaging it. Further, CPA's wing cut the Cameron Exploration Norseman's struts right off, causing it to veer up on shore about 200 feet into the willows, high and dry on floats, with one wing hanging down like a shot duck.

"The big question was how to get CPA's airplane going again with this damaged wing," MacLaren says. "Finally we decided to remove the black wing from Cameron Exploration's Norseman. They had caused the accident, after all, and they weren't going anywhere fast; their airplane was a wreck and would have to be shipped by train back to Edmonton because there was no road then. So we put this black wing on CPA's silver Norseman and it flew the rest of the season like that, with one black and one silver wing. It looked pretty strange, kind of lopsided."

But for all their trials with the big old aircraft, MacLaren still admires the Norsemen's toughness. Also, "there weren't many other kinds of bush planes around at that time on floats, outside of the old Fairchilds and the big Bellanca."

One of his most difficult repairs was rebuilding a Sikorski S-55 helicopter (CF-JTI) on an island in the Mackenzie River. "The parts stockroom wasn't 100 feet away," he notes dryly.

"The machine had blown a part that lets the blades free-wheel if the engine quits. It's like a clutch, anchored to the drive shaft," MacLaren explains. "When this thing disintegrated the blades were driving the drive shaft, and not anchored, flailing around like a six-foot baseball bat hammering out everything. As a result, the helicopter went in on this island, with great gravity, in forward speed. It didn't tip over, but it sheared off the front gear and collapsed one corner of the helicopter."

Sikorski (CF-JTI) now in the courtyard of the Aero Space Museum in Calgary. The repaired section is located in the area around the helicopter's call letters. (Photo: Aero Space Museum)

"There was one passenger in the cabin. He didn't open the sliding door, he just drove it off its tracks to get out, he was so scared it was going to catch fire."

Chuck MacLaren and his team flew parts to the site, and borrowed an air compressor and power unit from one of the boats that sailed the Mackenzie River. They camped in Fort Providence, using a Bell helicopter to ferry the crew back and forth.

This Sikorski helicopter is now displayed in the courtyard of the Aero Space Museum in Calgary. "Look at it closely," MacLaren says with a smile. "If you check out the left side you can see where there's a big repair that's been riveted back. That whole corner is what I fixed on that island."

When he retired from Eldorado Aviation in 1982 Chuck MacLaren went back to where he started: working on old airplanes, this time as a volunteer. The Alberta Aviation Museum, located on Kingsway Avenue in a hangar built in 1942 to house the British Commonwealth Air Training Plan's No. 2 Air Observer School, is once again his work site. He is as much a part of the museum's history as are the aircraft, and can remember the days when the hangar was filled with 80 Ansons at one time.

MacLaren can be found in the workshop of the museum six days a week, restoring one or another of the old birds to its former beauty. "I live fairly close and my car knows the route," he laughs.

He has worked on the restoration of every aircraft in the museum.

Gordon Cannam was the second of six children. He stayed on the farm until he was 20, when poor crops and hard times of the "dirty-30s" convinced Gordon and his older brother Glen to seek their fortune in gold. More precisely, they had heard of Goldfields on Lake Athabasca in northern Saskatchewan, where workers were being paid top wages to mine gold.

They first had to get a flight in, and so made their way to Edmonton where Gordon's cousin, Mickey Found, was flying for Mackenzie Air Service. Mickey agreed that the boys would likely find work in the North, and flew them up to Goldfields in Mackenze Air Service's Norseman (CF-BAN). That was Cannam's first flight, and an exciting introduction to aviation.

With the start of the war, Gordon Cannam's interest in aircraft led him to a job in the woodworking shop at Aircraft Repair's main base in Edmonton, operated under the British Commonwealth Air Training Plan (BCATP). The shop was run by Leigh Brintnell's Mackenzie Air Service, which had been chosen by the government for the wartime purposes of assembling, overhauling and repairing airplanes.

The next year was spent on Field Crews, repairing damaged aircraft at bases in North Battleford and Moose Jaw, Saskatchewan, and Penhold, Fort Macleod, and Lethbridge, Alberta. This was excellent training for Cannam. "We did all kinds of repairs to Ansons and Oxfords, including woodwork, engines, undercarriages, electrical, hydraulic and pneumatic systems."

The purpose of the Field Crews being sent to various operational bases was twofold: to avoid the long delay of dismantling the aircraft and shipping them to a main base, and secondly, to reduce costs by carrying out repairs in the field, thereby also increasing aircraft availability.

"Repairs carried out by Field Crews were due to landing accidents, emergency landing in nearby fields, even by taxiing into hangars," Cannam recalls. "During World War II there were thousands of trainee pilots who learned through the `learning curve' that applies to everyone."

Gordon Cannam returned to Edmonton and went on night shift for Aircraft Repair in charge of a crew repairing damaged Oxford wings and fuselages, or aircraft brought in for major inspections. This involved stripping the aircraft down to its bare bones.

The Oxford was similar in appearance to the Anson, Cannam says, both being twin-engine, low-wing monoplanes. While the Anson wing was comprised of a single unit (wing span of 56 feet 6 inches), the Oxford included a centre section with removable outer wing panels (wing span 53 feet 4 inches). As a point of interest, the Alberta Aviation Museum has recently restored an Anson Mark II which could possibly be one of the aircraft Cannam worked on during the war.

The major work on the Oxfords involved removing the outer wings, the centre section, then the plywood outer skin panels. The object was to inspect all the glue joints to ensure the aircraft was in a suitable condition to continue in service. The plywood skin panels were, of course, destroyed in the process of being removed so, after inspection of the structure and completing the necessary repairs, the wing skin was replaced with new plywood panels. Then components (centre section and wing panels) went to the paint shop, to the assembly line, and eventually the aircraft was returned to the flight line and sent to the various training bases.

No apprenticeship or diploma program was involved. "It was strictly, `get the job done for wartime purposes,'" Cannam says. "The experience I obtained there was very, very good."

Early in 1943, Gordon Cannam was sent to Moose Jaw (No. 32 Service Flying Training School) for two months and put in charge of a crew of 14 people. That is where he met his future wife, Lois Margaret Reid, who was working as a teletype operator for the CNR in Moose Jaw. They were married within a month of their meeting, on June 12, 1943.

Cannam spent that summer at Moose Jaw, doing major repairs on 16 different Airspeed Oxfords, and then came back to Edmonton in September with his new bride.

"I'd been working on deferments all this time because I was classed as working on a critical job, but I joined the Navy early in 1944 as a Shipwright, fourth class. I spent most of the next two years on Convoy duty in the North Atlantic."

By the time he was released from military service, the name of the Edmonton aircraft repair shop had changed to Northwest Industries. "Leigh Brintnell was still in charge of it and he was building Bellanca Skyrockets at that time. I worked on them, building wings, skis and various things, all from wood."

When Cannam became unemployed in February 1947, he applied at Associated Airways and was hired as a mechanic, largely to repair Ansons, which had gained popularity through being a major training airplane during the war. "I started with Associated Airways on March 3, 1947, on a temporary job, and remained with the same company until I retired in 1982," Cannam says.

One interesting salvage job that Cannam was involved in required them to ship the entire aft section of an Anson Mark V to Wabasca. The Anson had overshot the landing strip and had plummeted through a fence. Both the structural members of the fuselage and the horizontal stabilizer and elevators were damaged beyond repair. The propeller

The entire fuselage from midway between the aft windows had to be replaced, due to the aircraft belly-landing and overshooting the runway through a fence. Anson CF-FVQ, Wabasca, May 1949. (Photo: Cannam collection)

blades were curled back around the engine cowlings. Replacement parts were shipped in by truck to a point where the road became a trail through the bush, and horse-drawn vehicles then transported the parts the remaining 40 miles. Interestingly, the replacement components for this job were salvaged from T.P. (Tommy) Fox's "stubwing" Anson that he had flown back to Edmonton some time earlier, with nine feet of wingtips missing and the stubs evened-off and taped up.

"Since this Anson had come to rest in a farmer's field with the undercarriage retracted, it was lying flat on the ground – an ideal position to replace the damaged components, which included the entire aft section of the fuselage from the wing T/E [trailing edge] and aft. The propellers were also replaced from this ideal working height," Cannam recalls. "When the work was complete, the aircraft was jacked up and serviced. Then the pilot who had `put it in,' John Davids, came up and flew it out."

In May of 1947, based on his experience, Cannam obtained an engineer's licence and endorsements on various aircraft that Associated operated at the time. These included the Stinson 108, Norseman, Bellanca, Anson Mark V and Barkley-Grow T8P-1. After obtaining his basic engineer's licence, and writing qualifying exams on every aircraft type he worked on, he obtained his private pilot's licence in October 1947, and his limited commercial licence in February 1948.

"As I recall, all I did was work, study and write examinations – plus raise a family of three."

Early in 1950, Tommy Fox started Associated Helicopters and Cannam became qualified on the Bell 47 D1 helicopter as engineer. He spent the summers of 1951 and '52 maintaining the helicopter in northern Alberta, BC and the Northwest Territories. The helicopter proved extremely useful for transporting and supporting the oil industry, working in the mountains and other remote areas.

A memorable salvage job occurred on Victoria Island in the Arctic, 50 miles west of Cambridge Bay, in January-February 1957. By this time, Cannam was a supervisor, but as he was the only one qualified to do the anticipated work, he left his desk and headed North. With him was Les Bassnett to assist with the woodwork, and John Bosman to do the mechanical work. When they were dropped off at the site, the temperature was 30° below zero.

Serious damage had been done to the aircraft, an Anson Mark V (CF-INT). The right gear had collapsed, resulting in the right wing being broken off at the front spar, 10 feet from the wingtip. The rear spar was broken 13 feet from the wing tip. The only thing holding the wing on was the top plywood skin. When Cannam lifted it he realized that if he let it down hard it would break clean off.

"This was a major job in the wintertime because we had to work with glue and wood," Cannam says. They had to enclose the entire wing in tarps and heat it with a Herman-Nelson heater. The job was difficult and could not be hurried. "From the time we landed until we finished and took off, it was three weeks. In that period of time we burned 1400 gallons of gas in the heater, at an ungodly price of one dollar per gallon at that time."

They were fortunate that a camp, Site 17, was located a mile away, where they could buy fuel and also find board and room. When the repairs were completed, the aircraft was flown out to Edmonton. Because a major repair had been done to the wing, Cannam then had to make up the drawings and submit them to the Department of Transport. "They accepted them, just like that. So that was good."

Cannam's licences now permitted him to work on large aircraft up to the DC-3 and DC-4, the Bristol Freighter, the York, the Bell helicopter and numerous others. Later he acquired his "B" licence, which allowed him to sign out aircraft after major repairs, overhauls or modifications, and the present "M" licence, which allows him to certify that an aircraft is worthy for flight.

And so Cannam's career shifted with the tides of commerce, first working for Associated Airways on various fixed-wing aircraft, on helicopters, then back to fixed wing. When Associated Airways was bought by Pacific Western Airlines, Cannam spent the balance of his working life with that company. "It was a good period of time," he says, reflectively. "And then the Alberta government bought out PWA in a somewhat controversial move. I retired before PWA bought out Canadian Pacific Airlines and the name changed to Canadian Airlines International."

The Merger at the Museum

Chuck MacLaren and Gordon Cannam had first met in 1947, through their common membership in Westminster United Church.

"Chuck was then with Western Airmotive, and I knew Chuck had previously worked at Mackenzie Air Service as their welder and sheet metal man," Cannam says. "When I was with Associated Helicopters, Chuck did the welding on any of our helicopters that were damaged. Chuck would come in during the evening to work on it and invariably in the morning it would all be finished, ready for final inspection and painting, then final assembly, test flight, etc., before heading out on its next contract."

The Alberta Aviation Museum was incorporated under the Alberta Societies Act in 1980. The museum had actually been in operation for a number of years, but had experienced myriad growing pains since its inception in the late 1960s by the Edmonton Air Museum Committee, who'd begun to gather memorabilia for a future museum. But the group's energy faded, and, as Cannam says, "things fell apart." Many of the artifacts gathered by the original group ended up in museums in Yellowknife and Wetaskiwin.

Then, in 1980, the museum was reorganized and named The Alberta Aviation Museum Association. New members brought fresh ideas and contacts. They decided to check out a Fairchild 71C (CF-ATZ) that had been severely damaged in 1949 and had rested at its crash site on the shore of Lake Aristofats in the Northwest Territories for 31 years. The wreck had been stripped of instruments, fuel and oil tanks, basically everything removable. The wings had been broken in the accident, and weather had done the rest.

Nevertheless, the members of the museum decided it was worth salvaging, and made arrangements to bring it back to Edmonton to await the time when money, people and facilities became available to do something with it. In June 1981, a work party proceeded to Fort Smith, and on to Lake Aristofats. The remains of ATZ were taken to Great Slave Lake Fishing Lodge, and in September of 1981 were brought to Edmonton in a Hercules, courtesy of the Canadian Armed Forces.

Gordon Cannam had come to know ATZ in 1937 at Goldfields, where it was operated by Canadian Airways. During his tenure with Associated Airways he had seen it often, the last time while undergoing its Certificate of Airworthiness renewal at United Aircraft in Edmonton. The next time he spotted the old aircraft, in November of 1983, it was in storage at the Edmonton Flying Club, "piled in a heap." Cannam's first reaction was, "What a mess!"

"The Fairchild had been obtained in 1981 but had just sat around; there was no one to repair it, take hold of it. I was retired and wanted something to do," Cannam says. He laughs at the memory of acquiring this busy, unpaid job, and modifies his statement. "I don't know whether I *wanted* something to do or not, but I certainly got it!" He became involved late in 1983 and ATZ became his first restoration project.

Cannam's skills and abilities were welcomed by the fledgling museum, along with those of Chuck MacLaren, and there the two began to merge their talents.

The Products

Fairchild 71-C (CF-ATZ) (1933)

The Fairchild 71-C (CF-ATZ), manufactured in Montreal in 1933, had first seen service with Canadian Airways. It covered points north, flying first out of Winnipeg and then from Edmonton, to northern Saskatchewan, Northwest Territories, Alberta and BC. Legendary flyers such as Punch Dickens, Matt Berry, Wop May and Louis Leigh in turn sat at its controls.

Chuck MacLaren credits the Fairchild with uniting the forces that got the aviation museum going, "when Roy Faltinson and Stan McMillan brought that old Fairchild out of the bush." On January 5, 1984, the remains of the aircraft were moved to the PWA hangar (#13) at the west side of Edmonton Municipal Airport.

The aircraft was a familiar sight for MacLaren as well, who had worked on it in his CPA days. "I'd welded it together. So, I started working on it again, in a space that was part of PWA's old hangar across the field."

Gordon Cannam was called upon to do the wood restoration. Although many years had passed since he'd actually done woodwork, "those talents don't leave you." He also had experience on general aircraft repairs and maintenance, and had been in charge of various functions to salvage and repair aircraft. To the museum's aircraft restoration committee he seemed a natural choice to head the project. "So with the help of Chuck and several others, Jim Brown, Shorty Jungle and Ted Kopyn, we restored the Fairchild to its present status," Cannam says.

It was no easy job. The men who'd worked on so many wrecks in the past just looked at the old Fairchild and groaned. Cannam recalls the labor involved.

"The engine had sat at the edge of a lake, so it was full of sand and water, and was rusted and corroded. Shorty Jungle and Jim Brown took the cylinders apart – we had to hydraulic them off because they were rusted so badly. One cylinder just wouldn't come off, so we had to drill a row of holes all along the edge to let it expand a bit and then take it off mechanically.

"But," he adds proudly, "the engine that in the airplane now is the original one, with some replacement parts."

There was not much left of the fuselage, either.

"It's of a tubular metal structure, the same as the Stinson Reliant," Cannam says. "It was torn apart and wrecked, the controls and anything movable or removable had been wrecked or robbed, so we had to make up a lot of parts. The doors, instrument panel, seats, control system, all were missing. So, first of all, we had to put the fuselage together.

"Then we started on the wings. We had to make up new spars, new ribs, and initially we had no drawings to work with. We managed to get basic drawings for some parts, like the spars, from the Ministry of Transport and that helped to give us a start."

Juanita Elsden, who had once run a doll hospital, and Joan Woodman lent their expertise to the stitching work required on the Fairchild restoration, based on their former work in aircraft repair at Northwest Industries.

With the aid of such teachers, Chuck MacLaren expanded his talent base as welder, riveter and engine-changer to include tailoring, using a donated sewing machine that

Fairchild 71C (CF-ATZ), restored 1985-89. L. to R.: Vern Simmonds, Mickey Sutherland, Captain Joe McGoldrick. (Photo: Alberta Aviation Museum)

had once stitched up blue jeans in the Edmonton-based Great West Garments plant. The only area he shied away from was woodwork. "Gordie Cannam is the wood expert."

And so began the partnership of MacLaren and Cannam. Although they had worked for a lifetime in the aviation industry, in Edmonton, their different areas of expertise and employment histories had not brought them together until both were retired and the museum drew in these two talented men. The fact that they get along beautifully is an added bonus to their work relationship.

"I don't think anybody ever had trouble getting along with Chuck," Cannam says. "He's a fantastic fellow, as a mechanic and as a person. You can't want anyone better."

MacLaren says the same about Cannam.

The Fairchild, which took about six years and 14 000 hours of volunteer labor, became their first project. With good reason, its fuselage sports the name "Gordon Cannam."

Cranwell CLA4 (1926)

Following the success of the Fairchild restoration, the next designated project was a Cranwell CLA4. This small open-cockpit biplane was built in Edmonton in 1929-30 by a group of aviation enthusiasts. It flew locally out of Blatchford Field (Edmonton Municipal Airport) until it was wrecked in 1934 in a forced landing at 127th Street and 127th Avenue. Alf Want, a museum member and one of the Cranwell's original builders, had faithfully stored the wrecked Cranwell for 54 years. He donated it to the museum in January 1989, along with many parts and blueprints.

At this time, plans for having a real space for the museum began to form, as well as continued efforts to acquire artifacts and aircraft. The City of Edmonton offered the use of Building No. 14 at the airport, the last existing BCATP double-width and double-length wartime hangar.

Originally the home of the BCATP No. 2 Air Observer School, it had later been used, from 1946-57, by the City of Edmonton's 418 Squadron, RCAF. Primarily a Search and Rescue Tactical Air Command Squadron, they had 12 Mitchell bombers and two T33 jets stationed in the hangar. PWA had taken over operation of the hangar from 1957-61 during their work on construction of the Distant Early Warning (DEW) Line. At that point, the hangar was given to the City of Edmonton by the federal Department of National Defence, with the museum receiving permission for use of the building in 1991.

de Havilland Mosquito (Commercial Registration CF-HMQ)

The versatile Mosquito was the hero of the Royal Air Force fleet during World War II, and considered to be the fastest RAF aircraft from 1941 to 1944. The aircraft acquired by the museum was built in Christchurch, Hampshire, England, and after the war was purchased by Canada's Spartan Air Services Limited for use in aerial photography and survey work. Until 1963 it was used primarily in the Caribbean, Africa and in Canada's North.

Mosquito CF-HMQ, 1995 (restored 1993-95). L. to R.: Ross Grady, Gordon Cannam, Lindsay Deeprose. (Photo: Alberta Aviation Museum.)

The aircraft was then acquired by Jake Campbell, a Wing Commander of City of Edmonton 418 Intruder Squadron, RCAF, in World War II. His squadron had operated Mosquito Mark VIs as night fighters, and Campbell was credited with destroying many enemy aircraft.

The Mosquito had thus been restored to represent the Fighter Bomber version as flown by the 418 Squadron, with its new function being to guard the front gate of Namao Air Force Base. There it sat for a number of years before being donated to the City of Edmonton, when it was dismantled and trucked to City Archives.

The Mosquito's restoration presented a new set of challenges. "Chuck was mostly involved with fabricating parts and components," Cannam recalls. "There were a lot of parts missing and Chuck made up many of these. For instance he made the pilot's seat in its entirety. We were fortunate in being able to borrow the seat out of a Mosquito from the Aero Space Museum of Calgary for a pattern. We also had to make up the control column, and we modified the stick from an Anson Mark II dual-wheel type."

Cannam emphasizes that to take a used part from an Anson and modify it to look exactly like the part from a Mosquito is no small feat.

"And Chuck also made up the instrument panel and put in all the instruments. He did all the welding, for instance on the canopy, because we modified the model. It was originally a bomber with a V-windscreen and we modified it to a Fighter Bomber VI, which had a flat windscreen." The removal of the bar in the windscreen was to improve the pilot's vision when it became a fighter aircraft.

"When we got the Mosquito it was entirely stripped out because they had notions of hanging it in the Convention Centre, so everything was missing," MacLaren says.

"Gordie did most of the woodwork but there were quite a few people involved in the project. There was a *lot* of sanding involved, and we had to replace most of the wood."

The beautifully-restored Mosquito is equipped with two engines, although it was decided there was no point in running them up or attempting to make it airworthy. It bears the markings of an aircraft flown by Wing Commander Russ Bannock, one of the wartime commanders of 418 Squadron.

When asked about his role in restoring the Mosquito and other aircraft, Cannam acknowledges that he has been in charge of all the restoration projects at the museum since 1984, when they started work on the Fairchild. "Primarily my job is just to organize and coordinate things, see that they are getting the materials and so on, and money."

Ah, yes, money. The commodity that museums find in dishearteningly short supply.

"Fortunately, 418 Squadron had acquired about $25 000 for the restoration of this Mosquito. They made that available to us and that is what financed all the parts.

"Then we made a deal with the City of Edmonton, who owned it at this time, as the aircraft had been given to the city by 418 Squadron," Cannam explains. "Our promise was to restore it in a maximum time period of three years. That was in the spring of 1993, so that meant it had to be finished in 1996. However, we finished it in barely over two years. The unveiling project was given to Roy Woodburn, a member of the museum as well as of 418 Squadron, and he recruited a number of others to help him."

The roll-out, in September of 1995, was spectacular.

"The setting was made to simulate a wartime scene in England, at an aerodrome at night," Cannam says. "At first we could see nothing because a big sheet of material had been set in front of the aircraft to hide it. Then came the sounds of bombs falling – V-1 and others, whistling down, and then the sound of airplane engines starting up, taking off and flying. Strobe lights flashed on and off.

"Suddenly the curtain fell back and two mechanics came out to do a walk-around the aircraft, making a pre-flight inspection using flashlights, in the dark. It was eerie, and so real."

No one who witnessed the unveiling will ever forget it, especially MacLaren and Cannam, who had done so much work on the Mosquito. "It was touching, very well done," Cannam says simply.

Noorduyn Norseman (CF-EIH) (1944)

The history of CF-EIH was typical of the hardy, Canadian-made Norseman aircraft designed and manufactured in Montreal by the company headed by Dutch-born Robert Bernard Cornelius Noorduyn.

The Norseman Mark IV aircraft acquired by the museum began its life in March 1942 as Civilian Serial No. 94, later changed to Military (RCAF) No. 493. It was a large aircraft with a float-equipped, but unloaded, weight of 4441 pounds [lighter on wheels or skis], and a fully loaded weight of 6480 pounds. Its wingspan was 51'6", length 32'4" and height 13`9". Air speed was 150 mph, powered by a Pratt & Whitney 550 hp, nine-cylinder engine.

In August 1946 it was "struck off service" (SOS) by the RCAF, and on May 5, 1947, was sold by War Assets to Associated Airways of Edmonton for one dollar through Kashower Air Service Ltd. in Oshawa, and registered as CF-EIH. A major overhaul and replacement of component parts was immediately undertaken by Weston Aircraft Limited in Oshawa on behalf of the new owners, Associated Airways.

The large amount of work necessary to gain its Certificate of Airworthiness indicates that it had either been involved in a major accident or that it was assembled as a "hybrid unit." Some difficulty was experienced after it arrived in Edmonton, on floats, because of the many components that had been required during overhaul. On May 29, 1947, EIH was sold to McDonald Aviation Company Limited in Edmonton.

Gordie Cannam goes over the documented history of EIH. "Associated Airways often acquired airplanes and resold them, so it wasn't unusual that EIH was sold to McDonald Aviation," he comments.

According to a letter from J.J. Currie, Resident Inspector, Air Regulations, Edmonton, dated June 12, 1947, CF-EIH was indeed a hybrid. It had been registered as a Mark IV, yet Mark V landing gear was installed; the fuselage incorporated a detachable engine mount, not original to the Mark IV but rather a Mark V or VI. The instrument panel was not standard, and a survey of the worksheet in the aircraft logbook indicates that numerous new components had been fitted with no release note numbers quoted. Eventually these questions were somewhat resolved and temporary certificates of registration and airworthiness were issued on August 8, 1947.

The mongrel aircraft departed for Yellowknife early in August 1947 where it was operated through Charter Airways Ltd.

Its life was terminated just a few weeks later, on August 25, 1947.

The accident report, signed by the pilot and submitted to the District Inspector, Civil Aviation in Edmonton, on August 27, 1947, chronicles the last moments of the aircraft. "It had only a few hundred hours on it when they put it into the bush," Cannam says regretfully.

It was damaged beyond repair at Allin Lake on the Cameron River, 52 miles northeast of Yellowknife, during an attempted landing in a strong cross-wind. There were five persons on board, and all survived the accident.

Norseman CF-EIH lay on the shore of remote Allin Lake, abandoned and wrecked, half in and half out of the water, its body and reputation in shambles. It was finally salvaged in 1960, 47 years later, when Stan Edkins of Fort Smith, NWT, decided to bring out the miserable-looking mongrel and ship it home.

The Norseman was in seriously bad shape. All removable components such as flight controls, doors, floats, engine and instruments had been taken out by "visitors." A tree was growing through the spars of one wing. When the stump was cut to allow the aircraft to be lifted, 50 rings were counted on it. (The stump is now part of the museum's display.) The basic airframe was reasonably complete, however, and the missing components were considered not impossible to replace.

"We were fortunate to have it presented to us, in a sense, from Stan Edkins," Cannam says. "When he asked the museum if we wanted it we said, `Sure.' We gave him an income tax receipt for it and he brought it down. It was stored here for a period of time until we had completed the Mosquito."

The restoration of an aircraft of this vintage and condition could take a considerable amount of money, and the museum did not have the financial reserves for a project of this magnitude. They started work on the fuselage, however, utilizing steel tubing from a surplus Anson Mark II fuselage lying in the back yard.

Shortly thereafter, they received a letter from a local organization stating that an associated company in England wished to donate a sum of money to the restoration of some worthwhile project.

"Many thanks and much appreciation goes to The Mactaggart Third Fund and the Mactaggart family, headquartered in London, who provided these funds for restoration of our Norseman," says Cannam. "Maclab Enterprises and Alastair Mactaggart were also closely involved. The senior Sandy Mactaggart is a well-known Alberta businessman who has been involved with aircraft for many years, and has been a generous supporter of our museum. These benefactors provided something over $25 000, so the cost of the restoration of the Mosquito and the Norseman ran pretty close."

Gordon Cannam also credits another benefactor with helping the museum to build its collection. "We were very fortunate to have a good supporter in Joe McBryan, who owns Buffalo Airways (Yellowknife and Hay River). He was instrumental in helping to salvage the Fairchild CF-ATZ back in 1980-81, and over the years he has collected a tremendous number of Norseman parts and components. We received a lot of parts from him, including a set of wings."

The museum tries to "pay back" their benefactors, and when McBryan needs something, such as a part for a DC-3, and if the museum has that part, they reciprocate his kindness. Volunteers in all areas are the backbone of non-profit organizations, and the Alberta Aviation Museum fully acknowledges the help they receive from many sectors. "All the work, everything, done on the Fairchild, the Cranwell, the Mosquito and the Norseman, was performed with volunteer labor," Cannam says. "The only cash expenditure was for essential components, parts or work that we simply could not do in the shop, but that was very little."

In October 1997, when Norseman CF-EIH was partially restored, Gordon Cannam and Chuck MacLaren took a walk-around the aircraft.

"A lot of these old planes were brought out as a campaign to environmentally clean up the area, so getting them out of the bush was a form of recycling!" Chuck MacLaren says. "People would see airplanes that had been down for 40 years and report them, so a lot of them were picked up."

He produces photographs showing EIH being lifted from its shoreline resting place, including one of the tree dangling from one wing. "And here's the stump," he says, bringing the curved cutting from the storage room. "We really *did* count 50 rings on it."

"When we got EIH, there were about six feet missing from the fuselage," Cannam says. "We had a young guy helping us. He sanded it down and we got all the framework primed and painted. Then it was just a matter of building everything that was missing!" he laughs.

The missing parts that had to be rebuilt included a complete windshield, as well as an instrument panel, control column, and rudder pedals. It contained neither an engine nor engine mounts. The belly was ripped out and there was nothing inside.

"A whole section was missing from the tail," MacLaren adds. "We got quite a few pieces from Joe McBryan. He was real good to us. We did have the seats and they've been reupholstered, with a new floor. It will be just like a brand new airplane. We're going to display it on skis."

The skis, also donated by McBryan, are traditional, designed by the Elliot Brothers, who made many such types for different aircraft over the past 70 years. "Alas, the modern `wheel-ski' has completely replaced the all-wood Elliot Brothers ski," Cannam laments. Made from a number of longitudinal, formed strips of ash, secured with copper rivets and protected by a copper sheet also attached with copper rivets, these strong skis glided easily over the snow.

Gordon Cannam compares the structure of the ski pedestals, to which the skis were attached, to a hot dog. "The `bun' part is hollow and fits around an `air bag' – the `wiener'," he says. "The air bag is inflated to 35 pounds per square inch, which then acts like the tires of an automobile."

This extra shock-absorbing feature was necessary during takeoff and landings on rough snow or ice ridges often encountered on the unprepared landing surfaces throughout Northern Canada.

Another aspect of the work involved painting, performed in the museum's paint shop. "The belly and the front are going to be green," says MacLaren, "and all the horizontal parts, the wings and elevators and that, will be yellow." These Mackenzie Air Service colors were chosen because they stood out clearly, both in summer and winter.

In the paint booth area, MacLaren demonstrates one of his inventions: a circular turntable for holding the wing while it's being painted. "You have to work on every side of the wing, so this way you don't have to lay on your back or get six people to help you turn it over. You've no idea how heavy one of these wings is! Four guys can pick it up, but just. Then if you want to turn it over you had to have sawhorses underneath."

With the apparatus designed by Chuck MacLaren, the wing is inserted into clamps and can be turned over with one hand while being painted. The turntable is a simple invention that works, and is patterned after one he built 50 years ago while working on Ansons.

Chuck MacLaren with wing-turner system that he invented, holding Norseman wing (CF-EIH). (Photo: S. Matheson)

Inside the paint room are struts and elevators for the Norseman, ready to be put together, and all bright yellow. Next to these, also bearing a coat of yellow paint, sits the trusty old GWG sewing machine on which MacLaren sewed the fabric for the Norseman.

MacLaren used a special type of polyester thread for stitching the fabric for the wings. While not particularly heavy it's as strong as fish-line. "You can't break it." He also uses a poly-fibre material for covering the airplane. "There's lots of it here," he says, indicating bolts and bolts of the fabric. "It feels silky but it's a man-made fibre. It's not exactly authentic. When Norsemen were first built they used cotton."

Photos show MacLaren surrounded by yards of white material as he sews a giant "sock" to fit the fuselage as well as wing coverings for the Norseman. He patiently explains how one goes about making a sock for a 32-foot airplane.

"The fabric comes in various widths from four to six feet, so you just measure the top and run a seam down each corner, letting it hang down the side. It didn't go all the way around at the centre so I had to sew a wedge in it. Then I pinned it together, took it off, and came in here and sewed it.

"You've got a lot of cloth to handle," MacLaren acknowledges. "It's all around you. My wife might think I'm a lousy sewer – I *am* a lousy sewer – but I sewed that whole airplane together! And it turned out okay."

What's involved in "sewing an airplane together"?

"For the fuselage, you make the sock and pull it on in one piece, over the tail wheel and up to the windshield. Then, staple it on. It's forgiving because this cloth shrinks with heat. Usually you go over the whole thing with an iron."

So, you also "iron airplanes"?

"Yeah, I ironed the airplane," MacLaren says, jutting out his chin defensively. "I set my iron at 250° and went over the whole thing. Then I reset it at 350° – that shrinks the cloth up like a fiddle-string – and then it's ready for the dope."

The dope doesn't stick to the poly-fibre like it does to cotton so the first coat has to be thinned out to penetrate the weave and actually "lock on" behind. "There's no fuzzies on this poly stuff like there is in cotton, that's why the first coat has to go through, otherwise the fabric will peel off in big chunks," says MacLaren. "It happens. And from then on, you just put multiple layers of dope on it."

And then you did the wings?

"Yeah, the wing covers were sewed in lengths. We had a piece made up 25 feet long and about 14 feet wide. We wrapped it from the leading edge back. And then it was stapled on the back. When you do something like this, you bring the cloth around and cement it on the elevators, then on the other side you lap it over the one you already had glued to the frame, again using cement to secure this lapped fabric to the trailing edge. This lap joint is then covered with a four-inch width of tape."

And then what?

"Then you rib-stitch it. You have to anchor the cloth to the frame, especially on the wings and controls, otherwise they'd balloon. These stitches go right through and around the frame, double-knot, then onto the next stitch." He uses a special knot, described in many old books. Although books are helpful, MacLaren would surely have invented his own methods. "Well, I did rib-stitching long before these authors were born, probably."

MacLaren feels that it's good to learn new things and he encourages it in others. "People come here who want to do their own airplane. They figure this is a good place to come and practice, so they'll know all the rules when they get to theirs!" He laughs. "And that's allowed."

After 8000 hours of volunteer labor, and many contributions of parts and supplies, CF-EIH was rolled out on April 18, 1998. In attendance were Robert Noorduyn Jr., as well as a gathering of former Norseman pilots, engineers and other lovers of "Canada's Thunder Chicken." Inscribed on the fuselage is a name that will now live forever in the annals of Alberta Aviation Museum history, "Chuck MacLaren."

*Norseman CF-EIH
(dedicated to Chuck
MacLaren). (Photo:
S. Matheson)*

The aircraft is immaculate. Brightly-painted fabric and varnished wood glow under the spotlight – just like the two men who merged their trades and talents, along with a crew of dedicated workers, to bring a new and better life to once-wretched, and nearly-forgotten, old airplanes.

Futures

The museum's mission, to collect, preserve, restore, research and display the history of aviation in the City of Edmonton, and in the Province of Alberta, ensures there will be no end of interesting projects.

"We've got the gull-wing Stinson SR9 Reliant (1938) out here that is going to be a flying airplane, and we have an Anson Mark II as well," Cannam says.

Permanently on display are various other civilian aircraft such as an Ercoupe (1947), a home built Currie Watt, a Twin Beechcraft 18 and a Waco Model UIC (1933). Military aircraft on display or under restoration include Avro Ansons, a CF100 Canuck, Bomarc Missile, deHavilland Vampire, a Lockheed T33, McDonnell F101 Voodoo, a North American Harvard, and replicas of a Hawker Hurricane, a Vickers Viking Flying Boat and a Westland Lysander.

The cavernous hangar at the Alberta Aviation Museum also houses aircraft in various stages of being restored by independent groups. Chuck MacLaren points out a Lockheed PV-1 Ventura that was originally used for patrolling and bombing during World War II and later by Spartan Air Services Limited for aerial photography. It is being restored by the Venture Memorial Flight Association, who found it abandoned up North. "It was towed in on its own wheels all the way from Yellowknife like that."

MacLaren notes the flush riveting and the difficulty that its restorers will encounter. "This metal is so thin that you can't just drill and counter-sink the rivets. You have to punch each one with a set and dimple it. Then whatever you rivet it to has to be dimpled, so that doubles the work."

When one notes the size of the aircraft and the number of rivets, the workload involved in its restoration seems overwhelming. MacLaren agrees.

"It's a very slow process." He runs an experienced hand over the metal of the old airplane, like a doctor checking for sore spots.

When Chuck MacLaren and Gordon Cannam are asked to evaluate an aircraft for its value as a restoration project, they willingly offer their opinions on whether something could – or should – be fixed.

"Some people think, `Oh, I know where there's a wreck up North,' but a lot of times

The Masters: Chuck MacLaren and Gordon Cannam (Photo: S. Matheson)

it's just not worth the time and money that will be involved," MacLaren says.

"With most of them, we know whether or not they're worth fixing," Cannam echoes.

The two former farm boys plan to continue evaluating, organizing and doing much of the work to restore old airplanes. The Alberta Aviation Museum on Kingsway Avenue in Edmonton is ever grateful. These people, and the aircraft they so lovingly renew, represent a time in history that can never be repeated.

FIRST AIR REQUIRES AIRCRAFT GROOMERS

The Final Frontier

The world stands out on either side
No wider than the heart is wide;
Above the world is stretched the sky, –
No higher than the soul is high.

Edna St. Vincent Millay, "Voyage to the Moon"

How does a kid from Canada get involved in the exciting world of outer space?

A number have done so, including 10 who have become astronauts designated to fly on nine missions into space between 1983 and 1999.[1]

There are many careers available within the space program. One may work directly for the US National Aeronautics and Space Administration (NASA), which directed American space projects Mercury, Gemini and Apollo, operates the Launch Operations Center at Cape Kennedy, Florida, and the Johnson Space Center at Houston, Texas.

There are also space-related jobs to be found at a number of research and development installations throughout the USA and Canada. Calgary, for example, has five companies that are heavily involved in space technology and are building components for the new International Space Station.

The University of Calgary's Institute for Space Research has an instrument on ISIS II, launched in 1971, to observe the Earth's auroras from orbit. As well, medical personnel from the University have been invited to work at NASA as flight surgeons.

In 1962, Canada became the third nation in the world (after the US and the USSR) to design, construct and place a satellite in orbit (Alouette I, from a US base). There were four satellites in the series: Alouette I, Alouette II, ISIS I and ISIS II. All were very successful.

"Rocket experiments were conducted by the University of Calgary's scientists during the 1960s, so Alberta has a relatively long record of involvement in space science," states Dr. Leroy Cogger of the University's Department of Physics and Astronomy.

In the ensuing years, Canada has become a world leader in space technology and programs. We've launched numerous satellites, helped established international communications systems and developed the amazing Canadarm, a remote-manipulator system mounted on space shuttles and used in space to move payloads in and out of the shuttle bay. These pioneering achievements encourage our students to consider the many careers available in space.

Two Canadians who are involved in the space program, and who recently came to know each other through this common interest, are Brian Ewenson and Chris Hadfield. Although their careers have been quite different, their love of space exploration has connected them in friendship. When they met to participate in opening the Space Exhibit at the Aero Space Museum of Calgary in January 1998, it was like two pen-pals meeting for the first time.

Brian Ewenson is not an engineer, nor a scientist, nor even a pilot. In fact, his profession for the past 14 years has been a child care worker with the Boys and Girls Clubs of Canada, and more recently as Education and Programming Officer for the Aero Space Museum Association of Calgary.

How did he become so involved in space technology that he receives personal invitations (and eagerly-sought launch passes) from NASA to attend shuttle launches? And why is he so crazy about the space program that for his honeymoon he took his bride to the launch of space shuttle Columbia STS-78 at the Kennedy Space Center in Florida (which carried Calgary astronaut Bob Thirsk) – later calling this visit "the culmination of 17 years of dreams?"

Brian Thomas Ewenson was born in the city of Montreal, Quebec, on April 18, 1968. His father was a police officer for 30 years with the Montrea Urban Community Police, and his mother a homemaker. As Brian says, "We were a standard, working, middle-class family." Brian has a twin brother, Keith, and a younger sister, Karen. Keith is now a commercial pilot with Air Canada on their Airbus 320, and Karen is manager of a Toronto-Dominion bank.

When the boys were five years old, in 1973, the family took a trip to the Kennedy Space Center in Florida. The images Brian saw there became permanently etched in his mind. "Walking through the space center, and in particular through the Rocket Garden, I saw all these *huge* rockets. I was just stunned! At seven years old, while still in grade school, I started writing to some of the companies to get information and pictures. I was hooked."

Soon, he was getting up at three o'clock in the morning to flip on the television and watch the astronauts eat breakfast, be interviewed, suit up, walk out, and be strapped into the shuttle. He peppered corporations such as NASA and foreign space agencies for information, writing an average of five letters a week.

"When my brother and I were seven years old we'd take a bagged lunch and ride our bikes 10 miles, from Montreal out to Dorval International Airport, to watch airplanes on the runways. We were fascinated by aviation, how a vehicle that size could get off the ground."

Ewenson became involved with the Boys and Girls Clubs through his last year of high school. "A requirement of our mainstream courses was to do six months of volunteer work with an organization. I'd worked during high school with the YMCA as a summer camp counselor, so I chose the Boys and Girls Clubs as a place to do my six-month placement. I enjoyed meeting these kids and giving them experiences that they'd never had before."

He attended McGill University, graduating in 1992 with a Bachelor of Arts in Political Science. He then worked for several years with the Boys and Girls Club of Montreal.

When he learned that Nationair, a charter airline in Montreal, was looking for a flight attendant, he applied. Buoyed by his basic interest in aviation, an interest in travel and the fact that he was conversant in a number of languages, he felt it might be a good change from his past high-stress work.

Nationair

Brian was with Nationair for two years, in 1990 and '91. The company flew DC-8s (61s, 62s and 63s, different versions of a DC-8 indicating length, passenger capacity, etc.), and also Boeing 747s and 757s. He worked full-time for one year, and during his second year attended university and took weekend charter flights with the company. He returned to work full time at the Boys and Girls Club, and was also a football referee.

Brian was involved with one "incident" at his job with Nationair that could have resulted in a serious problem.

"It happened at Quebec City International Airport with the DC-8-63, in pouring rain and heavy fog," Brian recalls. "We came down on the runway and hit fairly hard. The DC-8 had a tendency to fishtail, especially when hydroplaning, because it was such a long aircraft. I was with another flight attendant, the in-flight director, sitting in the forward bulkhead facing the back end of the cabin, and we could see the horizontal (yaw) motion of the aircraft on the runway.

"As the ailerons and speed brakes came down, we didn't feel any deceleration. With both of us sitting right against the cockpit door we could hear alarms going off, and hear the commander and first officer fighting to keep the aircraft on the runway. As we were barreling down the runway, the flaps came back up to increase thrust. We thought we might get a rejected landing at that point and take off again. As we went down the runway, once again the flaps came down, probably in the area of 90 to 100 percent, speed brake, and we felt ourselves skidding. Both the in-flight director and myself assumed a brace position preparing for a crash, and started going through our shouted oral commands for people to brace."

The aircraft came to a stop within 30 to 15 feet of the end of the runway. Brian jumped from his seat, knocked on the cockpit door, opened it and asked the pilots if they were okay. The answer was affirmative, so he and the other attendants concentrated on looking after the 262 passengers.

"That was called an 'incident,' as we say in the aviation industry," Brian says. "You wonder what you'll do in an emergency situation, but the training just clicks in. We did everything that was supposed to be done, in the proper order. Once we'd got everyone off the aircraft, and the fire trucks were there and emergency crews were making sure the aircraft was okay to be towed, we sat back looking at the aircraft from a distance and how close we were to the end of the runway – that's when the shaking started."

But Brian has good memories of his work as a flight attendant, and still pays particular attention to the patter these people give at the start of a flight.

"One of the things that still bugs me are some business flyers who read their newspapers, not paying attention, while the flight attendant does the emergency briefing. And you have 30 to 90 seconds to get out of an aircraft alive in a situation! Even as a former flight attendant I don't get into the pattern of thinking I know where the emergency exits are and can ignore them. Our three 747s had different interior layouts. Each aircraft is different, the layouts are different, the procedures are different.

"Whenever I fly, I count seats forward and backward to exits right and left, and as well I check that the life vest and stuff is actually under the seat. I mentally check where the fire extinguishers are, and the oxygen. It drives my wife nuts."

Brian married Tammy Fioritti in 1996, and moved to Calgary.

Getting into Space

Brian Ewenson acknowledges that, until about 1997, he was just "Brian the Space Enthusiast." When he began to integrate space education into his programs with the Boys and Girls Clubs of Calgary, he became "Brian, the Space Enthusiast-Space Edu-cator."

Then he read an article in the Calgary *Herald* by science editor, Mark Lowey: "Aero Space Museum Looking for High-Flying Fashion." The Museum's president, Don Reed, had noted that the museum wanted to add something on space flight. Brian called. "I know a lot about space flight, how can I help you?" Within a month, he was advised of an upcoming election for the Board of Directors. "Get on the board and chair a committee," Reed suggested. So he did, and assumed the chair of the museum's Youth Committee.

"Being on the Board of the Aero Space Museum has given me a little more of a profes-

Brian Ewenson, April 9, 1997, Johnson Space Center, Houston, TX, in commander's seat of STS (space shuttle fixed-base simulator) (Photo: Ewenson collection)

sional image," Brian says, "although if you're an enthusiast, NASA will send you stuff. If you're an educator you'll get more stuff; but now I get much better contact with the people, more on a professional level."

And "stuff" is what Brian has, in abundance: file cabinets, storage boxes, library shelves, entire rooms all spilly with things inside: videos on space, NASA films, books, "kid-lit" books on space, paperback novels, complete dossiers on each and every astronaut, and a Bible personally signed by Jim Irwin who was on the Apollo 15 voyage to the moon.

Brian's walls are covered with certificates, naming him an Honorary Astronaut for having visited the Astronaut Hall of Fame in Florida and being part of the "Shuttle to Tomorrow" crew (June 14/96). He has a brick in his name at the Kennedy Space Center, having "proved" to NASA his support of the space program though his work in education programs, museum exhibits and newspaper articles.

He has models of shuttles on their launch pads, and models from explorations of Mars such as the Mars Rover, the Sojourner, Carl Sagan Station and the Orbiter, and of the Apollo Command and Service Module; polystyrene beads made on board the space shuttle Challenger on its 6th flight in 1983, a couple of Susan B. Anthony dollars, a number of classic, limited edition "G.I. Joe" astronaut dolls, one representing Alan Shepard on his first flight in a NASA flight suit. He has "every little toy" made that represents the space program, including a small space shuttle with a doll inside, put out by Burger King. He's collected flight patches from every manned mission dating back to the Mercury flights and including all shuttle missions; space cards, 27 scrap books, over 1000 photos, and four-drawer filing cabinets filled with all pre-and post-flight mission reports and fact sheets.

Brian explains his vast collection by saying, "I like to know a little bit about everything, but not everything about one thing." His books, videos and collected memorabilia range from light yet catchy, geared toward encouraging novices to learn about space, to heavy technical data. "I'm always seeking, always finding," Brian says. "Life is just too darn short to do everything you want to do."

Educating Kids on Space

"Brian the Science Guy" worked for the Boys and Girls Clubs, and a variety of children's organizations, for 14 years, and in 1999 became Education and Programming Officer for the Aero Space Museum.

"Within my arts and crafts and games that I play with the kids, I'm very, very strong on the educational side, whereas a lot of people are straight into the recreation," he says. "I like to do a balance of recreation, social work and education, particularly with math and sciences. The children, youth and teens that I work with come predominately from low-income backgrounds and troubled families. They don't get much exposure to the sciences and they tend to go into very traditional jobs for those types of communities – in restaurants, or working as cashiers, and they don't seem to have a whole lot of aspirations beyond that. We do need a service sector for our society to operate, yet we have a number of kids with latent talents that aren't being brought out in the schools or by parents."

One example is a project Ewenson undertook to grow canola grain seeds that had accompanied Calgary-educated astronaut Bob Thirsk on the space shuttle Columbia in June 1996. "Canolab" was Canada's first public plant biology experiment performed in space. The project proved that seeds that had spent 17 days aboard the space shuttle grew plants that were the same as those from seeds that had remained on Earth.

"I hope to inspire the kids to, not necessarily become astronauts, but get interested in the space program. There are seven people on each shuttle flight and you're looking at 40 000 people who've worked to prepare that vehicle. There is such a broad variety of jobs within the program. And people don't realize that you can work for the space program right here in Calgary! There are five companies in Calgary alone that are building components for the International Space Station!"

Canada in Space

When Brian Ewenson is asked who he believes was the most influential politician to bring Canada into the space picture, with our small population and relatively small amount of money, his response is surprising.

"The person very strong in it, actually through a huge mistake in Canadian policy, was John Diefenbaker and the demise of the Avro Arrow. A lot of Canadian engineers involved in the Avro Arrow packed up their bags when they were kicked off the Arrow project and went down to the States, and actually sent the first Americans into space. There were around 32 engineers from the Avro project who went to work for NASA directly in the Mercury and Gemini and Apollo programs. A lot of them did not return to Canada, but were very strong and influential in getting Canada into the space program. They were also the fellows who built the original Canadian satellite, Alouette, and then the follow-up on ISIS and Alouette II. Alouette was the first-ever satellite designed and built in Canada, but of course launched by the United States because we don't have a launch capability here."

There was an actual rocket range located in Churchill, Manitoba, run by the government and closed in the 1980s; an effort is presently being made to revive it as a private endeavor. "This private company expects to launch sub-orbital space craft as well as orbital space craft in Churchill, as Canada's only space port," Brian explains. "It will send unmanned sounding rockets, small satellite payloads, into polar orbit."

Brian feels that, while a person may move from one country to another because of work possibilities, such as the ex-Avro Arrow engineers, their roots remain here.

"It was just a bad political situation that led them to the other side of the fence where the grass was greener, and it *was* greener for them," Brian says. "Chris Hadfield is a classic example. He says, 'Yes, I work for the United States but I am still a Canadian astronaut.' One of the neat things about that is they can go down and work in the United States, contribute to the program in a great way, yet they still feel they're Canadian."

Colonel Chris A. Hadfield, born in Sarnia, Ontario, on August 29, 1959, is a prime example of a Canadian astronaut, a "sailor among the stars."

His interest in space started one night in July 1969 when, as a 10-year-old boy, he stood outside his family's cottage on Stag Island near Sarnia and stared up at the moon. An astronaut was walking around up there, right that very minute! Indeed, astronauts on the Apollo 11 mission, Neil A. Armstrong and Edwin E. Aldrin Jr., had landed the lunar module Eagle in the southwestern part of the Sea of Tranquility, then got out to walk about on the moon, while Michael Collins remained in orbit in the command module Columbia.

That night, Hadfield said to himself, "That would be a good thing to do when I grow up."

"It was too far-fetched to say out loud," Hadfield reflects, "so I just kept it as a quiet dream, and personal direction to head, in case it ever became possible."

But getting involved in the space program, and especially becoming an astronaut, takes a lot of down-to-earth work and determination. Chris Hadfield joined Air Cadets at age 13, where he learned to fly, receiving both his glider and powered wings. "I had my 15th birthday right at the end of the course, so I got to fly when I was 14."

On his first revolution of the earth, launched from Florida, the shuttle went around the world once and came across the field in southern Ontario from where he'd learned to fly. "So there I was, in a space shuttle going eight kilometres a second right over the field where I first learned to glide when I was 14 years old!"

After learning the basics of flight, he joined the military where he learned to fly jets. "I became a fighter pilot on CF-18s, then a test pilot for four years where I learned how airplanes really worked. And then I was hired by the Canadian Space Agency and learned how to fly in space."

Chris holds a Bachelor of Mechanical Engineering (Honors) degree from Royal Military College (1982). He graduated from the US Air Force Test Pilot School (1988), and took a Master of Aviation Systems degree from the University of Tennessee (1992). Added to his academic studies was a summer spent as a research engineer for the University of Waterloo, and three years as a fighter pilot with 425 Tactical Fighter Squadron at Canadian Forces Base Bagotville in Quebec. Here, he flew the first CF-18 intercept of a Soviet aircraft in Canadian airspace, and later represented Canada at the William Tell Fighter Weapons Meet at Tyndall Airforce base where the Canadian team won second place overall.

Chris Hadfield. (Photo courtesy of the Canadian Space Agency)

In 1989 Hadfield was named a Canadian Exchange Officer with the US Naval Air Test Center in Patuxent River, Maryland, and joined the Canadian Astronaut Program. Other accolades and "firsts" followed, including being selected in 1992 by the Canadian Space Agency to take training as a mission specialist at the Johnson Space Center in Houston, Texas. He was the first non-American to be assigned as Astronaut Support Personnel, representing the astronauts at the Kennedy Space Center, preparing the shuttles and crews for launch, and assisting the crews after landing.

Aboard Space Shuttle Atlantis in November 1995, Hadfield participated in STS-74, the second shuttle-to-Mir mission. He was the fourth Canadian in space, and the first Canadian to fly as a mission specialist, to board the Russian Space Station Mir and to operate the Canadarm in space. In the year 2000, he is scheduled to participate in a second space flight, Mission STS-100, which will orbit in space for 12 days or so, and will be the first Canadian to perform a spacewalk.

"I am technical," Hadfield says in an understatement, as he explains the rudiments of operating the Canadarm to an audience of young students and air cadets. He is in Calgary on a cold, blustery day in January 1998, accompanied by his 12-year-old daughter Kristin, on a visit organized by Brian Ewenson and the Aero Space Museum of Calgary.

Space Shuttle Atlantis – Mission STS-74 (November, 1995)

Chris Hadfield glances over photos of Space Shuttle Atlantis, the second in a series of nine space missions, and comes across a poetic line describing the launch: "Space Shuttle Atlantis breaks free from its earthly ties and soars toward the stars." Is that the thought that crossed his mind as they were taking off?

"No!" He laughs. "At that moment you're just gritting your teeth and hanging on. There's no 'soaring' at that point – just raw, brute power." He explains that the fuel lines that pump the hydrogen and the oxygen into the shuttle are *17 inches across*. Compared to a fuel line in a car being about 3/8" across, it's unthinkable. And there are two such lines on the shuttle, one for hydrogen and one for oxygen, with a turbo-jet type engine just for pumping the fuel into the motors.

Hadfield explains that the shuttle uses 12 tons of fuel a second. This is needed to propel the entire structure from the launch pad which, including a couple of million pounds of fuel, weighs 4.5 million pounds. The portion of the shuttle that goes into space weighs 200 000 pounds.

The crew of Space Shuttle Atlantis Mission STS-74 was comprised of Commander Kenneth D. Cameron, Pilot Jim Halsell and Mission Specialists Jerry L. Ross, Chris A. Hadfield and Bill McArthur. Part of the thrill for Hadfield was the fact that the shuttle carrying him into space was launched from the same pad as the Apollo II that had carried Armstrong, Aldrin and Collins on their historic mission.

Blast-off!

As the shuttle blasts off it immediately makes a turn to align with the orbit of the Mir Space Station. Hadfield explains that it was found to be cheaper to make the shuttle turn than to tear down the whole launch pad and build a new one.

It takes seven million pounds of thrust to send off a space shuttle, an amount of power that could lift up a seven-million-pound building based on the amount of thrust pouring out the back. There are three engines on the shuttle, providing 1.5 million pounds of thrust, and two large solid rocket boosters as well.

"It's an amazing amount of power and gives a very, very rough ride as it rattles and shakes and pushes you up off the pad, especially while you're in the air," Hadfield says. "As it's pushing you up through the atmosphere, it's really violent. We get up to about 500 knots before the air starts to thin out, then you really start going fast. It takes eight-and-one-half minutes total, from when the engines light until you're in orbit."

The shuttle must be travelling at just the right speed to stay in orbit. Any faster and you'd "wing out" into space; a little slower and the orbit would decay and you'd fall into the atmosphere. Hadfield compares the centrifugal force necessary to stay in orbit to that needed to keep a ball rotating on the end of a string. The speed required to stay in orbit is approximately five miles a second, or 17 500 miles an hour. At this speed, he compares a trip from Calgary to Edmonton, about 200 miles, taking just 36 seconds.

"In the shuttle, you boot around the world in 90 minutes, and across Canada, coast to coast, in nine minutes, so we're travelling at an incredible speed just to stay in orbit," Hadfield notes.

Whenever they passed over North America the astronauts would press their faces to the windows to view their home territory, so clear yet so far away. The first pictures Hadfield took from space were of his home town of Sarnia, the Chris Hadfield Airport and the island from which he'd watched the men on the moon, when he'd decided to become an astronaut.

Looking down through space, objects on Earth show clearly. "I think one of the questions asked in the game of Trivial Pursuit, is, 'What's the only manmade object that you can see from space?' and the answer given is 'The Great Wall of China,'" Hadfield says. "Well, that's wrong. You can't see the Great Wall of China from space because it's only about a dozen feet wide and it's all overgrown with trees and follows the hills. In fact, I was on the Great Wall of China and the tour guide made that comment. I said, 'That's not true, that's just a common myth.' You can, however, see all kinds of manmade things from space: you can see the streets of Calgary, you can see farms, buildings and all sorts of things."

He points to a photo showing a view out the back window of the shuttle. It is approaching sunset, where Earth shimmers golden in the background. "When you look down at the world, it's unbelievably beautiful."

Even more phenomenal are the Northern Lights, the Aurora Borealis, viewed from space. "You can see them from end to end, over 1000 miles."

Atlantis, the Canadarm and Mir

The term "astronaut," used to describe American space travellers, comes from two Greek words meaning "sailor among the stars." The term, "cosmonaut," used to describe Russian space travellers, comes from Greek words meaning, "sailor of the universe."

The primary purpose of the Atlantis STS-74 mission was to connect the shuttle with the permanently-orbiting Russian space station, Mir, enabling the astronauts and cosmonauts to visit each other's homes in space. This was to be accomplished via a Canadian invention, the remote-controlled robotic arm – appropriately named Canadarm – operated by Canadian astronaut Chris Hadfield.

This amazing apparatus, designed and built by Spar Space Systems (a subsidiary of Spar Aerospace) of Brampton, Ontario, is 50 feet long and weighs 1.5 tons.

"The people involved in designing this thought that since the Russians had built a place to go in space, and the Americans had built the delivery truck [the shuttle] that really didn't have any place to go, to combine the two programs made a lot of sense," Hadfield says. "And so about 1990 they started working on how to take a space shuttle to the Russian space station." The Canadarm would be the catalytic tool.

The concept of the space shuttle, in orbit, trying to catch up and connect to the also-orbiting space station, is mind-boggling. "We're about a half-million pounds of aluminum, going around the world at eight kilometres [five miles] a second, about 250 miles up, not very high, going round and round," Hadfield says.

Photo of space station Mir taken from STS-74 Atlantis, Chris Hadfield's mission. (Photo: courtesy of NASA)

The Russian Space Station, Mir, is an odd conformation, with seemingly dozens of arms and legs sticking out in all directions. Hadfield shows a photo and explains the purpose of some of its major appendages: "The white things are radiators where they get rid of their heat, these are solar arrays to collect electricity, and this long gantry with a boom on the end is a thruster to apply leverage. When you fire a thruster you can efficiently control which way Mir is pointing."

Mir was built piece by piece over the past 12 years. The first section, about the size of a school bus and weighing 40 000 pounds, went up in 1986, and other pieces have been added, with the newest about two years old.

The fundamental difference between a space station and a space shuttle is that a shuttle has to always stay "healthy enough" to come back to earth and land. In the case of an all-systems failure on the space station, if the problems can't be resolved in three days (the amount of air kept in reserve) the cosmonauts could get into their space ship and come home. The Progress space ship brings the cosmonauts supplies, fresh food and clean clothes, and new experiments to perform.

An IMAX movie, *Mission to Mir*, has been produced to familiarize viewers with this phenomenal space station that has been in orbit since 1986.

It is easy to see that there is really no place for a space shuttle to dock on Mir, and, as Hadfield explains, it's a fairly fragile structure. "Just one push of the thrusters and the shuttle could blow all the solar arrays off the side like sails, so we had to figure a way to safely attach the shuttle to the space station so we could transfer people across."

It had been decided, as an interim solution of how to take a space shuttle to a space station, to build another tunnel onto the end of one of the long appendages. The tunnel (approximately 15 feet long and weighing about five tons) was built in Russia, brought to Florida, and mounted in the back of the cargo bay of Space Shuttle Atlantis.

Hadfield's duty, to work the Canadarm to connect the tunnel from Atlantis to Mir, involved complete knowledge of the operation, split-second timing and a bit of luck. "We try and build in as much backup planning and redundant opportunities as you can get, but most things pretty much have to work. You're very time-critical on everything."

The first item of business was to activate the Canadarm. "It's built like your own arm with a shoulder, elbow and wrist. The shoulder can pitch and yaw, the elbow can just pitch, then the wrist can pitch, yaw and roll," Hadfield explains. "The arm on the shuttle has that combination of motion so you can move it around and grab onto things. That's what we had to do here: reach back with the arm, grab that orange tunnel, and assemble it onto the space station Mir.

"I was lucky enough to be the first Canadian to ever operate the Canadarm in space," Hadfield continues. A photo shows him upstairs, facing the back of the shuttle, flying the Canadarm with both hand controllers. "I could look out the window and see the arm, the tunnel just about to be installed on Mir, and in the background was Earth, its horizon, and then space."

An IMAX camera was on board to record one end of the docking module, or orange tunnel, being connected to the Atlantis space shuttle itself and the other end to Mir, with Hadfield running the controls of the Canadarm to put everything in place. Without the docking module, it would be impossible for the astronauts and cosmonauts to visit each other's space craft.

Hadfield's highly-technical and exacting job was to maneuver the Canadarm to pluck the docking module from its storage position, turn it and position it over the shuttle's docking hatch, using the Canadian-built Space Vision System (SVS) which would enable them to work in darkness and variable light conditions. Shuttle Commander Ken Cameron would then align Atlantis under Mir, and, when in position, fire the Atlantis thrusters to slam the docking module against the Mir space station's hatch. The operation was a success.

One photo, taken just after the tunnel had been installed, and looking out the back window of the shuttle as Hadfield was putting the arm away into a stowed position, caught the sun glinting off the Canadarm. "It was just so pretty, I gave the Prime Minister this picture when I got back. And he gave me my space wings, in fact," Hadfield says.

The space shuttle Atlantis in orbit over Earth, just as the Canadarm was being stowed away. This was the photo Hadfield presented to the Prime Minister. (Photo: courtesy of NASA)

Docking complete, they opened the hatch and entered the docking module, the first ever space-bridge. Now, two separate, sealed ecosystems were linked.

The three cosmonauts, fighter pilots Yuriy Gidzenko and Thomas Reiter (a German from the European Space Agency), and flight engineer Sergei Avdeyev, had been living on Mir for two-and-a-half months, and would be staying another three-and-a half months. All three men had come to Houston earlier to train with the astronauts, then the Americans had gone to Moscow to train with them, so it was like old friends meeting in their home in space. Members of both parties had learned a little of each other's language so communication was possible.

Inside Mir and Atlantis

The interior of Mir was somewhat of a mess. But, Hadfield cautions, if you went into your own kitchen, opened every cupboard door and then stuck everything to the walls and the ceiling and floor with Velcro, it would look the same. "Everything just sits where you put it, on the walls or on the ceiling. Put things where you like, they'll stay there forever! You have to get used to working in all three dimensions."

He champions the idea, though, of floating into your kitchen, seeing every single thing you own, and just reaching out to grab what you want. "When there's no gravity, that's a real good way to operate. You don't need to put stuff in a cupboard because nobody's going to poke into it. There are no pets running through, there's no dust because dust doesn't settle in space. You can just dump something on the floor and it will still be there five years from now. That's how they operate in Mir. These guys knew where everything was."

When the five astronauts joined the three cosmonauts in Mir, they had, of course, a party. For the Russians, fun times were long overdue.

"They would be there for six months and they couldn't take a weekend off," Hadfield says. "There was not a lot to do for variety. They had very few books, some movies and audio tapes of music, but they were living quite a monastic existence on the space station. They had an old acoustic guitar up there since 1982 when they'd launched it on an earlier space station and transferred it over to Mir, but it was kind of lousy and beat up. Also it's noisy on a space station because of the fans. Heat doesn't rise in space and it would get hotter and hotter. You actively have to cool everything, so there are fans and pumps and ventilators blowing.

Hadfield acknowledges that it's a little bit boring in space, "except when you look out the window and see the whole world going by. You can see everything you've ever read about. I saw Mount Everest 15 times."

In all, the astronauts transferred about a ton of material from the shuttle to Mir, including a couple of thermal electric freezers. "The old thermal electric freezers on board had a design flaw. They could overheat and burn out, so we designed new ones and replaced them. We transferred a lot of stuff between the two vehicles."

Water is, of course, of utmost importance. The shuttle creates water as it generates electricity, mixing hydrogen and oxygen to create electricity, heat and distilled water. The astronauts collected this distilled water for drinking, and any extra they put into ten 100-pound bags and gave to the cosmonauts, a real treat after relying on recycled water. Because Mir is powered by the sun it cannot generate water, so its occupants had to recycle. "They collected everything, urine, and all the humidity, and recycled that back into their water," Hadfield says.

While that system might sound disgusting, Hadfield says, with mock seriousness, "Yes, but all the water on earth is recycled dinosaur urine. It's true! Dinosaurs were here for 100 million years, they were big, they drank a lot of water and the water's all been recycled, so it's really nothing to worry about."

The two space ships were vastly different: the American shuttles bring fresh supplies with each mission and carry their waste back to earth. The station recycles. In Mir, many items are multi-purpose: a table folds to become an oven, a control panel becomes an exercise treadmill. The astronauts were able to take note of these systems used for longevity in space, which could perhaps be put into use when designing the International Space Station.

There was also quite a bit of work to be done in the shuttle, such as air quality checks which NASA would later analyze to test the efficiency of the shuttle's recycling equipment. They further made tests on any changes to the air quality with Mir attached. They checked the oxygen levels of the permanent crew on Mir, and supplied them with fresh oxygen.

One day, the astronauts cooked dinner for the cosmonauts. It certainly was cozy with eight people being crowded into Atlantis. The living space on the space shuttle is about the size of about two Dodge vans – a lot smaller than on Mir.

Hadfield shows pictures of their last supper together: "You can see the tortillas all over the wall. Here is our galley where we dispensed water on the space shuttle. We'd fill up a closed cup with water, put in a little straw with a shut-off valve, that's how we drank up there. We drank our coffee through a straw the same way.

"We had to bring back a lot of different experiments and medical samples," Hadfield says, "so rather than bring up an empty freezer we filled it with nine pounds of ice cream before we blasted off. We gave it to the Russians as a treat when we got up there."

As the only Canadian to ever go into the Russian space station, Hadfield had a patch designed to commemorate this mission. He took one up in the form of a large sticker. Just before leaving Mir, he stuck it on the wall of the docking module. On it he wrote Russian words, "STIKOVIACHNI OTSECK, which mean "Docking Module," signed his name, and proudly wrote, "Installed by a Canadian."

"So whenever you go into the Russian space station, there's Canadian graffiti on the wall," he laughs.

And then one day they carefully separated from the Russian space station, leaving the docking tunnel attached permanently onto Mir for future use. "We flew around Mir as we left, and took a bunch of pictures so the next crew would have a good description as they got ready for their flight."

Return To Earth

Then came clean-up of the shuttle, their home for the past 12 days. Again, lack of gravity made every chore more difficult, such as coiling up hoses. Everything floated all over the place.

Now the space shuttle, instead of being a dwelling, had to revert to an airplane to bring them home. Their return journey began by "falling" into the atmosphere.

"We had to stick the nose of the shuttle way up in the air. All that energy hit the bottom where thick ceramic tile soaked up all the heat, allowing the shuttle to slow from five miles a second down to landing speed. We did that gradually over an hour, coming down slowly through the air," Hadfield relates. "As it got thicker and thicker, we got slower and slower until we were at the point where we could tip over and start flying like an airplane about 300 mph."

It took much longer to get down to Earth than it had to come up. Compared to the eight-and-one-half minutes it took to go straight up, tip over and go into orbit, the ship now glided gradually, with low force.

"When they came back from the moon they just came screaming into the atmosphere, squished into the bottom of their space ship, and slammed down into the ocean," Hadfield recalls. "It was a rough ride. If they'd had any delicate experiments on board they would have been broken by the force of coming home.

"The shuttle, by contrast, came home very gently. We don't pull more than twice the whole force of gravity, and it took about an hour to slowly come down through the atmosphere, and travel the 12 000 miles back to base."

To illustrate the high speed of a shuttle, Hadfield compares it to travelling in a car. "If you stick your hand out a car window at 50 mph it's pretty powerful. At 60 mph, if you tried to turn your hand to the wind you could barely hold your hand out there. If you doubled your speed, you'd get four times as much energy because it increases with the square of velocity. You could get to a point where, if you stuck your hand out the window, it would just break your arm off. Well, a shuttle goes so fast that if you stuck your hand out the window you'd *burn* your arm off just from friction from the air."

To start decelerating, they fired their engines over Australia to allow the friction from the atmosphere to slow them down.

"A lot of the shuttles come right over Calgary on their way in to land. We came over Vancouver Island, across the Rockies, right over Calgary and turned all the way down to land in Florida, a nice, smooth, gentle process as we started falling to earth."

They came in for a landing at 230 miles an hour, diving at 20 degrees. Because the shuttle is so big, heavy and wide, they started their flare a kilometre above the ground. Then, still going about 230 miles an hour, they gently touched down on Runway 33 at Kennedy Space Center Shuttle Landing Facility, "one that we could see even from space," and rolled to a stop.

They were aided to their safe landing by a ground crew. The same airplane that had taken pictures of the launch had done a number of approaches just before their landing, to inform the astronauts of wind and weather conditions – and to keep the alligators off the runway – including Fred, the big one.

Mission STS-100 (scheduled for mid-2000)

In 1987, space agencies in Canada, the United States, Japan, Russia and the European community started to work on building a permanent, orbiting International Space Station. On Mission STS-100 (formerly called STS-99), Col. Chris Hadfield is scheduled to use the new Canadarm to attach equipment, this time to the International Space Station, which will entail making three space walks.

The new arm hasn't yet been named (in 1998 it was just called the Space Station Remote Manipulator System, or SSRMS). It is about 60 feet long, 20 percent longer than the Canadarm that was on the shuttle Atlantis in 1995, which was just under 50 feet, and weighs almost twice as much. Hadfield says it's a lot more powerful, with larger motors, and can move objects about 10 times as heavy, and can actually "walk" its way around the space station. It has been designed so it can be repaired in space because it's going to stay there, and any section can be replaced in a couple of hours.

The first arm used on the shuttle had a shoulder, elbow and wrist. The new one has an elbow and wrist on each end, enabling it to grab on in one place, walk to a new area on the station, let go at that end and walk somewhere else.

"When it grabs onto something it doesn't just grab mechanically, it plugs in electrically so we can power things, and it also plugs into a computer so it can 'talk' to things," Hadfield explains. "This arm is strong enough to grab the whole space shuttle and move it around."

With the purpose of his next flight being to attach this arm to the International Space Station, he is involved once again in an intensive training program. Because the Canadarm isn't functional under normal gravity, in order to do operational checks an air-bearing floor is used for two-dimensional work, with the rest performed by computer simulation.

"I'll get a chance to work on the arm in Brampton, to train with engineers and scientists who built it. I'll learn how all the mechanisms work, how to put it together and plug it in, so we can fix it if there are problems."

Chris Hadfield is looking forward to being the first Canadian to ever go outside the space shuttle and do a space walk. But how does one train for a space walk? Eighteen hours outside is about 13 times around the earth! There's no gravity – he might float away, like one sees in the movies, and be truly "lost in space."

Hadfield explains how training simulations can be done. "Old mines are used for drop experiments that last less than 10 seconds. You just drop down a hole, with a whole bunch of padding to soak up the impact." People, of course, can't be dropped down mine shafts for the experiments, thus the use of the airplane.

"They dive an airplane toward the ground, then pull it up quickly," Hadfield says. "Once it's pointed way up, they push it over. Everything 'floats' for about 30 seconds at the back of this airplane. Then, as the airplane pulls up, everything gets squished down onto the floor; then it pushes over and everything floats back up again, then squished down on the floor. You do this over and over again, in 30 second segments of weightlessness."

He refers to the "zero-G" segments in the movie, *Apollo 13*, which were filmed in the back of this airplane. "Every time you see Tom Hanks floating somewhere in that space ship, it's really in a sound stage at the back of this airplane. You can imagine what it's like when you are floating in weightlessness then squished to the floor, 40 times in a row. They also call this thing 'The Vomit Comet.'"

Although one can train for experiments that last less than 30 seconds, most jobs done in space last longer than that so other simulations of weightlessness are required. One system is by going under water. The astronauts don their space suits, complete with air hoses, to a point where they neither float nor sink, and remain suspended in weightlessness under water. These procedures are practiced in the Neutral Buoyancy Lab, a large underwater test facility located at the Johnson Space Center in Houston.

"It's the biggest swimming pool on earth, about two-thirds the size of a football field, and 40 feet deep, holding eight million gallons of water, which took a month to fill. They wanted everyone to have pressure in their showers in town so they took forever to fill it," Hadfield laughs.

"The whole thrust of the space program right now is building a space station and having people living permanently somewhere other than on the surface of the earth," Hadfield explains to a group of young people who have come to the Aero Space Museum in Calgary to meet the Canadian astronaut. "We're starting out with an International Space Station for the entire planet."

The project involves Canada, the US, Russia, Brazil, Japan and 11 European countries with cost-sharing worked out to pay the expected $60 billion price tag.

The International Space Station will be powered by the sun from large, outside solar collectors. Its construction is expected to take five years (to 2004), with 45 launches (36 American and nine Russian) bringing more than 100 main pieces up to the orbiting station. It will contain a laboratory the size of two football fields.

A crew of seven people is expected to live on the station full time, with the first three inhabitants initially proposed to arrive in early 2000. Eventually, 13 interconnecting main modules will provide living and work space, which should equal the interior passenger cabins of two Boeing 747 jetliners.

The initial module, named Zarya (the Russian word for sunrise), was launched November 20, 1998. The second module, a six-sided docking hub named Unity, left from the Kennedy Space Center via the shuttle Endeavour (named for Captain James Cook's British sailing ship) on December 4, 1998. Using Endeavour's Canadarm, the crew lifted Unity from the cargo bay and connected it to a tunnel-like docking port. Then, catching the orbiting Russian module, Zarya, and with the aid of Endeavour's thrusters to get everything in place, they stacked it on Unity and the docking port.

Two of the astronauts made three six-hour space walks over a period of six days, installing power and data cables on the modules and performing other tasks. Everything worked fine, except for the Russian delay.

It's a phenomenal project, and Canada has earned a place on board by contributing a major component – the Canadarm.

"I'll have a chance to ride on the end of the arm on the shuttle, which will be maneuvered by another astronaut, moving me around like someone on the end of a cherry-picker," Chris Hadfield states. "Imagine what it's going to look like when this arm reaches out from the International Space Station, with CANADA written on the forearm, which is our contribution, our ticket to be on board!"

Questions from the Crowd

Brian Ewenson stands with Chris Hadfield to help field questions from the audience of excited kids. They are well-prepared for this meeting, but who could quell the audiences' excitement at meeting a real live astronaut?

The first question is, **"How cold does it get in space?"**

Chris Hadfield asks, "What is the coldest it ever gets on earth?" The answer, between minus 56 and 62 degrees Celsius, or 70 to 80 degrees below zero Fahrenheit, also answers the question. "In space that's about the coldest it gets, too, but if you get *right* in the shade it's about minus 150 degrees (Celsius). But if you stuck your hand out into the sun, what's the hottest it ever gets on earth? Like in a place like Death Valley? About 60 degrees Celsius, or 140 degrees Fahrenheit. In space, it's 150 degrees Celsius."

"What happens to sweat in space?"

"Well, let's think about what happens when you take a shower in space," Hadfield says. "On earth when you take a shower, water comes out of the tap, hits your body, you lather up, scrub, it drains away, then you use your towel to dry off. In space, the water might come out of a jet and hit you, but you'd end up with a soapy film of water

around your body, with no way to get it off. Gravity isn't going to pull it off. So, you wipe it off with a washcloth and then you've got a bunch of wet washcloths, so a shower makes no sense. What we do is just use a wet washcloth and give ourselves a sponge bath.

"Sweat beads on your skin and you have to wipe it off with a towel. When we're doing that bicycle exercise, we end up with a thickening layer of sweat on our body, but it evaporates off or we wipe it off with a towel. But there's nothing to make it run anywhere, water just gets thicker and thicker."

"Why did you have a roll of duct tape in the shuttle?"

Hadfield laughs, referring to this handyman's aid as "400 mile-an-hour"

Chris Hadfield (L) and Brian Ewenson (R) at the Calgary Aero Space Museum. (Photo: S. Matheson) tape. "We used a lot of duct tape and actually left four rolls for the Russians on the space station [Mir] because it's handy stuff. We try not to use it on the International Space Station, though, because it doesn't remove very well. After 10 years or so, we'd have a lot of duct tape up there, so on the new space station we use elastics."

Another very practical question is, **"What happens if there was a medical emergency in the shuttle or on the Mir space station?"**

Hadfield replies that two people on the shuttle are trained to be the medical officers for every flight. "We could do basic surgery, pull a tooth, give needles, do advanced first aid. For ordinary nausea we take medication like Gravol to minimize the effects, and bring barf bags just like on airplanes. If it was something more serious, we'd shoot the person full of antibiotics and bring him home. The same thing on Mir. They're trained as first aid emergency medical technicians, and if it's serious they can get into their space ship and come home. A lot of astronauts are also medical doctors, so we often have a doctor on board to take care of us."

"Has any stuff ever exploded on Mir?" asks one young science-fiction fan.

"No," says Hadfield. "Mir has been up there for 12 years, and if anything happens they fix it, just like in any building on Earth. If there were any difficulties they could just get into their space ship and come home, so it's not as life-threatening as might be made out."

He notes two major events the cosmonauts had to deal with in 1997. In one, their oxygen-generating system caught fire. Then, when they were doing a docking test with one of their resupply ships, the docking system failed and it banged on the side of the space station, causing a slow leak in the attachment of the solar array panel. They had to close the hatch in that area. "But they dealt with those things, and fixed them," Hadfield says.

"What about 'time' in space?"

"We go by the same time as on earth," Hadfield replies, "but you go around the world 16 times in 24 hours. We normally worked on Houston time, or we set our watches to Moscow time, or to Greenwich Mean time, whatever, it was arbitrary. All the people in Russia have to get to mission control in Krunischev, Russia, by the Moscow subway system, and so the schedule on the Russian space station is driven by the schedule in the Moscow subway station. So, when we were docking at the space station Mir, we had to meet their ship on Moscow time."

"What was the scariest thing that happened to you in space?"

"We were on the dark side of the earth and we shut off all the lights in the space ship so we could look at Australia, at all the cities and the outlying coasts. Suddenly a great big meteorite burned up in the atmosphere underneath us. It was a big one, and we could see this long, flaming streak all across Australia. It was really cool to look at but then I had this odd feeling. This huge boulder had been whipping through space at five miles a second and it had just burned up in the atmosphere! If that boulder had hit us we'd have been dead! So that made me get a kind of itchy feeling on my back – and you can't train for that kind of thing.

"But," he adds, "Mir has been up there for 12 years and it doesn't have any meteorite holes in it, so you have to take the chance. And you're trained for it."

"What are the long-term effects on the body from being in space?"

"The Russians know more about what happens to the body in space than we do," Hadfield says. "The record for somebody staying in orbit is 14 months, by a Russian doctor. They reasoned that was the time it would take to get to Mars and they wanted to see how useful his body was after 14 1/2 months with no gravity, to see if he could explore Mars. He exercised on a bicycle and on a treadmill, with big elastics over his shoulders so he wouldn't float up off the treadmill, for two hours a day. And when he came back after 14 1/2 months he could walk, he could climb the steps to the bus, he did fine. Your body does pretty well.

"Some of the long-term effects are a higher radiation exposure, so you have to accept that. If you're going to Mars, when you get outside of the earth's magnetic field, you'll get a lot more radiation."

Another long-term effect is calcium loss. Your body doesn't need a heavy skeleton when there's no gravity, so it starts shedding calcium – basically, osteoporosis occurs.

"Some Americans who have been on Mir have had up to 15 percent calcium loss out of their bones," Hadfield says. "If you don't exercise while you're on Mir your bones get so soft that you can bend your lower leg, so you're not at all capable of coming back to earth. That's why they exercise so hard, and we're learning how to combat that with a high mineral diet and exercise, impacts on the lower legs, things like that. We're learning and we're getting better at it, but not many people have gone up."

"How long will it be before we have commercial flights into space?"

"We already have launched commercial flights and satellites into space for various purposes – things like cellular phones, television relays, that's all commercial," Hadfield replies. "There is some commercial use for human space flights also, and we carry some commercial payloads on the shuttles. Space Hab is a separate, commercial company that rents space in the shuttle and uses it as a business. The Russians have had commercial operations on Mir and they even had a Japanese journalist come up and stay for 10 days. They paid, I think, $25 million for him to go up to Mir and report on life in space as a documentary. So there are some commercial spin-offs."[2]

Brian Ewenson agrees. "There are thousands of spin-offs. Some people say, 'We've spent $25 billion to go to the moon and we brought back 750 pounds of rocks. Big deal!' But, per capita, Canada has spent the equivalent of two loaded hamburgers and a pack of bubble-gum on the space program," Ewenson says, making the comparisons immediately recognizable to the kids in the audience. "Show me another program that returns

\$7 to the economy for every \$1 spent? And think of the products that have been developed . . . the benefits are endless."

The audience breaks into a cheer following the litany of advantages, but they still want to know about commercial flights into space. **Like, when is an airline going to offer a vacation package?**

"As far as developing a tourism thing, we are still a generation away in safety and engine technology to make that possible," Hadfield cautions. "Right now, everybody on board must be a fully-trained crew member in order to make it safe. Once we come up with a smarter, more efficient engine, then we'll be in a position, I think, where we can start to take passengers on board."

A brochure is later sent to the author, however, that advertises "space voyages" by a company in Seattle, Washington. For a specified sum, participants can "take part in humankind's first commercial flights to the edge of the universe, to become space voyageurs of the new millennia," and thus earn Astronaut Altitude wings for reaching a height of 66 miles above sea level. These "astronauts" will view the earth's curvature, experience weightlessness, and fulfill their dreams of extra-terrestrial adventure. The first scheduled departure is December 1, 2001. Well, it's something to consider . . .

"Don't give them a dime!" Hadfield counsels.

The last question is a dandy, and the answer is eagerly awaited by the youthful audience: **"Did you see any aliens in space?"**

Chris Hadfield laughs. "No astronaut has ever seen aliens in space, despite all the garbage you might see on television. That's all just 'star wars' movies, that's not for real. But, my personal theory *is* that there is life in outer space, it just makes sense. There's an unlimited number of planets in space and the odds are pretty high that we're not the only one that has life. It's egotistical of us to think that we're the only life in the universe."

Brian and Chris

Both the space enthusiast-educator and the space astronaut are passionate about their interests, and share the feeling that if you want to somehow be involved in the space program the opportunity is there.

Brian Ewenson's mandate is to provide knowledge and material to interest and educate kids on the space programs.

"I have the only Boys and Girls Club in Canada that runs formal space education programs," Ewenson says. "For example, 'Rockets – a Teacher's Guide with Activities in Science, Mathematics and Technology.' NASA breaks it down to age groups so I can tailor my programs.

"We have to start bringing in youth to learn about the new technologies, and what is relevant to the youth today is space. My view is that, if this place [Earth] is going to exist 50 years from now, we had better keep up with the times. History is a continuum."

Colonel Chris Hadfield, Canadian astronaut, is appreciative of space-enthusiasts and educators such as Brian Ewenson, who go to great effort to organize visits from the astronauts and other space-related events.

During the past three years, Ewenson has hosted 10 astronauts in Calgary, introducing them to over 5000 youth on a personal basis. He has participated in growing space-flown canola and maple seeds, and sent 500 signatures on a CD-ROM disc stowed in the flight kit of John Glenn on the 95th shuttle mission Discovery in 1998.

In 1999, the University of Utah sent into orbit a basketball-sized, fully-educational, satellite to measure the thickness of the Earth's atmosphere through reflection from 900 mirrors, which had been polished and beveled by students from schools in 20 different countries. Brian makes use of the mirror from the Banded Peak Elementary School in Bragg Creek, Alberta, to discuss orbital discrepancies and show how kids can become involved in space programs.

Brian further designed and set up a permanent space exhibit in the Aero Space Museum of Calgary, and presents "Embrace Space!" programs to groups of all ages, where he explains the extraordinary achievements, benefits and opportunities to be found in the exploration and use of space. Through Brian's efforts, the Aero Space Museum of Calgary became the first ever international partner in the Lockheed Martin education/public awareness program outside of the United States.

In 1999, Brian Ewenson was invited by the Canadian Space Agency in Montreal to set up exhibits and tours for the agency's 10th anniversary celebration. Distinguished guests included Prime Minister Jean Chretien, Minister of Industry John Manley and Secretary of State for Science, Ron Duhamel.

Hadfield, on behalf of The Canadian Space Agency, gratefully acknowledges such efforts. "We try to go everywhere in Canada and tell people what's going on in space, but it takes a tremendous amount of organization to get one of us, and cover the costs to bring us up."

"At nine years old I decided to be an astronaut, and it was impossible then," Hadfield states. "But now, 50 people a year are sent into space on shuttles, and every eight months or so one of them is a Canadian. People from all around the planet are going to be living permanently in space, on space stations. And it's Canadian people, Canadian technology, the Canadarm, that's going to build this thing."

"It has been one, long continuum of learning," Hadfield says. "And I'm still in school, learning about how things work."

There are still frontiers to be flown.

Footnote

[1]Eight Canadian astronauts have flown to date, and three have retired from the program. The eight who have made flights are:

1.**Marc Garneau**, who conducted a set of experiments (CANEX-1) for Canadian scientists in space science, technology and life sciences during mission STS-41G (Oct. 5-13/84) on board *Challenger*. He also flew on board *Endeavour* on the STS-77 mission (May 19-29/96) and performed a number of experiments in the Spacehab module.

2.**Roberta Bondar** flew as Canada's first woman astronaut on STS-42 (Jan. 22-30/92). She was a payload specialist on the first International Microgravity Laboratory mission, on board the shuttle *Discovery*.

3.**Steve MacLean**, chosen to fly the CANEX-2 mission in 1985, which was rescheduled to STS-52 in 1992 following the *Challenger* tragedy. He flew on board *Columbia* (Oct. 22-Nov. 1/92) testing a new vision system for Canadarm.

4.**Chris Hadfield** flew *Atlantis* on STS-74 (Nov. 12-20/95) using the Canadarm to attach a new docking module to the Mir space station. He flew as Canada's first Mission Specialist, was first to use the Canadarm, and was the only Canadian to visit the Russian space station *Mir*.

5.**Robert Thirsk** flew as a Payload Specialist on board *Columbia* on STS-78 (Life and Microgravity Science mission, June 20-July 7/96) performing life science experiments.

6.**Bjarni Trygvasson** flew as Payload Specialist on board the shuttle *Discovery* STS-85 mission with his own experiment, the Microgravity Isolation Mount, in which products float free of vibrations from the craft.

7.**Dave Williams** who holds a degree in medicine and surgery, and a fellowship in emergency medical care, flew as Mission Specialist on board the shuttle *Columbia* (April 16/98) and conducted 26 experiments on the nervous system, e.g., studies on how humans adapt to different environments such as low-gravity conditions.

8.**Julie Payette** flew as Mission Specialist aboard the space shuttle *Discovery*, STS-96, from May 27 to June 6, 1999. She operated the Canadarm using the two-handed controls to point the arm and its television cameras into remote areas of the space shuttle that no human eye could see, to check the equipment installed in the shuttle's cargo bay in preparation for boarding the International Space Station. Two astronauts aboard the shuttle (Dan Barry and Tammy Jernigan) went space-walking on May 30th, to attach two cargo cranes outside the space station. Payette operated the arm for tests of Canadian Space Vision System, and Ellen Ochoa operated the arm for the space-walk.

[2]Mir's days may be numbered. An Associated Press article that appeared in the Calgary *Herald* (June 2, 1999) states that the 13-year-old space station may be abandoned in August 1999 and the cosmonauts return home, mainly because of lack of finances. It is estimated that the Mir operation costs the Russian government $365 million (Canadian) per year. "If there is no money to extend Mir's flight, its orbit will descend early next year (2000) to 200 kilometres above Earth from 400, and ground controllers will allow it to burn up in the atmosphere in February or March," said Vyacheslav Mikhailichenko, a spokesman for the space agency.